D0713874

Developing and Using Classroom Assessments

ALBERT OOSTERHOF
Florida State University

Merrill
Prentice Hall

Upper Saddle River, New Jersey
Columbus, Ohio

Library of Congress Cataloging-in-Publication Data

Oosterhof, Albert.
    Developing and using classroom assessments / Albert Oosterhof.—3rd ed.
        p. cm.
    Includes bibliographical references and index.
    ISBN 0-13-094204-9 (pbk.)
    1. Examinations—Design and construction. 2. Examinations—Validity. 3.
    Examinations—Interpretation. I. Title.

LB3060.65 .O67 2003
371.26'1—dc21

2002032584

Vice President and Publisher: Jeffery W. Johnston
Executive Editor: Kevin M. Davis
Editorial Assistant: Autumn Crisp
Production Editor: Mary Harlan
Production Coordination: Emily Hatteberg, Carlisle Publishers Services
Design Coordinator: Diane C. Lorenzo
Cover Design: Linda Sorrells-Smith
Cover Image: Eyewire
Text Design and Illustrations: Carlisle Publishers Services
Production Manager: Laura Messerly
Director of Marketing: Ann Castel Davis
Marketing Manager: Amy June
Marketing Coordinator: Tyra Cooper

This book was set in Garamond by Carlisle Communications, Ltd. It was printed and bound by R. R. Donnelley & Sons Company. The cover was printed by Phoenix Color Corp.

Pearson Education Ltd.
Pearson Education Australia Pty. Limited
Pearson Education Singapore Pte. Ltd.
Pearson Education North Asia Ltd.
Pearson Education Canada, Ltd.
Pearson Educación de Mexico, S.A. de C.V.
Pearson Education—Japan
Pearson Education Malaysia Pte. Ltd.
Pearson Education, *Upper Saddle River, New Jersey*

Copyright © 2003, 1999, 1996 by Pearson Education, Inc., Upper Saddle River, New Jersey 07458. All rights reserved. Printed in the United States of America. This publication is protected by Copyright and permission should be obtained from the publisher prior to any prohibited reproduction, storage in a retrieval system, or transmission in any form or by any means, electronic, mechanical, photocopying, recording, or likewise. For information regarding permission(s), write to: Rights and Permissions Department.

10 9 8 7 6 5 4 3
ISBN: 0-13-094204-9

 *For Darlene*

PREFACE

This book and the accompanying Web site provide a significant but succinct discussion of the development and use of classroom assessments. The book is designed for college courses and other settings for which a full survey textbook is inappropriate in terms of coverage and cost. *Developing and Using Classroom Assessments* is particularly appropriate in the following settings:

- An educational psychology course that includes a substantive discussion of assessment

- An integrated methods course in which assessment is taught as one of several components

- A full-length assessment course that uses a series of readings or involves the class in extensive field experience

- Self-study by school teachers and post-secondary instructors

FEATURES OF THIS BOOK

This book engages the reader. To illustrate, take time to page through the book and you will find numerous queries embedded in the text. Each is labeled "Apply What You Are Learning" and invites the reader to immediately apply recently learned concepts to realistic situations. Subsequent text often builds on these queries. This book also engages readers by drawing upon the considerable experience each of us has had with assessments as students and teachers. The introduction to each chapter uses familiar situations to establish relevance for issues to be addressed. Each chapter concludes with activities that connect the content of that chapter to real-world needs in the classroom.

Developing and Using Classroom Assessments also incorporates the broader context within which classroom assessments occur. For instance, the major implications of cognitive psychology to assessment are discussed throughout the book, such as the differences between declarative and procedural knowledge, the nature of problem solving, and options for assessing each. Similarly, in recognition that informal assessments represent a high proportion of classroom assessment activities, a full chapter is devoted to using informal observations and questions, and another chapter addresses their use to integrate assessment into instruction.

ORGANIZATION

Developing and Using Classroom Assessments is organized into four parts. Part I provides the teacher with a framework for assessing students. Components of this framework include determining how results of an assessment will be used, establishing the behaviors that indicate whether or not learning has taken place, gathering evidence to determine whether an assessment is valid, and establishing whether it is reasonable to generalize from observed performance to unobserved performance. These components of the assessment framework are illustrated with practical and familiar examples. This assessment framework is then applied extensively in Parts II, III, and IV of the book.

Parts II and III are concerned with the development, administration, and scoring of assessments. Part II focuses on written tests, including the essay, short-answer, and objectively scored formats. In Chapters 6 through 9, the reader learns when and how to use each format, including nontrivial attributes that should be built into each type of test item. The reader immediately practices what has been learned by critiquing a combination of well-constructed and faulty test items. Chapter 10 is concerned with helping students take written tests.

Part III focuses on alternative assessments, including informal observations and questions, performance assessments, and portfolios. Books on assessment often provide a cursory treatment of the casual observation and questioning of students, even though these informal assessments provide the basis for most formative evaluations in the classroom. Chapter 11 discusses these assessments in some detail. It identifies qualities critical to casual questioning and observation and illustrates their relevance through analogies to social interactions with which readers are very familiar. Two chapters are devoted to performance assessments. Chapter 12 addresses several factors to consider when using this powerful assessment medium, including characteristics, options for scoring, and things to do before creating each performance assessment. Chapter 13 describes in detail procedures to follow when creating performance assessments. The creation of five performance assessments is illustrated. Chapter 14 describes how to use portfolios to integrate assessment and instruction, including how to design portfolios and how to guide their use by students.

Part IV focuses on the *use* of assessments. Chapter 15 is concerned with integrating assessment into instruction. Particular attention is given to specific roles of assessment within cognitivist and constructivist approaches to learning. Chapter 16 describes how to report student performance to parents and others outside the classroom. Issues addressed include inferring what a student knows from what was observed, establishing performance standards, and assigning grades. Chapter 17 addresses the interpretation of students' scores on standardized tests. A significant section helps the reader evaluate common uses of standardized tests that directly affect classroom activities.

FEATURES OF THE WEB SITE

A Web site has been developed to supplement this book. Incorporating a Web site provides added flexibility, helps the book achieve relevance, and makes it easier to remain current within a rapidly evolving field. The address of the web site is *www.prenhall.com/oosterhof*.

The Web site is organized into three parts. The first part contains self-instructional modules and illustrations designed to supplement the book. For example, one illustration shows ways to use a word processor to produce written tests more efficiently. Another shows the effect that changing the number of observations has on the probability of correctly categorizing student achievement. The instructional modules deal with specialized topics that often are included in an introductory measurement course. For instance, one module helps the user understand the significant effect regression often has on test scores. Another shows what correction for guessing or formula scoring does and does not accomplish. A series of modules address standard deviation and correlation along with their role in computing reliability and validity coefficients.

The second part of the Web site describes a number of course projects that relate to topics addressed in the book. Many of these projects include worked-out examples created by practicing teachers and others.

The third part of the Web site provides links to a variety of sites on the Internet associated with educational measurement, particularly those concerned with assessments in the classroom. These sites provide access to current professional papers and reports, discussion of issues, information about school testing programs, and access to listservs, software, and search engines.

ACKNOWLEDGMENTS

I remain deeply indebted to the students, teachers, and other colleagues whose shared experiences have preceded the writing of this book. You will continue to find their ideas and insights incorporated throughout the present edition. I am grateful for the thoughtful and useful reviews of significant portions of this book provided by Laura L. B. Barnes, Oklahoma State University; Alexander W. Chizhik, University of Maine; Lee Doebler, University of Montevallo; and Marlynn Griffin, Georgia Southern University. I gratefully acknowledge the generous assistance of the editorial staff at Merrill/Prentice Hall. I owe special appreciation to Kevin Davis for his vital role in conceptualizing the initial edition of this book and his insights and guidance leading to the second and third editions. Special appreciation is acknowledged for the gentle hand that was provided by Mary Harlan during production, and the detailed editing provided by Carlisle Publishers Services.

Albert Oosterhof

BRIEF CONTENTS

CONTENTS

1

Introduction

Think for a moment of the number of tests you have taken since you entered school. If you averaged only 30 minutes of exams and quizzes per week within each of the basic subject areas, by the time you completed high school you have already answered over 1,000 hours of written tests. That amounts to 40 solid 24-hour days. This does not include tests you completed in college. Nor does it include the thousands of nonwritten assessments, ranging from how you held your pencil to how you conducted a science experiment. It does not include the hundreds of papers and projects you completed, nor the notebooks or portfolios you prepared. Although students may beg to differ, the demands that classroom assessments place on teachers is greater than the demands placed on students. It is estimated that more than 25% of a teacher's time is devoted to developing and using the various forms of classroom assessments.

We are constantly being assessed, and we are constantly assessing others, not only in classroom settings, but also in everyday life. We assess what others say to us, their facial expressions, their choice of words, and their attitudes. We evaluate their reactions to what we say and do. We often study who and what are around us to decide what to do or where to go.

This common experience we share with tests and other assessments is essential to working with the material presented in this book. For example, you know that some written exams are better than others; we will use this knowledge when we try to isolate qualities that create better tests. You are aware of specific problems that occur in tests, such as questions that are ambiguous and content that does not correspond to material covered in the course. You know that essays you write, math problems you complete, and portfolios you prepare would be scored inconsistently if graded by different teachers. You also know of the many problems associated with the use of assessments. Teachers sometimes distribute results long after a test is administered; results may be reported without explanations of areas that caused difficulty, and teachers often move on to subsequent instruction before addressing difficulties identified in tests. Portfolios often are reviewed several days, and sometimes weeks, after work samples have been completed, and sometimes only a portion of work in the portfolio can be reviewed in detail.

We know that teachers do and have to depend on informal assessments, such as casual observations and oral questions. Some teachers are more effective than others in their use of informal assessments and have a knack for knowing what is going on. Some teachers retain their initial impressions about students, whereas others effectively use informal assessments to detect changes in students or errors in initial perceptions. Some teachers effectively use informal assessments to guide students' learning; other teachers seem more oblivious to what students are learning. Our common experiences with all these situations will be invaluable as we present procedures for developing written tests, preparing performance assessments, asking oral questions, and observing what students do.

SIGNIFICANCE OF MEASUREMENT

Dictionaries list a number of related definitions for the verb **measure.** The definitions most useful to our discussion include determining the characteristics of something, regulating through the use of a standard, and making comparisons to a reference such as the performance of others.

Measurement is essential in virtually every discipline. In the physical sciences, measurement is used to determine characteristics of various substances or to ascertain when a material has achieved a particular property. In engineering, such qualities as loads, torque, friction, and thermal characteristics are constantly measured. In sports, measurements are used for making decisions, such as calling a strike in baseball, designating a first down in football, or calling a personal foul in basketball. Measurement is used in politics to anticipate the outcome of an election or to evaluate another government's reaction to a policy decision. Measurement is used in the performing arts when the director selects an actor for a particular role and when critics review the performance on opening night. Business relies on measurement data to determine the effectiveness of production techniques and to evaluate the impact of advertising.

Measurement is also critical to learning. Every theory of learning assumes the presence of feedback. Measurement, whether it originates from the teacher or the student, is a prerequisite to this feedback. Without good assessments, we cannot know whether effective learning has occurred.

In all disciplines, measurement is continuous. This is certainly true in scientific research, sports, the arts, business, and education. In each area, informal but deliberate observations are always taking place. In addition to continuous measures, planned formal observations must be used. The scientist must incorporate carefully developed measurements at selected points during and at the end of an experiment. A football coach must schedule times to analyze the progress of the team (for example, by viewing films after a game).

Teachers must also periodically develop and administer tests and other formal observations. Unlike ongoing informal observations, formal assessments are not spontaneous; they are deliberately scheduled and fully developed in advance. If teachers were to depend only on impromptu observations, the students' mastery of many crucial skills would go unexamined. The results of formal observations often guide the nature of subsequent, more frequent informal observations. Formal and informal assessments are both critical and are complementary.

Perhaps, unfortunately, measurement skills are not intuitive within any discipline, and experience by itself is insufficient for ensuring these measurement skills. For instance, watching the heavens at night does not provide the measurement skills essential to being an astronomer, even though that experience provides an important base from which to learn these skills. Driving a car does not provide the skills needed by traffic-control engineers to measure traffic flow, although it provides insights essential to interpreting these measures. Your experience with classroom assessments provides a context essential to learning the concepts discussed in this book, although you are likely to find many of the measurement concepts introduced in this book to be new. The application of measurement, particularly in the classroom, is dynamic and highly complex. Your experience, therefore, provides not only the context for learning measurement concepts, but also a basis for adapting, applying, and evaluating the educational measurement concepts we discuss here.

DISTINCTION AMONG MEASUREMENT, ASSESSMENT, AND EVALUATION

The terms **measurement, assessment,** and **evaluation** are often used interchangeably in education. For our discussion, it will be useful to maintain a distinction, although the differences among these terms are not absolute.

The distinction between measurement and evaluation is the easiest to establish. In education, measurement is concerned with establishing characteristics of individuals or groups of individuals, usually students. Measurement does not associate value with what we see. Evaluation, however, combines our measures with other information to establish the desirability and importance of what we have observed. Evaluation is the outcome of measurement after value has been added. Here are some contrasts between measurement and evaluation:

Measurement: Performance on a test indicates that a student is unable to spell number words less than one hundred.

Evaluation: This performance is of significant concern, because spelling number words is a prerequisite to the next unit on writing checks.

Measurement: A teacher observes a student speaking in class without first raising her hand.

Evaluation: This behavior is encouraging because that student has never participated in class discussion.

Measurement: In education, we observe that the terms *measurement* and *evaluation* are often used interchangeably.

Evaluation: Equating measurement and evaluation is undesirable because it confuses issues discussed later in this book.

The linkage of evaluation to measurement sometimes makes it difficult to discuss measurement and evaluation separately. For example, erroneous measures lead to inappropriate evaluations. In addition, establishing what should be measured is determined by the values we expect to attach to our observations. This book focuses more on classroom applications of educational *measurement* than on evaluation. It will provide ideas for determining what should be measured and how to interpret student performance on these measures. Evaluation is important; however, your professional expertise in your content area is fundamental in establishing what to measure and determining the significance of what you observe. Evaluations also depend on the context of your educational measures and cannot be discussed fully in the absence of that context.

The distinction between measurement and assessment is less concise. *Assessment* is often used as a stylistic alternative to *measurement*. Some sentences sound better if you use the word *assessment* rather than *measurement*. Sometimes, measurement is perceived as quantitative, cold, and less desirable, whereas assessment is seen as qualitative and warm.

Let us clarify what is meant by measurement. It is often described only in quantitative terms. Statements such as "Measurement is the process used to assign numbers to attributes or characteristics of persons" are fairly common. These statements fit well with notions of validity and reliability that are limited to statistical conceptualizations. Such statements are also consistent with the view that test scores are always numbers.

However, *measurement* is often given a broader meaning. Dictionary definitions such as those noted earlier do not limit measurement to quantification. Likewise, people who describe themselves as measurement specialists do more than merely associate numbers with attributes. The same can be said about books with "educational measurement" in their titles. Even the term **test score** is not necessarily a number. Messick (1989a) put it this way:

> The term "test score" is used generically here in its broadest sense to mean any observed consistency, not just on tests as ordinarily conceived but also on any means of observing or documenting consistent behaviors or attributes. This would include, for instance, any coding or summarization of observed consistencies on performance tests, questionnaires, observation procedures, or other assessment devices. This general usage also subsumes qualitative as well as quantitative summaries and applies, for example, to protocols, clinical interpretations, and computerized verbal score reports. (p. 5)

In our discussion, **educational measurement** will refer to the process of determining a quantitative or qualitative attribute of an individual or group of individuals that is of academic relevance. **Test** will refer to the vehicle used to observe that attribute, such as a written test, an observation, or an oral question. **Test score** will refer to an indication of what was observed through the test.

Assessment generally has broader connotations than does measurement. Were measurements limited to assigning numbers to attributes, assessment might be thought of as combining qualitative and quantitative attributes. Or, if measurements were limited to paper-and-pencil tests, assessment might be said to involve all techniques including observations and oral questions. In our discussion, however, measurement, not assessment, will be used to represent all these activities.

Airasian (1997) defines assessment as the "collection, synthesis, and interpretation of information to aid the teacher in decision making" (p. 4). This definition is broader than what we have defined as measurement. It is, however, unclear at what point assessment supersedes measurement. For instance, does determining a quantitative or qualitative attribute of an individual include only the collection of information, or does it include the synthesis of information, or, possibly, naming the characteristic being described? If the validation of test scores is concerned with how the scores are to be interpreted and used, then the meaning of measurement might be as broad as that of assessment.

As with many synonyms, measurement and assessment have similar meanings, yet they also have subtle differences. The subtleties are often useful, but not always applied consistently. In our discussion, assessment will be viewed as having broader connotations than measurement. Assessment will refer to a related series of measures used to determine a complex attribute of an individual or group of individuals. Portfolios, which include planned collections of student work, are an example of an assessment. Performance assessments, in which student performance on a complex task is observed, are assessments. A series of related but informal observations used to determine complex attributes of one student or a group of students is also an assessment. Each of these types of assessments involves collecting, synthesizing, and labeling information. At what point a measurement becomes an assessment, however, remains undefined.

DISTINCTION BETWEEN FORMAL AND INFORMAL ASSESSMENTS

The basic distinction between formal and informal assessments lies in their spontaneity. Formal assessments are devised in advance, whereas informal assessments happen on the spur of the moment.

Formal assessments include final exams, unit tests and quizzes, graded homework, critiques of

prepared speeches, and judgments of performances in science labs. Formal assessments also include tryouts for athletic teams and roles in a school play. Details of how each of these assessments will be implemented are established prior to their occurrence.

Informal assessments, although more numerous, are less obvious. Informal assessments occur when a teacher listens to a student's questions or watches her facial expression to determine whether she understands the concept being taught. Informal assessments occur when a teacher arrives at first-day impressions of a student's ability by watching where he sits, looking at what he wears, and listening to what he says. Informal assessments include talking through a math problem to find out why the student gave a wrong answer or asking questions while teaching a concept to determine whether students are learning what is being taught.

Because formal assessments are devised in advance and informal assessments are spontaneous, they differ in a number of ways. A basic difference is that informal assessments can and do occur while instruction is being delivered, whereas formal assessments often require a pause in instruction. As a result, informal assessments can be particularly effective at redirecting instruction as it occurs. However, informal assessments are more likely to be unsystematic and more often lead to faulty conclusions about student performance.

Formal assessments are used when more controlled measures are required, whereas informal assessments are used when more frequent and responsive measures are needed. Because of their respective advantages and limitations, the use of formal versus informal assessment depends to a large extent on the role assessment is to play in the classroom.

ROLES OF ASSESSMENT IN THE CLASSROOM

Bloom, Hastings, and Madaus (1981) proposed that assessment is used to facilitate formative, summative, and diagnostic evaluations. We will add a fourth role: preliminary evaluations.

Preliminary evaluations occur during the first days of school and provide a basis for expectations throughout the school year. They are obtained mainly through a teacher's spontaneous informal observations and oral questions and are concerned with students' skills, attitudes, and physical characteristics. These evaluations are basically the same as those you establish whenever you meet new people. They happen naturally, and they are essential to guiding our interactions with others and with students.

Formative evaluations occur during instruction. They establish whether students have achieved sufficient mastery of skills and whether further work with these skills is appropriate. Formative evaluations are also concerned with the attitudes students are developing. The purpose of formative evaluations is to determine what adjustments to the present learning environment should be made. Formative evaluations are based primarily on continuous informal assessments, such as listening to what students say, using oral questions to probe comprehension, and watching students' facial expressions and other behaviors. Formative evaluations are also based on formally developed assessments such as quizzes, seat work, homework, and group projects. Most assessments that occur in the classroom lead to formative evaluations.

Summative evaluations occur at the conclusion of instruction, such as at the end of a unit or the end of the year. Summative evaluations are used to certify student achievement and assign end-of-term grades. They serve as the basis for promoting and sometimes for grouping students. Summative evaluations also help determine whether instructional strategies should be changed before the next school year. Unlike in formative evaluations, the role that assessment plays within summative evaluations is not to establish student proficiency with each skill, but instead to provide an overview of achievement across a number of skills. With summative evaluations, each skill might be measured by just one test item, which is not enough to establish with confidence proficiency with individual skills. Often, only a sampling of skills are tested. Summative evaluations are based on formal assessments.

Diagnostic evaluations occur before or, more typically, during instruction. Diagnostic evaluations are concerned with skills and other characteristics that are prerequisite to the current instruction or that enable the achievement of instructional objectives. During instruction, diagnostic evaluations are used to establish underlying causes for a student's failing to learn a skill. When used before instruction, diagnostic evaluations try to anticipate conditions that will negatively affect learning. In both cases, the role of measurement is to assess a student's performance in specific prerequisite skills not typically taught in the present classroom setting. Diagnostic evaluations are based mostly on informal assessments, although formal measures, such as standardized tests, are sometimes used.

Figure 1.1 illustrates the relationship among the four evaluative roles of classroom assessment. Preliminary evaluations feed into formative evaluations. Formative evaluations occur during instruction and are based on frequent assessments. Diagnostic evaluations are concerned with problems that might be or, more typically, already are preventing students from learning. Summative evaluations follow instruction.

As indicated in Figure 1.1, preliminary, formative, and diagnostic evaluations depend mostly on informal assessments. These evaluations require measures of student performance that are highly responsive to immediate situations. They require assessments that can occur without a pause in instruction. Summative evaluations, in contrast, require the more controlled measures provided by formal assessments. Summative evaluations do not depend on the spontaneous and responsive characteristics of informal assessments.

MAXIMUM VERSUS TYPICAL PERFORMANCE

Maximum performance and **typical performance** refer to whether students are performing at

Preliminary Evaluations

Purpose
Provide a quick but temporary determination of students' characteristics

When it occurs
During the first 10 days of school

Techniques used
Mostly informal observations and questions

Diagnostic Evaluations

Purpose
Identify problems that will prevent or are preventing a student from learning

When it occurs
When difficulties in learning new knowledge are anticipated; or more typically, after difficulties in learning have been observed

Techniques used
Typically informal observations and questions; sometimes formal assessments such as a teacher's written test or a standardized test

Formative Evaluations

Purpose
Determine what students have learned in order to plan instruction

When it occurs
Continuously, during instruction

Techniques used
Mostly informal observations and questions; also, written and oral quizzes, classroom activities and performance assessments, homework, and portfolios

Summative Evaluations

Purpose
Certify what students have learned in order to assign grades, promote students, and refine instruction for next year

When it occurs
At the conclusion of a unit of instruction

Techniques used
Mostly formal assessments, including written tests, performance assessments, projects, and portfolios

Figure 1.1
Four roles of classroom assessment

their best or at their normal level. Formal assessments such as written tests, portfolios, structured performance assessments, and graded homework tend to encourage maximum performance. These assessments establish a student's ability to perform when motivated, but the performance does not necessarily generalize to other settings. Determining that a student can distinguish between statements of fact and opinion on a test, for instance, does not indicate the student will apply this skill when reading newspapers. Likewise, determining that a student has achieved knowledge in history, mathematics, or reading does not mean that she will use these skills beyond the classroom.

Typical performance is more concerned with attitudes than with academic skills. Attitudes influence students' interest in applying what they learn as well as in learning it in the first place. Typical performance is usually measured by informal assessments, particularly observation. Observations or other measures have to be unobtrusive to assess typical performance.

Whether teachers should develop and administer measures of typical performance pertinent to the content they are teaching is unclear. Certainly, values are important and can be taught. The way in which a teacher facilitates learning in the classroom affects the attitudes students develop about a subject. Whether a teacher should measure these attitudes with the intent of modifying student behavior can be argued both ways. For instance, consider the following questions:

- Should a study of world religions include measures of students' beliefs or interests in religion?

- Should a study of political history include measures of political preferences or interests in politics?

- Is it appropriate for a teacher of meteorology to measure students' attitudes toward meteorology or interest in weather systems?

Because we often are uncertain whether measuring typical performance is appropriate, particularly if the intent is to modify undesired attitudes,

we might answer in the affirmative to all, part, or possibly none of these questions.

Typical performance can be measured only to a degree. To be valid, observations of typical performance may need to be conducted without students being aware that they are being assessed. Often, obtaining unobtrusive measures of attitude is not possible, and, as a result, students fake typical responses.

SUMMARY

It is quite appropriate to examine closely the issues related to classroom assessment. Assessment is germane to everything that goes on in the classroom. Students do not learn effectively unless they receive feedback, which is obtained through assessments. Teachers similarly cannot be effective without information gained through their assessments.

Each of us has already had an extensive amount of experience with assessments, gained from years of involvement with written tests and other assessments. Our experience with assessments also derives from informal interactions with others. We can recognize the considerable differences in the quality of assessments and in the effectiveness with which they are used. This experience will be invaluable as we discuss the development and use of classroom assessments.

Several terms were defined in this chapter. *Educational measurement* refers to the process of determining a quantitative or qualitative attribute of an individual or group that is of academic relevance. *Assessment* refers to a related series of measures used to determine a complex attribute of an individual or group. A *test* is any vehicle used to observe that attribute, and includes written tests, performance assessments, portfolio systems, and casual observations and questions. A *test score* is an indication of what is observed through the test and can be quantitative or qualitative in nature. *Evaluation* combines measures and assessments with other information to establish the desirability and importance of what we have observed.

Four types of evaluation have been identified. *Preliminary evaluations* occur during the first

2 weeks of school and provide a quick determination of students' characteristics. *Formative evaluations* occur continuously during instruction to determine what students are learning and to enable instruction to be adjusted accordingly. *Diagnostic evaluations* identify problems that are preventing students from learning. *Summative evaluations* occur at the conclusion of a unit of instruction and are used for tasks such as certifying what students have learned, assigning grades, and refining instruction for the next year. Preliminary, formative, and diagnostic evaluations rely more heavily on informal assessments but often include formal assessments. Summative evaluations involve formal assessments.

The remainder of this book is divided into four parts. Part I describes how to establish a framework for assessing your students. This framework involves four interrelated components, including identifying student performances to be observed, establishing how results from assessments will be used, obtaining evidence that appropriate capabilities are being assessed, and determining whether observations of student performance will generalize to other settings.

Part II describes how to develop and score written tests. We will also discuss "testwiseness" and other issues that help students successfully complete written tests. Part III explains how to develop and score alternative assessments. We will discuss informal observations and questions, performance assessments, and portfolio systems. These alternative techniques help evaluate skills that cannot be assessed through written tests.

Part IV describes how to use assessments and report results. This discussion will pertain to students as well as to audiences outside the classroom, such as parents. Topics of integrating assessment into instruction, grading, and standardized tests are included in this discussion.

PART I

How to Establish a Framework for Assessing Your Students

A framework for assessing students has many parallels to the framework of a house. The framework of a house includes all the components that provide structure: floor joists, wall studs, headers that span the distance above doors and windows, and roof trusses. Although each of these components can be constructed individually, they depend on each other; that is, they provide structure only if used together. This framework represents only a portion of a house, and in most cases, little or none of the framework can be seen when the construction of the house is finished. Yet it is futile to construct a house without a strong framework.

You probably can anticipate how this analogy relates to establishing a framework for assessing students. As with a house, an assessment framework involves several components:

- Purpose, which establishes how results from assessments will be interpreted and used

- Specifications, which establish the knowledge to be assessed and corresponding performance to be observed

- Validity, which is concerend with evidence as to whether appropriate capabilities are being assessed

- Consistency, which is concerend with whether observations of student performance will generalize to other settings

As with the framework of a house, these components depend on each other. For example, establishing the knowledge to be assessed is of little help unless one also establishes how results from assessments will be interpreted and used.

Also, the assessment framework provides only the structure on which assessments are developed, a structure that ultimately is invisible to students and others. For example, this framework will be unnoticed by students when they take a test or develop a portfolio. Nonetheless, it is futile to develop and use classroom assessments without a strong framework.

The four components of our assessment framework are diagrammed in Figure 2.1 and are discussed in the next four chapters. The first component involves establishing purpose; how assessments will be interpreted and used. In Chapter 1, we indicated that assessments are used to help evaluate students. Four types of evaluations were identified: preliminary, diagnostic, formative, and summative. In Chapter 2, we expand this discussion of evaluation and look at specific references for interpreting and using classroom assessments.

Chapter 3 then describes how to specify the knowledge to be assessed and select the types of student performance to be observed. Determining what to observe is complicated, because a teacher generally cannot see what is being learned or what another person knows or is thinking. The teacher must therefore carefully select student behaviors that provide an appropriate **indication** of what students have learned.

Because a teacher can observe only indications of learning, it is important to find evidence that the appropriate capabilities are being assessed. This gathering of evidence, called **validation,** is covered in Chapter 4.

When using student behaviors as an indication of what has been learned, it's important to recognize that only a sample of each student's relevant behaviors can be observed. The component of the assessment framework discussed in Chapter 5 involves determining whether what is observed generalizes to what was not observed. That is, would consistent results be obtained had the same capability been assessed in a different way?

Again, although the structure provided by this assessment framework is critical, its existence is largely invisible to students. Removing any component of this framework, however, severely weakens our classroom assessments regardless of whether they involve informal assessments, written tests, performance assessments, or portfolios.

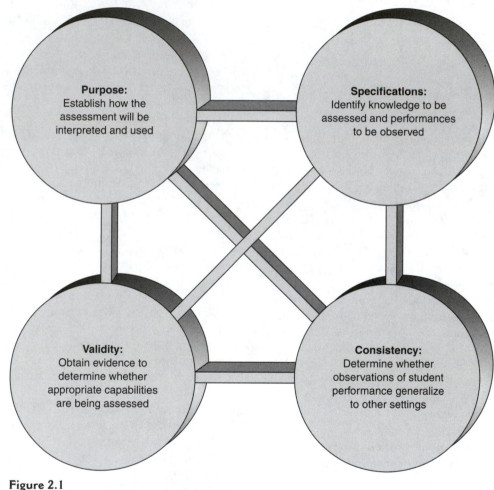

Figure 2.1
The assessment framework

2

Determining How Your Assessments Will Be Interpreted and Used

A teacher hands back your test. All that is written on it is a number. You got a 37. What is the first question you are probably going to ask? Most likely it will be something like, "What does 37 mean?" or, "Is this a high score or a low score?" Basically, you need a frame of reference to interpret that score. Any measure of performance needs a reference in order to be interpreted.

Any of several references can be used for interpreting performance. You probably thought of at least one of these references when you were pondering how to interpret the score of 37. Some examples of references are

If I got 37, how did others do?

Is 37 high or low with respect to what I can do?

Does 37 mean I have improved?

What does 37 mean I can and cannot do?

Each question is asking for a frame of reference. We will observe, however, that some frames of reference are more useful than others. This chapter emphasizes criterion-referenced and norm-referenced interpretations of performance, which are typically the two most useful frames of reference in the classroom. However, we will also review the characteristics of two other widely used frames of reference.

Further, this chapter helps you achieve four skills:

- Identify frames of reference that help interpret student performance
- Recognize the meaning of criterion-referenced and norm-referenced interpretations
- Recognize when criterion-referenced and norm-referenced interpretations are preferable
- Identify qualities desired in criterion-referenced and norm-referenced tests

FRAMES OF REFERENCE FOR INTERPRETING PERFORMANCE

We will consider four approaches to interpreting student performance:

Ability-referenced, in which a student's performance is interpreted in light of that student's maximum possible performance

Growth-referenced, in which performance is compared with the student's prior performance

Norm-referenced, in which interpretation is provided by comparing the student's performance with the performance of others or with the typical performance for that student

Criterion-referenced, in which meaning is provided by describing what the student can and cannot do

Table 2.1 summarizes characteristics of these four frames of reference.

Ability-Referenced Interpretations

Ability-referenced interpretations are a comparison of a student's performance to that student's potential performance. Statements such as "That's about all this student can do" or "This student can do better if given more time" are examples of ability-referenced interpretations.

The key to using ability as the frame of reference is having a good estimate of the student's maximum potential. Therein lies the problem. Teachers usually have only tentative, broad ideas of what each student is capable of doing. Although previous work and information from

Table 2.1
Four references commonly used for interpreting classroom assessments

	Interpretation Provided by This Reference	Condition That Must Be Present for This Reference to Be Useful
Ability-referenced	How are students performing relative to what they are capable of doing?	Requires good measures of what students are capable of doing; their maximum possible performance
Growth-referenced	How much have students changed or improved relative to what they were doing earlier?	Requires pre- and postmeasures of performance that are highly reliable
Norm-referenced	How well are students doing with respect to what is typical or reasonable?	To whom students are being compared must be clearly understood
Criterion-referenced	What can students do and not do?	Content domain that was assessed must be well defined

other teachers provide ideas about a student's general ability, little information is available concerning specific abilities that are pertinent to the student's present performance. Furthermore, previous performance establishes what a student *has* done, not what the student is capable of doing.

Standardized aptitude tests including "intelligence tests" provide teachers with estimates of students' ability, but these estimates also are general and of limited use in interpreting a student's performance. Furthermore, standardized aptitude tests typically indicate which students will achieve the most rather than how much a particular student can achieve. As with all measures of ability, scores on aptitude tests are usually confounded by other variables, such as student background, prior achievement, and motivation.

Perhaps the greatest limitation of ability estimates is that we usually do not know precisely which abilities are prerequisite to the skills we are trying to teach. Because ability-referenced interpretations depend on having accurate measures of specific abilities relevant to a skill, which are difficult to obtain, abilities provide a limited frame of reference for interpreting student performance. We usually do not have a good understanding of a student's maximum possible performance.

Growth-Referenced Interpretations

Growth-referenced interpretations compare a student's present skills to prior performances. This is a natural frame of reference in the classroom, since improvement in skills is highly relevant.

Growth, of course, implies change over time; that is, a change in performance between earlier and later measures of student performance. For the measure of growth to be reliable, both the earlier and present measures must individually be reliable. If the earlier measure is simply a teacher's present recollection of each student's earlier performance, this "measure" of earlier achievement will likely have very low reliability and, likewise, so will the growth-referenced interpretations.

Portfolio systems used by many teachers help get around this problem. They typically provide actual samples of earlier work to which present performance can be compared. As long as measures of the same skills can be obtained from the earlier and present work, and both work samples are reliably scored, then growth-referenced interpretations can be meaningful. In fact, the reliable measure of growth is one of the potential strengths of portfolio systems.

Growth-referenced interpretations are often combined with what we later identify as norm-referenced interpretations. Norm-referenced interpretations involve the comparison of a student's performance to that of others. Statements such as "This student has improved more than others" or "This is one of the best classes I have had in terms of how much students have learned" combine growth- and norm-referenced interpretations. Interestingly, the reliability of interpretations that combine growth and norm references becomes very low as the correlation between how students perform on the earlier and present measure becomes high. This is because reliable differences observed on the present measure are subtracted out if the same relative differences are observed on the earlier measure.[1]

Unless actual samples of a student's earlier performance with the same skill are available, growth-referenced interpretations tend to have significant problems, and generally should be replaced with norm-referenced and criterion-referenced interpretations. For summative evaluations, only norm-referenced and criterion-referenced interpretations should be used.

Norm-Referenced and Criterion-Referenced Interpretations

Norm-referenced interpretations involve comparing the student's present performance to a range of previously observed performances, usually the performances of other students. We often make comparisons with other individuals or events to help interpret what we see. How well a student did on a test is often described in terms of how others in the class did. Similarly, measures such as how much it rained, how fast you were driv-

---

[1]Expressed as a formula, the reliability of growth-referenced scores becomes

$$r_{growth} = \frac{\dfrac{r_A + r_B}{2} - r_{AB}}{1 - r_{AB}}$$

where r_A and r_B are the reliability of scores on the earlier and present measures of students' achievement and r_{AB} is the correlation between scores on the earlier and present measures.

ing, and how you feel today are often interpreted through comparison with other similar events. It rained less than it usually does, I have never driven this fast, and so on. These are all norm-referenced interpretations.

For describing student performance, norm-referenced interpretations are limited in that they do not define what a student can and cannot do. However, they do help answer such questions as what is typical and what is reasonable.

Criterion-referenced interpretations, in contrast, involve comparing a student's performance to a well-defined **content domain.** Examples of content domains include the ability to locate a word in a dictionary; to associate famous composers of music with historical periods, such as baroque, classical, and romantic; or to solve an algebraic equation involving whole numbers and one unknown.

The key to making a criterion-referenced interpretation is having a well-defined domain. A criterion-referenced interpretation describes student performance within that domain. That is, a criterion-referenced interpretation indicates what a student can and cannot do with respect to the content domain. However, unlike norm-referenced interpretations, criterion-referenced interpretations do not answer questions of what is typical and what is reasonable.

Criterion-referenced and norm-referenced interpretations are generally the most useful frames of reference for describing student performance; hence, our focus on these two references.

MEANING OF CRITERION- AND NORM-REFERENCED INTERPRETATIONS

Criterion-referenced means that a score is being interpreted in terms of the skills the test measures. To permit a criterion-referenced interpretation, the description of what is being measured does not necessarily have to be elaborate, but it must be concise. Indicating that a student can type 37 words per minute allows a criterion-referenced interpretation of an individual's performance. So does stating that a student can perform 12 chin-ups, list the 50 states, spell two-digit numbers, or convert temperatures from the Fahrenheit to the Celsius scale. Each of these examples establishes a specific skill that a student can perform and, therefore, represents a criterion-referenced interpretation. Note that each result can be interpreted even without reference to how other students performed. For instance, knowing that a particular student can spell two-digit numbers provides useful information about that student even without knowing what other students have achieved.

In contrast, a test is said to be norm-referenced if it compares a student's performance with the typical range of performances. Indicating that a student can type faster than 60% of the students completing a typing class represents a norm-referenced interpretation of performance, as does indicating that a student can do more chin-ups than 30% of other students the same age, can spell better than half the other students in the class, or is the best violinist in the orchestra. The group of people to whom the student is being compared is the **norm group.**

Note that in the examples of norm-referenced interpretations, the student's skill can be described in general terms. Saying that a student is "the best violinist in the orchestra" indicates that the individual performs better than other violinists in the orchestra but does not describe the violinist's specific skills—what this violinist can and cannot do. Norm-referenced interpretations can be made using more general descriptions of the domain than can criterion-referenced interpretations. Stated differently, content domains that cannot be well defined favor, or even require, norm-referenced as opposed to criterion-referenced interpretations.

Although norm-referenced interpretations can be made with more general descriptions of the content domain, they do require a well-defined norm group. A description of the violinist as the best in the orchestra provides meaningful information only if we have a clear understanding of which orchestra is being referenced.

✿ 2.1   Apply What You Are Learning

Do each of the following allow a criterion-referenced or norm-referenced interpretation of performance?

1. Katherine won the 100-meter race.
2. Willis ran one mile in 5 minutes, 12 seconds.
3. Raul scored near average on the final chemistry exam.
4. Carmen can separate alcohol from water through distillation.
5. In geometry, David cannot bisect an angle.
6. Brandy obtained the best score on the geometry test.

Answers can be found at the end of the chapter.

Both criterion-referenced and norm-referenced interpretations can be and usually are applied to a performance. For instance, we might observe that the student who types 37 words per minute is faster than 60% of the other students in the class. Both perspectives provide useful information.

It is possible for a test to be neither criterion-referenced nor norm-referenced. This condition is undesirable because without a good reference, a score lacks meaning. This point was illustrated at the opening of the chapter, when we observed that a score of 37 had no meaning when given without reference, such as what the test measured or how others did on the test. This fact is so obvious that few teachers would report a score in this manner without elaboration.

For less-obvious reasons, however, many classroom tests lack both criterion-referenced and norm-referenced interpretations. This situation typically occurs when a teacher wants to use a criterion-referenced test but does not understand that a criterion-referenced interpretation requires a well-defined content domain. The following examples illustrate this point.

Example 1: Ellen scored 92% on an algebra exam.

This performance cannot be given a criterion-referenced interpretation because the specific skills measured by the exam are not detailed. We do not know what Ellen can or cannot do. Nor is it possible to specify what instruction she should now receive. Scoring 92% may represent a high degree of competence if the exam measures difficult skills or low competence if the exam measures exceptionally easy skills. Converting scores to percentages does not in itself allow a criterion-referenced interpretation of a test. Ellen's performance cannot be norm-referenced either, unless comparison scores are also given.

Example 2: Natalie surpassed the criterion score of 80% and, therefore, passed the spelling test.

Again, this performance cannot be given a criterion-referenced interpretation because the specific skills measured by the test are not described. Unless the types of words sampled by this test are known, we cannot tell whether scoring above 80% (or any other passing score) indicates a high or low proficiency in spelling. Establishing a passing score, sometimes called a criterion score, does not by itself allow for a criterion-referenced interpretation. We will see later that passing scores are applicable to both norm-referenced and criterion-referenced tests. Also, both norm-referenced and criterion-referenced interpretations can be given to test scores with or without specifying a passing score.

Largely because of a short article by Glaser (1963) published in the *American Psychologist,* criterion-referencing of tests gained considerable popularity. This trend has been healthy because knowing what students can and cannot do is a critical element to effective assessment and instruction. With the increased popularity of criterion-referencing, however, numerous, varying definitions emerged, not all of which were appropriate. An article written by Nitko (1984) stressed the importance of a well-defined domain of skills to making criterion-referenced interpretations. According to Nitko, the nature of a well-defined domain may be ordered or unordered. When a domain is ordered, indicating a student's position within the domain also indicates what

that individual can and cannot do. Here are examples of well-defined, ordered domains:

- A list of words ordered according to their spelling difficulty
- A series of pictures depicting finger positions on piano keys ranging from an untrained position through progressively more appropriate finger positions
- A series of math items ordered such that correctly answering each item (or a group of items) requires mastery of a skill more complex than the skill needed to master the preceding item in the series

In the first example, noting the most difficult word a student can spell identifies specific words the student can and cannot spell. Similarly, identifying the picture that most closely resembles a student's finger positions on piano keys indicates what the student must still learn. A similar interpretation can be given to a student's score on an ordered series of math items. In practice, domains tend not to represent perfect orders. For instance, a student may be able to spell some more difficult words and not some easier ones.

Nitko (1984) pointed out that a large number of important school learning outcomes represent unordered behavioral domains. The skills and, consequently, the test items that are included in a domain are clearly established (well defined), even though the skills cannot be ordered. Here are examples of well-defined, unordered domains:

- The addition of pairs of three-digit numbers that require regrouping
- Correctly lighting a Bunsen burner
- Locating words in a dictionary

These examples may require a student to perform a particular sequence of behaviors; however, measuring the student's proficiency with these skills would probably not pinpoint that individual's performance on a continuum within the domain. In contrast, if a student's mastery of the lighting of Bunsen burners required knowledge of gas burners whose complexity in lighting ranged from simple to complex, this would represent an ordered domain.

Nitko proposed various approaches to defining unordered domains. Two of them are to specify the stimulus and response attributes or to specify only the stimulus attributes of test items that belong in a domain. Another approach is to define a domain in terms of a common error made by students, for example, erroneously inverting the letters *ie* when spelling words.

Note that a passing score is not essential to a criterion-referenced interpretation of test performance. For either criterion-referenced or norm- referenced tests, however, a passing score may be administratively convenient and useful. For instance, tests used by colleges and employers to help select the best applicants are norm-referenced. Cutoff scores are commonly used with these tests. A teacher who uses a mastery learning strategy establishes a cutoff score to determine which students will be provided further instruction. Unless the test measures a well-defined domain, however, the presence of a cutoff score does not facilitate a criterion-referenced interpretation. Educators often mistakenly believe that preset cutoff scores, rather than the well-defined domain, allows for criterion-referenced interpretations.

❧ 2.2   Apply What You Are Learning

Indicate whether each of the following allows a criterion-referenced interpretation, a norm-referenced interpretation, or neither.

1. Tyrone obtained a score of 100.
2. Using a periodic table, Donna can name each of the elements.
3. Using graph paper, a ruler, and a protractor, Kristin can determine the sine, cosine, and tangent of angles.
4. Pablo scored 90 on a history exam.
5. Using a map of the United States, Ricky can show the location of the 10 largest Civil War battles.
6. Suzanne passed the geography test.
7. Yao can select the specified number of objects when verbally given the numbers 1 through 12.
8. In terms of grade-point average, Kirk graduated 194th among 210 students in his high school class.
9. Donna passed the oral portion of her Spanish final exam.
10. Henry knows more vocabulary words than 80% of his second-year German class.

Answers can be found at the end of the chapter.

We must emphasize that the usefulness of a test depends largely on how well the domain being measured is defined or how adequately the norm group to whom students are being compared is described. Not all classroom or standardized tests are equal regarding these important qualities. The best criterion-referenced tests determine within a specific domain exactly what each student can and cannot do. The best norm-referenced tests give a statement of a student's ability through comparison with a clearly defined and relevant group of other individuals. Many tests deviate from these ideal standards. Unfortunately, some classroom and standardized tests provide no reference at all from which to interpret their scores.

CHOOSING THE APPROPRIATE INTERPRETATION

The type of interpretation to use depends on the parameters available and the information needed from the results. Criterion-referenced interpretations are indicated when content domains can be well defined and it is important to determine what students can and cannot do. Norm-referenced interpretations are preferred when a relevant and well-defined norm group can be established and it is important to describe student performance in terms of what is typical or reasonable. As noted earlier, it is common to use both references, with one emphasized over the other based on the situation.

The type of evaluation often influences the reference used for the interpretation. For instance, assessments used for preliminary evaluations may occur in the absence of norms. In such a case, assessments have to be criterion-referenced. However, measures used for summative evaluations may involve content domains too broad to be well defined. These measures then have to be norm-referenced. Let us next examine the influence of the type of evaluation on the selection of a frame of reference.

Interpretations for Preliminary Evaluations

Preliminary evaluations occur when you first meet students, usually within the first 2 weeks. Either norm- or criterion-referenced interpretations are emphasized, depending on circumstances.

When preliminary evaluations involve general or overall assessments of students' knowledge and attitudes, norm-referenced interpretations are required. These general assessments of what students know or what their attitudes are involve domains too broad for criterion-referenced interpretations. As always when norm-referenced interpretations are used, it is important to identify your norm group. Are you comparing the new students with each other, with previous students when they were new, with previous students at the end of last year, or possibly with what you consider to be ideal students? Each reference may be appropriate, but it is important to recognize what the comparison group is.

A student may be her or his own norm group. During preliminary evaluations, you often establish what is reasonable or typical for individual students. This norm becomes useful for interpreting later performance.[2]

_____

[2]When is a comparison like this norm-referenced and when is it growth-referenced? It is norm-referenced when you compare a student's performance with her or his range of previous performances. Then you are answering the question, "How does the present performance compare to what is typical for this student?" In contrast, the interpretation is growth-referenced if you are asking, "How much has this student improved or otherwise changed compared to a previous observation?" However, growth-referenced interpretations are problematic unless there is clear documentation of the student's prior performance. When careful documentation of prior performance does not exist, norm-referenced interpretations are preferable to growth-referenced interpretations.

Assessments leading to preliminary evaluations may be criterion-referenced instead of, or as well as, norm-referenced. Is a student a loner? Does he volunteer ideas or ask questions? Does she know the names for numbers? Does he know what is meant by electrolysis? Each of these can be a well-defined domain. Each is a domain that can be used to describe what a student can and cannot do (or in the case of attitudes, does or does not do). Each can also be norm-referenced when used to describe what is reasonable or typical.

Interpretations for Diagnostic Evaluations

Diagnostic evaluations are used to judge students' level of performance prior to instruction or to establish the source of the problem when students seem unable to achieve during instruction. Diagnostic evaluations are concerned with prerequisite or enabling skills.

Diagnostic evaluations usually require criterion-referenced interpretations as they involve knowing what a student can and cannot do. Thus, prerequisite or enabling skills must be expressed as well-defined domains. However, it is often difficult to understand fully what the prerequisite skills are or to have the time to measure each of them. For this reason, diagnostic evaluations tend to be sporadic or constrained.

Although diagnostic evaluations emphasize criterion-referenced interpretations, they also may be norm-referenced, for instance, if it is important to know whether a student's problem is typical. You may respond differently if the problem is common to most students rather than unique to a few students.

Interpretations for Formative Evaluations

Formative evaluations occur during instruction. Their purpose is to monitor learning in order to determine whether instruction should continue, should be modified, or should cease. Determining what students can and cannot do is central to formative evaluations. Criterion-referenced interpretations are required.

Most classroom assessments lead to formative evaluations. The majority of these assessments involve the teacher's informal observations and questions, but also include paper-and-pencil quizzes, and products included in portfolios. To be criterion-referenced, these formative evaluations must involve well-defined domains. This process becomes a significant challenge for teachers—in terms of both difficulty and importance. During instruction, the teacher must always perceive instructional goals in terms of well-defined domains. The domains must allow the teacher to describe what students can and cannot do.

Interpretations for Summative Evaluations

Summative evaluations follow instruction and typically involve unit tests, midterm and final exams, and projects or other end-of-unit assignments. Summative evaluations usually use general or global content domains. Often, only a sample of specific content domains is assessed. Summative evaluations typically require norm-referenced interpretations.

Portfolios are being used increasingly for some academic subjects to accumulate samples of students' work. If these samples represent well-defined domains, criterion-referenced interpretations of these summative evaluations are possible. This kind of information is particularly useful for parents and other teachers because it describes what the child can do rather than simply indicating how the child compares with others.

SUMMARY

To be interpretable, scores on a test or any measure must have a frame of reference. Four interpretations commonly used by teachers are ability-referenced, growth-referenced, norm-referenced, and criterion-referenced. Of these, the norm-referenced and criterion-referenced interpretations tend to be the most useful. Norm-

referenced interpretations require a clearly defined norm group. Criterion-referenced interpretations require a well-defined content domain.

Often, both norm and criterion references are used to interpret student performance, although specific settings tend to emphasize one interpretation more than the other. Diagnostic and formative evaluations emphasize criterion-referenced interpretations. Preliminary evaluations rely heavily on both. Summative evaluations emphasize norm-referenced interpretations.

ANSWERS: APPLY WHAT YOU ARE LEARNING

2.1. 1. norm-referenced; 2. criterion-referenced; 3. norm-referenced; 4. criterion-referenced; 5. criterion-referenced; 6. norm-referenced.

2.2. Items 2, 3, 5, and 7 allow criterion-referenced interpretations because each refers to a well-defined domain. From each of these items, one can indicate what the student can and cannot do relative to the domain. Items 8 and 10 allow norm-referenced interpretations. Although the specific skills that are referenced by these two items are not well defined (e.g., all that is known for sure about the vocabulary words is they are German), both of these items relate student performance to the performance of others. Items 1, 4, 6, and 9 allow neither criterion-referenced nor norm-referenced interpretations. None of these latter items establishes a well-defined domain. For example, the skills that are included in the geography test or the oral portion of the Spanish exam are not specified. In addition, none of these latter items relates student performance to the performance of others.

SOMETHING TO TRY

- Think of a paper-and-pencil test you recently administered as a teacher or a test you took as a student. Was an ability-, growth-, norm-, or criterion-referenced interpretation used with this test? Why did you come to this conclusion? (Very often, more than one reference is used to interpret a particular test.) If an ability-referenced interpretation was used, was the maximum possible performance of each student well understood? If a growth-referenced interpretation was used, was the earlier level of performance well documented? If a norm-referenced interpretation was used, was the group with which students were being compared clearly understood? If a criterion-referenced interpretation was used, was the content domain well defined?

- Think about a recent assessment that was not a paper-and-pencil assessment, such as a portfolio assessment or an informal observation or question. What were its references? Why did you come to that conclusion?

ADDITIONAL READING

Berk, R. A. (Ed.). (1984). *A guide to criterion-referenced test construction*. Baltimore, MD: Johns Hopkins University Press. Each chapter focuses on an issue important to criterion-referenced testing, such as describing alternative types of criterion-referenced tests, specifying what is to be measured by a test, determining test length, validating a test, and estimating the reliability of test scores.

Bloom, B. S., Madaus, G. F., & Hastings, J. T. (1981). *Evaluation to improve learning*. New York: McGraw-Hill. Chapters 4 through 6 provide a detailed discussion of formative, diagnostic, and summative evaluations.

Fremer, J. J. (1994). A 30-year retrospective on criterion-referenced testing (Special issue). *Educational Measurement: Issues and Practice, 13,* 4. This issue provides an overview of the criterion-referenced testing movement. Articles are written by Glaser, Hambleton, Linn, Millman, and Popham, all of whom are recognized for contributions in this area. The series of articles begins with Glaser's original 1963 article, and concludes with a separate article by Glaser in which he addresses issues that remain unresolved related to criterion-referenced testing.

Glass, G. V. (1978). Standards and criteria. *Journal of Educational Measurement, 15,* 237–261. This article provides a useful elaboration on the meaning of criterion in the term criterion-referenced and shows the word was not intended to imply a minimum performance standard.

3

Measurable Objectives and Goals

This chapter is concerned with making learning visible. Unless a teacher can see, hear, or use other senses to detect a student's learning, the teacher cannot know whether learning has taken place. A teacher cannot assess a student's learning unless there is observable evidence of that learning.

Making learning visible, however, is difficult. Most of a person's knowledge and mental actions are invisible to others. Because we cannot see a person's thoughts, we depend on indicators that suggest the nature of his or her knowledge. To illustrate, consider the following:

How could you indicate that you know the universe is very large and that it contains a very large number of objects?

How could you indicate that you know the concept of multiplication?

In both cases, you might provide evidence of your knowledge as follows:

Regarding the magnitude of the universe, you might say the universe is large because it contains Earth, other planets, and our sun. The sun is one of billions of stars in our galaxy, and individual stars are light-years away from each other. Our galaxy, although very large, is but one of millions of galaxies in the universe.

Regarding the concept of multiplication, you might use several illustrations to show

that multiplication is repeated additions. For example,

$$4 \times 3 = 3 + 3 + 3 + 3$$

To provide evidence of your knowledge, you must do things that others can see. Likewise, to assess a student's knowledge, a teacher must ask students to do something visible that indicates presence of that knowledge. A description of what students will be asked to do is called a **performance objective.** (Alternative names for performance objectives are *behavioral objectives* or *instructional objectives;* these names are interchangeable.) A performance objective describes an observable event that will indicate that a student has learned the targeted knowledge.

Performance objectives can be categorized by underlying capabilities or learning outcomes. Associating each objective with one of these categories helps assure that the correct learning outcome is being measured. Otherwise, as performance objectives only describe a visible manifestation of a skill, the visible performance may be the result of a capability other than the one being assessed. For example, a teacher may ask a student to solve a multiplication problem, such as 4×3, intending to measure the student's comprehension of multiplication; in fact, however, the teacher is measuring knowledge of multiplication tables.

This chapter helps you achieve five skills:

- Recognize categories of learning outcomes
- Identify characteristics of performance objectives
- Select your own performance objectives
- Communicate performance objectives to students
- Distinguish between performance objectives and instructional goals

CATEGORIES OF LEARNING OUTCOMES

The following exercise will help demonstrate that different types of learning are involved. Two people or two groups of people are needed.

Ask the first person to watch you, and tell the second person seated nearby to look away. Hold up three fingers, and ask the first person to state how many fingers are shown. The first person will say three. Ask the person who is looking away to state how many fingers are being shown. The second person will also say three. The demonstration can be continued using different numbers of fingers.

From outward appearances, the performance of both persons in this demonstration is the same. However, very different capabilities are involved. The first person is illustrating the capability of counting. The second person is illustrating the ability to recall information. Although the first and second person may each have both capabilities, this may not be the case for students in the process of learning the concept of counting. A teacher must carefully structure observations so that the student's performance is a true indicator of the capability being measured.

You can improve the chances of measuring the appropriate capability by knowing the types of capabilities involved. Bloom (1956) and Gagné (1985) proposed the separate categories of knowledge that are listed in Table 3.1. Both sets of categories, particularly Bloom's, are widely used in education.

Bloom devised his categories through a series of informal conferences that he led from 1949 to 1953, during which a large number of performance objectives, primarily from college-level courses, were reviewed. His taxonomy actually was an attempt to categorize behavioral objectives rather than establish the nature of knowledge. Development of the taxonomy was governed by

Table 3.1
Categories proposed by Bloom and Gagné

Bloom's Taxonomy	Gagné's Capabilities
Knowledge: Information, such as specific facts, principles, trends, criteria, and ways of organizing events	*Verbal Information:* Same as what Bloom calls Knowledge
Intellectual Skills	*Intellectual Skills*
Comprehension: Use of information without necessarily applying this information to new situations and without fully understanding the implications of this knowledge	*Discriminations:* Reacting to stimuli such as visual images and determining whether they are the same or different
Application: Use of an abstract concept in a specific but previously unused situation	*Concrete Concepts:* Identifying physical objects or images that have a specified characteristic
Analysis: Breaking a concept or communication into its component parts	*Defined Concepts:* Understanding of an abstract classification
Synthesis: Putting elements together into a cohesive whole	*Rules:* Applying principles that regulate the relationship among classes of objects or events
Evaluation: Making a judgment about the value of products or processes for a given purpose	*Higher Order Rules:* Combining a series of rules into a single more complex rule or into the solution of a problem

Note: In addition to the categories shown in the table, Gagné adds *cognitive strategies, motor skills,* and *attitudes.* Bloom lists motor skills and attitudes as separate domains that he refers to as the psychomotor and affective domains. Other individuals have proposed taxonomies for the psychomotor and affective domains.

educational, logical, and psychological considerations, in that order of importance, with emphasis placed on developing categories that matched "the distinctions teachers make in planning curricula or in choosing learning situations" (Bloom, 1956, p. 6). Bloom referenced three domains—cognitive, affective, and psychomotor—but he developed categories for only the cognitive domain.[1]

Gagné took a different tack. He borrowed from historical models derived from experimental psychology to propose conditions that must occur in order for learning to take place. These models included reinforcement models such as those associated with behaviorism, and information processing models that have been used more recently by cognitive psychologists. From the models, Gagné proposed that there are "several varieties of performance types that imply different categories of learned capabilities" (Gagné, 1985, p. 17).

As Table 3.1 suggests, categories proposed by Bloom and Gagné share some basic similarities, yet there are important differences. What Bloom refers to as *knowledge* is the same thing that Gagné calls *verbal information*. Although not widely known, Bloom refers to his remaining five categories as *intellectual skills*. Gagné uses this same name, although Bloom and Gagné suggest very different structures for these skills. Bloom refers to the affective and psychomotor domains that were noted earlier. Gagné adds to *verbal information* and *intellectual skills* the capabilities he calls *cognitive strategies, motor skills,* and *attitudes*.

Cognitive psychologists use somewhat similar categories of learning outcomes, but refer to them as **declarative knowledge** and **procedural knowledge.** Declarative knowledge is equivalent to what Bloom calls knowledge and Gagné calls verbal information. Declarative knowledge is knowing that something is the case. It is information that can be conveyed in words; that is, knowledge that can be declared.

---

[1]Krathwohl, Bloom, and Masia (1964) proposed a taxonomy of educational objectives for the affective domain. Harrow (1972) similarly proposed a taxonomy for the psychomotor domain.

Procedural knowledge is roughly equivalent to what Bloom and Gagné both refer to as intellectual skills, although the overlap is not complete. Although Bloom's taxonomy remains widely used in education, the subcategories Bloom associates with intellectual skills depart substantially from what is now known about the structure of procedural knowledge (Confrey, 1990; Gierl, 1997; Snow, 1989; Tittle, Hecht, & Moore, 1993). Procedural knowledge is knowing how to do something. Procedure knowledge involves making discriminations, understanding concepts, and also applying rules that govern relationships. Cognitive psychologists find that procedural knowledge often includes motor skills and cognitive strategies.

In modern cognitive psychology, **problem solving** is presented as a third category. The ability to solve problems builds on declarative and procedural knowledge. Problem solving may involve domain-specific strategies, suggesting that different strategies are employed when solving problems in different content areas, such as math and writing.

Because they are assessed differently, it is important to look at the differences between declarative knowledge, procedural knowledge, and problem solving. We will also briefly look at attitudes, which in classroom settings are typically assessed through informal assessments.

Declarative Knowledge

Declarative knowledge refers to information one can state verbally. Declarative knowledge includes the recall of specific facts, principles, trends, criteria, and ways of organizing events. An example is *recalling* that you saw three robins as opposed to looking at the robins and determining that you see three birds. Other examples include recalling the definitions of words, recalling physical and chemical characteristics of elements and compounds, and recalling that the trend each year is for an increase in the number of cars on the highway. Recalling that books can be categorized as fiction and nonfiction is also an example of declarative knowledge, as is recalling that Ohm's law pertains to the relationship among electrical resistance, voltage, and amperage.

It is important to understand the difference between declarative and procedural knowledge. Asking students to state what they know measures only declarative knowledge, not procedural knowledge. A very broad range of questions can be used to ask students to declare what they know. For example:

Tell me what is meant by relative humidity.

What is the difference between air and oxygen?

Why do interest rates affect the stock market?

Contrast the geography of northern and southern Africa.

Why do heavy objects like ships float in water?

Each of these examples measures declarative knowledge. None measures procedural knowledge, which we will learn requires the use of very different types of questions.

Often the importance of declarative knowledge is downplayed, even to the extent of discouraging the teaching and assessment of this type of knowledge. This happens in part because declarative knowledge is wrongly thought of as being limited to the memorization of facts. Although knowledge of facts is part of declarative knowledge, so is knowledge of trends, abstractions, criteria, and ways of organizing events. As we note later, declarative knowledge is fundamental to one's ability to solve intellectual problems.

Procedural Knowledge

Procedural knowledge is knowledge of how to do things. Examples of procedural knowledge include demonstrating conversions between the Fahrenheit and Celsius scales; correctly classifying whales, sharks, porpoises, salmon, and other sea animals as fish or mammal; and identifying which object in a picture is a tree. Other examples include visually discriminating between a $1 and a $5 bill, and predicting whether an object will float or sink in water.

Although the same content is often involved in both declarative and procedural knowledge, these two capabilities are distinct. For example, being able to state that most assessments in a classroom are informal rather than formal (declarative knowl-

edge) is different from being able to observe and correctly classify assessments as informal or formal (procedural knowledge). Likewise, being able to explain that transmissions with a cellular phone are routed from one transmitting tower to another as one travels (knowledge that can be declared) is different from being able to identify which cordless phones are cellular phones (knowledge that requires invoking a classification procedure). Unfortunately, it is common to assume that a student has achieved both types of knowledge after examining only one of these two capabilities.

🌑 3.1   Apply What You Are Learning

One situation in each of the following pairs is an example of declarative knowledge, whereas the other is an example of procedural knowledge. Indicate which (A or B) is an example of procedural knowledge.

1. A. Knowing that a touchdown in football is worth 6 points
   B. Distinguishing between a touchdown and a safety
2. A. Looking at the fish caught by each of several individuals and determining who caught the most fish
   B. Recalling the next day who caught the most fish
3. A. Naming the capital cities of each state
   B. Given descriptions of several cities, identifying which are capital cities
4. A. Describing the difference between declarative knowledge and procedural knowledge
   B. Classifying descriptions as examples of declarative knowledge and procedural knowledge

---

Answers can be found at the end of the chapter.

From a measurement prospective, it is useful to subdivide procedural knowledge into **discriminations, concepts,** and **rules.** Each presents a different way to assess different aspects of procedural knowledge.

Discriminations. Discriminations are the most basic procedural skill. They involve reacting to stimuli, such as visual images, and determining whether they are the same or different. Examples are determining whether two pencils are the same or whether two sounds are the same. The student is not told what characteristic is being compared, nor asked to give a name to what is being observed or to describe in what ways (if any) the stimuli are different. Instead, discriminations are concerned with whether a student is sensitive to a relevant difference.

Students, particularly older students, learn most relevant discriminations on their own. With young children (such as in early elementary grades), many discriminations are deliberately taught and assessed. Forming letters and numbers involves fine discriminations, such as the difference between p and q, or between l and 1. When a student is having trouble learning a skill involving procedural knowledge, the problem may be that he or she is missing an important discrimination. Discriminations are implicit within concepts such as weight, color, shape, and size. A student who exclaims, "Now I see what you are talking about," may be conveying the importance of a missing discrimination.

Again, discrimination is a very basic procedural skill and does not involve a student describing or explaining a difference, or even calling it by name. For instance, having a student pick up multiple objects that are identical in every way except for one being heavier than the others would assess discrimination associated with weight. The student would be asked to identify the object that is different from the others. To assess discrimination, the student would *not* be told to "identify the one that is heavier" than the others, or to describe in words how the one object is different from the others. Discriminations often are prerequisite to concepts. For instance, being sensitive to the quality of weight is prerequisite to learning the concept "weight."

Concepts. Concepts involve a characteristic that can be used to classify physical objects or abstractions. To assess concrete concepts, have students point at or otherwise identify objects or images that have the specified characteristic. Examples include identifying which objects are balls, or circling the letter *d* within words.

The examples to be classified should be provided by the teacher rather than the student. The examples should involve previously unused illustrations of the concept that include characteristics relevant to their classification as examples versus nonexamples. If students provide the examples, or if previous illustrations are reused, it is possible that knowledge of information rather than knowledge of the concept is being assessed. That is, a *declarative* rather than *procedural* representation may be involved.

Because a concept involves a *class* of things, it should be assessed under a variety of conditions. If, for example, the concept of "rectangle" is being taught, the student should be asked to identify rectangles that have light or heavy lines, those with lengths close to and much longer than the widths, and those displayed at different angles. The student similarly should recognize that circles, triangles, and other shapes that have light or heavy lines are not rectangles. To demonstrate mastery of a concept, a student must perceive all qualities relevant to the concept and disregard all qualities irrelevant to the concept. To learn a concrete concept, a student must have already learned *discriminations* that are inherent in the concept.

Abstract concepts involve understanding a classification of nontangible objects, events, or relations. That is, unlike concrete concepts, abstract concepts involve things that cannot be touched or directly sensed. Examples include the concepts of sailing, the game of basketball, or a mystery novel. Another example is the meaning of a tax shelter. Abstract concepts typically incorporate concrete concepts. For instance, sailing involves boats, wind, water, sails, and many other concrete items that can be touched or otherwise sensed. However, the concept of sailing also involves abstractions such as right-of-way rules and the boat's center of gravity. Because abstractions cannot be touched or pointed at, students are asked to distinguish between examples and nonexamples of the concept. And here again, students should be assessed under a variety of conditions.

The distinction between concrete and abstract concepts is not always clear because concrete and abstract concepts often share the same name. For example, the basic shape of a rectangle is learned as a concrete concept. However, conceptualizing a rectangle as "a closed plane figure formed by four line segments that intersect at right angles" is an abstract concept. These are different concepts, knowledge of which would have to be assessed separately.

Rules. Rules involve the application of principles that regulate the relationship among classes of objects or events. For example, a rule pertains to using the indefinite article *a* or *an* in sentences. Another example is applying Boyle's law (the product of the volume of a confined gas and its pressure is a constant) by calculating what the pressure of air in a pump would become if its volume were decreased by 90%. Rules in this sense are *not* statements of proper procedure such as leaving the classroom only after obtaining permission. Instead, a rule involves abstract functional relationships such as those previously referenced.

To assess a rule, students should be asked to apply the rule. Rules regarding the use of the indefinite article *a* or *an* in sentences can be assessed by asking students to supply the indefinite article within sample sentences. Boyle's law can be assessed by having students solve problems in which air pressure and volume must be computed for varying conditions.

As with concepts, the teacher and not the student should provide the situations to which the rule is to be applied. Directions to the student might even suggest which rule is to be applied, as in the problem "Convert 75° Fahrenheit to Celsius." The examples should involve previously unused applications of the rule. Obtaining unused applications is often very simple, such as using a different Fahrenheit temperature, or using unknown words when measuring students' knowledge of spelling words involving *ie.*

Being able to state a rule (information) is different from using the rule. Stating, "The product of the volume of a confined gas and its pressure is a constant," is not equivalent to applying Boyle's law, nor is stating Boyle's law a prerequi-

site to understanding this rule. Information often facilitates learning concepts and rules but is not a prerequisite to, and certainly is not equivalent to, a working knowledge of concepts and rules.

✤ 3.2 Apply What You Are Learning

Listed here are some educational goals or general objectives. Which type of knowledge (declarative or procedural) does each reference? If procedural knowledge is involved, indicate whether discrimination, a concept, or a rule is involved.

1. Recalling information published in the newspaper
2. Correctly spelling words involving *ie,* such as receive and piece
3. Identifying animals by name, when each is seen on a farm
4. Stating names of animals that were seen at a farm
5. Classifying an example as a preliminary, diagnostic, formative, or summative evaluation
6. Stating the difference between a rule and concept
7. Seeing a difference in marks made by a pencil and pen, although not being able to describe the difference in words

---

Answers can be found at the end of the chapter.

Procedural knowledge is of course different from motor skills, but the demonstration of procedural knowledge often involves motor skills. Particularly in early elementary school, it may be more effective to have students physically group objects to demonstrate knowledge of a concept. For instance, students could demonstrate knowledge of what a nail is by separating diverse nails into one group and similar-looking objects such as screws and thumbtacks into another. Similarly, to demonstrate knowledge of a rule governing subject–verb agreement, it may be necessary for students to write sentences using paper and pencil or a computer. The ability to appropriately use gestures when speaking or to correctly determine the weight of an object using a balance scale are other examples of procedural knowledge whose assessment involves motor skills. So is climbing a rope, writing with a pencil, sanding a piece of wood, tuning a violin, or lighting a Bunsen burner. Because procedures such as these so heavily involve motor skills, performance assessments rather than written tests must be used for evaluating a student's knowledge.

Problem Solving

A problem to be solved exists when one has a goal and has not yet identified a means for reaching that goal (Gagné,[2] Yekovich, & Yekovich, 1993). An example of problem solving would be the process a student must go through when required to write an expository paper or prepare a persuasive speech. Another example would be the process required by a student to identify the best route to take when traveling by car to a distant city.

By "problem solving," we are not referring to one's ability to solve a math problem such as multiplying pairs of two-digit numbers. That skill involves procedural knowledge, specifically a rule. Once that rule is learned, the student can apply the procedure to multiply other pairs of numbers. With experience, implementation of the rule is likely to become automated.

A student's ability to solve a problem is assessed in a manner somewhat similar to that used for assessing rules. Both involve presenting a specific situation in which students can apply their skill. However, in assessing problem solving, students are not told which relationships are involved; instead, they are asked to generate a solution from the knowledge they have or, more simply, to solve a problem. Often, any of several responses represents a legitimate solution to the problem. Thus, written tests involving multiple-choice or even essay items do not provide effective measures of problem solving. Performance assessments, in which students are observed, often individually and under controlled conditions, are a better alternative.

---

[2]Robert M. Gagné authored *Conditions of Learning* in 1985. Ellen D. Gagné, with Carol Walker Yekovich and Frank R. Yekovich, authored *The Cognitive Psychology of School Learning* in 1993.

Attitudes

Attitudes are the learned mental states that influence a student's typical behavior. Choosing to go to a movie rather than a play illustrates the existence of an attitude. So are many other choices a person makes such as looking for alternative points of view rather than accepting a single point of view, or rereading a sentence that is unclear rather than accepting what is understood on the first reading. Cultures tend to reinforce selected attitudes, although often inconsistently.

Assessment of attitudes involves measuring typical rather than maximum performance. Teachers, however, measure maximum performance more often than they measure typical performance. In part, this is because it is difficult to structure an assessment that accurately elicits typical performance. Also, it is often unclear when an attitude should be measured with the intent of modifying behavior perceived as undesirable. As noted earlier, one is more likely to use informal assessments such as casual questions or observations to assess attitudes.

🌑 3.3 Apply What You Are Learning

Listed here are descriptions of behaviors. Use the following options to identify the category each behavior represents:

    A. Declarative knowledge
    B. Procedural knowledge
    C. Problem solving
    D. Attitude

1. Listing the letters of the alphabet
2. Naming the letter of the alphabet being shown
3. Placing a coat on a hanger
4. Determining which computer will best meet your needs
5. Reading a science fiction book rather than a mystery
6. Using a learned procedure to classify paintings by historical period
7. Naming the oceans of the world

8. Determining what clothes are appropriate to wear when visiting a country with which you are not familiar
9. Identifying the category each of the foregoing behaviors represents (that is, what capability have you just been demonstrating?)

Answers can be found at the end of the chapter.

COMPONENTS OF PERFORMANCE OBJECTIVES

You are aware that another person's knowledge cannot be seen. One must infer knowledge from what we see the other person do. A performance objective establishes what students will be asked to do in order that we can make reasonable inferences about what they know. That is, the performance objective prescribes the observable events that provide a reasonable basis for concluding that knowledge has been achieved.

When declarative or procedural knowledge is involved, performance objectives can be used to identify the student performance that is to be observed. Goal statements are used when problem solving is involved. In this section, we divide a performance objective into four components: **name of capability, behavior, situation,** and **special conditions.**

Name of Capability

For each objective, it is useful to indicate the type of capability being assessed. Again, as performance objectives only describe a visible manifestation of knowledge, there is always the danger that a student's performance is the result of a capability other than the one being assessed. Particular behaviors provide good indicators of the various types of capability. Naming the capability involved alerts us to the type of behavior we should use to assess the knowledge being evaluated. Table 3.2 lists the type of behavior used to assess each type of capability.

Table 3.2
Type of performance used to assess each type of capability

Type of Capability	Performance Used to Assess Capability
Declarative Knowledge	
Information, such as specific facts, principles, trends, criteria, and ways of organizing events	Ask students to state what they know
Procedural Knowledge	
Discrimination, such as reacting to visual images, sounds, or other sensory stimuli and determining whether they are the same or different	Provide students several identical examples, except one that is different with respect to the stimuli to be discriminated; ask students to identify the one that is different from the others
Concept, such as identifying physical objects or images that have a specified characteristic, or understanding an abstract classification	Ask students to classify diverse and previously unused illustrations as examples versus nonexamples of the concept
Rule, such as applying principles that regulate the relationship among classes of objects or events	Provide students a relevant but previously unused example and ask them to apply the rule
Problem Solving	
Using declarative knowledge and procedural knowledge, and often specific strategies, to reach a goal for which a means of reaching the goal has not yet been identified	Ask students to generate a solution to the problem

The strategy proposed here is to actually include the name of the capability as part of the performance objective. Whereas one might use the formal names of capabilities, I recommend abbreviated names. Instead of "declarative knowledge" I use the name *information* since declarative knowledge always involves verbally conveying information. As noted earlier, it is useful to subdivide procedural knowledge into what we refer to as discriminations, concepts, and rules, since each presents a different way to assess different aspects of procedural knowledge. Therefore, instead of writing out *procedural knowledge* in our performance objectives, I simply state the appropriate subcategory: *discrimination, concept,* or *rule.*

Behavior

A learning outcome can be measured only if it can be observed. To create an observable event, a student must exhibit a behavior. The central role of a performance objective is to identify a behavior that indicates that the targeted learning has occurred.

To be most useful, the behavior should be specified in a manner that can be observed directly; that is, no inferences should be required to indicate whether the behavior has occurred. The performance objective must specify exactly what you will see.

🌐 3.4   Apply What You Are Learning

Listed here are pairs of events. Within each pair, one event can be observed directly, the other cannot. The event that can be observed directly is the better candidate for a performance objective. For each pair, select the event that can be directly observed.

1. A. Knows letters of the alphabet
   B. Orally names all letters of the alphabet
2. A. Points to a specified letter in a word
   B. Describes the letter in the word to which you are pointing
3. A. States the name of the historical period during which a painting was created

   B. Is able to associate paintings correctly with historical periods
4. A. Knows how to find a word in the dictionary
   B. Opens the dictionary to the page containing the targeted word

Answers can be found at the end of the chapter.

Notice that in the first pair, one cannot directly observe "Knows letters of the alphabet." Within the second pair, "Describes the letter" requires an inference to determine whether a description has occurred; the event "describe" is not directly observable. When writing performance objectives, it is tempting to use descriptions of the skill rather than a direct statement of what students will be observed doing. To be most useful, the performance objective must state the behavior that will be observed. One must establish what that behavior will be in order to construct test items that will require students to perform that behavior.

By attaching the name of the capability to the statement of behavior, we create a performance objective. Here is what they would look like:

Information: Orally names all letters of the alphabet

Concept: Points to a specified letter in a word

Concept: States the name of the historical period during which a painting was created

Rule: Opens the dictionary to the page containing the targeted word

Situation

Often the context in which the student exhibits the behavior is relevant. May a dictionary be used when translating sentences from another language? May a calculator be used when solving math problems? Will the student be allowed to select the topic when asked to give an extemporaneous speech? Most characteristics of a situation are not specified either because they are obvious (such as the language in which the speech is to be given) or because they are judged not to be critical to defining the skill (such as the topic of the material being translated to another language).

Judgments have to be made about which if any situations will be specified as part of the performance objective. Including the following situations might help clarify the preceding objectives (the situation is italicized):

Concept: Points to specified letter in a word *when the teacher points to a word in a book and names a letter.*

Concept: *When shown an unknown painting that is clearly characteristic of the period,* states the name of the historical period during which the painting was created.

Special Conditions

Sometimes it is appropriate to place conditions on the action (for example, indicating how quickly the student must point to the appropriate letter within a word) or to establish a standard (such as the need to make a correct identification 80%, or possibly 100%, of the time).

Special conditions are sometimes confused with situations. A situation specifies the context in which the behavior will occur. Special conditions, in contrast, specify conditions that must be present in the student's behavior in order to conclude that the targeted knowledge has been learned. As with situations, judgment must be used about which, if any, special conditions are to be specified. Here is an example of a special condition in a performance objective (the special condition is italicized):

Information: Orally names all letters of the alphabet *in ABC order*

Special conditions are not always specified in a performance objective. Thus, a performance objective does not necessarily include a performance standard or passing score. Not all authors agree with this point of view. For example, Mager (1984) proposes that a performance standard should always be included within the objective to define a successful performance, a practice that is still widely followed. Later in the book, we will show that establishing a passing score on a test is not always possible or necessary. Even when passing scores are used, it may be appropriate to establish

the passing score *after* the test has been administered and the performance of students evaluated. In some situations, then, it would be inappropriate to specify a performance standard in the objective.

🌀 3.5 Apply What You Are Learning

Each of the three performance objectives listed here has been partitioned with brackets, and the partitions are numbered. Within these objectives, indicate whether each partition is a capability, behavior, situation, or special condition.

[Concept]:[1] [Within two seconds,][2] [point to the specified letter within a word].[3]

[Rule]:[4] [Given sentences orally spoken in English,][5] [orally state equivalent sentences in German].[6]

[Concept]:[7] [Given two sounds whose pitches are discrepant in frequency by 1%,][8] [orally state whether the first or second sound has the higher frequency].[9]

Answers can be found at the end of the chapter.

SELECTION OF PERFORMANCE OBJECTIVES

Ultimately, the teacher selects or creates performance objectives for her or his own class. However, the following four guidelines may facilitate selection of a useful set of objectives:

1. Describe the *results* of learning rather than strategies for facilitating learning

2. Use behaviors that are relevant indicators for the capability that is to be learned

3. Obtain indicators of all critical aspects of the knowledge being assessed

4. Obtain indicators for an appropriate sample of all knowledge that is to be learned

Describe the Results of Learning

Performance objectives specify what one will be able to see the student do if the student has learned the targeted knowledge. According to

Linn and Gronlund (2000), to name consequences of learning that are observable, performance objectives should *not* be specified in terms of the following characteristics:

- *Teacher performance,* such as saying, "Students will be taught to spell correctly."
- *Learning process,* such as stating, "The student will learn how to add numbers."
- *Course content,* such as indicating, "The student will know the difference between criterion- and norm-referenced tests."

To avoid these problems, always ask what you will be able to see the *student do* after the knowledge being taught has been learned.

Use Relevant Behavior as Indicators

Performance objectives do not describe knowledge. They describe indicators of knowledge. Considerable care must be taken to make sure the behavior specified in the objective is relevant to the knowledge that is being assessed. Table 3.2 lists the type of behavior used to assess each type of capability.

Again, different behaviors serve as good indicators for the various types of knowledge. You are encouraged to include the name of the capability as part of the performance objective. Although it does not assure that relevant behaviors will be used, naming the capability can help make you aware of the type of behavior that is appropriate.

Assess All Critical Aspects of the Knowledge

Because only indicators of knowledge are being described, it is probable that one performance objective by itself does not address all critical aspects of a particular knowledge. Attending to all critical aspects of the knowledge, more than anything else discussed in this chapter, requires the abilities of a highly intelligent and perceptive teacher. The teacher must have mastery of what is being taught so that critical aspects of a concept or rule are evident. The teacher must be perceptive

of how these critical aspects can be seen in the behavior of another person. Reading periodicals, such as *Reading Teacher* and *Arithmetic Teacher,* among others, and talking with other teachers are useful tools in developing this knowledge.

Assess an Appropriate Sample of Knowledge

It is likely that the teacher will not be able to assess all knowledge that is to be learned within the course of a school year. When this is true, the teacher must select an appropriate sample of knowledge, a sample that is representative of overall content and does not exclude important skills.

To determine areas for which performance objectives are to be selected, the teacher should work from a general domain to a specific set of objectives. A way to accomplish this is to prepare a table such as Table 3.3. Column headings are types of capabilities, and row headings are content areas. For this illustration, the content areas are for an elementary school math class. The Totals column provides estimates of the percentage of time to be associated with each content area. These percentages are judgments of the teacher and are used to help match objectives to priorities of the class. In this illustration, objectives related to discriminations are not included.

The numbers within each cell are estimates of the emphasis to be placed within a content area on each of the capabilities. For example, the first content area is physical measurements. The first cell within this role indicates that 5% of overall learning will involve *information* within the physical measurements area. The numbers in each row add up to the total percentage for that row.

The percentages in the table appear to be highly precise statements concerning the amount of learning that should occur in each pairing of content and capability. However, they are not precise. These numbers represent subjective estimates that help identify where emphases within the class occur. In using such a table, whether this number is 2 or 3 is irrelevant; what is important is whether the number in a particular cell is relatively large or small.

Table 3.3
Framework for selecting objectives in an elementary math class

	Declarative Knowledge	Procedural Knowledge		Problem Solving	
	Information	Concepts	Rules		Totals
Physical measurements	5	5	5	-	15
Time	2	3	-	-	5
Money	4	2	4	-	10
Counting numbers	2	3	5	-	10
Addition and subtraction	3	5	8	4	20
Multiplication and division	3	5	8	4	20
Fractions	2	3	5	-	10
Geometric shapes	6	4	-	-	10

Selecting performance objectives is tedious and time-consuming. It is work to be shared with others who are or have been teaching the same material. Curriculum supplements typically provide teachers with lists of objectives or cite sources of objectives. Many educational organizations and state agencies also have and publish lists of objectives. These objectives always need to be reviewed critically and must be selected within the context of content and capabilities to be taught in the class.

CONVEYING PERFORMANCE OBJECTIVES TO STUDENTS

Performance objectives should be communicated to students. Knowing what is expected can help motivate them and also helps students determine when a skill has been achieved.

Communicating performance objectives does not necessarily imply that students are to be provided with a list of objectives; a student who lacks the skill about to be taught may be unable to comprehend the meaning of the stated objective. Also, research conducted some time ago revealed no improvement in learning when students are provided objectives before instruction (Duchastel & Merrill, 1973; Melton, 1978). Teachers can convey performance objectives to students simply by illustrating the behavior that is to be learned.

The method used to communicate objectives should take into account the category of performance that is to be taught. Table 3.4 lists the categories we discussed earlier and proposes a technique for conveying each type of capability to students. For example, a teacher who wants students to describe the different types of clouds (information) might tell students they will be expected to recall what each type of cloud looks like. However, if the teacher wants students to be able to associate weather patterns with various types of clouds (a rule), the teacher might show students pictures of some clouds and illustrate the ability to forecast weather associated with these clouds.

GOALS VERSUS PERFORMANCE OBJECTIVES

Goals are broader than performance objectives. As we have noted, a performance objective details the specific *behavior* that indicates that the student has obtained the capability being assessed. For instance,

Rule: Given sentences orally spoken in English, orally state equivalent sentences in German.

The assessment of a well-written performance objective requires no inference. No inference is

Table 3.4
Techniques for informing students of the objective

Type of Capability	Instructional Technique
Declarative Knowledge	
Information	Describe what students will be expected to recall
Procedural Knowledge	
Discriminations	(Learner is informed later)
Concepts and Rules	Demonstrate the activity to which the learner will be asked to apply the concept or rule
Problem Solving	Demonstrate the situation to which the learner will be asked to solve the problem

required in the above objective because one can observe this behavior directly.

Goals are stated more generally than objectives. For example,

Orally translates from English to German

A goal is often the equivalent of several objectives. With performance assessments, it is quite natural to use an instructional goal rather than performance objectives, since the skills being assessed are often highly complex in terms of the number of behaviors involved. Similarly, a group of several goals is used to provide the context for a portfolio. The use of goals rather than equivalent sets of objectives allows brevity. With complex skills, instructional goals may provide more practical descriptions than provided by performance objectives.

Inferences are required to assess whether a student has achieved a goal. This allows flexibility in terms of the specific criteria that will be used to judge a student's performance. This flexibility can be damaging though, because it increases measurement error resulting from subjectivity in developing an assessment and scoring results. For this reason, when we discuss performance assessments and portfolios in later chapters, we give careful attention to how one selects performance and products to be included in performance assessments and portfolios, and how one evaluates a student's work.

SUMMARY

Student performance can be categorized into capabilities. Research in cognitive psychology indicates the existence of three dominant types of capability: declarative knowledge, procedural knowledge, and problem solving. For brevity, in this book we refer to declarative knowledge as information. We subdivide procedural knowledge into three subcategories: *discriminations, concepts,* and *rules.* Being aware of the type of capability involved is important, because different kinds of student performance are used to assess the different kinds of capabilities.

Performance objectives specify the behaviors that indicate that targeted knowledge has been learned. Performance objectives include up to four components: the name of the capability, the behavior, the situation, and special conditions. Naming the capability helps the teacher focus on appropriate indicators of knowledge. The behavior is central to the objective and specifies what will be seen when learning has occurred. The situation describes the context in which the student will be asked to indicate achievement. The special conditions, if necessary, specify conditions that must be met for the student's performance to be judged successful.

Performance objectives are best selected from a general domain, such as a table that lists the content and capabilities to be learned. Objectives can be conveyed to students without actually being stated.

Particularly with performance assessments and portfolios, goals are substituted for objectives. Goals are stated more generally, and assessing whether a student has achieved a goal requires inference. The flexibility inherent in goals increases subjectivity in both the development and scoring of student assessments.

ANSWERS: APPLY WHAT YOU ARE LEARNING

3.1. 1. B; 2. A; 3. B; 4. B.

3.2. 1. declarative; 2. procedural (rule); 3. procedural (concept); 4. declarative; 5. procedural (concept); 6. declarative; 7. procedural (discrimination).

3.3. 1. A; 2. B; 3. B; 4. C; 5. D; 6. B; 7. A; 8. C; 9. B.

3.4. 1. B; 2. A; 3. A; 4. B.

3.5. 1. capability; 2. special condition; 3. behavior; 4. capability; 5. situation; 6. behavior; 7. capability; 8. situation; 9. behavior.

SOMETHING TO TRY

• A student's outward performance may provide an inaccurate or misleading indication of the student's learned capabilities. Can you recall personal experiences when a teacher or other person used an individual's outward behavior to make an incorrect conclusion about that individual's knowledge or attitude? What are strategies you might use to reduce the number of inaccurate conclusions drawn from outward behaviors?

• This chapter (and most of the other chapters in this book) includes several *Apply What You Are Learning* exercises. They in essence are self-assessments. Look at some of these exercises and try to identify which capability is being assessed by the exercise.

• Think of a *capability* you would try to teach your students. (Be sure not to confuse *capability* with *performance*. An example of a capability is knowing the concept of addition or knowing a rule such as that describing the relation between the density of an object and its ability to float on water.) Then list student *performances* that would be good indicators of whether this capability has been learned. Identify by name the type of capability you have described.

ADDITIONAL READING

Bloom, B. S. (Ed.). (1956). *Taxonomy of educational objectives: Handbook 1. Cognitive domain.* New York: McKay. Discusses the technique used to classify objectives, describes categories of the cognitive domain, and presents example objectives and test items within each category. Part 2 of this book presents the familiar taxonomy and includes numerous illustrations. Section 1 of Part 2 discusses *knowledge,* what contemporary psychologists call *declarative knowledge.* Bloom's illustrations provide one of the best demonstrations that declarative knowledge goes well beyond the memorization of facts.

Gagné, E. D., Yekovich, C. W., & Yekovich, F. R. (1993). *The cognitive psychology of school learning.* New York: Harper Collins. This book provides a very readable discussion of cognitive psychology, and carefully discusses implications to learning in classroom settings. Separate sections are devoted to learning mathematics, science, reading, and writing.

Gagné, R. M. (1985). *The conditions of learning* (4th ed.). New York: Holt, Rinehart, and Winston. Discusses the nature of learned capabilities and conditions required for students to learn each capability.

Gronlund, N. E. (1999). *How to write and use instructional objectives* (6th ed.). Upper Saddle River, NJ: Merrill/Prentice Hall. This small book describes how to write objectives for attitudes as well as intellectual and performance outcomes. Suggestions are given for using objectives within instruction.

4

Gathering Evidence of Validity

Validity pertains to the degree to which a test measures what it is supposed to measure.[1] More than on any other factor, the quality of a test depends on its validity. If a test does not measure what it is supposed to measure, it is useless. Validity is the most central and essential quality in the development, interpretation, and use of educational measures.

Validity is an abstraction. We cannot directly see validity any more than we can directly see a student's knowledge we wish to assess. Instead of directly observing validity, we depend on various evidence that indicates the presence or absence of validity. Much like the evidence Agatha Christie's famous detective Hercule Poirot uses to solve a mystery, an educator uses evidence to determine whether a test is measuring what it is supposed to measure.

The various types of evidence that Hercule Poirot uses can be divided into familiar categories, such as physical, eye-witness, and circumstantial evidence. These categories provide a useful way to structure a discussion of evidence,

but they also are arbitrary and alternative categories have been devised.

The same applies to validity evidence related to educational tests. The categories of evidence currently most widely used are those presented in the 1985 *Standards for Educational and Psychological Testing* (AERA, APA, NCME, 1985), which groups validity evidence into three interrelated categories: construct-related evidence, content-related evidence, and criterion-related evidence. As we will observe, the distinctions among these categories are not clear, and one type of evidence does not negate the need for other types.

Construct-related evidence establishes whether the student performance to be observed represents a legitimate indicator of the capability or psychological construct the teacher hopes to assess. Content-related evidence establishes how well the actual content of questions, tasks, observations, or other elements of a test corresponds to the student performance that is to be observed. Criterion-related evidence indicates how well a student's performance on a test correlates with her or his performance on relevant criterion measures external to the test.

Our discussion of gathering evidence of validity will use these three categories. Later in this chapter, we will introduce an expanded view of validity proposed by Messick (1989a) and also describe the categories of validity evidence more recently proposed in the 1999 *Standards for Educational and Psychological Testing* (AERA, APA, NCME, 1999).

You have very likely observed evidence (or perhaps lack of evidence) of validity in tests you have taken. For instance, you may have observed that some written tests developed by some teachers more adequately sample the content covered in the course than do others. You may have noticed that the wording or structure of questions on some tests more accurately measures what you have and have not learned. Perhaps you have noticed how effective teachers are careful to substantiate conclusions they draw from assessments. Each of these situations

---

[1] As noted in Chapter 1, *educational measurement* refers to the process of determining a quantitative or qualitative attribute of an individual or group of individuals that is of academic relevance. *Test* refers to the vehicle used to observe that attribute, such as a written test, a performance assessment, an informal observation, or an oral question.

involves collecting evidence of validity. In this chapter, we will look at specific ways to develop and apply that evidence to classroom assessments.

This chapter helps you achieve three skills:

- Recognize types of evidence used to establish validity
- Apply these types of evidence to formal and informal classroom assessments
- Recognize the role of validity in the interpretation and use of tests

CONSTRUCT-RELATED EVIDENCE OF VALIDITY

Construct-related evidence establishes a link between the underlying but invisible construct we wish to measure and the visible performance we choose to observe. The constructs of greatest relevance to teachers are those of learned knowledge. As with any psychological construct, learned knowledge cannot be directly seen. We cannot see what a student knows or is thinking. Therefore, to establish construct-related evidence of validity, we must establish that the visible student behaviors we choose to observe are legitimate indications of the student knowledge we wish to evaluate.

In Chapter 3, we learned that what a student learns involves declarative knowledge, procedure knowledge, and the ability to solve problems. A different type of behavior is used to assess each of these capabilities. Therefore, to establish construct-related evidence of validity, we need to be aware of which type of capability is involved, and then ensure that our assessment involves a type of performance that provides a good indication of achievement for that particular capability. Let us look in further detail at the type of performance used to assess each of the three types of capabilities.

Declarative Knowledge

Declarative knowledge pertains to knowledge that can be recalled, including facts such as his-

torical dates, names of cities, or chemical properties of common elements. Declarative knowledge also includes knowledge of principles, trends, and ways of organizing events. An example of a principle is knowing that deciduous trees lose their leaves in the winter. An example of a trend is recalling that the population of cities has generally increased over time. All such knowledge can be assessed by asking students to state what they know. A teacher can measure a student's declarative knowledge through oral questions or any format of items used in written tests. We are using *information* to refer to declarative knowledge.

Assessing procedural knowledge requires observing different types of performance. Instead of stating something, the student must do something. For example, if a student knows a *concept,* the student can identify examples of that concept in very different settings. Take our earlier example of the concept of "rectangle." Simply asking a student to define or describe a rectangle does not measure the student's knowledge of the concept. Instead, it measures *information*—the student's ability to recall the definition or characteristics of a rectangle.

Procedural Knowledge

Procedural knowledge involves concepts, rules, and discrimination. Knowledge of the concept of a rectangle would be measured by asking a student to point to examples of a rectangle. The student should be expected to identify those examples within the context of other objects that are not rectangles. The student should also be able to identify diverse examples of rectangles (for instance, rectangles with very similar or very different lengths and widths).

Knowledge of concepts can be measured through oral questions and by most formats used in written tests. For instance, even true-false items can ask a student to select which of several illustrations are correct examples of the concept. Alternately, a student can mark examples of a concept, such as circling words within a paragraph that are verbs. Completion items, however, tend not to provide a good format for measuring a concept. Having a student write one or even several words in a blank usually does not help determine whether that student can distinguish between correct and incorrect illustrations of a concept.

Assessing a student's knowledge of a *rule* requires observing a different kind of performance. Consider, for example, knowledge of Ohm's law, an equation that specifies the relationship among electrical voltage, amperage, and resistance. Having a student state or describe Ohm's law would not measure the student's understanding of the rule. It would measure information—the student's ability to describe or declare information about Ohm's law. Asking a student to provide an example of Ohm's law could easily involve recall of information if the student used previously learned examples. To measure a student's knowledge of a rule, the teacher must ask the student to apply the rule to concrete situations. For example, a student might be asked to determine electrical voltage when given amperage and resistance. As with concepts, knowledge of rules is assessed by asking a student to apply the knowledge in diverse settings. For instance, the student might also be asked to determine what happens to electrical voltage if resistance is decreased while amperage remains constant.

The same test formats used to measure knowledge of concepts can be used with rules. For instance, oral questions are an effective technique for asking students to apply a rule. With the multiple-choice format, students might have to select the options that represent a correct application of a rule. The essay format can be used to describe what a particular rule indicates will happen under specified conditions. Again, the completion format generally is not able to measure students' ability to apply a rule. There are, however, notable exceptions. For instance, when application of a rule, such as Ohm's law, results in a single number, a completion item can be used to elicit a student's response. Similarly, when application of a rule, such as selecting the appro-priate tense of a verb, results in a single word, a completion item can be used to obtain a student's response.

Discrimination involves reacting to stimuli and determining whether they are the same or different. Discriminations are a very basic form of procedural knowledge that are formally assessed much more often in early elementary grades than with older children. Discriminations involve any stimuli, such as hearing, seeing, and touch. An example of a discrimination is detecing a difference in pitch of two sounds. The student is not told what characteristic is being compared, nor asked to give a name to what is being observed or to describe in what ways the stimuli are different. The student is only asked to detect whether there is any difference. For instance, a student would listen to a small series of sounds that are identical in every way, except the pitch of one sound is of a different pitch than others in the series. The student would be asked which sound was different from the others. Again, note that the student is not asked to describe the difference or give it a name. Discriminations are prerequisite to concepts. That is, learning a concept is not possible unless the student is sensitive to discriminations. Learning discriminations are justified in terms of their relevance to concepts. Declarative and procedural knowledge are largely justified through their importance to solving problems.

Problem Solving

Problem solving involves reaching a goal when a means for reaching that goal has not yet been identified. The solution will require use of previously learned information, concepts, and rules. An example of a goal would be establishing a strategy for locating two floats of different sizes under an object so that the object floats level in the water. Students who are able to solve this problem would likely use various strategies and utilize different subsets of concepts and rules. To efficiently solve problems, students must have established useful structures that organize their declarative knowledge, and must also have automated relevant procedural knowledge in the sense that concepts and rules can be applied without having to think through the process.

To assess problem solving, a teacher must be aware of the characteristics of different approaches, each of which represents a legitimate solution of the problem. Of equal importance, the teacher must use assessment procedures that provide students flexibility in selecting appropriate and inappropriate approaches. Written tests, including the essay format, generally do not provide this flexibility. Student proficiency with problem-solving skills usually must be determined through performance assessments. Portfolios may provide a useful approach to managing the assessment of problem solving. As with declarative and procedural knowledge, construct-related evidence of the validity of assessments involving problem solving depends on establishing the nature of the capability, which is an invisible process that goes on in the mind, and determining whether the performance that will be observed represents a legitimate indicator of that capability.

CONTENT-RELATED EVIDENCE OF VALIDITY

Content-related evidence of validity indicates how well the content of a test corresponds to the student performance to be observed. (Remember, the term *test* covers written tests, performance assessments, portfolios, informal observations, and oral questions.) You can think of content-related evidence as an extension of construct-related evidence. Through construct-related evidence, we determine the nature of knowledge we need to assess and establish student behaviors that will provide good indicators of that knowledge. Through content-related evidence, we determine how well our test incorporates those behaviors.

Poor planning or lack of planning by the teacher may result in a test that does not incorporate targeted behaviors. You probably have found evidence of this in some of the written tests you have taken or in the poor choice of observations some teachers use for making judgments

about their class. You probably have also noticed how some teachers carefully plan what they are going to observe when they informally assess students during instruction.

Another reason that a test may not incorporate targeted behaviors is that a test always involves sampling; that is, it includes only a sample of the behaviors that could be assessed, mainly because of lack of time and other resources. With informal observations, there is only enough time to observe a small fraction of what goes on in the classroom. Written tests, performance assessments, and portfolios similarly involve only a small sample of potential student behaviors. Some samples, however, are better than others. Including a representative sample of content within a written test or informally observing a representative sample of students is better than using unrepresentative samples.

Content-related evidence of validity is often established *while an assessment is being planned*. It involves a systematic analysis of what the test is intended to measure. Two techniques are commonly used for defining the intended content of a test: the first involves the establishment of a table of specifications; the second uses performance objectives.

Table of Specifications

A table of specifications consists of a two-dimensional chart. The vertical dimension of the chart lists the content areas to be addressed by the test. The horizontal dimension lists the categories of performance the test is to measure. Table 4.1 illustrates what a table of specifications might look like for an astronomy unit in science related to our solar system. The vertical dimension lists the three basic content areas addessed within that unit. The horizontal dimension lists the three capabilities that are involved.

A table of specifications is similar to the framework described in Chapter 3 for selecting performance objectives (see Table 3.3). Both that framework and a table of specifications use the same two dimensions: content and capabilities.

Table 4.1
Table of specifications for an astronomy test on the solar system

	Information	Concepts	Rules	Totals
Physical characteristics of planets, asteroids, and comets	6	5	—	11
Location of planets, asteroids, and comets	3	—	6	9
Terms used to describe orbits of planets	4	—	—	4

However, the framework for selecting objectives includes content for the entire school year or term. A table of specifications is much easier to develop since it lists only the content to be covered by a single written test or other assessment.

Table 4.1 indicates that the three capabilities judged to be the most central to this astronomy unit are information, concepts, and rules. On another assessment, another combination of capabilities might be used, including discrimination and problem solving.

The numbers within the table of specifications indicate the number of test questions to be associated with each content area and capability. A greater number of questions indicates that more emphasis or importance is given to that particular content area and capability. To establish these numbers, the teacher must determine the following:

First, the total number of items to be included in the test

Then, the number of items to be associated with each content area, entering these numbers in the Totals column

Finally, the number of items within a content area to be associated with each capability

---

🌑 4.1   Apply What You Are Learning

Based on the table of specifications illustrated in Table 4.1, answer the following questions.

1. How many items should be concerned with the physical characteristics of planets, asteroids, and comets?

2. Of the items that are concerned with the physical characteristics of planets, asteroids, and comets, how many should measure information?
3. How many items on the overall test should measure information?
4. What is the total number of items in this test?

Answers can be found at the end of the chapter.

A table of specifications is quite easy to construct. It does play an important role in the development of a test, and is most commonly used with written tests. A table of specifications establishes content-related evidence of validity because its use will control the content of the test. One is much more likely to construct tests that are valid if the overall content of tests are planned out prior to their development. A table of specifications provides one means of implementing that planning.

Performance Objectives

Another good approach for establishing content-related evidence of validity is to work from performance objectives. A performance objective can be thought of as the intersection of a row and column within a table of specifications, because each performance objective identifies both the content and the performance category of a skill. Chapter 3 suggests that each objective begin by stating the performance category or capability that is involved. The content is then specified through the behavior, situation, and special conditions components of the objective. In essence, a list of performance objectives can substitute for a table of specifications.

Table 4.2 lists performance objectives that are equivalent to the table of specifications presented

Table 4.2
List of performance objectives for an astronomy test on the solar system

	Number of Questions
Information: State the physical characteristics of each of the planets with respect to size, rotation, basic surface features, and physical state.	6
Information: Draw a picture that shows the relative location of orbits of planets, asteroids, and comets.	1
Information: Using original wording, state the meaning of each term used to describe the orbit of a planet.	4
Rule: Given a star chart that shows the planets and Earth's moon, point in the direction in the sky where each of these objects will be located.	3
Concept: Classify an object as a planet, asteroid, or comet when shown its picture.	5
Rule: Given a diagram from *Dance of the Planets* showing the location of the planets at a given time, mark the location of a specified planet one year later.	3
Information: State the reasons the planets and our moon change their apparent location in the sky when viewed from Earth.	2

in Table 4.1. The number of questions that will be used to measure each objective is specified, indicating the emphasis each skill is to receive in the test.

Applications to Formal Classroom Assessments

A table of specifications or the list of objectives is developed before the test or other assessment is constructed. This then becomes a blueprint or plan for determining test content. When the test is completed, the table or list of objectives is used to help judge the validity of the test.

When developing a test, a teacher uses judgment to determine how specific the test plan should be. As with blueprints that guide constructing projects, the amount of detail required in a test plan depends on the significance of the test. A simple construction project such as building a birdhouse probably does not require a blueprint; remodeling a porch might require establishing some specifications; building a three-bedroom house calls for a fairly detailed blueprint; and constructing a large commercial building requires highly detailed plans specifying how parts of the

framework will be joined and where ventilation ducts will be routed.

Similarly, a short quiz often can be developed without a formal table of specifications or list of objectives, and content-related validity probably can be established by using the teacher's idea of what is to be measured. Even if a major error in judgment results and the quiz has low validity, the implications of constructing one invalid quiz are minor.

However, any assessment that covers several weeks of instruction should be based on formal specifications. Such assessments include written exams, such as essay or objectively scored tests; performance assessments, such as of a student's speech; and major take-home projects used for summative evaluations.

As occasionally happens when carpenters build houses, teachers constructing important assessments may overestimate how well they can develop the assessment without a formal plan. For example, without a written plan, a teacher might develop a test by selecting the more innovative test questions from among those included with curricular materials. Likewise, a teacher might focus on questions that will challenge students, instead of first establishing the content that is to be assessed. The carpenter who misjudges the need for specifications must adjust for or sometimes accept the errors that result. The teacher who misjudges the need for specifications often uses an assessment whose content is inconsistent with the focus of the class. The resulting low validity of such an assessment is a significant concern because the quality of each classroom assessment depends on its validity more than on any other factor.

● 4.2   Apply What You Are Learning

Indicate (yes or no) whether each of the following statements describes a correct procedure for establishing content-related evidence that a written exam is valid.

1. Look through all existing questions, remove questions that do not match one of the objectives, and use the remaining questions on the test.
2. First determine how many questions should be used to measure each objective. Then construct a test so that the number of questions measuring each objective matches this specification.
3. Use a set of test questions whose difficulties correspond to the range of students' abilities.
4. First develop a table of specifications. Then construct a test so that the content of questions included in the test corresponds to this specification.
5. Use questions that have been proven to distinguish between students who have acquired specific knowledge and those who have not.

Answers can be found at the end of the chapter.

Applications to Informal Assessments

Informal assessments are by nature spontaneous. Also, they typically are directed toward one student at a time, with wide variation across students. It is unlikely that a formal plan, such as a table of specifications or list of objectives, will be used, at least outwardly, with informal assessments.

Nevertheless, all assessments, including those that are informal, must be valid. Otherwise they are useless. Thus, content-related evidence of validity is relevant to informal assessments.

With informal assessments, content-related evidence is addressed before and after the assessments. Before instruction, while instructional activities are being planned, establish what will be observed and the type of informal questions that will be asked to determine whether students are learning important skills. Ask yourself whether declarative knowledge, procedural knowledge, or problem solving is involved so that the behaviors your questions require students to perform are appropriate. After instruction, or when planning the next day's activities, look back at what has been observed and ask what evidence, if any, confirms whether or not students have mastered critical skills. Frequently ask (1) what you should know about students, (2) what you know now about students, and (3) how you know what you know. Because informal assessments are spontaneous, it is easy to base evaluations on what was seen rather than on a representative sampling of content. By frequently looking back at what has been assessed, the representativeness of informal assessments can become quite good.

The content of what is observed varies widely from student to student. Knowledge about individual students gained through informal assessments, therefore, is much less complete than is knowledge learned about the class as a whole.

CRITERION-RELATED EVIDENCE OF VALIDITY

Criterion-related evidence indicates how well performance on a test correlates with performance on relevant criterion measures external to the test. Conceptually, criterion-related evidence of validity is quite simple. It asks, basically, "If a test is valid, with what other things should performance on the test correlate?" If, for example, a teacher's informal assessment of a student is valid, observations made through the informal assessment should be expected to correlate reasonably well with other knowledge the teacher has about the student. If it does not, one is inclined to question the validity of the informal assessment.

(The terms *criterion-related evidence of validity* and *criterion-referenced interpretations of performance* are sometimes confused. The meaning of these terms is distinct. Like norm, ability, and growth references, *criterion-referenced* refers to the frame of reference used to interpret performance on a test. It requires describing concisely the domain being measured by the test, and establishes what a student or group of students can or cannot do. In contrast, *criterion-related validity* is concerned with whether performance on a test correlates with other measures that should provide similar results. In fact, criterion-related evidence of validity is appropriate for criterion-referenced and norm-referenced tests.)

With criterion-related validity, the adequacy of the criterion is an important concern. As an example, a teacher's prior knowledge of a student often serves as the criterion for informal assessments. Therefore, it is important to ask how adequate the teacher's prior perceptions are.

Applications to Formal Classroom Assessments

With formal classroom assessments, criterion-related evidence of validity is obtained casually. Although this evidence is obtained casually, most teachers appropriately believe that using information beyond that obtained on a test is important. If a student's performance on a test is atypical, particularly if it is lower than expected, the teacher might question whether the test is valid. If a student has difficulties with a particular test format, such as essay or multiple-choice, the teacher might become suspicious about the validity of that format for the student.

It is always appropriate to look at performance on other measures as an indication of the validity of a formal assessment. Although not an infallible indication of validity, performance on other measures does provide some evidence of what the assessment measures.

Criterion-related evidence, as with all approaches discussed in this chapter, is also appropriate for establishing the validity of stan-dardized tests. Statistical correlations are often used to provide criterion-related evidence with these tests. For example, correlations are calculated between scores on the standardized test and scores on another relevant test, or even with scores on some later measure of academic performance, such as course grades. With classroom tests, however, statistical correlations usually are less useful than the teacher's determination of whether students' scores make sense in light of what else is known about their performance.

Applications to Informal Assessments

As with formal assessments, a teacher should use other indicators to help judge the validity of informal assessments. This is difficult, however, because of the spontaneous nature of informal assessments. By looking back intermittently at what else is known about individual students and the class in general, informal assessments can benefit from criterion-related evidence of validity.

VALID INTERPRETATION AND USE OF TESTS

Our discussion of validity has followed quite closely the framework established in the 1985 *Standards for Educational and Psychological Testing* (AERA, APA, NCME, 1985). Messick (1989a, 1989b) broadened this framework to include issues related to the use of test scores, including consequences associated with its interpretation and use. More recently, representatives from the organizations that devised the 1985 *Standards* reconvened and in 1999 published an update to the 1985 *Standards*. The update to the *Standards* incorporates elements of Messick's expanded view, and also restructures the framework within which validity evidence is discussed. Discussion of validity in the 1999 *Standards* is sophisticated, and also, unfortunately, not readily understandable by large segments of the population to which discussion of test validity must be directed (see, for example, comments by Fremer, 2000a, 2000b). Because of this problem, and also because the construct, content, and criterion-related categories of validity evidence are likely to dominate for the next several years, I have chosen to use the framework contained in the 1985 *Standards* in our preceding discussion of validity evidence. Nonetheless, important ideas and issues are raised by Messick's expanded discussion and the 1999 *Standards*. Each is introduced here.

Messick's Expanded View of Validity

Discussions of validity have traditionally focused only on evidence of what a test measures. Messick (1989a, 1989b) has described how this perspective is limited. He reasons that test validation is inseparable from the interpretation and intended use of tests.

Table 4.3 summarizes Messick's ideas. As illustrated in the table, Messick views validity in two dimensions, or facets. One dimension pertains to outcomes of a test, specifically, test interpretation (What do scores on the test mean?) and test use (What actions should result from having these scores?). The other dimension concerns justifications for the testing. It involves evidence that justifies interpretations and uses of the test as well as consequences of these interpretations and uses of the test.

This two-by-two matrix results in four cells. The upper-left cell concerns evidence supporting interpretations of the test, that is, evidence of what the test measures. Included here are the types of evidence discussed earlier in this chapter: how well the test measures relevant constructs, descriptions of test content, and awareness of how performance on the test correlates with other measures. All this evidence allows interpretation of test performance.

The remaining three cells within the matrix address issues traditionally not included in discussions of test validity. The upper-right cell concerns evidence supporting proposed uses of a test, in other words, evidence that the test is relevant and useful for its intended application. This aspect of validity is especially relevant to classroom tests. For instance, many classroom tests are formative in nature in that they are meant to help the students or the teacher determine what to do next. An important question, then, is whether such a test is relevant and useful for this formative role. For example, in language arts, does a writing assignment provide relevant and useful information for helping the student improve writing performance? In math homework or in a written test that requires solving binomial equations, does student performance provide the teacher relevant and useful information concerning how to help students solve binomial equations?

Table 4.3

Messick's expanded view of validity

	Test Interpretation	**Test Use**
Evidence	Evidence of what the test measures	Evidence that the test is relevant and useful for its intended application (*requires evidence of what the test measures*)
Consequences	Knowledge of appropriateness of what the test measures in light of society's values (*requires evidence of what the test measures*)	Consequences to society of using the test (*requires* (a) *evidence that the test is relevant and useful for its intended application,* and (b) *knowledge of appropriateness of what the test measures in light of society's values*)

Source: Adapted from S. Messick. (1989). Meaning and values in test validation. *Educational Researcher, 18*(2), 5–11.

Published tests also play significant roles within the classroom, and evidence as to the appropriateness of their interpretation *and* use in the school and classroom is highly relevant. Among other applications, standardized tests are used to group students and to evaluate the effectiveness of teaching and of teachers. As with classroom tests, the validity of published tests depends on evidence that they are relevant and useful for their typical applications. Research shows, with some significant exceptions, that students do not benefit from being grouped. Evidence also shows that published tests often are not useful for evaluating teachers, in part because the content of a given test does not correspond fully with what teachers are expected to teach.

Evidence supporting the interpretation and use of classroom and published tests is also relevant to students with special needs. The following are some additional questions that must be addressed when special needs are involved:

- What is the relevance or usefulness of a test administered in English to a student whose best language is Spanish or another language?

- How can scores on an intelligence test be interpreted when the test depends on cultural experiences and language previously irrelevant or unknown to some of the students?

- How useful are tests that require written and oral responses for students whose physical impairment affects how they write or speak?

These issues show that virtually any test is invalid for some, if not many, situations. The question is, for which interpretations and uses is a particular test valid? It is inappropriate to conclude that a test is invalid for every application when evidence indicates that it is valid for some, but not all, applications.

The lower two cells of Table 4.3 pertain to consequences of test interpretation and use. The lower-left cell concerns consequences of test interpretation, specifically knowledge of the appropriateness of what a test measures in light of society's values. It is unlikely that conse-

quences are examined for each classroom test, but they have a very real role when a teacher formulates the overall assessment strategy. Furthermore, issues of societal values are relevant to issues that affect classroom tests, such as school policies, goals and content of instruction, establishment of expectations, and grade assignment.

The lower-right cell of Table 4.3 concerns consequences of test use, that is, the consequences to society of using the test. An example is using tests (including assessments obtained through teacher observations) to place students in special education programs. One consequence is the labeling of students. Another is providing additional resources for the students.

As noted in the table, the consequences to society (including students) of using a test depend on (a) evidence that the test is relevant and useful for its intended application and (b) knowledge of the appropriateness of what the test measures in light of society's values. These prerequisites both require evidence of what the test measures. This dependence, Messick argues, shows how an examination of the evidence and consequences of the interpretation and use of a test is consolidated into an expanded, yet unified, view of validity.

The 1999 *Standards*

The recently published *Standards for Educational and Psychological Testing* (AERA, APA, NCME, 1999) reflect discussions that have occurred as a result of Messick's expanded view of validity. The current *Standards* replaces the more familiar framework of construct, content, and criterion-related evidence of validity with the five "sources of validity evidence" listed in Table 4.4. Similar to both Messick's expanded view of validity and the 1985 *Standards,* the 1999 *Standards* indicates the various sources of evidence "illuminate different aspects of validity, but they do not represent distinct types of validity. Validity is a unitary concept" (AERA, APA, NCME, 1999, p. 11).

Although perhaps an oversimplification, one might view the 1999 *Standards* as a restatement of the 1985 *Standards,* with amplification, along

Table 4.4
Sources of validity evidence addressed in the 1999 *Standards for Educational and Psychological Testing*

Source of Validity Evidence	Issues Addressed
Evidence based on test content	Does the content of the test, including themes, wording, item format, and administration and scoring guidelines, match the construct being measured?
Evidence based on response processes	Do the cognitive processes examinees use to respond to items on the test match those associated with the construct being assessed?
Evidence based on internal structure	Do the relationships among items within the test match the nature of the construct? If the construct involves a single dimension, do the test items establish a one-dimensional scale? If the construct involves multiple dimensions, is status on each of the dimensions established when the test is scored?
Evidence based on relations to other variables	Do scores on the test correlate in reasonable ways with other measures? That is, do scores correlate highly with other variables when, given the nature of the construct, high correlations are expected? Similarly, are correlations low when low correlations with other variables are expected?
Evidence based on consequences of testing	Does reasonable interpretation and use of test scores result in the positive consequences proposed for the test? Are the negative consequences identified, and are interpretation and use of the test justified in light of these negative consequences?

with an inclusion of Messick's expanded view of validity. As indicated in Table 4.4, the first source of validity evidence, evidence based on test content, incorporates our earlier discussion of content-related evidence. It clarifies this discussion by addressing the relevance of variables such as item format and scoring procedures to the "content" of the test. The second source of validity evidence, evidence based on response processes, is consistent with our discussion of construct-related evidence. The 1999 *Standards* reiterates the critical importance of establishing a reasonable linkage between the nature of the construct and the examinee behavior that will be elicited by the test.

The third source of validity evidence, evidence based on internal structure, in essence indicates that items used in a test, and the resulting scores on the test, should correspond to the structure of the construct. If the construct involves just one quality, examinee responses to the items within a test should not measure more than one factor. Similarly, if the construct involves multiple qualities,

examinee responses and resulting scores should again correspond to this structure. There are statistical techniques available to help establish the internal structure of a test, some of them referenced in the 1999 *Standards*. Teachers will not and need not use these statistical techniques. The prudent teacher, however, looks beyond scores on a test to determine the nature of students' responses, and makes judgments as to whether these responses make sense in light of what the test is measuring. This is close to the essence of internal structure.

The fourth source of validity evidence, evidence based on relations to other variables, in part raises the question we have addressed in criterion-related evidence—does performance on the test correlate with variables outside the test with which performance on the test is expected to correlate? The 1999 *Standards* expands this to also ask whether performance on the test has a low correlation with outside variables with which the construct being measured is not expected to be related? Evaluating expected low correlations helps establish what the test does *and does not* measure, and is a strategy often included in discussions of construct-related evidence. Teachers wisely will watch for problems of validity signaled by test performance being correlated with things it should not, such as performance on assessments being influenced by reading ability, attention span, or student background, where it would seem these variables are unrelated to the achievement being examined.

The fifth source of validity evidence, evidence based on consequences of testing, reflects Messick's concerns that we discussed previously. As with much of the *Standards,* the focus here is on standardized tests. When a testing progam involving standardized tests is implemented with an expectation that benefits will be realized, it is appropriate to determine whether or not the proposed benefits are realized. Likewise, with classroom assessments, consequences should be evaluated, and should be responsive to the purpose for which the assessment procedures are intended. For instance, if reasons for using portfolios include actively involving learners in self-assessment and improving the effectiveness of formative evaluations, then the realization of these consequences needs to be addressed. If the purpose of giving unannounced "pop quizzes" is to encourage students to work harder and improve achievement, the realization of these consequences should be addressed.

SUMMARY

Validity pertains to how well a test measures what it is supposed to measure. It is the single most important quality in the development, interpretation, and use of any educational measure.

Validity is an abstraction. Instead of observing validity, we evaluate various evidence pertaining to the interpretation and use of the test. Evidence associated with interpretation is conventionally grouped into construct-, content-, and criterion-related categories.

Construct-related evidence establishes whether a test matches the capabilities or psychological construct that is to be measured. With classroom

tests, learned knowledge is usually the construct of greatest relevance. Declarative and procedural knowledge are the two dominant types of learned knowledge.

Content-related evidence concerns how well elements of a test relate to the content domain being assessed. A table of specifications and list of performance objectives are two common techniques used to guide the establishment of content-related validity. Content-related evidence is gathered when the test is being developed.

Criterion-related evidence of validity indicates how well performance on a test correlates with performance on relevant-criterion measures external to the test. With informal and formal classroom assessments, the teacher gathers criterion-related evidence by observing whether performance on an assessment agrees with other relevant indications of student performance.

Test validity applies not only to evidence of what the test measures, but also to evidence supporting applications for which the test is to be used. Validity also pertains to the appropriateness of what a test measures and to the consequences that result from the use of the test. These dimensions of validity are interrelated. An evaluation of validity often indicates that a test is valid for some, but not all, applications for which it might be used.

ANSWERS: APPLY WHAT YOU ARE LEARNING

4.1. 1. 11 questions; 2. 6 questions; 3. 13 questions; 4. 24 questions.

4.2. 1. no; 2. yes; 3. no; 4. yes; 5. no. Although the strategies suggested in questions 1, 3, and 5 may identify good items, collectively these items may not provide a representative sample of the skills the test should be measuring. Content-related evidence of validity will be established only if the skills to be measured and the emphasis to be given to each skill are specified first. Only then should the required test items be assembled. Experience (including yours) has shown that tests often are not content-valid unless the content of the test is planned prior to selecting items for the test.

SOMETHING TO TRY

• For a subject area you would likely teach, think of specific examples of knowledge you would try to help your students learn. Try to think of separate examples for each of the following types of capability: information, discrimination, concept, rule, and problem solving. For each example, describe what you might ask your students to do to indicate what they have learned. Make sure each description takes into account the nature of the capability being assessed (see Table 3.2).

• Prepare a lesson plan for a 1-hour class you would likely teach. (An existing lesson plan would be fine.) Describe how you would informally assess students during this lesson. State types of construct-, content-, and criterion-related evidence that could be used to establish the validity of these informal assessments.

ADDITIONAL READING

Messick, S. (1989). Validity. In R. L. Linn (Ed.), *Educational measurement* (3rd ed., pp. 13–103). New York: American Council on Education. This chapter provides an extended discussion of test validation, beginning with a description of the historical development of concepts of validity.

5

Generalizing Observed Performance to Unobserved Performance

When a teacher formally or informally assesses students, the teacher observes only a small fraction of what might be observed. A written test incorporates only a portion of applicable items; a performance assessment typically asks a student to complete just one task of the many that the student might have been asked to perform; a portfolio usually includes only a fraction of the student's work. With informal assessments, a teacher casually observes a given student for only a fraction of the time during which the student might be observed. Likewise, when a teacher spontaneously asks questions during instruction, those questions represent but a small number of possible questions.

That assessment involves only a small sample of potential observations raises an important question. Would the conclusions drawn based on what was observed be different if what was not observed were included? If what a teacher observed does not generalize to what was not observed, the conclusions are useful only within the narrow context of the observation.

Because the usefulness of assessments is significantly reduced if the observations fail to generalize, it is important for us to be aware of the conditions that reduce generalizability. In this chapter, we will review these conditions and also discuss strategies to counteract these conditions. Within this context, this chapter helps you achieve three skills:

- Identify why observations often do not generalize
- Describe ways to detect inconsistencies associated with lack of generalizability
- Identify techniques for improving generalizability

WHY OBSERVATIONS DO NOT GENERALIZE

A measure of student performance will not generalize when there is inconsistency in the measurement. Any of a number of sources of inconsistency will cause what is observed to not generalize to samples of student performance that were not observed. For example, if a student does not know the answer to a multiple-choice item, the student will guess the answer. Sometimes the student will guess correctly and sometimes not. This inconsistency in guessing reduces the ability to generalize student performance from one multiple-choice item to another, and to a lesser degree, between two multiple-choice tests.

A different source of inconsistency can be illustrated with the assessment of reading comprehension. To assess reading comprehension, students often are asked to respond to questions related to a passage they have just read. Students' prior familiarity with the content of the reading passage affects how well they comprehend what they read. Comprehension appears to change depending on whether the reading passage involves less familiar or more familiar content. The student's ability to comprehend what is read is not changing, only the prior familiarity with what is being read. This inconsistency reduces the ability to make generalizations about reading comprehension based on only one assessment.

Still another example of inconsistency pertains to differences *among* students. Usually some students perform a particular task better than others. If we observe just one student performing a task, we are not able to generalize from that observation to other students whom we have not observed. Similarly, if we observe a nonrepresentative group of students performing a task, we cannot make generalizations from that group to other students.

The good news is that each of these inconsistencies causes problems *only* if we try to generalize beyond what we observe. The bad news, however, is that a teacher usually has no choice but to generalize. A teacher can observe only a small fraction of potential student performances and realistically must generalize beyond that. To understand problems of generalizability better, we will first look at the types of inconsistency that can limit a teacher's ability to make generalizations. Later in this chapter, we will describe strategies that help reduce these inconsistencies when assessing students.

Inconsistencies between Earlier and Later Measures

Inconsistencies between student performance on earlier and later measures are common. When these inconsistencies occur, it is important to determine whether the teacher is trying to make generalizations.

Here is an example that does *not* involve generalization. At the beginning of a lesson, a teacher usually anticipates that student performance before instruction will be different or inconsistent with performance after instruction. For this reason, a teacher does not make generalizations about a student's achievement after instruction based on achievement observed before instruction. At the conclusion of instruction, a teacher reassesses student achievement. Because the teacher is not making a generalization, this inconsistency is not a concern.

However, through preliminary evaluations, a teacher often makes judgments about student attitudes based on assessments during the first 2 weeks of school. The teacher uses earlier assessments of attitude to make generalizations about what later judgments would indicate. If students' attitudes change over time (which they often do), the teacher's prior generalizations will be in error.

Teachers also need to be concerned with retention. Will students' performance at the conclusion of a unit of instruction generalize to a later point of time when the assessed knowledge

becomes a prerequisite skill within a subsequent unit? If students' forget some of what they learned (which they usually do), this inconsistency means the earlier performance will not fully generalize.

Inconsistencies between Tasks That Supposedly Measure the Same Skill

Typically, more than one test item is used to measure each skill being assessed on a written test. Similarly, a teacher will orally ask more than just one question to determine whether students understand a particular concept. The use of multiple test items, oral questions, or other observations is a good technique. Multiple measures increase our confidence in what we observe.

Inconsistencies in student performance on test items that supposedly measure the same skill are a concern. In fact, this anticipated lack of consistency among items causes us to use multiple items to measure each skill. If we expected each student to perform the same regardless of which multiplication problem was used, we would use a one-item test to measure students' multiplication skills—more than one test item would be redundant. Instead, however, we use several items to average out the inconsistency and increase our confidence in the measure. We will later observe that the use of several test items, oral questions, or observations is one of the most effective techniques for improving the generalizability of our assessments.

Students perform inconsistently on items that supposedly measure the same skill for a variety of reasons. One explanation is that students often guess at the correct answer and their guesses are inconsistently lucky. This problem occurs not only with multiple-choice and true-false items, but also with other formats, such as essays, performance assessments, and oral questions.

Another reason for inconsistent performance across items is that many test items pose vague questions. In this case, students differ according to what they perceive is being asked and therefore they give inconsistent answers. To help reduce this source of inconsistency, we will place considerable emphasis in subsequent chapters on techniques for asking concise questions.

Another reason for inconsistent performance is that test items designed to measure the same skill often end up measuring different skills. The skills that students are expected to learn are extremely complex. Even a task as narrowly focused as knowing the multiplication tables involves different skills—which is why, for example, it is easier to multiply numbers by 0 or by 5 than by, say, 6 or 7. Also, each student's prior experience influences what a test item measures. For instance, asking a student to use aerodynamics to explain why a kite flies may involve recall of information if the relevance of aerodynamics to kites had previously been explained to the student. However, the student would have to generalize aerodynamic principles from other applications if the student had not been taught or did not recall the application of these principles to kites.

Sometimes, two *groups* of items, such as two versions or forms of a test, that supposedly measure the same skill are involved. For example, if a teacher is using a mastery learning strategy, one form of a test might be used to evaluate student achievement after initial instruction and an alternative and, hopefully, equivalent version of the test would be used later with students who needed further instruction. Although both versions of the test are designed to be equivalent, there might be some inconsistency between the groups of items that make up the two versions of the test. This inconsistency is undesirable and threatens the ability to generalize student performance from one form of the test to the other.

Inconsistencies between tasks that supposedly measure the same skill pertains to tasks that are thought to be interchangeable. This might involve two algebra problems that require students to solve for one unknown, two reading passages where students are asked to identify the main idea, or two very similar products, either of which the student could have selected for inclusion in a portfolio. As we note in the next section, inconsistencies also result when it is obvious that the two tasks are different from each other.

Inconsistencies among Alternative Skills in the Same Content Domain

The complexities of skills that are taught in the classroom create another source of inconsistency within student assessments. We often combine distinct skills into a single performance objective or a single content domain to make instruction and assessment manageable. Alternatively, we might be unable to subdivide a complex skill into fully meaningful subparts. A student who is proficient in one skill may be less proficient in another skill included in the same domain. The particular set of skills measured in an assessment, then, affects the teacher's judgment of the student's performance.

For instance, when assessing a student's ability to deliver a persuasive speech, it is impractical and inappropriate to divide the delivery of a speech into its hundreds of component skills. A teacher can measure only a sampling of these skills when assessing a student's speech. The particular skills that end up being measured during the speech are largely determined by multiple factors that are not easily controlled, such as the topic and illustrations the student selected for the speech, the student's and teacher's prior experience with the topic and illustrations, the instructional goals on which the teacher is concentrating, and even the confidence and attitude the student has going into the speech. The teacher's assessment of the speech does not fully generalize, say, to a persuasive speech the student would make on a different topic. The teacher's intention of measuring the student's ability to deliver a persuasive speech becomes a more limited measure of that student's ability to deliver a speech within particular circumstances.

Complex assessment techniques, such as portfolios and performance assessments, are particularly vulnerable to inconsistencies among alternative skills. The sample of work included in a portfolio, and even the student's and teacher's understanding of how to select samples of work to include in a portfolio, largely determine the assessment that will be made of each student's performance. Likewise, the attributes of student performance a teacher chooses to rate within a performance assessment significantly affect the score each student will receive as a result of her or his performance. It is common to accept inconsistencies in portfolios and performance assessments as an inevitable characteristic of these techniques or even as a desirable attribute of these flexible procedures. However, inconsistencies caused by the assessment procedure rather than by actual differences in student performance reduce the generalizability of the assessments. The inability of these assessments to generalize beyond the specific sample of student actions included in a particular portfolio or performance assessment is a significant limitation and not an asset. As we discuss portfolio and performance assessments in later chapters, we will pay particular attention to techniques that help improve their generalizability.

Other techniques used to assess students are also vulnerable to inconsistencies in performance among skills in a domain. The informal observation in which a teacher engages naturally during instruction is highly susceptible to the specific skills the teacher happens to observe. For instance, in a chemistry lab, a student needs to use equipment correctly, make accurate measurements, follow a reasonable sequence of actions, and work safely. For a given student the teacher will probably observe a subset of these actions; if a different subset of actions were observed, a different assessment of the student's performance might be obtained. What students allow or encourage the teacher to see also affects observations. Again, observation of other actions may result in different judgments of performance.

Because skills taught in school are complex, virtually every content domain involves multiple skills that are distinct and diverse. Inclusion of a particular subset of skills in an assessment provides a different judgment of student performance than would be obtained from an alternative subset of skills. The ability to generalize from what we observe to what we do not observe cannot always be realized in educational measurement, in large part because of the complexities of the skills being assessed. Our goal is to take deliberate steps in the development and administration of student assessments toward maximizing generalizability.

Inconsistencies Internal to a Test Score

Inconsistencies internal to the test score may be built into a test, reducing our ability to generalize from that score.

One cause of this internal inconsistency is the use of a single score to report student performance on multiple, unrelated qualities, for example, using one score on an essay test to indicate both the correctness of answers to questions *and* the correctness of spelling. Scores in this case would not be internally consistent. For some students, a low score would indicate problems with answering the questions; for other students, a low score would indicate problems with spelling. Using one score to report performance on unrelated qualities lowers the internal consistency of test scores.

Imagine an automobile that uses sensors to measure the amount of fuel remaining in the tank and another set of sensors to measure the temperature of the engine. If readings of the fuel sensors are reported using a fuel gauge and readings of the temperature sensors are reported with a separate temperature gauge, the information provided by the two gauges is very useful. However, because fuel and temperature readings are unrelated, the reading would be meaningless if both fuel and temperature were combined into one gauge.

For the same reason, one test score should not be used to report unrelated qualities. As with the combined fuel and temperature gauge, combining unrelated factors into a single test score reduces the internal consistency and the usefulness of the score. This is a potential problem with any test in which student performance is reported as a numerical score. Lack of internal consistency is also a problem when qualitative scores, such as narrative descriptions, are used. For instance, if a teacher uses the same words to describe two unrelated characteristics of a student, this qualitative description lacks internal consistency and its usefulness as a description is diminished.

Table 5.1
Some situations that tend to affect internal consistency

Situations That Tend to Cause Higher Internal Consistency

On a math test, the use of one score for addition and subtraction problems

On a history test, the use of one score for questions concerning significant dates and the names of significant people

On a French test, the use of one score for vocabulary and translation

---

Situations That Tend to Cause Lower Internal Consistency

Within a social studies essay exam, the use of one score for accuracy in contrasting democracy versus totalitarianism and accuracy in spelling

Within a science homework assignment, the use of one score for quality of work and timeliness (i.e., not turning in a late paper)

Within Olympic competition figure skating, the use of one score to indicate technical quality and artistic interpretation

---

A test has *internal consistency* if everything that contributes to the score is related. Table 5.1 lists some situations that will cause higher versus lower internal consistencies. Situations in the upper half of the table tend to have higher internal consistency because the students who do best in one quality being scored tend to be the students who do best on the other quality. For instance, the same students tend to do best on addition and subtraction problems or on listing historical dates and names of significant people. In contrast, students who are most knowledgeable in social studies often are not the best spellers. Higher internal consistency would result if separate scores were used to report knowledge in social studies and the ability to spell. Similarly, technical quality and artistic interpretation in figure skating are not highly related. For higher internal consistency, Olympic judges should and do use separate scores to report performance in these two areas.

Problems with internal consistency occur within every assessment technique. For example, a portfolio assessment of writing might include assessments of students' ability to communicate ideas in writing, to use appropriate grammar, to use good penmanship, and to assemble samples of work into a portfolio properly. If one overall score (such as an overall qualitative description) is given to each student's portfolio, the score will lack internal consistency. However, if separate scores or descriptions are provided for each of these attributes, each score will have higher internal consistency.

Informal assessments, such as ongoing observations and oral questions, can lack internal consistency also. The reliability of observations is improved if unrelated attributes, such as a student's attitude, facial expressions, and performance, are kept as separate assessments rather than combined into an overall judgment of the student. Unrelated attributes can help qualify or explain student performance, but they should be retained as distinct assessments.

Random attributes also threaten internal consistency. Students' guessing of the correct answer is an example of this type of threat. Other examples of random attributes include students' guessing at what is being asked by an ambiguous question and teachers' using inconsistent standards from paper to paper when grading student work. Random attributes pose a particularly difficult problem for internal consistency since it is impossible to separate out their effects. With non-random attributes, such as grammar and spelling, it is possible to establish separate scores. It is not possible, however, to determine separate scores for students' ability to identify correct examples of a concept versus students' good fortune to guess correctly at examples of the concept. Nor is it possible to separate differences in the quality of students' responses that result from ambiguities within the questions or inconsistencies among scores that result from inferior methods used to score student work.

Internal consistency caused by random attributes presents a serious problem for educational measurement. Later chapters will describe techniques that reduce random effects such as those associated with guessing and vagueness in task descriptions.

Inconsistencies among Raters of Scores

A useful practice when students' responses must be subjectively scored is to involve more than one rater. Although often not practical, it is beneficial to have more than one rater read students' papers, review portfolios, observe students during performance assessments, and even informally observe students in class.

Although more practical, using only one rater to assess each student's performance hides inconsistencies that would become visible if multiple raters were involved. This inconsistency, again, reduces the ability to generalize. In this case, it reduces the teacher's ability to anticipate whether other teachers or parents would make the same judgments about a student's performance. Since the use of multiple raters is usually impractical, we will emphasize techniques that reduce inconsistencies in one teacher's ratings. Reducing these inconsistencies would have the indirect benefit of improving consistencies among different raters were different raters used.

Inconsistencies in Decisions Based on Student Performance

A passing score is often set for a test. With standardized tests, passing scores are sometimes used to make decisions about whether a student is eligible to receive a high school diploma or be admitted to a particular college. With classroom tests, passing scores are used to determine whether further instruction should be provided or a student should be placed with a particular group of students. When test scores are numerical, the passing score is also expressed as a number, possibly a percentage. When test scores are qualitative descriptions, a passing score might be an explicit or implicit description of a student's performance in relation to a minimally acceptable performance.

Misclassifications of students relative to a passing score usually are a by-product of other sources of inconsistency we have already discussed. For instance, subtle differences between otherwise equivalent items used on separate forms of a test may cause a student who scored just below the passing score on one form of the test to score just above what appears to be a comparable passing score on the other form of the test. Similarly, because students will perform differently on a small sample of tasks than they would have had the teacher been given the opportunity to observe the student on all possible tasks, students who truly lack sufficient proficiency will often be misclassified as having sufficient proficiency, based on the sample of items.[1]

Classroom measures, particularly those that involve informal assessments, such as casual observation, include substantial inconsistencies. Although some inconsistencies are unavoidable, steps to minimize them will reduce inconsistencies in decisions. It is important to be aware that many decisions based on observations of student performance are in error; that another, comparable observation might have resulted in a different decision.

METHODS FOR DETECTING INCONSISTENCIES

A variety of statistical methods are used for detecting inconsistencies in test scores. These methods are seldom used with classroom assess-

---

[1] If you have Microsoft® Excel on your computer, go to the web site associated with this book and download the file entitled Correct Classification Probabilities. With this demonstration, you can see how often students are misclassified under various conditions.

ments; however, teachers often see references to these methods within the context of standardized testing. This section provides you a conceptual overview of what these methods do.

We will look at two approaches for detecting inconsistencies. The first involves reliability coefficients, and is typically used with the traditional standardized written tests. The second approach involves generalizability theory, and is more often used with performance assessments and portfolios when used in large-scale assessments.

Reliability Coefficients

Reliability coefficients involve computing a correlation coefficient between two sets of scores, or estimating what would have been obtained if a correlation coefficient were computed. The two scores might be students' scores on two different forms of a test, or scores obtained on an earlier and later administration of the same test. In each case, both sets of scores are obtained using the same students. That is, when two forms of the test are involved, the same students would complete both forms, resulting in two scores for each student. When an earlier and later administration of the same test are used, both administrations would involve the same students, again resulting in two scores for each student.

The reliability coefficient is the computed correlation between these two sets of scores. The reliability coefficient ranges between 0.00 and 1.00, where zero indicates no reliability and one indicates perfect reliability.[2] A reliability coefficient of 0.00 would result if variability among students' scores were entirely the result of inconsistencies. A reliability of 1.00 would indicate that no inconsis-

tency was involved in the variability of students' scores. A reliability coefficient could be anywhere between zero and one, with values close to 1.00 preferable. Oosterhof (2001) is one of a variety of sources that illustrate how the correlation coefficient is computed.

Test–Retest Method. Possibly the most obvious method for judging whether a test measures something consistently is to readminister the test to the same students, and compute the correlation between scores obtained on the two administrations. If, on the readministration, the students who originally obtained the highest scores continue to achieve high scores, the middle-scoring students continue to achieve the middle scores, and so on, the test is probably measuring something that remains consistent over time.

With most classroom assessments and standardized achievement tests, the test–retest method is not relevant because one *does expect* student performance to change over time. The amount of change likely will be inconsistent across students. In these situations, because inconsistency in scores over time is to be expected and is not a concern, the test–retest method is not used.

However, there are situations in which inconsistency over time is a concern and should be monitored. For instance, schools that used standardized tests to place students in groups for extended periods of time are assuming that the test is measuring something that is stable over time. Here the test–retest method is relevant. The developers of the standardized tests should use a sample of examinees to establish whether there is a high correlation between test scores between the beginning and end of the year. (As a separate validity issue, one should also evaluate whether placing students in static groups benefits student learning.)

A teacher may also assume that important student traits, such as initiative, attitude, and motivation, remain constant. This happens when the teacher at the beginning of the year makes judgments concerning students' traits, and anticipates they will remain constant throughout the year.

---

[2]Correlation coefficients can be negative as well as positive, which means their value can range from −1.00 to +1.00. Correlations within the negative range indicate an inverse relationship, where high values on one variable tend to correspond with low values on the other variable, and vice versa. With standardized tests, correlation coefficients, when used as a reliability coefficient, invariably are positive numbers.

Although test developers can establish test–retest reliabilities, it usually is not practical for teachers to compute correlation coefficients between earlier and later measures. Nonetheless, prudent teachers do repeat assessments, at least through informal observations, to determine whether changes in student traits are occurring.

✿ 5.1   Apply What You Are Learning

For each of the following, indicate (yes or no) whether consistency over time is a relevant concern.

1. A teacher assesses a student's portfolio by comparing the student's present work with similar work completed earlier in the year.
2. A judgment of each student's ability to learn is made during the first week in school. This judgment is the basis for grouping students throughout the year.
3. A teacher informally observed the work of five students in class. The teacher wonders if these five students' work is a good indication of what the rest of the class is doing.

Answers can be found at the end of the chapter.

Alternate–Form Method. Instead of readministering the same items to students, another common way to check for inconsistency is to administer to a sample of students a second form of the test that contains a different set of similar items that measure the same skills. The second form might be administered to the same students immediately after the first, or at some later time. The correlation between students' scores on the two forms is then computed.

Because two forms of a test involve different samples of items, the alternate–form method has a distinct advantage over the test–retest method. It checks for inconsistencies associated with using different items. As we noted earlier, it is important to know whether students would perform the same were a different sample of similar items used in the test.

To use the alternate–form method, two forms of the test must exist. Many standardized tests have at least two forms of each test to allow later retesting without reusing the same items, or to help maintain security by assigning different forms to students sitting next to each other. In fact, whenever two forms of a test are being used interchangeably, it is important for the test developer to administer both forms to a sample of students to establish that scores on the two forms are highly correlated.

Teachers often use alternate forms of a test, such as when students are later retested after addressing problems found on an earlier test. However, a teacher seldom has the opportunity to have the same students complete both forms to check for inconsistencies, so different procedures are needed. If the purpose of using alternate forms is simply to control copying, a preferred solution is to generate two forms of a test by using the same items, but in a different order. Research has for some time shown that the order in which items are presented on a test has a minimal effect on the scores of examinees (Marso, 1970).

When alternate forms are developed so that students can be administered a retest later, distinct (although similar) items should be used on the different forms of the test. In this situation, a reasonable option is to take steps to ensure the equivalence of the forms. This might involve writing items from carefully developed specifications and then randomly assigning items that measure each skill to the respective forms of the test.

Split–Half Method. The split–half method is similar to the alternate–form method in that the consistency of results on two forms is determined. Unlike the alternate–form method, the split–half method involves the administration of only one form of a test. Two forms are artificially created by splitting test questions from a single form into two groups. The consistency of students' performance on the two parts of the test is then analyzed, often by computing the correlation between scores on the two halves. Because the split–half method requires the administration of only one form of a test, this method often is more practical for classroom tests.

Unlike the test–retest method, the split–half method does not indicate whether test results will be consistent over time. Also, unlike the alternate–form method, the split–half method does not indicate whether two forms of a test are interchangeable. The split–half method does provide an estimate of whether the use of alternate samples of items provides the same results.

Kuder–Richardson Methods. Kuder and Richardson (1937) devised formulas that provide estimates of alternate–form reliability, but from a single administration of one form of the test. In that sense, their methods are similar to the split–half technique. Formulas 20 and 21 within their published paper became particularly widely used, and often are referred to as the *KR-20* and *KR-21* reliabilities. As with the split–half technique, the Kuder–Richardson methods provide an estimate of whether different samples of items provide consistent results. In addition, the Kuder–Richardson techniques determine whether test scores reflect a single attribute, what earlier in this chapter we referred to as internal consistency.

The *KR-20* and, to a lesser degree, the *KR-21* are used to estimate the reliability of many traditional standardized written tests. Reliability coefficients above 0.85 are the norm. When classroom tests are computer scored, Kuder–Richardson reliabilities often are computed. Diederich (1973) showed that a 1-hour classroom test should have a reliability between 0.60 and 0.80, with shorter tests expected to have somewhat lower reliabilities.

When a computer is not used to score classroom tests, computing reliability coefficients is impractical. Although more subjective, a teacher can simulate the Kuder–Richardson methods by judging whether students' performance across tasks within an assessment is correlated. For instance, when hand-scoring essay or completion items, is there consistency with respect to which students do better and worse from item to item? If so, this suggests a higher reliability than if there is little consistency from item to item. Higher consistency indicates that similar performance would be observed were a different sample of items that measure the same task used in the assessment.

Interrater Method. With subjectively scored assessments, such as essay tests and judgments of products produced by students, considerable inconsistency may arise in the scoring. Two raters, if they separately review students' work, may derive very different judgments of each student's performance. The interrater method can be used to detect this inconsistency. Basically, two teachers independently score each student's performance. Thus, as with each of the techniques described earlier, the interrater method creates two scores or judgments for each student, in this case, one from each rater. These scores or judgments are then compared for each student. With numerical scores, the interrater reliability is said to be high if the ranking of students is approximately the same by both raters. When qualitative judgments are involved, the descriptions given by the two raters should be approximately the same for each student.

Generalizability Theory

Generalizability theory represents a second approach to detecting inconsistencies within test scores. The name "generalizability" very appropriately refers to why it is we are concerned with inconsistencies in test scores. Every assessment, whether it be a written test, a performance assessment, portfolio, or informal observation, involves only a sample of the possible observations that could be made. The critical question discussed in this chapter is, "Does the performance that was observed generalize to performances that were not observed?" Inconsistencies in scores is what prevents observations from generalizing.

Generalizability theory, like the computation of reliability coefficients, uses statistical techniques to estimate the degree to which inconsistency is present in test scores. An important difference with generalizability theory is that the technique used is able to detect the specific source of inconsistency. We learned earlier that any of a number of sources of inconsistency can cause what is observed to not generalize to samples of student performance that were not observed. The application of generalizability theory does not identify all possible sources of inconsistency. However, the statistical procedures will, within the limits of how a research study is designed, detect specific sources of variability in students' scores that is causing inconsistency.

Generalizability theory has been particularly useful in studying inconsistencies associated with performance assessments and portfolios. Studies show that, with adequate scoring plans and training, raters appear able to control inconsistencies in scoring so that scores assigned to student performance would generalize to scores assigned by other raters. Studies have also shown that performance on one task often generalizes poorly to what would have been observed if the assessment had required students to perform a different task associated with the same instructional goal (see, for examples, studies by Shavelson with others, 1997; and Um, 1995).

More so than with reliability coefficients, the statistical techniques associated with generalizability theory do not lend themselves to the day-to-day classroom assessments. Research that has been done using this approach have provided important insights into where inconsistencies must be addressed to improve the generalizability of performance assessments and portfolios. We make considerable use of these findings in later chapters. In the next section, we summarize the major findings.

TECHNIQUES FOR IMPROVING GENERALIZABILITY

To improve the generalizability of classroom assessments, one must anticipate the conditions that cause inconsistency within educational measures and then take actions to control those conditions. For example, the complexity of the content domains being taught in the classroom is a major cause of inconsistency in measurement. A student's score on a given test is a function of the sample of specific skills from the domain that are measured by the test. One can generalize from the student's performance on this test only to the extent that the test adequately samples all relevant skills within the content domain being measured. To improve generalizability, one must improve the sample of skills measured by the test by increasing the number of items or student observations in the test and/or improving the representativeness of skills measured by the test.

Four general techniques for improving the generalizability of test scores are described here. The first includes a series of actions that can be used to improve the quality of observations of student performance. The second technique involves improvements in how the student performances observed are scored or judged. The third technique involves increasing the number of observations included in a test. The fourth technique is concerned with including a sufficient sample of diverse tasks within the assessment.

Improving the Quality of Observations

The next several chapters describe in detail a variety of techniques used to improve the quality of observations. Chapters 6 through 9 describe techniques that apply to written tests, such as those using completion and multiple-choice questions. Chapters 11 through 14 describe how to improve observations of student performance obtained from informal assessments, student portfolios, and performance assessments.

Ambiguities in a test are a major threat to generalizability. When a test presents a vague task, students' reactions and responses are inconsistent. Ambiguities can be reduced by a variety of means, depending on the test format. For example, with multiple-choice items, using a stem that presents a concise problem to be addressed by the student reduces ambiguity. Problematic words and sentence structures in the stem and options can be avoided. With completion items, the item needs to be constructed so that only a homogeneous set of words will represent a correct answer when written in the blank. For portfolios, the categories of work samples to be included are identified, and within each category, the concise conditions or characteristics that a work sample should have are specified. Conciseness can work against the flexibility that is an asset of some formats, such as essays and portfolios. The trick is to determine the conditions that must be specified or controlled while providing students flexibility in how to meet those conditions.

Tests can also be improved by controlling students' ability to guess the correct answer for reasons unrelated to the skill being tested. Guessing presents a significant problem, particularly with the true-false and multiple-choice formats. We will look at ways to make the wrong answer plausible to students who lack the knowledge being tested without decreasing the likelihood that knowledgeable students will select the correct response. Guessing is also a serious problem with casual oral questions. *Leading questions* may tell students the correct answer, even if they do not have the knowledge being assessed.

Improving the Scoring of Performances

The scoring process can pose a serious threat to generalizability, particularly for some formats, such as essay items. Two raters may assign quite different scores to the same paper. Because the student's written answers obviously do not change, the difference between raters is caused by something other than the proficiency being assessed. Inconsistency between raters is undesirable.

A teacher would not score a multiple-choice test without first developing a scoring key, yet even though essays are much more difficult to score, many teachers do read answers to essay tests without first creating a scoring plan. An effective way to increase the generalizability of essay tests is to improve the scoring procedures.

Development of a scoring plan is also an integral part of constructing performance assessments and portfolios. A scoring plan can be used with either quantitative or qualitative scoring of performance. Procedures for developing scoring plans are discussed in chapters concerned with the use of these formats.

Observations and oral questions are also subjectively scored. Observations and oral questions are usually informal and spontaneous. Thus, their scoring plans have to be responsive to this spontaneity. Having clear goals for these assessments is central to the ability to determine spontaneously how to score and interpret what is observed.

Increasing the Number of Observations

Increasing the number of observations is an effective way to improve generalizability for educational measures just as it is for physical measures. When one uses a micrometer to measure the thickness of an object, multiple observations are obtained by repeatedly loosening and retightening the instrument's screw. These observations are then averaged to obtain one best measurement. Similarly, the pH of soil is established from several samples. With physical measurements, the degree of consistency among the repeated measurements is often used as evidence of the reliability of those measurements.

With educational measurement, there are various ways to increase the number of observations, any one of which increases reliability or generalizability. One method is to include more items in a test; another is to have more than one person score each assessment; still another is to combine the observations of individual students to obtain a measure of performance of a *group* of students.

Increasing the number of observations reduces inconsistency because it tends to average out the randomness that is inherent in all assessments. For instance, including several multiple-choice items in a test averages out the gains made from a student's guessing. Including multiple samples of each type of work in a portofolio significantly improves the generalizability of these assessments. Using multiple readers to score an essay test averages out the inconsistency among persons scoring the test. Likewise, estimates of how the class as a whole is performing are more generalizable than are estimates of how individual students in the class are performing. In each instance, consistency of the measure is improved by increasing the number of observations.

Expanding the Breadth of Observations

As we have noted, only a sample of tasks can be included in any formal or informal assessment. The assessment is of limited value if what we observed does not generalize to other tasks within the same content domain that we did not observe. It is natural, and very important, to be concerned with whether this generalization occurs.

Unfortunately, as we noted earlier, research suggests that performance tends not to generalize very well across tasks. For instance, the ability to establish classifications from observations is a fundamental skill in science, yet students' ability to successfully apply classification techniques in one setting did not generalize well from one setting to another, even though a homogeneous content area was involved (Shavelson et al., 1997). The ability to write an expository paper from a prompt is an essential skill in language arts, yet the quality of students' writing did not generalize well when the prompt was changed (Um, 1995). We know that young children often cannot consistently identify the shape that is a rectangle if geometric objects are presented in diverse shapes, orientations, and contexts.

A particularly effective way to increase generalizability is to observe a student during performance of a task across multiple, diverse instances of the task. Thus, a teacher should ask a student to write papers in response to multiple prompts, or to identify rectangles presented in diverse situations and orientations.

In terms of breadth of observations, standardized tests are at a substantial disadvantage,

particularly when the test includes only a few exercises because of the amount of time required to complete each task. Particularly when standardized tests involve performance assessments, skills are often assessed with just one item, such as assessing writing skills with one essay written from one prompt. With classroom assessments, the teacher can usually base evaluations on a greater breadth and number of observations than can be included in a standardized test.

Increasing the breadth of observations is a particularly effective technique for increasing the generalizability of assessments. Each of the three previous techniques, however, is prerequisite to this concern. Recall that the first technique involves improving the quality of observations, such as by reducing ambiguities in questions or tasks presented to the student. The second technique involves improving the scoring of observations. Unless observations are of high quality and performances are carefully scored, the individual components of an assessment will contain considerable error, and students' performance will not generalize, even if the breadth of observations is increased. All assessments contain random error, and an effective way to reduce this error is to implement the third technique: increasing the number of observations. The fourth technique, expanding the breadth of observations, is actually a form of increasing the number of observations. To help assure that what we do observe regarding students will generalize to what we did not observe, each of these four techniques for improving generalizability must be implemented.

● 5.2   Apply What You Are Learning

For each pair, indicate which strategy (A or B) improves generalizability.

1. A. Asking students to perform a large number of tasks
   B. Asking students to perform a small number of tasks

2. A. Based on an assessment, inferring what individual students can do
    B. Based on an assessment, inferring what the class as a whole can do
3. A. Being flexible about which qualities will be scored in each student's answer
    B. Being structured about which qualities will be scored in each student's answer
4. A. Within the content domain being assessed, asking a student to perform several very similar tasks
    B. Within the content domain being assessed, asking a student to perform several diverse tasks

Answers can be found at the end of the chapter.

RELATION OF GENERALIZABILITY TO VALIDITY

The generalizability of an assessment has an important relationship to its validity. Basically, an assessment cannot have a high degree of validity unless its generalizability is also high. Recall that validity is concerned with whether an assessment measures what it is supposed to measure. Validity is critical because an assessment is of no use unless the capability being evaluated is in fact being measured. Generalizability represents a very important attribute because it is a prerequisite to validity.

The following example illustrates why generalizability is a prerequisite to validity. Two teachers have agreed on the criteria to be used for scoring an essay test that students have completed. However, as is often the case, the teachers assign inconsistent scores to many of the students' tests; that is, scores assigned by one teacher do not fully generalize to scores assigned by the other. The students have completed the essay test and are no longer adding to or changing their answers; therefore, the inconsistency in students' scores has nothing to do with changes in students' performance. Therefore, the scores assigned by the teachers are being influenced by something other than the students' performance on the test. *When there is inconsistency in scores, something is being measured instead of, or at least in addition to, what the assessment was designed to measure.* Inconsistency in the scores indicates that the validity of the test is threatened.

Generalizability, therefore, is a prerequisite to validity. The assessment of a student is not valid unless students' observed performance generalizes to performance that the evaluator did not have the opportunity to observe. The need for generalizability is seen in inconsistencies between different teachers who might potentially score the test, but also in inconsistencies among test items that supposedly measure the same skill, and inconsistencies among alternative skills in the same content domain. For this reason, subsequent chapters place considerable emphasis on techniques that are known to improve the generalizability of our measures.

Although generalizability of observations is critical to validity, consistency is not by itself a sufficient condition for validity; unfortunately, we can measure the wrong capability with possibly even perfect consistency. Consistency in scores is a necessary but not a sufficient condition for validity. This book emphasizes techniques that reduce inconsistency in students' scores on written tests, performance assessments, and portfolios. At the same time, we must be very careful to ensure that in addition to being consistent, our assessments are also valid measures of the abilities we are trying to evaluate.

SUMMARY

Generalizability is the degree to which observed student performances generalize to those that were not observed. Assessments must have generalizability because only a small sample of potential student performances are observed. To use assessments effectively, a teacher must be able to generalize beyond what has been observed.

A teacher will have problems making generalizations whenever certain types of inconsistencies are present in the performance being observed. These inconsistencies come from different sources. There are inconsistencies between earlier and later measures of student performance, among test items that are designed to measure the same skill, and among measures of alternative skills in the content domain. There also are inconsistencies internal to a test score, for example, when one score is used to indicate performance on more than one unrelated trait, and there are inconsistencies in how different raters score a student's response.

Not all sources of inconsistency are relevant to a particular assessment. A source of inconsistency normally is relevant only if a generalization is involved. For instance, a student's performance always changes over time. When a teacher assesses students following instruction, the teacher is not making a generalization from assessments that occurred before instruction. However, if early in the school year a teacher makes judgments about students' attitudes, unless the teacher reassesses students' attitudes, the teacher is making a generalization. In this latter situation, inconsistencies that occur over time restrict the teacher's ability to generalize.

Reliability coefficients and generalizability theory are two statistical approaches often used for detecting inconsistencies in test scores. Reliability coefficients may involve the computation of scores between two sets of scores, such as between scores on a test and a later retest, or scores on two alternative forms of a test, or between scores assigned to students by two different teachers. The widely used Kuder–Richardson reliabilities estimate from a single administration the correlation that would be obtained between two parallel forms, if both forms were administered to students. Reliability coefficients are most often used with standardized written tests. Generalizability theory is more typically used with standardized tests that involve performance assessments or portfolios. Depending on the design that is used, generalizability theory is more effective than reliability coefficients at detecting specific sources of inconsistencies.

Unless a computer performs the computations, teachers typically do not use statistical procedures. Instead, a teacher uses judgments such as to whether there is a relationship between how students perform between different parts of an assessment. A teacher can use several techniques to improve overall consistency and therefore improve generalizability. These include reducing the ambiguity within test items and tasks, improving the scoring of student performance, increasing the number of observations, and expanding the breadth of observations.

ANSWERS: APPLY WHAT YOU ARE LEARNING

5.1. 1. No. The teacher hopes there will be change in students' work, and probably anticipates differences in how much individual students do change. 2. Yes. If the same grouping is used throughout the year, it is assumed the original judgment concerning each student's ability does not change. Inconsistency over time with respect to this judgment is an important concern. 3. No, because no duration in time is involved. The teacher is wondering whether the work of the five students is similar to the work of other students in the class.

5.2. 1. A; 2. B; 3. B; 4. B. Increasing the number of tasks improves generalizability. This can be accomplished simply by using a large number of questions or by making inferences to the class as a whole rather than to individual students. Using a carefully structured scoring plan when scoring students' answers considerably reduces error. With essays, performance assessments, and portfolios, a structured scoring plan specifies what qualities will be scored, but provides students flexibility in how they will demonstrate those qualities. Selecting diverse rather than highly similar tasks from a domain to include in a test facilitates generalizability. The use of diverse tasks increases the chance that student performances that were not observed are similar in nature to performances that were observed.

SOMETHING TO TRY

- At the beginning of this chapter, in the section entitled **Why Observations Do Not Generalize,** six sources of inconsistencies are described. Try to list at least one example for each of the six. If possible, use examples from recent assessments that were administered to you or recent assessments that you administered to students.

ADDITIONAL READING

Feldt, L. S., & Brennan, R. L. (1989). Reliability. In R. L. Linn (Ed.), *Educational measurement* (3rd ed.). New York: Macmillan. This chapter provides a detailed and highly technical discussion of reliability theory.

Harvill, L. M. (1991). An NCME instructional module on standard error of measurement. *Educational Measurement: Issues and Practice, 10*(2), 33–41. Standard error of measurement is a useful way to indicate the amount of inconsistency in test scores; it estimates the variability in scores, expressed as a standard deviation, associated with inconsistencies within the scores. This instructional module explains the use and computation of standard error of measurement.

Nitko, A. J. (2001). *Educational assessment of students* (3rd ed.). Upper Saddle River, NJ: Merrill/Prentice Hall. Chapter 4 provides an alternate discussion of inconsistencies that cause measurement error, and also ways to estimate reliability.

Oosterhof, A. C. (2001). *Classroom applications of educational measurement* (3rd ed.). Upper Saddle River, NJ: Merrill/Prentice Hall. Chapter 5 discusses reliability and its relation to validity. Chapter 20 includes a discussion of standard error of measurement and illustrates how it relates to measurement error.

Traub, R. E., & Rowby, G. L. (1991). An NCME instructional module on understanding reliability. *Educational Measurement: Issues and Practice, 10*(1), 37–45. This module provides an understandable explanation of reliability theory.

PART II

How to Develop, Administer, and Score Written Tests

In Part II, we discuss the development, administration, and scoring of written tests. From experience, you know that written tests are widely used in schools, starting in the upper-elementary grades. Our discussion will include the standard completion, essay, multiple-choice, and alternate-choice formats, as well as variations to these formats. We will look at ways to improve substantially the clarity with which these items are written. Clarity is essential because ambiguity of test items is a major reason that many classroom tests lack the necessary degree of validity and often are scored inconsistently.

Written tests have significant limitations in the skills they can measure. Their rigid structure prevents them from measuring what we have called problem solving. A student's ability to solve complex problems can be assessed only if the test provides students an intricate problem that requires synthesis of multiple concepts and rules, and also allows flexibility in how to solve the

problem. Performance assessments, portfolio systems, and even informal observation and questions can assess one's ability to solve complex problems, but written tests cannot. Written tests also cannot effectively measure skills involving extensive motor skills, such as assembling objects, speaking, playing a musical instrument, or performing a lab experiment. Because written tests require students to read and write, their use is problematic with young children and some students with special needs. Written tests are generally not useful for measuring attitudes.

Written tests, however, can very effectively assess students' ability to recall information. Written tests can also measure knowledge of concepts and the ability to apply rules. These capabilities are prerequisite to solving complex problems, and to many tasks involving motor skills. The learning and assessment of these skills consumes a substantial amount of time in most classes. Compared with performance assessments, written tests more efficiently measure the recall of information and the understanding of concepts. Within a limited amount of time, a written test can, therefore, more thoroughly assess students' mastery of these skills. Other assessment tools, performance assessments in particular, should be used when written tests cannot. Using written tests and alternative assessments to complement one another provides the more effective approach to assessing student knowledge.

Chapters 6 through 9 discuss the development and scoring of various types of written test items. Chapter 10 discusses "testwiseness" and describes how to help students learn to take written tests. Part III then addresses the use of alternative assessments.

6

Completion and Short-Answer Items

For all practical purposes, the completion and short-answer formats are equivalent. Their most significant distinction is appearance. A completion item consists of a sentence containing one or more blanks; the student is expected to identify the word or short phrase represented by each blank.

> The Italian artist who painted the ceiling of the Sistine Chapel is (Michelangelo).

A short-answer item rewords this incomplete sentence as a question.

> Which Italian artist painted the ceiling of the Sistine Chapel?

Virtually any completion item can be rewritten as an equivalent short-answer item and vice versa. For expediency, the term **short-answer item** will be used when discussing attributes common to both completion and short-answer formats.

Short-answer items are widely used in elementary and secondary schools, and also in many post-secondary situations. Short-answer items are used in academic contests in which small teams of students from different schools compete against each other, and in television game shows. Short-answer items may be used more often than written items in all other formats.

Because short-answer items are used frequently, you should be familiar with their char-

acteristics, including their advantages, limitations, and desired attributes. Evaluation of short-answer items used in the classroom reveals some major flaws. For example, many items present ambiguous questions for which diverse responses would qualify as appropriate answers. This chapter describes and illustrates the characteristics preferred in short-answer items. After discussing these characteristics, you will be asked to apply your understanding of these characteristics to evaluate a series of short-answer items.

This chapter helps you achieve three skills:

- Identify the advantages and limitations of short-answer items
- Identify qualities desired in short-answer items
- Evaluate short-answer items for these qualities

ADVANTAGES AND LIMITATIONS OF SHORT-ANSWER ITEMS

Advantages of Short-Answer Items

Short-answer items have three advantages over written items in other formats. First, short-answer items are easy to construct. Second, as with the essay format, short-answer items require students to produce an answer rather than to select an answer from alternatives. Third, unlike the essay format, many short-answer questions can be included in a single exam.

1. *Short-answer items are easy to construct.* The ease of constructing short-answer items is a function of two characteristics. First, short-answer items generally can measure recall of information, but not procedural knowledge, such as concepts and rules: Items that measure recall of information are easier to construct. Second, creating short-answer items does not require the detailed scoring plans needed to create essay items, nor the need to construct the list of options associated with multiple-choice items. For settings in which the short-answer format is appropriate, this efficiency in item construction is a major asset.

2. *Short-answer items require the student to supply the answer.* The multiple-choice and, even more so, the alternate-choice formats are negatively affected by guessing. Students often give the correct answer to items without solving the problem presented. Because guessing is a source of inconsistency, answers to short-answer tests tend to generalize better than answers to multiple-choice or alternate-choice items. As a result, short-answer tests achieve a higher degree of reliability with a given number of items.

3. *Many short-answer items can be included in a test.* The inclusion of many items allows one test to provide a more adequate sampling of content, particularly compared with the essay format. This ability increases the generalizability of test scores and potentially also their validity. This advantage occurs with a limitation; more than with other formats, however, short-answer items have difficulty measuring procedural knowledge.

Limitations of Short-Answer Items

Short-answer items have two limitations. First, as already noted, short-answer items are generally restricted to measuring recall of information. Second, they are more likely to be scored erroneously than are objectively scored formats, such as multiple-choice and alternate-choice tests.

1. *Short-answer items are generally limited to measuring recall of information.* You may have noticed that most short-answer or completion-item tests you have taken or given examined knowledge of facts, such as names of people, places, and procedures. Because the student must answer this format of items with a short sentence or often a single word, the skills that short-answer items measure are limited.

Many short-answer items are exceedingly difficult, such as those used in local and regional competitions staged for teams of high school students, in spelling bees, even in game shows such as *Jeopardy*. These questions test recall of verbal information rather than procedural knowledge such as concepts and rules.

As we noted before, the importance of declarative knowledge must not be understated. This type of knowledge represents the foundation on which many cognitive actions must be based. However, knowledge of concepts and rules generally must be assessed using other item formats.

2. *Short-answer items are more likely to be scored erroneously than are the objectively scored formats.* Short-answer questions often can be answered with a variety of responses, any one of which might be the desired response. The question "Who discovered America?" could be referring to the name of a person, a nation, or a culture from any of a variety of historical periods. Errors are likely to be involved in scoring potentially correct but divergent responses to short-answer items. To reduce this problem, each short-answer item should be constructed so that knowledgeable students respond with homogeneous answers.

🌐 6.1 Apply What You Are Learning

In this part of the book, four different formats of written tests are discussed: short-answer, essay, multiple-choice, and alternate-choice (such as true-false items). Try to anticipate the item formats described by each of the following statements.

1. These two formats require the student to produce rather than to select an answer.
2. These two formats are the fastest to score.
3. These two formats are *least* likely to involve errors in scoring.

Answers can be found at the end of the chapter.

IDENTIFYING QUALITIES DESIRED IN SHORT-ANSWER ITEMS

This section identifies specific criteria for evaluating short-answer items. In the next section, you will be asked to use these criteria to evaluate some short-answer questions.

1. *Does this item measure the specified skill?* For any test to be valid, items must measure the skills the test is designed to assess. Using performance objectives or a table of specifications are helpful in this regard. Any test item should be selected or constructed only after the skill to be measured has been identified.

Short-answer items are generally limited to measuring declarative knowledge. If the skill to be assessed involves a concept or rule, a different format may have to be selected.

2. *Is the level of reading skill required by this item below the students' ability?* Chapter 5 described how internal consistency is decreased when a test measures more than one trait. If a test measures a student's proficiency in (1) a given content area and (2) reading ability, the internal consistency of the test decreases because more than one quality is being measured simultaneously. Students should learn to value good reading skills. Unless, however, the purpose of a test is to measure reading proficiency, the classroom test is not the place to measure reading ability. The level of reading skill required for understanding each item on a test should be *below* that of the students taking the test.

3. *Can this item be answered using one or two words or a short sentence?* Most short-answer items can be answered using one or two words. If more than a few words or a short sentence is required to answer the question, the item is probably a brief-response essay item and should be evaluated with the criteria discussed in Chapter 7.

4. *Will only a single or very homogeneous set of responses provide a correct response to the item?* The most major cause of errors in scoring short-answer items is using questions for which several responses represent legitimate answers. The way to reduce this error is to construct items so that only a single or very homogeneous set of responses represents a correct answer. Also, if potentially correct answers are restricted, teaching aides and students can assist with scoring the tests.

☙ 6.2   Apply What You Are Learning

Correct answers to two of the five items are restricted. Which two items are they?

1. What makes it different from a car is that an SUV has _____.
2. What is the name given to scientists who study weather?
3. A country that has no direct access to the sea is _____.
4. In the U.S. Congress, the House of Representatives includes how many members?
5. What do you call a store where you buy food?

Answers can be found at the end of the chapter.

To develop items with restricted responses, Ebel and Frisbie (1986) proposed that teachers first determine the desired answer and then construct a question for which that answer is the only appropriate response. This is a very effective technique.

5. *Does the item use grammatical structure and vocabulary different from that contained in the source of instruction?* A common but unwise approach to constructing completion items is to select important sentences from a textbook or other source and replace a key word with a blank. Two problems are associated with this practice. First, it encourages students to memorize rather than comprehend what is read. Second, because most sentences derive some of their meaning from adjacent sentences, extracting sentences creates vague test items. Note the vagueness of the following items. Each is an important sentence appearing earlier in this book.

Although norm-referenced interpretations can be made with more general descriptions of the content domain, they do require a _____.

The distinction between concrete and defined concepts is _____.

The intended answers are "well-defined norm group" and "not always clear."

The suggestion made by Ebel and Frisbie (1986) is again relevant: First determine the word or phrase that represents the correct answer, and then construct the question for which that answer is the only appropriate response.

6. *Does the format of the item (and the test in general) allow for efficient scoring?* Short-answer items are more time-consuming to score than are questions written in the multiple-choice and alternate-choice formats. Except for the youngest students, the efficiency of scoring can be improved by having students write answers in a column to the side as illustrated here.

1. The artist who is responsible for
   the artistic style known as
   Cubism is __(1)__ .   1. _Picasso_

2. The French artist who did a series
   of paintings of water lilies
   is __(2)__ .   2. _Monet_

3. The artist who created the
   painting entitled The Scream
   is __(3)__ .   3. _Munch_

7. *If the item requires a numerical response, does the question state the unit of measurement to be used in the answer?* Consider the following question:

> What is the sum of 24 inches and 12 inches?
> __36__ inches

Had "inches" not been specified to the right of the blank, correct answers would have included 3 (feet) and 1 (yard). You can score answers more quickly and accurately if students use a common unit of measure.

The remaining criteria pertain only to completion items.

8. *Does the blank represent a key word?* If the blanks in completion items fail to represent key words, the test will measure reading comprehension more than knowledge of a particular content area. In fact, a technique for measuring reading comprehension is to have students fill in blanks representing every fifth word of a paragraph. Taylor (1953) named this procedure the "cloze" technique. Because every fifth word versus key words is substituted with blanks, the cloze technique does not (and is not intended to) provide an effective measure of the knowledge portrayed in the paragraph.

● 6.3   Apply What You Are Learning

To make a completion item, which underlined word in each sentence is the key word and could be replaced with a blank?

1. <u>Mercury</u> is the <u>planet</u> closest to the <u>sun</u>.
2. The minor <u>planets</u> located <u>mostly</u> between Mars and Jupiter are called <u>asteroids</u>.
3. The <u>name</u> of Jupiter's <u>moon</u> that has active <u>volcanos</u> is <u>Io</u>.

Answers can be found at the end of the chapter.

9. *Are blanks placed at or near the end of the item?* The efficiency with which students answer completion items can be improved somewhat by placing blanks at or near the end of each item. This way, students can answer the items when they first come to a blank and avoid having to reread part of the item. Therefore, item 1 in the preceding examples should be rewritten as follows:

1. The planet closest to the
   sun is __(1)__ .   1. _Mercury_

10. *Is the number of blanks sufficiently limited?* An excessive number of blanks within a completion item can cause problems. Too many blanks increases the amount of time required for students to determine what is being asked. If fewer blanks are used, more items can be included in a test, improving coverage of content and hence potential validity.

Another problem caused by the use of too many blanks is that the resulting test item often has a variety of unintended but legitimate answers. How many answers can you generate for this item?

> A _____ is _____ of _____.

Some possibilities include the following:

A <u>gulf</u> is <u>south</u> of <u>Pensacola</u>.

A <u>midget</u> is <u>kind</u> of <u>small</u>.

A <u>branch</u> is <u>part</u> of <u>a tree</u>.

A <u>great aunt</u> is <u>the sister</u> of <u>your grandparent</u>.

Although this example is rather extreme, completion items tend to have multiple solutions as the number of blanks increase. Remember, multiple correct answers are the major source of errors when scoring short-answer items.

11. *Is the physical length of each blank the same?* The tendency to provide a longer blank when the correct response is a longer word gives a clue to the answer.

PRACTICE APPLYING THESE DESIRED QUALITIES TO SHORT-ANSWER ITEMS

The previous section examined 11 criteria for evaluating short-answer items. Figure 6.1 lists these criteria. This section will help you apply these criteria by examining some example items.

The objective being assessed by the following items and the proposed correct responses are provided to help you evaluate each item. Each example fails to meet at least one of the criteria listed in Figure 6.1. A critique follows each item. Numbers in parentheses preceding each critique indicate which of the criteria the example item has failed to achieve. Try to identify these problems before reading the critique.

The following example items are intended to measure this objective:

Information: When given its definition, name the literary figure of speech being defined.

Example 6.1

1. A (1) compares two
   different things by using the
   word "like or "as."   1. simile

Critique for Example 6.1

(9) This completion item should be worded so that the blank appears near the end of the sentence. This improves the item's efficiency by allowing students to respond immediately. Here is an improved version of this item:

1. A comparison of two different
   things by using the word "like"
   or "as" is called a(n) (1) .   1. simile

Figure 6.1
Criteria for evaluating short-answer items

1. Does this item measure the specified skill?
2. Is the level of reading skill required by this item below the students' ability?
3. Can this item be answered using one or two words or a short sentence?
4. Will only a single or very homogeneous set of responses provide a correct response to the item?
5. Does the item use grammatical structure and vocabulary different from that contained in the source of instruction?
6. Does the format of the item (and the test in general) allow for efficient scoring?
7. If the item requires a numerical response, does the question state the unit of measurement to be used in the answer?

Additional criteria for completion items

8. Does the blank represent a key word?
9. Are blanks placed at or near the end of the item?
10. Is the number of blanks sufficiently limited?
11. Is the physical length of each blank the same?

Example 6.2

2. The statement "he eats like a bird" illustrates what figure of speech?   2. simile

Critique for Example 6.2

(1) Mechanically, this is a good short-answer item but may not measure the targeted performance objective. If the phrase "he eats like a bird" was not previously used as an illustration of a simile, or a student does not recall its use, then the item is asking a student to classify new illustrations as examples of a concept, this being a good procedure for assessing procedural knowledge.

Example 6.3

3. (3) imply resemblances such as from human physiology to other objects; for instance, "the mouth of a river" or "the eye of a needle."   3. metaphors

Critique for Example 6.3

(9) Again, this completion item should be worded so that the blank appears near the end of the sentence. Here is an improved version of this item:

3. Implied resemblances such as from human physiology to other objects, for instance, "the mouth of a river" or the "eye of a needle," are called (3) .   3. metaphors

Example 6.4

4. In what way are similes and metaphors similar and different?

Intended answer: Both similes and metaphors use vocabulary that is already familiar to describe what is less well known. Similes accomplish this through comparisons, typically using "as" or "like," for instance, "He eats like a bird." In contrast, metaphors attribute a resem-

blance to a familiar object, for example "the mouth of a river."

Critique for Example 6.4

(1, 3) This item does not measure the objective. Also, students should be able to answer short-answer items with one or two words or a short sentence. This is an example of a brief-response essay item. (The essay format is discussed in the next chapter.)

SUMMARY

Despite differences in appearance, the completion and short-answer formats are equivalent and can be used interchangeably. Completion and short-answer items are the most widely used item format in written tests. There are three basic advantages to the short-answer format: ease of construction, student-generated answers, and the option of including many items within one test. Short-answer items have two basic limitations: they are generally limited to measuring recall of information (declarative knowledge), and they are more likely to be scored erroneously than are objectively scored items. Several desirable qualities of short-answer items were discussed and are listed in Figure 6.1.

ANSWERS: APPLY WHAT YOU ARE LEARNING

6.1. 1. essay and short answer; 2. multiple-choice and alternate-choice; 3. multiple-choice and alternate-choice.

6.2. Correct answers to items 2 and 4 are restricted. Possible answers to item 1 include "4-wheel drive," "greater room inside," and "greater weight." Possible answers for item 3 are "landlocked" and the name of a landlocked country such as "Switzerland." Correct answers to item 5 include "grocery store," "convenience store," or names of stores where food is sold such as "Winn-Dixie" and "Seven-Eleven."

6.3. 1. Mercury; 2. asteroids; 3. Io.

SOMETHING TO TRY

- If you have access to some previously written short-answer items, use the qualities listed in Figure 6.1 to evaluate these items.
- Prepare some short-answer items that measure this objective:

  Information: Given a geological feature, name the region of the country where this feature exists.

Use Figure 6.1 to evaluate these items.

- Similarly write and then evaluate several items for an objective within your academic specialization.

ADDITIONAL READING

Wesman, A. G. (1971). Writing the test item. In R. L. Thorndike (Ed.), *Educational measurement* (2nd ed.). Washington, DC: American Council on Education. This chapter reviews the item-writing literature and discusses ideas for producing various formats of objectively scored test items.

7
Essay Items

The essay question represents a very flexible test format. It can potentially measure any skill that can be assessed with other formats of written tests. An essay item is also uniquely able to assess a student's ability to communicate ideas in writing. However, the essay format has a number of weaknesses, which, if uncontrolled, can substantially reduce the usefulness of a test. For example, answers to essay questions are often scored differently depending on which teacher does the grading. Also, a variety of student characteristics other than the adequacy of the student's response often affect essay scores.

Some essay items more effectively exploit the advantages of the format and avoid the limitations. This chapter describes characteristics typically associated with the better-quality essay items. You will be asked to apply these characteristics by evaluating a series of essay questions. Many of the limitations of the essay format pertain to the scoring of students' responses. Techniques that can improve scoring accuracy are described in this chapter. These include using a model answer, concealing the identity of students, and grading all responses to one question at a time.

The essay format of course relies heavily on a student's writing skills; therefore, writing proficiency can significantly confound measures of achievement when this format is used. For this reason, the essay format is predominantly used in secondary schools and post-secondary settings.

Recall that one assesses declarative knowledge by having students state what they know.

This is exactly what essay items require students to do. Essay items certainly are able to measure procedural as well as declarative knowledge, but they are less efficient at doing so. For instance, knowledge of a concept is assessed by having students classify diverse illustrations as examples versus non-examples of the concept. Although an essay question can provide an illustration to be classified and then have the student explain the rationale behind the classification, the effort spent on the explanation might in fact be demonstrating declarative rather than procedural knowledge.

This chapter helps you achieve four skills:

- Identify advantages and limitations of essay items
- Identify qualities desired in an essay item
- Evaluate essay items for these qualities
- Score students' responses to essay items

ADVANTAGES AND LIMITATIONS OF ESSAY ITEMS
Advantages of Essay Items

Essay items have three advantages over test questions written in other formats. First, essay items tend to measure more directly the behaviors specified by performance objectives. Second, essay items examine the student's ability to communicate ideas in writing. Third, as with short-answer items, essay items require the student to supply the response instead of selecting from among responses provided by the test.

1. *Essay items tend to measure more directly behaviors specified by performance objectives.* More so than other written formats, the essay item can directly measure the performance specified by the performance objectives. For instance, if the objective is that students will be able to state the relative advantages of fluorescent and incandescent light bulbs, the corresponding essay item might simply be

State the relative advantages of fluorescent and incandescent light bulbs.

Other test formats, as illustrated by the following true-false items, must infer student competence through a series of *indirect* measures:

For a given amount of light output, incandescent light bulbs consume more electricity than fluorescent light bulbs. (true)

Incandescent light bulbs last longer than fluorescent light bulbs. (false)

As we will see later, the tendency for essay items to measure more directly the skill specified by an objective may be a result of how the objectives are stated rather than a characteristic of the essay format. Research has not been conclusive on whether the essay format provides a more valid measure of learning than do other types of written tests.

2. *Essay items can examine students' ability to communicate ideas in writing*. Given the importance of writing skills, this quality of essay items is significant. However, when essay items are used to assess a student's ability to communicate ideas, writing proficiency and comprehension of content should be reported in separate scores. Recall that the usefulness of test scores is reduced when a single score is used to describe simultaneously more than one outcome of instruction.

Caution must be used not to overgeneralize the advantage of essay items in assessing writing skills. For example, the essay test does not represent an appropriate environment for *training* students to write. Students are more inclined to learn appropriate grammar and to develop their writing skills when their abilities are shaped through frequent writing experiences outside examination settings. The use of essay items as a means of improving writing skills is likely to fail because of examination pressure, such as the need to write answers quickly.

3. *Essay items require the student to supply the response*. The multiple-choice and alternate-choice formats both allow the student to select an answer from among options provided on the test. In working from a list of alternative answers, students may actually generate correct responses

that they would have been unable to generate had no answers been suggested.

The essay format prevents students who have not acquired the knowledge from giving a correct answer through a blind guess. Guessing reduces the precision of test scores. If a guess is truly blind (i.e., based on no information), the student's response represents a random action that tends to lower the reliability of the scores. However, because test reliability can be improved by increasing the number of items on the test, the ability to include a greater number of items in a multiple-choice or alternate-choice test more than offsets this particular advantage of the essay format.

🌐 7.1   Apply What You Are Learning

Can you remember the three advantages of the essay format? List these advantages on a separate piece of paper and then check your answers.

Answers can be found at the end of the chapter.

Limitations of Essay Items

Essay items have three limitations relative to test items written in other formats. First, exams that use the essay format tend to provide a less-adequate sampling of the content being tested. Second, the scoring of essay items is less reliable. Third, essay items take longer to score.

1. *Essay items usually provide a less-adequate sampling of the content*. Time constraints usually allow inclusion of only a few essay items on one exam. As a result, one essay test will measure a relatively small portion of skills that students are expected to learn. Some time ago, Posey (1932) demonstrated that when as few as 10 items are included in a test, a student's score is largely determined by whether these items happen by chance to sample content with which the student is knowledgeable. One conceivably might use broad essay questions to cover a greater percentage of skills with each item. This strategy, however, tends to reduce the quality of an essay test.

For instance, broad questions are very difficult to score accurately.

It is interesting to note that most of a student's time during an essay test is not spent solving the problem posed by the question. Most of the time is spent writing out the answer. If a student is fairly knowledgeable about the concept being questioned, relatively little time is needed to read the essay item and formulate a response. If some way other than writing could be established for recording the students' answers to essay questions, substantially more skills could be assessed by one test. If students did not write out their answers, however, the essay's distinctive advantage of being able to assess the ability to communicate ideas in writing would be lost.

Because so few items can be included in an essay test, instructors often conclude that an advantage of the format is that less time is required to develop a test. The time required to develop each high-quality essay item, however, is generally greater than that required to develop a good item written in any alternative format. The inclusion of fewer items in an essay test results from a limitation of the essay format; time constraints allow for the measurement of only a few skills.

Furthermore, some teachers believe essay tests are easier to develop because they construct essay items without also creating a plan for scoring these items. This important issue is discussed later in the chapter.

2. *The scoring of essay items is less reliable.* Because of the subjective aspect of scoring essay items, scores assigned to a set of student responses are often inconsistent. Different readers will assign scores ranging from very low to very high to a given essay response. That is, scores assigned by one teacher may generalize poorly to scores assigned by another. Factors such as penmanship, expected achievement, difficulty in reading a student's writing, and sex and race of the student have been found to affect significantly scores assigned to essays. Various teachers, often unconsciously, differentially weight these and other factors. Chase (1986) and Rafoth and Rubin

(1984) found that factors other than a student's proficiency with the skill being assessed had a substantial effect on the scores assigned. The subjective scoring of essay tests, combined with the relatively small number of items that can be included, usually reduces the generalizability of scores on these tests. Techniques described later in this chapter can help reduce this significant limitation of the essay format.

3. *Essay tests are more time-consuming to score.* Scoring essay exams is obviously time-consuming. No other written test format takes as long to score. If fairly detailed scoring procedures are followed and student responses are graded by more than one reader (both techniques are desired), the amount of time required to score essay items can be substantial.

🌰 **7.2   Apply What You Are Learning**

Can you remember the three limitations of the essay format? List these limitations on a separate piece of paper and then check your answers.

Answers can be found at the end of the chapter.

IDENTIFYING QUALITIES DESIRED IN ESSAY ITEMS

Before considering specific qualities, a distinction should be made between **brief-response** and **extended-response** questions. Although extended-response essay items have unique assets, these same qualities limit the usefulness of the essay format in classroom tests.

Desirability of Using Brief-Response versus Extended-Response Questions

An essay question qualifies as a brief-response item if students can read and fully answer the item within 10 minutes. A question requiring a longer response is considered an extended-response item. The required length of the answer is generally established by the nature of the task presented to the students. An extended-response item presents a broader task. The task may be broader simply because it asks students to do quantitatively more rather than to do a qualitatively different kind of task. Alternatively, an extended-response item may allow students to demonstrate such skills as creativity, selecting and organizing a number of ideas relevant to a given issue, and communicating ideas in writing. Either way, the appropriateness of using an extended-response essay question to achieve these characteristics should be evaluated.

If the purpose of using an extended-response question is to have students demonstrate a greater number of skills, the extended-response question can generally be broken into shorter questions that, individually, can be answered within 10 minutes. This tactic will significantly improve the consistency with which answers are scored and will generally allow assessment of a better cross-section of skills.

Not all extended-response essay questions can be subdivided. To determine whether subdivision is possible, look at the types of capabilities that are being assessed. If the capabilities involve recalling information or demonstrating knowledge of concepts or rules, the extended-response question generally can be rewritten as a series of brief-response questions, and doing so will be advantageous.

However, if the extended-response question requires diverse strategies to solve a complex problem, then brief-response questions may not suffice. Be careful here. A task should not be classified as complex problem-solving simply because it is difficult, is academically important, or requires students to do a lot. Complex problem-solving involves but *does not* require students to demonstrate their knowledge of information, concepts, or rules. If the extended-response question does require students to do these things, it likely is not measuring a problem-solving skill. Complex problem-solving requires students to draw on and synthesize information, concepts, and rules *in order to solve a problem,* and in solving the problem, the students' recall of information and knowledge of concepts and rules generally is not documented in their written responses. Again, if the essay question is asking for a statement of knowledge of informa-

tion, concepts, and rules, the essay question generally is not assessing a problem-solving skill and usually can be rewritten as a series of brief-response questions.

If a proposed essay question will require an extended response because it truly is measuring a complex task, such as problem solving, alternative formats other than a written test should be considered. Usually, complex problem-solving skills are more adequately assessed through the use of portfolios and performance assessments. Asking a student to demonstrate a problem-solving skill within the context of a written exam tends to be contrived, and more often than not distorts and invalidates an important assessment.

Criteria for Evaluating Essay Items

This section examines criteria that characterize high-quality essay items. In the next section, you will be asked to use these criteria to evaluate a series of essay questions. The last section of this chapter describes techniques that can be used to facilitate accurate scoring of essay tests.

1. *Does the item measure the specified skill?* As noted earlier, for a test to have content validity its items must collectively measure the skills specified in the performance objectives or outlined in a table of specifications. An item should be selected or constructed only after the skill to be measured has been identified. With every test item, regardless of format, it is essential to ask whether the item is measuring the targeted skill.

● 7.3   Apply What You Are Learning

Here is an objective and two essay items intended to measure that objective. Which item (A or B) provides the best measure of this objective?

Concept: Given descriptions of manmade objects in space, state with an explanation whether or not it is a satellite of Earth.

A. The mission of the Hubbell Space Telescope is to photograph far away objects from its orbit above Earth. Is the Hubbell Space Telescope a satellite of Earth? Explain your reasoning.

B. What determines whether an object rocketed into space is an Earth satellite? Explain your reasoning.

_____

Answers can be found at the end of the chapter.

Sometimes instructors allow students to choose the subset of essay items they will answer. This practice lowers the content-related validity of the test, because the set of questions included is determined by student preference rather than by a systematic plan. Allowing students to select questions creates two additional problems as well. First, to the degree that students avoid difficult questions, the test is less likely to detect areas with which they need help. Second, test scores based on subsets of items that measure different skills are difficult to interpret.

However, it often is appropriate to provide students options in how they respond to a question. For instance, students might be allowed to write about the scientist of their choice in order to illustrate the scientific method of inquiry. The essay question might even list the names of scientists from which the students may choose. Allowing students a choice in how they respond to a question is appropriate as long as the same capability is being assessed regardless of a student's choice, and the same scoring plan can be applied to all students' responses.

2. *Is the level of reading skill required by this item below the students' ability?* As with other formats, measures of reading ability and achievement will be confounded unless the reading skills required to understand the test item are below those of the students taking the test. Each sentence should use simple construction and words with which all students are proficient.

3. *Will all or almost all students answer this item in less than 10 minutes?* An essay question that requires students to take more than 10 minutes to formulate and write a response is not a brief-response essay item. As discussed earlier, extended-response items should be avoided within the context of a classroom test.

4. *Will the scoring plan result in different readers assigning similar scores to a given student's response?* Consistency in scoring is essential with all item formats. The need for consistency is more obvious for objectively scored items, such as multiple-choice items. For instance, if two people grade the same answers to a multiple-choice exam but derive quite different scores, the scoring process is likely to be judged inadequate. Consistency in scoring is equally important for essay items. Scoring inconsistency is as damaging to the generalizability of scores of an essay test (and, therefore, to its validity) as it is to any objectively scored tests. *The scoring plan for each essay item must be designed so that different readers will assign similar scores to a given student's response.*

To facilitate reliable scoring, the scoring plan should incorporate the three characteristics listed in Figure 7.1. First, the total number of points the item is worth must be specified. *The points associated with each essay item should be proportional to the relative importance of the skill being tested.* The importance of a test item should not be equated with the amount of time students need to answer the item. The increased time required to write a response to an essay item is not an appropriate reason for assigning more points to essay questions than to items in other formats.

Second, the attributes to be evaluated must be specified. Figure 7.2 provides an example of how

---

1. Total number of points assigned to the item based on its importance relative to other items
2. Specific attributes to be evaluated in students' responses
3. For each attribute, criteria for awarding points, including partial credit

---

Figure 7.1

Three characteristics to be included in the scoring plan of each essay item

Test Item

A strong cold front approached Florida and a severe storm resulted. As the front approached, sustained winds from the southwest increased to 50 miles an hour with some gusts higher than 80. As the front passed, the wind switched to the northwest and then slowly diminished. Was this storm a hurricane? Explain your conclusion, briefly describing how each piece of information presented above was used in drawing your conclusion.

Attributes to Be Scored

1. Classifies the storm as not a hurricane

2. Identifies absence of a closed circulation around a calm center

3. Identifies absence of sustained wind above 74 miles per hour

4. Identifies three characteristics of this weather system that are not defining characteristics of a hurricane

Figure 7.2
Illustration of attributes with a scoring plan

1 point	1. Classifies the storm as not a hurricane
2 points	2. Identifies absence of a closed circulation around a calm center (no partial credit)
1 point	3. Identifies absence of sustained wind above 74 miles per hour
2 points	4. Identifies three characteristics of this weather system that are not defining characteristics of a hurricane (1 point if two characteristics identified)

Figure 7.3
Illustration of a scoring plan

attributes should be specified. First, let us state the objective being assessed:

Concept: Given a description of a storm involving strong winds, state with explanation whether or not it is a hurricane.

Figure 7.2 shows an essay item that measures this objective and specifies the four attributes in students' responses that are to be scored. If these four attributes are judged to be appropriate for scoring this item, misspellings or errors in grammar will not count. Information that students provide that is superfluous to the criteria specified in the scoring plan will not count, regardless of the accuracy of this information. (Such qualities would be scored only if included in the scoring plan.) Therefore, answers to essay items often will include errors that are not scored. This does not mean that such errors are

to be ignored; these errors can be marked (but not scored), and students can also be required to correct important errors after test papers have been returned.

The third criterion to be included in a scoring plan pertains to how points will be awarded. The four criteria of a scoring plan are illustrated in Figure 7.3: The total number of points the essay item is worth has been set at 6; the attributes to be evaluated are specified; and the points associated with each attribute (or combination of attributes) are also specified.

A scoring plan must be precise enough for the reader to know when and when not to award a point. If more than one point is associated with a given quality, the guidelines should indicate if and how partial credit is to be awarded. A scoring plan can be written using abbreviated or telegraphic statements.

There is an erroneous tendency to equate points to the number of attributes being scored. For instance, the four attributes within Figure 7.3 might be thought to require a total of 4 points. Total points associated with an essay item should be influenced only by the *relative* importance of the skill being measured.

The scoring plan should be established for each essay item *when the item is written*. Creating an essay question without simultaneously establishing how it is to be scored is analogous to creating a true-false item without establishing whether the item is true or false.

One might incorrectly conclude that the presence of a scoring plan prevents essay items from measuring more than factual knowledge. This conclusion would be justified were a scoring plan thought of as a specification of the correct answer; however, this is not what a scoring plan is. Instead of establishing the correct answer, the scoring plan specifies attributes of the correct answer. For instance, an essay item might ask students to take a position on a controversial issue and defend that position. The scoring plan would not be concerned with the position the students chose. Instead, the scoring plan would be concerned with the conciseness with which students expressed their positions and the nature of the defense they gave in support of their respective positions. *The scoring plan delineates attributes that distinguish adequate from less-adequate responses to the essay item.*

🌑 7.4 Apply What You Are Learning

The preceding discussion identified three characteristics to use in developing a scoring plan. These characteristics are summarized in Figure 7.1. Which of these characteristics are not addressed in the scoring plans to each of the following essay items?

Item 1. In an orchestra, what are the differences between wind and string instruments?

Scoring plan: 1 point for each correct answer

Item 2. Support or critique this statement: "A satellite can be launched with less rocket power from the European Spaceport (northern coast of South America) than from either the Kennedy Space Center (Florida) or the Vandenburg Air Force Base (California)."

Scoring plan:

- Reference to boost provided by Earth's rotation when satellite is launched toward the east rather than to the south, as from California
- Reference to greater boost provided at the European Spaceport because its closer proximity to the equator results in greater speed from Earth's rotation than in Florida

Answers can be found at the end of the chapter.

In the above exercise, Item 1 is vague. There are a variety of differences between wind and string instruments that could be listed, probably some that the item writer did not anticipate. For instance, wind instruments are used in marching bands, they often are not made of wood as are string instruments, and they always are placed up to or partially into the player's mouth. Had the item writer thought through the scoring plan as the item was developed, the vagueness of this item would have been detected before the test was administered. Have you had to answer essay items where it was obvious a scoring plan had not been thought through?

5. *Does the scoring plan describe a correct and complete response?* The purpose of any test is to determine how proficient students are in a particular skill. This purpose can be realized only if test items are constructed so that students who have acquired that knowledge tend to give a correct answer and students who have not acquired that knowledge give an incorrect or incomplete response. This result can be accomplished, in turn, only if the person scoring the test can describe a correct and complete response. With an essay item, the correct response is described through the scoring plan.

It is difficult to construct a scoring plan that describes a correct and complete response if the essay item asks a broad question. This difficulty is a major reason for encouraging the use of essay questions that can be answered fully within 10 minutes; items that require more than 10 minutes tend to ask broad questions.

It is also difficult to develop a good scoring plan when the correct answer is a matter of opinion. Asking students to choose and defend a particular opinion or asking students to identify opinions is appropriate, as long as the scoring plan can specify characteristics of an appropriate response.

● 7.5   Apply What You Are Learning

For which item (A or B) of the following pairs would it be *more difficult* to develop a scoring plan that content experts would agree describes a correct response?

1. A. What is a map?
    B. Describe information that is included in a road map.
2. A. What are the major differences between a conservative and liberal economic policy?
    B. Which is better, a conservative or liberal economic policy?

Answers can be found at the end of this chapter.

Colleagues who teach similar classes often can help each other develop or proof a scoring plan. One strategy is to ask a colleague to answer the essay question orally. If the colleague's response differs significantly from your own scoring plan, either modify the scoring plan or the item itself. An alternative strategy is to ask a colleague to score some of your students' answers using your scoring plan. Usually, a colleague will quickly detect any significant problems that exist in your scoring plan.

6. *Is the item written in such a way that the scoring plan will be obvious to knowledgeable students?* If students proficient in the area being assessed are unable to describe how an item will be scored, the item cannot fulfill its role; that is, the item will be unable to determine the proficiency of students because it will not distinguish between students who have acquired the knowledge and those who have not. Proficient students will be able to give correct answers only if they can determine from the item the characteristics of a correct answer.

The same conditions that facilitate development of a scoring plan also help communicate to students the qualities desired in the answer. The essay item must pose a specific task for which the attributes of a correct response are not simply a matter of opinion. In addition to stating the essay question, it is sometimes helpful to state briefly the *characteristics* of a correct response. Also, to communicate how the item will be scored, state within the test how many points each essay item is worth.

PRACTICE APPLYING THESE DESIRED QUALITIES TO ESSAY ITEMS

The previous section presented six criteria for evaluating essay items. Figure 7.4 lists these criteria. This section will help you apply these criteria by examining some example items.

Each example states the performance objective that is to be measured, an essay item designed to measure that objective, and the scoring plan that was proposed for scoring responses to the item. When administered, only the essay item would be shown to students. Use Figure 7.4 to evaluate each example. Each essay item and/or its scoring plan fails to

1. Does the item measure the specified skill?
2. Is the level of reading skill required by this item below the students' ability?
3. Will all or almost all students answer this item in less than 10 minutes?
4. Will the scoring plan result in different readers assigning similar scores to a given student's response?
5. Does the scoring plan describe a correct and complete response?
6. Is the item written in such a way that the scoring plan will be obvious to knowledgeable students?

Figure 7.4

Criteria for evaluating essay items

meet at least one of these six criteria. Compare your evaluation to the critique that follows each example.

Example 7.1

Objective: *Concept:* Given a description of heat being transferred, classify the heat transfer as predominantly conduction, convection, or radiation (and provide logic behind this classification).

Essay item shown to students: A pan of water is being heated on the stove. Although the water is not being stirred, the water can be seen moving around within the pan as the temperature of the water increases. Is heat being transferred within this water mostly by conduction, convection, or radiation? What is happening in this water that causes this transfer of heat? (3 points)

Scoring plan: The student shows heat is being transferred by convection.

Critique for Example 7.1

The item, as written, is good. The scoring plan, however, does not provide criteria for awarding points. Without these criteria, different readers would likely assign dissimilar scores to each student's response. Here is a better scoring plan:

1 point	States heat transferred by convection
1 point	Indicates that convection transfers heat by movement and thus mixing of the heated fluid
1 point	Indicates that convection movement is caused by fluid expanding when heated, thus becoming more buoyant and rising

Example 7.2

Objective: *Concept:* When given an illustration of a change in a substance, classify it as a physical change (i.e., altering the shape, form, volume, or density) or a chemical change (i.e., producing new substances with different characteristics).

Essay item shown to students: Explain the difference between a physical and chemical change in a substance. (3 points)

Scoring plan: Determine whether the student correctly explains the difference.

Critique for Example 7.2

Example 7.2 fails to meet almost all the criteria in Figure 7.4. Let us evaluate this item by examining each of the six criteria:

1. Asking the student to explain the difference between physical and chemical change does not measure the targeted performance objective. Notice that this objective involves a concept. To measure a concept, students should be provided an illustration they have not previously used in this context, and then should be asked to classify the illustration. As worded, this essay item measures recall of information, specifically, the distinction between physical and chemical change. A better essay item for measuring this objective would be the following:

   A piece of wood has burned. Is this an example of a physical or chemical change? Explain why.

2. To this item's credit, the level of reading skill needed to understand this question is appropriately lower than the reading level of those taking the test, assuming the item is directed at typical readers of this book.

3. Again to this item's credit, most students can answer it within 10 minutes.

4. The scoring plan is vague, and different readers will likely assign quite different scores to a given student's response. In essence, the scoring plan states students should give a correct answer, without specifying attributes to be evaluated or how points are to be awarded. Here is an improved plan for awarding the 3 points associated with this item (although improving the scoring plan does not negate this item's other problems):

   2 points Associates physical change with altering shape, form, volume, or

density (or 1 point if 3 of 4 are listed); otherwise, 0 points

1 point   Associates physical chemical change with producing a different substance

5. The original scoring plan does not describe a complete response, to a large part because of the lack of conciseness in the scoring plan. As originally worded, the vagueness of the scoring plan makes it difficult determining what constitutes a fully correct response.

6. The essay item does not communicate to the student how answers will be scored, mainly because the task presented to the student is vague. Often, vague essay items result from having only a vague scoring plan in mind when the item is written. If the revised scoring plan presented above in point 4 were used, here is how the essay item could be rewritten:

What changes in a substance, if they occur, would be classified as physical changes? Likewise, what change in a substance would be classified as a chemical change?

Example 7.3

Objective: *Rule:* Given a constant force applied to an object moving through space, draw and explain the path this object will take through space as the force is continually applied to the object.

Essay item shown to students: An object is initially moving through space from left to right. A constant force from above, perpendicular to its initial movement, is applied to the object. Draw the path the object will take over an extended period of time as a result of the force being applied. Explain why the object will follow the path you have drawn. (4 points)

Scoring plan: An appropriate path is drawn and explanation given.

Critique for Example 7.3

The item is well written. It measures the objective and can be answered within 10 minutes. This item is written so that the scoring plan probably would be obvious to knowledgeable students.

The scoring plan is carelessly written and as a result is vague. Assuming the person reading students' answers is knowledgeable, the scoring plan in this well-written item can be implied from the item; therefore, we may not have a serious problem here. Regardless, creating a vague scoring plan is a bad practice because it encourages writing vague essay items. The scoring plan should specify the attributes to be evaluated in students' responses, as well as criteria for awarding points for each attribute. Here is an improved scoring plan:

1 point   Drawing shows downward change in object's path

1 point   Change is smooth

1 point   From explanation, obvious that student recognizes that the rate of motion from left to right remains unchanged

1 point   From explanation, obvious that student recognizes downward motion increases at a constant rate

Example 7.4

Objective: *Rule:* Demonstrates that for a given perimeter, area of a rectangle increases as the length and width of the rectangle become closer to equal.

Essay item shown to students: An architect is drawing a classroom for a new school. The perimeter of the room is to be 160 feet. Determine whether the room will have more floor space if made in the shape of a rectangle or square. (3 points)

Scoring plan:

3 points   Uses square and sequence of at least three rectangles, all with perimeter of 160 feet, to demonstrate area increases as length and width become close to equal (2 points if proper sequence of at least four rectangles are given, but no square)

Critique for Example 7.4

The scoring plan matches the objective better than the essay item. Given the information provided in the scoring plan, the instructor who wrote this item probably had the objective clearly in mind when writing the item, but has not used the item to clearly communicate the intended task to students. Note that because students can fully answer the essay item by simply stating the square room has the larger area, a student would have a legitimate complaint if that answer received less than full credit.

In terms of the criteria listed in Figure 7.4, the teacher failed to write the item in such a way that the scoring plan would be obvious to knowledgeable students. Here is an alternative essay item that more adequately conveys the scoring plan:

Drawing a sequence of four rectangular rooms and computing their areas, show that the maximum floor area is obtained when the length and width of the room are equal. Use a perimeter of 160 feet for all four rooms. (3 points)

This particular item might be considered a performance assessment rather than an essay item. (Chapters 12 and 13 discuss performance assessments.) In some cases, the distinction between essay items and performance assessments is unclear.

SCORING STUDENTS' RESPONSES TO ESSAY ITEMS

Analytical versus Holistic Scoring

Responses to essay items usually are scored analytically or holistically. *Analytical scoring* uses a detailed scoring plan to evaluate the answers to a given question. As described earlier in this chapter, the scoring plan identifies specific attributes to be judged in students' responses and indicates the number of points associated with each of these attributes. In a sense, the scoring plan can be thought of as a checklist, with the reader checking off the desired attributes contained in a given response.

As the complexity of an essay question increases or as students are given more flexibility in terms of how they may respond to a question, the quality of a student's overall response becomes less adequately represented by the sum of highly explicit parts. In such cases, *holistic scoring* often works better than analytical scoring. Holistic scoring involves reading the answer to each item in its entirety and then evaluating the overall quality of that answer.

One common approach to holistic scoring involves placing a student's paper into one of three groups, representing low, medium, and high categories of judged quality. Often, the reader reevaluates students' answers within each group to subdivide responses into additional categories. The final number of categories might correspond to the number of points associated with the essay item.

The advantages of holistic scoring are that it (1) is relatively fast and (2) can be used with items for which answers cannot be subdivided into components. Weaknesses of holistic scoring are that it (1) usually results in less-reliable scores and (2) provides limited information to the student as to why an answer was judged appropriate or not so judged.

Because less time is required to read students' responses with holistic scoring, having a second reader independently score each response can offset the lower reliability. The two scores for each response are averaged. This approach is more practical in some situations, such as when teachers are working as a team or are using a common exam.

An alternative procedure for improving the quality of holistic scoring is to establish model answers for each question. Model answers help clarify the attributes sought in students' responses; in addition, distributing model answers to students can supplement the limited feedback associated with holistic scoring. When using a model answer, the teacher might read the responses of a few students before finalizing the model answer so that any unanticipated qualities may be included in the model.

A final procedure for improving holistic scoring involves what is called a scoring rubric. A scoring rubric consists of several different descriptions, each for a different level of quality, often ranging from a poor response to an excellent response. Generally, descriptions at each level address the same elements within a response. Therefore, the scoring rubric defines the elements in students' responses that are to be scored. When scoring answers, a student's response is assigned to the one description within the scoring rubric that best matches the quality of that response. Typically, numbers are assigned to the descriptions within the rubric. For example, if the scoring rubric includes six descriptions, these descriptions are numbered 1 through 6, with 1 point assigned to the description of a poor response and 6 points assigned to the excellent response. In Chapter 12, we look more closely at scoring rubrics within the context of performance assessments.

Reading Responses to Multiple versus Single Items

With other formats, such as short answer and multiple-choice, all of one student's answers are read before reading the responses of the next student. With essay items, all students' responses to a given item should be evaluated before reading responses to the next item. From a practical perspective, working with one item at a time focuses the reader's attention and speeds up the scoring process—which are significant advantages in grading essay exams. More important, reading all responses to a given item improves scoring accuracy. Focusing on a single item helps the reader maintain a clear perception of the standards being used to evaluate answers to that particular essay question. Also, reading the responses of all students to a single item reduces the tendency to bias the evaluation of one item in light of the quality of a student's response to previous items.

Reading Students' Papers in a Variable versus Consistent Order

A number of studies have shown that the quality of the previously scored essay affects the score assigned to a subsequently read response. Daly and Dickson-Markman (1982) and Hughes, Keeling, and Tuck (1980) demonstrated that a high-quality essay deflates the score assigned to a subsequent paper. Hughes and Keeling (1984) found this still to be true even when responses were being judged against model answers. To reduce the cumulative effect this biasing might have across items on each student's test score, the order of student papers should be rearranged after each question is read.

Concealing the Identity of Students

Previously referenced studies by Chase (1979, 1986) found that factors such as expected achievement, as well as the sex and race of the student, significantly affect scores assigned to essays. To prevent this biasing, student identity should be concealed to the extent possible when scoring essays. Such techniques as having students write their names on the back of a paper or using temporary identification numbers can facilitate this concealment. Unfortunately, a teacher is likely to learn to recognize the identity of students through writing style and penmanship. Full concealment of identity is generally not possible.

Using Multiple Readers

It is more practical to use multiple readers for holistic rather than analytic scoring because the former method takes less time. Averaging scores across multiple readers, however, will increase the reliability of tests, regardless of scoring technique. Coffman (1971) encourages having a different reader score each question when it is not possible for each reader to score the responses to all questions.

Using Diversity of Responses as an Indicator of Item Ambiguity

Often, students read questions other than those intended in an essay item. This problem can be minimized by carefully constructing the item and scoring plan, using the qualities listed in Figure 7.4 to evaluate the item, and having colleagues review questions before they are administered to students.

Diversity of students' responses, in which students appear to be interpreting the essay question differently, should be viewed as an indication of item ambiguity. If an essay question is ambiguous, the teacher, in essence, is giving students the option to interpret the question as they choose. This situation is similar to allowing each student to select questions to be answered and causes the same problems with content validity and with interpreting performance on the test. Essay questions that generate diverse responses should be revised before being reused.

SUMMARY

Essay items have some advantages over other written-test formats: They tend to measure targeted behaviors more directly, and they facilitate examination of students' ability to communicate ideas in writing. Relative to short-answer and completion items, essay questions much more readily assess intellectual skills. In contrast to objectively scored items, essay questions require students to supply the response. Essay items have basic limitations: They usually provide a less-adequate sampling of content to be assessed; they are less-reliably scored, and they are more time-consuming to score. Six qualities that should be incorporated into essay items were discussed and are listed in Figure 7.4.

When constructing essay items, it is also important to create a scoring plan. The scoring plan often specifies the characteristics as opposed to the content of a correct response. The plan may involve analytical or holistic scoring. The latter is appropriate when characteristics of a correct response cannot be subdivided into a series of separately scored characteristics. Other relevant scoring considerations include the desirability of scoring the responses of all students to one item before scoring the next item, rearranging the order of students' papers before reading the next item, concealing the identity of students when scoring responses, and using multiple readers whenever possible.

ANSWERS: APPLY WHAT YOU ARE LEARNING

7.1. The three advantages of essay items are that (1) they allow for more direct measurement of behaviors specified in performance objectives; (2) they assess students' ability to communicate ideas in writing; and (3) they require students to provide an answer rather than to select one from alternatives provided.

7.2. The three limitations of essay items are (1) less-adequate sampling of content resulting from the limited number of questions that can be included in one test; (2) errors in scoring answers resulting from inconsistency between readers and from evaluating irrelevant variables; and (3) greater time required to score students' responses.

7.3. Item A provides the better measure. Notice that item B is asking students to recall information, whereas item A requires students to determine whether or not a new illustration is an example of a concept. Always be alert to the type of capability involved.

7.4. 1. Neither the total number of points nor the attributes to be evaluated is specified. 2. Neither the total number of points nor guidelines for awarding points is specified.

7.5. 1. A; 2. B. Within the first pair, item A is so general that a knowledgeable student could cite a variety of correct answers that were not included in the scoring plan. Within the second pair, the correct answer for item B is largely a matter of opinion or circumstance.

SOMETHING TO TRY

- If you have access to some previously written essay items, use the qualities listed in Figure 7.4 to evaluate these items, including the scoring plan.

- Prepare an essay item with a scoring plan that measures the following objective:

  Information: Using an actual example, describe the procedure Congress is to follow for attempting to override a presidential veto. Use Figure 7.4 to evaluate this item. An essay item written to measure this objective probably can be answered using two to four sentences. Although this represents a minimal essay question, it provides a useful context for writing a concise essay item and scoring plan.

- Prepare an essay item with a scoring plan that measures the following objective:

  Information: State the relative advantages of various types of motor vehicles such as full-size cars, compact cars, SUV's, and light trucks, including a statement concerning the cause of each advantage.

  Construct the essay item so that it requires approximately 5 minutes to answer and involves a comparison of two specified types of vehicles. Use qualities listed in Figure 7.4 to evaluate the item. This includes being sure that the task specified by the essay question closely matches the scoring plan.

- Similarly, write and evaluate essay items, with scoring plans, for an objective within your academic specialization.

ADDITIONAL READING

Coffman, W. E. (1971). Essay examinations. In R. L. Thorndike (Ed.), *Educational measurement* (2nd ed.). Washington, DC: American Council on Education. This chapter provides a thorough discussion of advantages, limitations, and research issues related to essay questions as well as a description of procedures for improving the development and scoring of essay questions.

8

Multiple-Choice Items

The multiple-choice format is one of the most popular item formats used in educational testing. Many group-administered standardized tests consist entirely of multiple-choice items. The multiple-choice format is also used extensively in classroom tests, particularly in the middle grades through college.

The multiple-choice item traditionally consists of a *stem* that describes a problem and a series of *options,* or *alternatives,* each representing possible answers to the stem. Normally, one option is correct, with the remaining alternatives referred to as *distractors,* or *foils.*

The suggestion is often made that the multiple-choice format is limited to testing recall of information. Because the correct response is always included among the item's alternatives, this type of item sometimes has been nicknamed multiple-guess and assumed to be unable to measure skills assessed by the essay and short-answer formats.

The multiple-choice format does have distinct limitations; however, effectively constructed multiple-choice items also have significant advantages. Many multiple-choice items used in classroom tests could achieve these advantages if they were constructed more effectively. Based on your own experience with multiple-choice tests, you probably will anticipate many of the qualities desired in multiple-choice items, such as a clearly expressed statement of the problem in the stem and judicious use of the "all of the above" option.

This chapter will help you identify the qualities inherent in the better multiple-choice items. You will be asked to use these qualities to evaluate a series of multiple-choice items.

Considerable flexibility exists within the multiple-choice format. This flexibility will be easier to anticipate by broadening the traditional definition of multiple-choice options. Although the stem presents a problem to be addressed by students, the options should not be thought of as possible solutions to this problem. Instead, these options are the means through which students *transform* proposed solutions to a mark recorded in the test booklet or on an answer sheet. Look at the multiple-choice items illustrated in Figure 8.1. The directions serve as the stem in that they present the problem to be addressed. The multiple-choice options are the lines into which the individual sentences are formatted. These options *do not* represent alternative solutions to the problem presented by the stem. They do control how students mark their answer sheets. The options are designed so that students who are

---

Directions: For each sentence, mark on your answer sheet the letter identifying the line that contains an adjective. Mark "E" if the sentence contains no adjective

1. A. Krueger National
   B. Park is a
   C game reserve
   D. in South Africa.
   E. (No adjective)

2. A. This park was
   B. established in 1898
   C. to protect wildlife
   D. in the region.
   E. (No adjective)

Figure 8.1

Illustration of multiple-choice items using embedded options

unable to solve the problem will typically mark a different answer than will those who understand the concept.

Some variation of the multiple-choice format can be used at all grade levels, although they are more widely used in secondary schools and post-secondary settings. Although standardized tests are increasingly using performance assessments and various construct-response formats, the multiple-choice item still dominates and is likely to continue to do so for some time. This encourages the introduction of multiple-choice items in early grades. Computer-aided lessons often incorporate multiple-choice items because it often is difficult for a computer to adequately process answers students provide with other item formats.

This chapter helps you achieve five skills:

• Identify the advantages and limitations of multiple-choice items
• Identify qualities desired in multiple-choice items
• Evaluate multiple-choice items for these qualities
• Identify variations of multiple-choice items
• Determine the optimal number of options to be included within a multiple-choice item

ADVANTAGES AND LIMITATIONS OF MULTIPLE-CHOICE ITEMS

Advantages of Multiple-Choice Items

Multiple-choice items have four basic advantages over some of the other formats. First, they often provide a more adequate sampling of content. Second, these items tend to structure the problem to be addressed more effectively. Third, they can be quickly scored. Fourth, responses to multiple-choice items are objectively scored.

1. *Multiple-choice items allow a test to obtain a more adequate sampling of content.* Multiple-choice items often can provide a more-adequate sampling of content for two reasons. First, compared with essay items, multiple-choice tests can involve many more items, mainly because students need less time to record responses. Therefore, more content can be sampled by using the multiple-choice rather than the essay format.

Second, compared with the short-answer format, multiple-choice items (and essay items) can more readily measure procedural knowledge. Short-answer items require students to construct a response that consists of one or two words or, at most, a short sentence. Short-answer items, therefore, are usually limited to questions that involve the recall of *information*. In contrast, the stem to a multiple-choice item can ask students to identify an example of a particular *concept*. The options can include examples and non-examples of this concept. The student can demonstrate the ability to classify illustrations related to the concept by identifying the appropriate response. Multiple-choice items can similarly ask students to apply a particular *rule*. The options to such items can include correct and common incorrect solutions resulting from the application of the rule. The options might also contain descriptions of the characteristics of correct and common incorrect solutions instead of solutions. A short-answer item usually cannot do this.

2. *Multiple-choice items tend to structure the problem to be addressed more effectively.* The responses to a multiple-choice item often help define the problem being addressed. Consider the following items:

Short answer: When backing a car out of a garage, what should one do first?

Multiple-choice: Which among the following should be done first when backing a car out of a garage?

A. Lock the car doors
B. Place the foot on the brake pedal before shifting into reverse
C. Start the engine
D. Walk behind the car looking for obstacles

A knowledgeable student answering the completion item might anticipate several actions, any of which could occur first when backing a car out of a garage, such as opening the garage door. The context provided by the options makes it easier to structure a problem with a multiple-choice item than with other written formats.

3. *Multiple-choice items can be quickly scored.* Because students respond to each item with a single mark, multiple-choice items are scored very quickly. Except with students in early elementary grades, scoring efficiency can often be improved by having students mark responses in a blank to the side of each item, or on a separate answer sheet.

When responses are marked on a separate answer sheet, tests can be scored by machine. In the past, scoring machines were expensive and, if available at all, were located at a remote central site. Smaller, more economical scoring machines are now available and are accessible in many school buildings and in some individual classrooms. These machines score answer sheets for an entire class in a few minutes. Scoring machines often print each student's score on the answer sheet and mark incorrect answers. Many of these scoring machines will enter each student's responses into a computer so that patterns in students' answers can be quickly tabulated and used diagnostically.

4. *Responses to multiple-choice items are objectively scored.* As noted earlier, essay tests usually suffer from inconsistencies in scoring students' responses. Unless carefully constructed, short-answer items have a similar problem. Inconsistency in scoring is negligible with multiple-choice items. When given the answer key, two individuals are likely to assign the same score to a given student's responses. Because multiple-choice items are objectively scored, they can be scored by students, teacher aides, or machine.

Although objectively scored, multiple-choice tests contain other sources of inconsistency. We will look carefully at this issue later in the chapter.

8.1   Apply What You Are Learning

Which item format has each of the following qualities?

A. Short answer or completion
B. Essay
C. Multiple-choice

1. Students' answers can be quickly scored.
2. Test items can be quickly constructed.
3. A knowledge of several concepts can be more adequately sampled within a single test.
4. Students' ability to express ideas in writing can be evaluated.
5. Students' responses can be scored with minimal error.

Answers can be found at the end of the chapter.

Limitations of Multiple-Choice Items

Multiple-choice items have three limitations we will address. First, these items are somewhat susceptible to guessing. Second, multiple-choice items usually must indirectly measure targeted behaviors. Third, multiple-choice items are time-consuming to construct.

1. *Multiple-choice items are somewhat susceptible to guessing.* More so than with the essay and short-answer formats, multiple-choice items can be answered correctly by guessing. This would represent a significant problem were it not possible to include many multiple-choice items in a test.

The probability of successfully guessing improves if a student can eliminate some of the distractors to a number of items. The more distractors the student can eliminate in a test, the higher the test score. If the distractors represent common errors, this increase in score is desirable from a measurement perspective because a student who can avoid common errors should obtain a higher score.

Guessing negatively affects the generalizability of performance on a test. To the degree that guessing is involved, a student's performance will be inconsistent from item to item. Increasing the number of items on the test is an effective way to offset the results of guessing and to increase the generalizability of test scores.

Because guessing is less of a problem for short-answer items, they tend to be more reliable than are multiple-choice items. Within the context of quantitative word problems, Oosterhof and Coats (1984) found that fewer than two-thirds the number of completion items would provide reliability comparable to that of multiple-choice items. Using the smaller number of short-answer items can reduce test preparation and administration times and potentially offset the greater scoring time required by the short-answer format.

Relatively few items on multiple-choice tests are answered correctly by blind guessing. Later in this chapter, we will look at techniques that help make incorrect answers more plausible to students who have not yet learned the knowledge being assessed.

2. *Multiple-choice items often must indirectly measure targeted behaviors.* Direct measures are always preferable to indirect measures. Indirect measures, however, are frequently used in many disciplines. An astronomer estimates the temperature of a star by measuring its color. Chemists measure the acidity of a liquid by judging the color of litmus paper. Similarly, an educator must make judgments based on indirect observations. As long as the relationship is understood between a first quality that can be observed and the second quality that is of interest, measures of the second quality can be inferred from observations of the first.

In education, we sometimes forget that all assessments involve indirect measures of knowledge. We cannot see what a student knows or is thinking. Instead we make inferences from student behaviors we can observe. For instance, how would a science teacher establish whether students know how to use observations to test scientific hypotheses? One of the more convincing ways would be to present students with a hands-on experiment, and observe them formulating and evaluating scientific hypotheses from their observations. Better still would be to repeatedly observe students using observation techniques within the context of a large number of diverse experiments. Yet all of these, from an assessment perspective, involve making *inferences* about students' knowledge from observed performances.

Often the wording of our performance objectives or instructional goals misleads us into thinking we have a direct measure of knowledge. For instance, the following type of instructional goal is common:

Explains how to use observation to test scientific hypotheses

This goal, literally interpreted, suggests this essay item:

Explain how one uses observation to test a scientific hypothesis.

Although the *wording* of this essay item is highly consistent with the instructional goal, students' *knowledge* of using observations to test a scientific hypothesis can similarly and still indirectly be measured by a series of multiple-choice items, such as the following:

In an experiment, a student filled two different glasses half full of water and then placed both glasses in a large container of water. Both glasses floated. The student then very slowly added more water to each glass. The first glass still floated after it was completely full of water, but the second glass sank before it was completely filled. Which one of the following hypotheses is supported by this observation?
A. The first glass has a different shape than the second.
B. The first glass is larger than the second.
C. The first glass is made from different material than the second.

As with all test formats, multiple-choice items do not allow teachers to observe directly what the student was thinking or why students selected particular wrong answers. Essay tests sometimes, but not always, provide an indication of the student's thought process. With multiple-choice math tests, work sheets often can be used to help diagnose problems. Similar documentation is usually not present in other content areas. However, the overall information that can be gained from using the multiple-choice format sometimes is more useful than that obtained from an essay test. For example, more skills can be measured within a given amount of time by the multiple-choice test. Also, time saved by not scoring essay test items can be used to diagnose specific deficiencies through informal assessments and provide remedial instruction, focusing on the students found to be having problems.

3. *Multiple-choice items are time-consuming to construct.* More time is required to build a test with multiple-choice items than is required with any other written format. Considerable time is needed to develop effective alternatives within each item. Essay tests, in particular, require less time to develop, primarily because fewer essay questions can be included in a test. (However, when one includes the need to develop the scoring plan, the time required to develop each essay item is often comparable to that required to develop each multiple-choice item.)

● 8.2 Apply What You Are Learning

Identify the item format being described by items 1 through 5:

    A. Short answer or completion
    B. Essay
    C. Multiple-choice

1. Least likely to measure procedural knowledge such as concepts and rules
2. Because of guessing, least likely for a student's performance on one item to generalize to performance on other items
3. Because of inconsistencies in scoring, least likely for a student's performance on one item to generalize to performance on other items
4. Because of the limited number of items used, least likely for a student's performance on the overall test to generalize to other skills in the same unit of instruction

Answers can be found at the end of the chapter.

IDENTIFYING QUALITIES DESIRED IN MULTIPLE-CHOICE ITEMS

This section examines criteria for evaluating multiple-choice items. In the next section, you will be asked to use these criteria to evaluate a series of multiple-choice questions.

1. *Does this item measure the specified skill?* As with any format, each multiple-choice item must be constructed or selected to measure a specific skill. Often, several multiple-choice items are needed to assess a particular skill, with each item within the set measuring a different aspect or perspective of that skill.

2. *Is the level of reading skill required by this item below the students' ability?* Again, this concern is relevant to test items written in all formats. Unless the level of vocabulary and sentence structure are sufficiently low, a test item will confound the measurement of reading ability with that of the skill being measured.

3. *Does the stem clearly present the problem to be addressed?* When the stem to a multiple-choice item is not self-sufficient, students end up reading the options without knowing what problem they are supposed to solve. The stem by itself should communicate what the student is expected to do.

● 8.3 Apply What You Are Learning

Listed below are pairs of item stems. Within each pair, which stem more adequately presents the problem to be addressed?

1. A. Validity is
    B. A test is said to be valid if it

2. A. When riding a bicycle at night
    B. Which color of clothing is best to wear when riding a bicycle at night?

3. A. Which one of the following scales is used to measure the magnitude of an earthquake?
    B. Earthquakes are often very powerful and can be measured by seismographs over long distances. The Richter scale

Answers can be found at the end of the chapter.

A useful technique for improving the clarity of the stem is to present it as a question rather than as an incomplete sentence. Notice how this technique improved the clarity of the stems within items 2 and 3 in the previous exercise. Individuals who have had limited experience in constructing multiple-choice items find that writing the stem as a question helps formulate the problem being addressed and tends to improve the clarity of the entire item.

4. *Are all options parallel in type of content?* When options vary in type of content, the item is asking students to make a single judgment about two or more distinct qualities, like comparing apples to oranges. Note in the next example that because the options are not parallel in content, more than one alternative may represent the correct response.

Which of the following represents the warmest temperature?

A. 100 degrees Celsius
B. 200 degrees Fahrenheit
C. 300 degrees Kelvin
D. An oven set at medium

The first three options are all specific temperatures on well-defined scales. The fourth option represents a range of temperatures and uses an undefined scale (e.g., is this a drying oven used by a chemist or a food-baking oven?). The correct answer conceivably could be either A (the highest temperature among the first three options) or D.

Before constructing alternatives to a multiple-choice item, first think of the specific characteristics that all options will have in common. Then write options that match those characteristics. This approach helps maintain a focus for the item and reduces the chance of distractors inadvertently becoming correct responses. Usually, options fail to be parallel in content because the stem does not present a concise problem. Unfortunately, two very common problems with multiple-choice items are failing to establish a concise problem in the stem and unintentionally creating multiple correct answers because the options are not parallel in content. It is good to be particularly alert to these two problems.

5. *Do the options avoid repetitive words?* The following item would be more efficient if the words repeated in each option were relocated to the stem:

Physics is

A. the science that deals with the structure of matter.
B. the science that deals with the composition, structure, and properties of substances.
C. the science that is more concerned with solids than liquids.

Not only would this editing result in a more efficient use of words, but the modified stem would more clearly state the problem being addressed. Sometimes, a limited amount of repetition across options helps reinforce the idea presented in the stem or makes the options easier to read. However, excessive repetition should be avoided.

6. *Is extraneous content excluded from the stem?* The purpose of the stem is to present a specific problem to the student. The use of words or other content extraneous to this problem causes the item to measure how well students can determine what you are asking. The stem to each item should state the problem as simply as possible.

❧ 8.4   Apply What You Are Learning

Listed here are stems to multiple-choice items. Within each pair, which stem is most free of extraneous words and content?

1. A. The percent of homes that have at least one computer has increased each year, reaching what percentage at the end of last year?
    B. At the end of last year, what percentage of homes had at least one computer?
2. A. In miles per second, what is the speed of light?
    B. Although it is believed physical objects cannot go this fast, the speed of light is

---

Answers can be found at the end of the chapter.

7. *Are adjectives or adverbs emphasized when they reverse or significantly alter the meaning of a stem or option?* Whenever a single word significantly changes the meaning of a sentence or phrase within a test item, that word should be underlined or capitalized to draw attention to its presence. Otherwise, a student may read over the word and misinterpret the item. Here are some examples in which a word has been underlined because it alters the meaning of the phrase:

Which of the following conditions least affects the speed at which wind blows?

All of the following represent a field of science except

Which of the following is not a major cause of forest fires?

The word *not* is particularly troublesome within multiple-choice items because most phrases make grammatical sense if *not* is included or omitted, even though the meaning of the sentence changes dramatically. Potentially, the test item becomes a measure of how carefully students can read rather than a measure of the skill that the item was designed to target. The word *not* should be excluded from items whenever possible.

However, the negative is sometimes used within the stem to determine whether students can detect an exception. For instance, one might want to ask "Which of the following is not a major cause of forest fires?" If it is important that students identify exceptions, replacing *not* with *except* and locating except at the end of the stem is more effective. Here is what the item would look like:

All of the following are major causes of forest fires except

The word *not* should always be excluded from the options of multiple-choice items. Its inclusion makes a normally correct response incorrect and, if it is a double negative, it makes a typically wrong response correct. The difficulties caused by using *not* are illustrated here:

Which of the following is not an item format?

A. Not recall
B. Not short answer
C. Not reverse video
D. Not test–retest

Such a poorly constructed item would probably never be included in a test, but it demonstrates the confusion that can be generated by using *not* in the stem or in any of the options. (Note how clear the previous item becomes if all the nots are removed.)

8. *Is each distractor plausible?* Ideally, multiple-choice items should be constructed so that (1) students proficient with the skill select the correct option and (2) every student who has yet to achieve the skill selects a distractor. This ideal is unrealistic, however. Most academic skills are complex enough that students cannot simply be classified into two groups: those who have mastered and those who have not mastered the skill. The elusive perfect item is unable to divide students into such distinct groups because this grouping does not exist.

The perfect multiple-choice item is elusive for a second reason. Students who have not achieved the intended proficiency often select the correct answer by guessing, by detecting fallacies in the distractors, or by observing something in the correct response that is compatible with their misconception. Therefore, multiple-choice items can be substantially improved by making sure that each distractor is at least as attractive as the correct response for students who have not learned the skill being measured.

Techniques that make distractors more plausible are illustrated in Figure 8.2. First, distractors can represent common misconceptions as seen in items 1 and 2. In item 1, options B and C represent common misconceptions because orange and red, being bright colors, are thought to be highly visible at night. White clothing reflects more light and is the better choice when bicycling at night. (Clothing with reflective tape is even better.) With respect to item 2, many people believe that echoing causes thunder to

1. When bicycling at night, which of the following colors of clothing is it best to wear?

   A. Blue

   B. Orange

   C. Red

   D. White

2. Although the duration of a lightning bolt is very short, the resulting sound of thunder usually lasts for several seconds. Why does the duration of thunder last so much longer than that of the lightning?

   A. Some parts of a lightning bolt are closer to the observer than other parts.

   B. The heat generated by lightning requires time to dissipate.

   C. Thunder echoes off nearby objects such as buildings and hills.

3. In baseball statistics, which of the following would represent the highest batting average?

   A. .000

   B. .300

   C. 100

   D. 1,000

4. A large number of fish swimming together is referred to as a

   A. cluster.

   B. gathering.

   C. group.

   D. school.

Figure 8.2
Illustrations of plausible distracters

linger. In reality, because a lightning bolt is several miles in length, the sound from thunder caused by closer parts of the lightning bolt reaches an observer several seconds before thunder caused by more distant parts.

Distractors also can be made more plausible by making them sound correct to the untrained reader, as illustrated by items 3 and 4. In item 3, unin-formed sports fans will find options C and D attractive since 100 and 1,000 sound like perfect or high values. (Batting average is the ratio of base hits to official times at bat, with 1.000 being the highest possible average and values less than .300 being common.) In item 4, the words used for options A through C sound like labels one might associate with a number of fish swimming together. These distractors do not represent common misconceptions. Students would select "cluster" because of ignorance rather than because of a misconception.

Distractors are often made plausible simply by being reasonably close to the correct answer. With items involving numerical answers, distractors will be more attractive if they represent common errors fairly close to the correct response. Students who can approximate but not correctly solve the problem presented by an item will consider such options. Although the use of distractors similar to the correct response improves their plausibility, care must be taken so that knowledgeable students continue to select the intended answer as the correct response.

Writing plausible distractors may seem devious. This perception is inaccurate when the purpose of the test item is kept in focus. To the degree possible, each item should distinguish between those students who have and those who have not gained a relevant skill. If knowledgeable students perceive distractors as the correct response, an item loses its usefulness. Similarly, if students who have not yet learned the relevant skill are more attracted to the correct response than to the distractors, the item again loses its usefulness.

9. *Is the grammar in each option consistent with the stem?* In the next illustration, can you identify the correct answer even though you may not know the concept being tested?

In item response theory, the one-parameter model assumes that each test item

A. discriminates equally well.

B. students perform equally well.

C. students score the same across items.

D. guessing affects all items the same.

In this item, the stem grammatically matches only option A, which happens to be the correct answer. The correct answer sounds correct.

All responses should be written so that they grammatically match the stem. When they do not, the item provides clues to the answer that are not relevant to student achievement. A grammatical mismatch usually occurs when the stem represents an incomplete sentence but one or more of the options do not adequately complete the sentence. This problem can be avoided by writing the stem as a question rather than as an incomplete statement. Whenever incomplete statements are used as a stem, each of the options should be checked for grammatical consistency with the stem.

10. *Does the item exclude options equivalent to "all of the above" and "none of the above"?* Phrases such as "all of the above" and "none of the above" are often included in multiple-choice items. Their typical role is to increase the number of options. "None of the above" is sometimes used to avoid giving clues to students when their incorrect solutions are inconsistent with each of the options included with the item. Although the rationale for using such options is good, their effect on test items is not beneficial.

When "all of the above" is used, a multiple-choice item actually behaves as if the number of options has been reduced. If any two of the options can be identified as correct, the student can be quite certain that "all of the above" is correct, in effect eliminating the role of the remaining responses. Similarly, if just one option can be identified as incorrect, the "all of the above" option can also be eliminated.

Sometimes, each of the distractors within a multiple-choice item contains a degree of truth, often unintentionally. When "all of the above" is used in this context, students are placed in an unfair dilemma by being expected to select between the superior option or "all of the above."

"None of the above" has similar problems. If a fallacy can be seen in each option, "none of the above" represents the logical response. Students, however, usually have difficulty determining whether the erroneous qualities were intentional and serious enough for the teacher to judge the option wrong. The only way to avoid this problem is to use options that are unequivocally correct or incorrect, and developing such options is difficult.

Spelling and computation skills do lend themselves to unequivocal statements. "None of the above" is often used in multiple-choice items testing these skills so that students will not assume that the correct solution is among the options. The effect of using "none of the above" with computational items was investigated by Oosterhof and Coats (1984). Replacing the last option with "none of the above" was actually found to lower reliability. "None of the above" served as an effective option only when it was the correct answer. As less-knowledgeable students seldom selected "none of the above," it became an effective distractor only when it was the correct response. However, constantly using "none of the above" as the correct response is obviously not recommended.

11. *Unless another order is more logical, are options arranged alphabetically?* Correct answers should be distributed evenly among the alternative positions of multiple-choice items. Because items often are constructed before they are assembled into a test, this situation may be hard to achieve. Another approach is to alphabetize the options within each item. This strategy will counteract the common tendency to place the correct option in the same location.

Sometimes, arranging options in an order other than alphabetical makes it easier for students to contrast the options. For example, options representing numerical values, dates, or points along a scale should be listed sequentially from low to high.

● 8.5 Apply What You Are Learning

The options in each of the following items are alphabetized. With which items would an order other than alphabetical be appropriate?

1. In soccer, how many players does each team have on the field?
   A. Eight
   B. Eleven
   C. Nine
   D. Seven
   E. Ten
2. When using a credit card to purchase gasoline at a location that uses "pay at the pump," when must you provide your credit card?
   A. After pumping the gas
   B. Before pumping the gas
   C. While pumping the gas
3. All of the following are sufficient to establish a specific triangle, <u>except</u>
   A. knowing all three angles.
   B. knowing all three sides.
   C. knowing one side and its two adjacent angles.
   D. knowing two sides and the angle between them.

Answers can be found at the end of the chapter.

PRACTICE APPLYING THESE DESIRED QUALITIES TO MULTIPLE-CHOICE ITEMS

Figure 8.3 lists the 11 criteria for judging multiple-choice items that we have just discussed. This section will help you apply these criteria by examining some example items.

The objective being assessed and the proposed correct response are provided to help you evaluate each item. Each example fails to meet at least one of the criteria addressed in this checklist. A critique follows each item. Numbers in parentheses preceding each critique indicate the criteria within Figure 8.3 that the example item failed to achieve. Try to identify these problems before reading the critique.

The first examples pertain to a rule in astronomy; specifically, that objects in lower orbit travel faster than objects in higher orbit. Examples 8.1 through 8.3 are intended to measure knowledge of the following objective:

Rule: Given smaller objects within space in orbit around a substantially larger object, use

1. Does this item measure the specified skill?
2. Is the level of reading skill required by this item below the students' ability?
3. Does the stem clearly present the problem to be addressed?
4. Are all options parallel in type of content?
5. Do the options avoid repetitive words?
6. Is extraneous content excluded from the stem?
7. Are adjectives or adverbs emphasized when they reverse or significantly alter the meaning of a stem or option? Is the word *not* excluded from options, and preferably from the stem also?
8. Is each distractor plausible?
9. Is the grammar in each option consistent with the stem?
10. Does the item exclude options equivalent to "all of the above" and "none of the above"?
11. Unless another order is more logical, are options arranged alphabetically?

Figure 8.3
Criteria for evaluating multiple-choice items

the relative height of orbits to identify which object is traveling fastest in its orbit.

Example 8.1

The artificial satellite with the highest orbital speed
A. is the most recently launched satellite.
B. is the satellite in the higher orbit.
C. is the satellite in the lower orbit.
D. is the satellite with an orbit closest to the equator.

Critique for Example 8.1

(1, 3, 4, 5) This item is not measuring the skill specified by the objective. To measure knowledge of a rule, the item should be providing students a situation that requires application of the rule. This item measures declarative rather than procedural knowledge. Another problem with this item is the stem does not clearly describe the problem students are to solve. This is partly because each option repeats a significant amount of information that should be included in the stem. Also, the options are not parallel in content, perhaps because the stem does not establish a concise problem. Here is an improved version of the item, although it still measures declarative knowledge:

Does the artificial satellite in higher or lower orbit have the higher orbital speed?
A. The satellite in higher orbit
B. The satellite in lower orbit
C. The satellites have the same orbital speed

Example 8.2

Ganymede and Callisto are moons of Jupiter with approximately equal mass. Ganymede orbits 1.1 million miles above Jupiter, whereas Callisto orbits 1.9 million miles above the planet. Ganymede has
A. the faster orbital speed.
B. more impact craters.
C. will fall out of orbit sooner.

Critique for Example 8.2

(3, 4, 9, 11) This item *does* measure procedural knowledge, but the stem again does not clearly establish the problem students are to solve and the options are not parallel in content. Recall that the problem with using options not parallel in content is that more than one of the options often is unintentionally correct. That has happened here. For instance, more impact craters tend to exist on the moon closer to a planet because the planet's gravity attracts small objects to its vicinity, such as meteorites. If the item writer had first constructed a stem that clearly established the problem to be addressed, the options would likely have become parallel in content.

The present item has two other problems. Notice that option C is not grammatically consistent with the stem. When the grammar of an option does not match the stem, it provides clues to the answer that are not relevant to student achievement. The other problem is that options are not ordered alphabetically. Unless another order is more logical, arranging options alphabetically helps randomize the location of the correct answer.

Here is an improved version of Example 8.2. Notice that the stem more clearly presents a problem, which in turn forces the options to be parallel in content. Although options are not listed alphabetically, they are in a logical order.

Ganymede and Callisto are moons of Jupiter with approximately equal mass. Ganymede orbits 1.1 million miles above Jupiter, whereas Callisto orbits 1.9 million miles above the planet. Which moon has the faster orbital speed?
A. Ganymede has the faster orbital speed.
B. Both moons have the same orbital speed.
C. Callisto has the faster orbital speed.

Example 8.3

When a planet has more than one moon, which of the following best explains why the moon closest to a planet has the highest orbital speed?
A. The closest moon has to travel faster to offset the greater gravitational pull of the planet.
B. The closest moon tends to be the youngest moon and has maintained more of its original speed.
C. The closest moon usually is smaller than the other moons and therefore travels faster.

Critique for Example 8.3

(1) Mechanically, this item is well constructed, but it does not measure the performance objective. Because the objective pertains to a rule, the

item should ask students to apply the rule to solve a previously unused problem. Instead, this item is measuring declarative knowledge, or knowledge of information. The item asks students to identify correct statements of factual information. Declarative knowledge is important and students must be able to state what they know; however, the present performance objective is concerned with knowledge of a rule, not declarative knowledge.

Items in Examples 8.4 through 8.6 are intended to measure the following objective:

Information: Identifies basic characteristics of instruments commonly used in a symphony orchestra.

Example 8.4

Which of the following characteristics is not a difference between a trumpet and a trombone?
A. Both are made primarily of metal.
B. Both can play notes an octave below middle C.
C. Both change pitch primarily with valves.
D. All of the above
E. None of the above

Critique for Example 8.4

(7, 10) The word *not* should be underlined since it significantly alters the meaning of the stem. Better yet, *not* should be excluded from test items. In this case, the stem can be changed to a positive statement, as illustrated in the revision. The item also includes "all of the above" and "none of the above" as options, which should be avoided. Here is an improved version of this item:

Which of the following is true of both trumpets and trombones?
A. They are made primarily of metal.
B. They can play notes an octave below middle C.
C. They change pitch primarily with valves.

Example 8.5

A symphony orchestra includes many instruments. They can be classified into strings, brass, woodwinds, and percussion sections. The percussion section
A. includes the chimes.
B. includes timpani which can be tuned to different pitches.
C. involves drums as well as other instruments.
D. is where you place the glockenspiel.
E. All of the above.

Critique for Example 8.5

(3, 6, 10) The stem contains extraneous content. And once again, the stem does not clearly establish the problem to be addressed. The intended answer, "all of the above," becomes the obvious answer to students who know any two of the preceding options are correct. ("All of the above" also causes problems if the options for the item vary from being fully correct to partially correct.) Here is an improved version of this item:

Within a symphony orchestra, the percussion section includes all of the following instruments except
A. bassoon.
B. chimes.
C. drums.
D. glockenspiel.
E. timpani

Example 8.6

Which one of the following instruments uses reeds to make sound?
A. Oboe
B. French horn
C. Glockenspiel
D. The conductor
E. None of the above

Critique for Example 8.6

(8, 10, 11) Most students, even without knowing what a reed is, will recognize that the conductor is not an instrument; that option is not plausible and should be replaced. "None of the above" is more acceptable here than in many items because each of the options is unequivocally correct or incorrect. However, research cited earlier in this chapter suggests the item would be improved by replacing "none of the above" with an option that directly answers the stem. Finally, unless there is another more logical order, the options should be alphabetized. This helps randomize the location of the correct response. Here is an improved version of the item:

> Which one of the following instruments uses reeds to make sound?
> A. Flute
> B. French horn
> C. Glockenspiel
> D. Oboe
> E. Vibraphone

VARIATIONS OF MULTIPLE-CHOICE ITEMS

This section describes some of the variations possible within the multiple-choice format. In each variation, the stem presents a problem to be addressed by students. However, rather than presenting possible solutions, the options provide a means through which students transform proposed solutions to a mark in the test booklet or answer sheet.

Options Representing Ranges of Values

When testing computational skills, distractors to multiple-choice items usually represent solutions derived through common errors. These distractors do not usually represent all the errors that students are likely to make. Students who do not find their solution among the options are unintentionally told that an error has been made. Figure 8.4 illustrates how ranges of values can be used as options to computational items. Using ranges of values has two advantages: the solution to the problem pre-

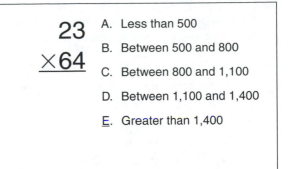

Figure 8.4
Illustration of multiple-choice items using options with ranges of values

sented in the stem is not included among the options; and it usually takes less time to construct options representing ranges of values than to construct distractors representing specific errors.

The following guidelines should be observed when constructing ranges of values for options:

- Each range should have upper and lower limits that represent common numbers, such as multiples of 5, 10, and 25.
- The width of intervals should be the same, except for the first and last options. Intervals should be selected that capture common student errors.
- The interval containing the correct solution should not include common incorrect solutions.

Matching Items

Matching items are a special case of the multiple-choice format in which several items share a common set of options. All the qualities listed in Figure 8.3 apply to matching items.

Figure 8.5 illustrates two sets of matching items. For items 1 through 8, students must identify dates on which events related to the formulation of the

For items 1 through 8, use the options listed in the right column to identify the date on which each of the events listed in the left column occurred.

1. First Continental Congress is convened	A. 1770
2. Second Continental Congress is convened	B. 1771
3. Articles of Confederation are written	C. 1772
4. Articles of Confederation revised in Philadelphia	D. 1773
5. Bill of Rights is written	E. 1774
6. Constitution of the United States is written	F. 1775
7. Articles of Confederation are ratified	G. 1776
8. Constitution of the United States is ratified	H. 1777
	I. 1778
	J. 1779
Answers	K. 1780
1. E 5. T	L. 1781
2. F 6. R	M. 1782
3. H 7. L	N. 1783
4. R 8. S	O. 1784
	P. 1785
	Q. 1786
	R. 1787
	S. 1788
	T. 1789
	U. 1790

For items 9 through 12, use the options listed in the right column to identify the person primarily responsible for each of the events listed in the left column.

9. Published proceedings of the Philadelphia Convention in which the Articles of Confederation were revised	A. Franklin
	B. Hamilton
10. Favored a government controlled by landowners	C. Madison
11. Authored the Bill of Rights	D. Mason
12. Refused to support ratification of the Constitution without inclusion of the Bill of Rights	E. Washington

Answers

9. C   10. B   11. C   12. D

Figure 8.5

Illustration of matching items

United States Constitution occurred. To answer these items correctly, students are required to identify the sequence in which these events took place. For items 9 through 12, students must identify the role played by individuals in the development of the Constitution.

As with all multiple-choice items, options associated with a matching item should be parallel in content. This quality was established in Figure 8.5 by keeping the lists of options separate for the two groups of items. Unfortunately, teachers sometimes increase the list of answers, ostensibly to reduce guessing, by combining heterogeneous content into one set of matching items.

Matching items represent a highly efficient means of testing students. A large number of matching items can be both developed and administered in a test within a short period of time. This efficiency also poses a danger to the matching format. Too much emphasis can be given to a single skill in a test by measuring that skill with a set of matching items. Planning in advance the number of test items to be used to assess each skill can prevent this problem.

Ranking of Options

Students can be asked to rank multiple-choice alternatives on a number of qualities. In essence, the first eight items in Figure 8.5 ask students to order historically a series of events. Other examples include asking students to identify the order in which steps should be completed in a laboratory experiment, to rank preferences for which of several medications should be given to patients, or to order alternative routes on a map according to distance.

As with all multiple-choice items, options must be parallel in content when students are asked to put them in some order. If a set of options represents more than a single dimension, knowledgeable students may use a defensible but unanticipated ordering.

Interpretive Test Exercises

Interpretive test exercises comprise a written presentation followed by a series of items examining students' ability to interpret the material. The written presentation might consist of a brief story, a newspaper article, a musical score, a patient's history, a chart, or a table, as illustrated in Figure 8.6. The questions can be concerned with facts contained in the presentation, interpretations and inferences, or issues requiring the student to draw on previously learned information. For example, within Figure 8.6, items 1 and 3 can be answered directly from information contained in the table. Item 2 requires a simple calculation. Items 4 and 5 require students to make an inference from the fact that Key West, being surrounded by water, has a smaller range in average temperatures than does Miami. Therefore, having freezing temperatures would be more abnormal for Key West, although Miami would be more likely to have a higher temperature on a given day in January. From a map of Florida, students could also answer questions about the effects of latitude and proximity to water on temperature.

Giving more than a brief introduction to interpretive exercises is beyond the objectives of this book. Wesman (1971) provides a good treatment of this assessment technique and is listed as an additional reading at the end of this chapter. Interpretive exercises should be used prudently because they can require a substantial amount of time to develop and administer. Capabilities such as knowledge of concepts and rules often can be tested with less-elaborate items. However, the interpretive exercise is a useful procedure for assessing students' ability to read and evaluate printed material. As with all multiple-choice items, it is very difficult for interpretive exercises to assess complex problem-solving tasks for which students must be allowed to apply any of several possible successful strategies. Performance assessments, which are discussed in later chapters, provide a better approach.

January Weather Data for Selected Florida Cities

	Average Daily Low Temperature	Average Daily High Temperature	Average Number of Days with Precipitation
Jacksonville	45	65	8
Key West	66	76	7
Miami	59	76	7
Orlando	50	71	6
Tallahassee	41	64	10

Respond to the following questions using weather information obtained in the above table. The options for each of these questions are

   A. Jacksonville

   B. Key West

   C. Miami

   D. Orlando

   E. Tallahassee

1. Which city tends to have the lowest temperature in January?
2. Which city tends to have the smallest range of temperatures in January?
3. Which city is <u>most</u> likely to experience precipitation on a typical January day?
4. Which city is <u>least</u> likely to experience precipitation on a typical January day?
5. Which city is likely to experience the <u>highest</u> temperature sometime during January?

Figure 8.6
Illustration of an interpretive test exercise

OPTIMAL NUMBER OF CHOICES

For classroom tests, the *most important* factor in determining the number of options to include in multiple-choice items is the number of appropriate distractors that can be created. Incorporating distractors that are not plausible or are not parallel to the content of other options will contribute to the ambiguity of items.

The optimal number of choices to be included in an item might be less than expected. Lord (1977) compared four approaches for establishing this optimal number. Results varied somewhat, depending on the theoretical assumptions being made. In general, however, three options per item were found to produce the most reliable test scores *as long as the total number of options across items in the test was constant*. For example, 20 items involving three options tend to provide more reliable scores than 12 items involving five options. Two options per item were found to be the next best. Four, and then five, options per item were found to be less effective.

This research into the optimal number of choices per item made one assumption that often is not true—that the total number of options a student can complete is the same regardless of how the options are grouped into items. It was expected that the same amount of time would be required to answer 60 alternatives divided into 30 two-option, 20 three-option, 15 four-option, and

12 five-option items. Budescu and Nevo (1985) investigated the appropriateness of that assumption with vocabulary, mathematical reasoning, and verbal comprehension tests. Each item in the vocabulary test could be read and answered quickly. The stems of the mathematical reasoning tests, however, required examinees to solve a computational problem before responding. The verbal reasoning items required examinees to read a paragraph before answering questions. Therefore, more time was required to administer 30 two-option mathematical reasoning items than 12 five-option mathematical reasoning items. The same was true with the verbal reasoning items. Adjusted for different amounts of testing time, five-option mathematical and verbal reasoning items were more reliable.

When a significant amount of time is required to solve the problem being addressed by the item, using fewer items, with more options per item, is the better strategy. *If items can be answered quickly,* it is preferable to use more items with fewer options per item. Thus, it seems that two-option items, such as alternate-choice items, have some potential! That is the topic of the next chapter.

SUMMARY

A multiple-choice item consists of a stem and a set of response options. The stem can be any stimulus or problem situation that might be presented to students. The response options may present correct and incorrect solutions to this problem. Alternatively, the response options can be very broadly defined; they simply represent any means through which students transform proposed solutions to a mark in the test booklet or on an answer sheet. This broader definition of response options provides considerable flexibility within the multiple-choice format.

The multiple-choice format has certain advantages. It can assess a relatively large number of skills within one test, it tends to structure a problem more effectively for students,

and it can be quickly and objectively scored. Limitations of the multiple-choice format are its susceptibility to guessing, its more indirect assessment of procedural knowledge such as concepts and rules, and the amount of time required to construct each multiple-choice item. Eleven qualities that should be incorporated into multiple-choice items were discussed and are listed in Figure 8.3.

The best strategy for determining how many options to include in a multiple-choice item is to see how many plausible distractors can be created. It is counterproductive to include poorly constructed distractors just to obtain a certain number of multiple-choice options. For items that can be read and answered quickly, using more items, each with fewer options, is preferable. For items that require more time to answer, fewer items, each with more options, is best.

ANSWERS: APPLY WHAT YOU ARE LEARNING

8.1. 1. C; 2. A; 3. C; 4. B; 5. C. *Item 1:* Short-answer items can be scored quickly, but multiple-choice items are more quickly scored, particularly when machines are used. *Item 2:* One short-answer item can be constructed more quickly than one essay item, largely because the essay format requires development of a detailed scoring plan. Considerable time is necessary to prepare options to multiple-choice items. *Item 3:* Multiple-choice allows better sampling than essay because more items can be included in a single test. Short-answer items often will provide less-adequate sampling of content than will multiple-choice when the measurement of concepts and rules are involved. *Item 4:* With written tests, only the essay item format can assess students' ability to communicate ideas in writing. *Item 5:* Responses to multiple-choice items are more consistently graded than are responses to essay or short-answer items.

8.2. 1. A; 2. C; 3. B; 4. B. *Item 1:* The short response required by short-answer items usually limits this format to measuring declarative knowledge, rather than procedural knowledge such as concepts and rules. Unlike with short-answer items, the student's response to multiple-choice items (usually an A, B, C, D, or E) is not the actual solution to the problem presented by the item. Instead, answers to multiple-choice items provide an indirect indicator of whether the student has solved the problem presented by the item. *Items 2–4:* Guessing significantly affects the reliability of multiple-choice items. However, inconsistency in scoring more significantly reduces the reliability of essay items. This is because, unlike the essay format, multiple-choice items can offset this threat to reliability by including a substantial number of items in a single test; but so can the short-answer format whose reliability is not affected significantly by guessing. Therefore, the short-answer test is likely to have the highest reliability.

8.3. 1. B; 2. B; 3. A.

8.4. 1. B; 2. A. Note that the stems with extraneous material are longer than necessary. This extraneous material may also unintentionally provide information that students can use to answer other questions within the test.

8.5. Options in item 1 should be ordered numerically. Options in item 2 should be ordered in their logical sequence of *before, while,* and *after* pumping the gas. Within item 3, listing options alphabetically should be sufficient.

SOMETHING TO TRY

• If you have access to some previously written multiple-choice items, use the qualities listed in Figure 8.3 to evaluate these items.

• Prepare some multiple-choice items that measure this objective:
  Rule: Distinguish between safe and unsafe bicycling practices.
  Use Figure 8.3 to evaluate these items.

• Similarly write and then evaluate several items for an objective within your academic specialization.

ADDITIONAL READING

Carlson, S. B. (1985). *Creative classroom testing.* Princeton, NJ: Educational Testing Service. This book discusses types of objectively scored test items that teachers often overlook when constructing classroom tests. Several of the item types described are variations of the multiple-choice format. A number of examples and work sheets are provided in the discussion.

Haladyna, T. M. (1999). *Developing and validating multiple-choice test items* (2nd ed.). Mahwah, NJ: Lawrence Erlbaum. This book provides an extended discussion of developing multiple-choice items and validating item responses.

Osterlind, S. J. (1997). *Constructing test items: Multiple-choice, constructed response, performance, and other formats* (2nd ed.). Boston: Kluwer Academic Publishers. This book provides an extensive treatment of constructing test items, particularly those using the multiple-choice format. Emphasis is on methods for identifying and minimizing measurement error during item construction and later review.

Wesman, A. G. (1971). Writing the test item. In R. L. Thorndike (Ed.), *Educational measurement* (2nd ed., pp. 113–128). Washington, DC: American Council on Education. This chapter reviews the item-writing literature and discusses ideas for producing various formats of objectively scored test items. See pages 113–120 for a discussion of the construction of multiple-choice and matching items; see pages 122–128 for the construction and characteristics of multiple-choice items within interpretive exercises.

9

Alternate-Choice Items

Alternate-choice items present a proposition for which one of two opposing options represents the correct response. The most common example of the alternate-choice format is the true-false item. However, the alternate-choice format is quite general, and a number of its variations look nothing like the traditional true-false item. Because the true-false format is familiar, it does represent a useful starting point.

True-false items appear to have distinct limitations. Students with no knowledge of the content being tested can blindly guess the correct answer to half the items. Many true-false items measure trivia. True-false items are often stated ambiguously. However, because true-false items are quickly answered, they can sample a considerable amount of content within a single test. Because of their simpler structure, alternate-choice items can be used with younger students than multiple-choice. Also, true-false and other alternate-choice items, when carefully constructed, measure procedural knowledge such as concepts and rules.

This chapter describes qualities desired in alternate-choice items. You may anticipate many of these qualities, such as the need to use statements in true-false items that can be categorically classified as true or false. After we discuss qualities desired in alternate-choice items, you will be asked to use these qualities to evaluate a series of items.

The alternate-choice format can be used in a variety of creative ways. For example, Figure 9.1 illustrates a spelling test in which items are embedded in a paragraph. Students indicate whether each word is correctly spelled. Numbers given to the right of each word reference item numbers on the answer sheet. (Alternately, students could circle underlined words that are incorrect.) By listing words in the context of a paragraph, the test becomes a more authentic assessment of what students are expected to do; that is, check the spelling of words within a context rather than spelling words in isolation.

Although response options are not limited to *true* and *false,* or even single words, options to an alternate-choice item always come in pairs. Each option represents an opposite of the other. As illustrated in Figure 9.1, an item does not need to be a sentence. Items can consist of a word within

---

Indicate whether each underlined word is correctly spelled. For each word, mark your answer sheet as follows:

    A. Correctly spelled
    B. Incorrectly spelled

Back in 1990, NASA launched[1] the Hubble Space Telescope. Since that time, this 12-ton telescope has allowed astromoners[2] to peer[3] into the outer limits of the universe[4] where large eliptical[5] galaxies are seen as they appeared near the begining[6] of time. The space telescope is as large as a school bus and uses an 8-foot-diameter[7] mirror to collect light. The telescope obtains electrical power from two 40-foot solor[8] panels[9]. Their combined output is 2400 watts[10].

Answers

1. A	6. B
2. B	7. A
3. A	8. B
4. A	9. A
5. B	10. A

Figure 9.1
Illustration of embedded alternate-choice items

a sentence or, as will be demonstrated later, even an element within a checklist or matrix.

This chapter helps you achieve four skills:

- Identify variations of alternate-choice items
- Identify the advantages and limitations of alternate-choice items
- Identify qualities desired in alternate-choice items
- Review alternate-choice items for these desired qualities

VARIATIONS OF ALTERNATE-CHOICE ITEMS

The most familiar version of the alternate-choice format is a true-false item; however, considerable variation from the true-false format is possible. At a superficial level, the options *true* and *false* can be replaced with words such as *yes* and *no,* or *correct* and *incorrect.* Considerable flexibility also exists in the physical appearance of these items. This section describes some of these variations.

Traditional True-False Items

Most of us are very familiar with the true-false item. A single statement is made, usually consisting of one sentence. Students are asked to indicate whether the statement is true or false.

When high school and college students are asked which item format they like the least, true-false items often come to the top of the list. This format suffers a terrible reputation. As noted earlier, true-false items are often thought to measure trivia and to be stated ambiguously. Some of this reputation is deserved. For example, true-false items are often ambiguous because subtleties make the item true or false. When writing the true-false item, it is difficult for the teacher to construct a statement that focuses students' attention on the element within the item that students are to judge as true or false without also giving away the answer to the item.

We will look at a number of techniques for minimizing this problem.

True-False Items Requiring Corrections

A common variation of true-false items is asking students to rewrite false items as correct statements. Students' corrections can provide insights into how well they understand concepts. Giving students credit only when a false item is correctly rewritten may recover some of the test reliability lost when students give correct answers for the wrong reason.

Brown (1983) recommended that students identify the false element within each item instead of simply rewriting false statements as true sentences. This approach reduces trivial revisions. For example, most false true-false items can be made true by strategically inserting the word "not."

Requiring students to correct false statements is equivalent to creating a series of short-answer or, possibly, brief-response essay items. In addition, associated limitations with the essay format would be expected to appear. For example, the number of items that can be included in the test will be reduced, and subjectivity in scoring answers will be increased. If students' responses are kept short, however, these limitations will be minimized.

Embedded Alternate-Choice Items

A series of alternate-choice items can be embedded in a paragraph. The spelling test illustrated in Figure 9.1 illustrates this approach. Each item consists of an underlined word or group of words. Students are asked to indicate whether each underlined element represents a particular quality such as a correctly spelled word or a factually correct statement.

Figure 9.2 illustrates embedded items used to determine if students can identify the verbs within a sentence. The items in Figure 9.3 test students' knowledge of historical facts. Figures 9.1 through 9.3 illustrate embedded alternate-choice

Indicate whether each underlined word is used as a verb. For each item, mark your answer sheet as follows:

A. Used as a verb
B. Used other than as a verb

Sailing has[1] many advantages as[2] a recreational sport. You can[3] sail[4] by yourself or with[5] others. You can participate[6] in leisurely day sailing or competitive racing.[7] You need[8] not be physically strong to enjoy the sport. And while[9] important basic techniques[10] can be learned[11] quickly, you can spend[12] a lifetime developing your sailing[13] skills.

Answers

1. A	6. A	11. A
2. B	7. B	12. A
3. A	8. A	13. B
4. A	9. B	
5. B	10. B	

Figure 9.2
Embedded alternate-choice items measuring knowledge of the concept of a verb

Indicate whether the underlined words make the sentence historically correct. For each item, mark your answer sheet as follows:

A. Correct
B. Incorrect

Christopher Columbus was a native of Italy.[1] His first voyage to the New World involved four[2] ships and over 100[3] men. This voyage began in Portugal[4] in 1491.[5] Approximately one year[6] was required to reach the Western Hemisphere. He first landed in what is now called Bahamas.[7] Columbus made a total of four[8] voyages to the New World. He was rich[9] and famous when he died in 1506. Before his death, he knew that he had yet to reach Asia.[10]

Answers

1. A	6. B
2. B	7. A
3. A	8. A
4. B	9. B
5. B	10. B

Figure 9.3
Embedded alternate-choice items measuring historical knowledge

items which can assess both procedural knowledge such as rules and concepts, as well as the recall of information.

Multiple True-False Items

A conventional multiple-choice item consists of a stem and a list of options. Usually, one of the options is correct, and the others serve as distractors. An alternative would be to allow any number from none to all of the options to be correct. In essence, each of the options represents a true-false item. When a group of items shares a common stem in this manner, they are called "multiple true-false items."

Figure 9.4 illustrates multiple true-false items. Note that the options are numbered as separate items. This numbering procedure is important when scoring answers by machine. Many scoring machines compare the density of students' answers to each item and assume the darkest mark represents the student's intended response. Lighter marks are presumed to be poor erasures. Treating each option as a separately numbered test item increases the accuracy of scoring.

Multiple true-false items are more similar to true-false than to multiple-choice items. Each of the series of items must present its own proposition, even though several items share a common stem. These propositions must be unequivocally true or false. In contrast, multiple-choice items allow students to select the best answer among a series of options, all of which may contain some truth and some falsity.

Read each option and indicate which are correct.

In comparison with North America, Africa has a larger

1. land area.
2. population.
3. energy consumption.
4. number of countries.

Correct options: 1, 2, 4.

Figure 9.4
Illustration of multiple true-false items

Sequential True-False Items

A series of true-false items can be presented in sequence, the correct response to each item being dependent on conditions specified in the previous item. For example, Figure 9.5 presents an incorrect solution of an algebraic problem. From the series of four items following this incorrect solution, the student must determine where the solution is wrong. This item can measure the ability to locate inconsistencies in mathematical logic.

Sequential true-false items can be used in a number of settings where solution of a problem requires a series of steps, each providing information to the next stage. For example, many exercises in geometry and trigonometry can be divided into sequential items, as can problems in other subjects requiring students to apply logical reasoning.

Focused Alternate-Choice Items

A conventional true-false item requires students to classify a proposition as true or false. When constructing the item, it is often difficult to highlight the element within the proposition that is to be evaluated without also giving away the answer to the item.

The items shown in Figure 9.6 illustrate how the alternate-choice format can explicitly state the focus within each item. The student is asked

Items 1 through 4 represent a student's attempt to solve for *x*. Evaluate this solution by determining whether each equation is equivalent to the *immediately preceding* equation.

In comparison with multiple-choice items, advantages of the true-false format are

A. This expression is *equivalent* to the preceding equation.

B. This expression is *not equivalent* to the preceding equation.

Solve for *x*:

$(4x - 3)(3x + 8) = (3x + 4)(3x + 6)$

1. $12x^2 - 24 = 9x^2 + 24$
2. $3x^2 = 48$
3. $x^2 = 16$
4. $x = 8$

Answers: 1. B; 2. A; 3. A; 4. B.

Figure 9.5
Illustration of sequential true-false items

1. The probability of precipitation increases as barometric pressure (A. increases; B. decreases).
2. The atmosphere near the equator flows to the (A. east; B. west).
3. Wind direction between centers of high and low pressure is (A. parallel; B. perpendicular) to a line connecting the two centers.

Answers:
1. B; 2. B; 3. B.

Figure 9.6
Illustration of focused alternate-choice items

to identify which of two key words or phrases accurately completes the statement. Notice that this is not simply a two-option multiple-choice item. Within any alternate-choice item, the two responses must have opposite or reciprocal meanings.

Ebel (1982) compared the reliability of scores from conventional true-false and the focused alternate-choice items. Students enrolled in a college course were administered eight unit tests. Each test included two forms consisting of true-false and focused alternate-choice items, respectively. For six of the eight tests, scores on forms using the alternate-choice items were more reliable. This increase in reliability probably results from helping students focus on the element within the item that is to be evaluated.

Checklists

A checklist consists of a series of statements. The student must read each statement and then indicate whether the quality described in the statement is present or absent.

Checklists can be used to facilitate instruction or assess students in a variety of content areas. For example, the lists of characteristics that have been used within the last several chapters to evaluate test items can be used as a checklist. You have been asked to use these lists to determine the status of various qualities within test items. These lists could also be incorporated into an exam to assess your ability to evaluate test items.

Language students can be given checklists to evaluate the grammatical structure of sentences. Student pilots can use checklists to facilitate instruction and examination in pre-flight procedures. Sometimes, students are expected to continue the use of a checklist after instruction has been completed. This is the case with the checklists used by airplane pilots. Teachers can also use checklists to structure observations of students, such as within performance assessments. This procedure is discussed in later chapters.

A checklist can be thought of as a series of alternate-choice items. Each element of the checklist represents an item. The two possible responses to each item have opposite meanings, although a variety of pairings can be used as responses such as yes/no or acceptance/non-acceptance.

ADVANTAGES AND LIMITATIONS OF ALTERNATE-CHOICE ITEMS

Advantages of Alternate-Choice Items

Alternate-choice items have four advantages. First, they allow a test to obtain a more adequate sampling of content. Second, they are relatively easy to construct. Third, alternate-choice items can be efficiently scored. Fourth, responses to alternate-choice items are objectively scored.

1. *Alternate-choice items allow a more adequate sampling of content.* As with the short-answer and multiple-choice formats, a substantial number of alternate-choice items can be included in a single test. This permits a more adequate sampling of content than can be achieved by, particularly, the essay format. In fact, students may be able to answer twice the number of alternate-choice versus multiple-choice or short-answer items within a given period of time. Unlike short-answer items, students need not write out a response. Unlike multiple-choice questions, students answering alternate-choice items need not read through a list of options. This makes the alternate-choice format particularly strong in its ability to sample content.

Alternate-choice can provide a more adequate sampling of content, not only with respect to the number of items that can be included in a test, but also the categories of knowledge they can assess. Unlike the completion or short-answer format, alternate-choice items easily measure procedural knowledge such as concepts. Recall that an effective way to measure knowledge of a concept is to provide students multiple illustrations, each of which is to be classified as an example or non-example of the concept. Using the true-false variation, a test can include a series of statements to which students indicate, true or false, whether or not each statement is an example of the concept. With young children, a series of pictures or drawings can similarly be provided, with students asked to circle the illustrations that are examples of the concept.

2. *Alternate-choice items are relatively easy to construct.* Alternate-choice items do not

require the construction of scoring plans associated with essay items or the list of options required by the multiple-choice format. As a result, more alternate-choice than essay or multiple-choice items can usually be produced within a given period of time.

The similarity of the structure of alternate-choice items to the way that we structure learning also may facilitate their construction. Ebel (1982) proposed that learning consists of formulating relationships among concepts. Assuming each relationship can be expressed as a proposition, achievement can be assessed by asking students to identify whether each in a series of propositions is correct or incorrect. The true-false format, in particular, parallels this pattern. If the teacher has identified the relevant propositions that express these relationships, the development of true-false items simply consists of writing a series of accurate and erroneous versions of these propositions.

3. *Alternate-choice items can be efficiently scored.* As with the multiple-choice format, alternate-choice items can be quickly scored by hand or machine.

4. *Responses to alternate-choice items are objectively scored.* Essay and, to a lesser degree, short-answer items are subjectively scored. As a result, two readers often assign different scores to a given student's answers. Essay tests in particular lose reliability because of scoring inconsistencies. Because multiple-choice and alternate-choice tests are objectively scored, their reliabilities are not threatened by inconsistencies in scoring. (However, students' guessing at answers adds inconsistency to multiple-choice and particularly alternate-choice tests.)

Limitations of Alternate-Choice Items

Alternate-choice items have three limitations. First, these items are susceptible to guessing. Second, alternate-choice items can be used only when dichotomous answers represent sufficient response options. Third, alternate-choice items typically must indirectly measure

performance objectives related to procedural knowledge.

1. *Alternate-choice items are susceptible to guessing.* Because one of two responses to an alternate-choice item must be correct, the probability that a student will give the correct response from a blind guess is 50%. With no understanding of the skills being tested, a student is expected to correctly answer 5 items on a 10-item test or 50 items on a 100-item test.

This threat of guessing is more perceived than real. Student knowledge hopefully is never tested with just one item, regardless of item format. In addition, 5 of 10 items or 50 of 100 items generally would not be considered passing scores on a test. If students did answer alternate-choice items with blind guesses, fewer than 10% of the students would correctly answer *more* than 7 of 10 or 56 of 100 items on a test. The chances of a student blindly achieving a score greater than 70% on a 100-item alternate-choice test is less than four in a million. Increasing the number of items included in a test will control the threat of guessing answers to alternate-choice items. Students typically can answer two alternate-choice items per minute. Therefore, including sufficient items within a test is feasible.

Nevertheless, guessing does reduce the reliability of alternate-choice items. Increasing the number of items included in a test reduces but does not negate this problem. In general, when comparing tests that require equal amounts of time to administer, short-answer tests provide the highest reliability, followed by multiple-choice, alternate-choice, and essay tests, in that order (Frisbie, 1973; Oosterhof & Coats, 1984; Oosterhof & Glasnapp, 1974). Even with the problems caused by guessing, tests that use the alternate-choice format can obtain acceptably high reliabilities (Ebel, 1982).

2. *Alternate-choice items can be used only when dichotomous answers represent sufficient response options.* Many statements cannot be answered with simply a *yes* or *no,* or a *true* or *false.* To function properly, an alternate-choice

item must be answered without qualification, using these or similar dichotomous answers. Later in this chapter we look at some techniques that help alternate-choice items address this constraint.

3. *Alternate-choice items usually must indirectly measure targeted behaviors.* As noted in the opening chapter, educational measurement is not alone in its dependency on indirect measures. Most measures in the physical sciences, for instance, rely on well-understood indirect measures of phenomena and properties. Similarly, all measures of knowledge use student behaviors as an indirect measure of knowledge because teachers cannot directly see what a student knows or is thinking. Chapter 7 points out that essay tests in particular appear more able to directly measure skills one is trying to teach, but this often is simply the result of wording performance objectives in a manner more similar to the wording of essay questions. It is critical to recognize that student performance is always an *indirect* measure of a student's knowledge. More fundamental than choosing a particular item format is selecting the type of student behavior that provides a well-understood indirect measure of the knowledge being assessed. This is why, beginning in Chapter 3, emphasis has been placed on identifying the type of behaviors that provide good measures of different types of knowledge, such as information, concepts, and rules. We must recognize that alternate-choice items often indirectly measure performance specified in instructional objectives, however all assessments are indirect measures of knowledge. With all item formats, particular attention must be placed on constructing items that involve student behaviors known to be good indicators of the targeted knowledge.

❧ 9.1 Apply What You Are Learning

Indicate whether each of the following statements is true or false:

1. The reliability of a 20-item alternate-choice test is generally higher than that of a 20-item short-answer test.

2. Students tend to get higher scores on multiple-choice tests than on alternate-choice tests.
3. Scoring errors diminish the reliability of an alternate-choice test more than that of a short-answer test.
4. More time is usually required for students to complete a 30-item multiple-choice test than a 30-item alternate-choice test.
5. Students spend a greater portion of time solving problems on an alternate-choice test than an essay test.
6. Compared to alternate-choice items, the essay format more adequately measures procedural knowledge.
7. More time is required to construct an alternate-choice test than an essay test.
8. A multiple-choice item usually requires more time to construct than an alternate-choice item.

Answers can be found at the end of the chapter.

IDENTIFYING QUALITIES DESIRED IN ALTERNATE-CHOICE ITEMS

This section examines specific criteria for evaluating alternate-choice items. In the next section, you will use these criteria to evaluate a series of alternate-choice questions.

1. *Does the item measure the specified skill?* As with any format, each alternate-choice item must be constructed or selected to measure a specific skill. This, of course, means the item must measure appropriate content. It also means that the item must take into account whether declarative or procedural knowledge is involved. Often, several items are used to assess a particular skill, with each item within the set measuring a different aspect or perspective of that skill.

2. *Is the level of reading skills required by the item below the students' abilities?* Again, this concern is relevant to test items written in all formats. If reading skills are above or even at the limit of a student's capability, the test confounds the measurement of reading ability with that of the skill being measured.

3. *Is one of the two response options unequivocally correct?* This quality is relevant to all variations of alternate-choice items. It is particularly difficult to achieve with true-false items. The problem results from having to create a single statement that is, in isolation, unequivocally true or false. A technique that often eliminates the problem is to contrast two ideas. To illustrate, the following true-false item has been improved through such a contrast:

Without contrast: In the temperate zone, average outside air is cold in the winter.

With contrast: In the temperate zone, average outside air is cooler in the winter than the spring.

In some locations within the temperate zone,[1] outside air temperature is fairly warm throughout the winter, such as in the southern United States. Also, the meaning of the word *cold* is indefinite and may or may not be thought to include moderately cool temperatures. By using a contrast, one option becomes unequivocally correct; within the temperate zone, average outside air in the winter is cooler than in the spring everywhere.

Alternate-choice items must function as unequivocally correct or incorrect propositions *from the perspective of students with whom the items will be used.* It may be unrealistic to write items that content experts, for instance, would judge to be unequivocal. If your knowledgeable students consistently answer an item correctly, this is evidence that the item is constructed appropriately. If, however, some students present defensible explanations for selecting the wrong response, you have reason to believe the item is deficient.

4. *Does the item present a single proposition?* An alternate-choice item becomes ambiguous when it contains two propositions, one that may be true and the other that may be false. To avoid this source of ambiguity, alternate-choice items should always state a single proposition.

---

[1]The temperate zone is the region between the tropic of Cancer and the Arctic Circle or between the tropic of Capricorn and the Antarctic Circle.

❧ 9.2   Apply What You Are Learning

Indicate "yes" when the alternate-choice item contains more than one proposition; otherwise indicate "no":

1. In the summer, Phoenix has higher temperatures than New Orleans; however, New Orleans has more rainy days.
2. Fog is more common in London than in Paris.
3. From Salt Lake City one can see mountains that contain popular ski resorts.

Answers can be found at the end of the chapter.

5. *Is the item stated as simply as possible?* This point parallels the need to exclude extraneous material from the stem of a multiple-choice item. In either format, the use of words or other content extraneous to the problems being presented may cause the item to measure how well students can determine what the question is asking. Identifying what is being asked represents an important skill. However, if that is not the skill being tested, including extraneous material in an item confounds the measurement of the intended skill. You will not know if students missed the item because they did not comprehend the question or because they have yet to master the skill being tested. Each alternate-choice item should state its proposition as simply as possible.

❧ 9.3   Apply What You Are Learning

Listed below are pairs of true-false items. Within each pair, which item (A or B) is most free of extraneous words and content?
1. A. In the United States, high-definition television uses (A. analog; B. digital) signals.
   B. High definition television, more so in the United States than some countries, uses (A. analog; B. digital) signals.
2. A. One of the rules in volleyball is that a team scores points only when it serves the ball. (true)
   B. In volleyball, only the team that served the ball can score a point. (true)

Answers can be found at the end of the chapter.

Stating an alternate-choice item as simply as possible helps restrict the item to a single proposition. In the above examples, when an item was not stated simply, multiple propositions were created. To state items simply, clearly establish in your mind the proposition to be addressed, and then include in the item only words that are critical to communicating that proposition.

6. *Are adjectives or adverbs emphasized when they reverse or significantly alter the meaning of an item?* Individual words that by themselves significantly change or reverse the meaning of the item should be underlined or capitalized to give emphasis. Failing to do so often results in students reading around these critical words. In effect, the item becomes a measure of reading ability that confounds the measurement of the skill being tested.

The word *not* is a particularly troublesome adverb in alternate-choice items. Demonstrate this to yourself. Which of the following statements are true?

When water changes from liquid to ice, its density does *not* decrease.

When pressure increases, the boiling point of water does *not* increase.

An egg *cannot* cook as quickly in boiling water when air pressure decreases.

Only the last statement is true. Note how much easier these alternate-choice items become when the word *not* is deleted:

When water changes from liquid to ice, its density decreases. (true)

When pressure increases, the boiling point of water increases. (true)

An egg cooks as quickly in boiling water when air pressure decreases. (false)

Most adjectives and adverbs that significantly alter the meaning of a sentence can be used in alternate-choice items if they are emphasized. The adverb *not* is an exception and should never be used in alternate-choice items.

7. *Are adjectives and adverbs that imply an indefinite degree excluded?* Words such as *frequent, often,* and *sometimes* specify indeterminate quantities. Each of these and similar words have a broad range of meanings. The sentence, "Students *often* spelled the words correctly," could mean they correctly spelled several out of 100 or almost all of the 100 words. Words with indefinite meanings should be excluded from alternate-choice items. They prevent items from being classified as unequivocally correct or incorrect. Which of the following alternate-choice items can be answered unequivocally?

Cities *usually* have *many* taxis.

Large cities *frequently* have subways.

Cities *typically* have light pollution at night.

None of these items can be answered unequivocally. The italicized words within each item have indefinite meanings. Here is how each of these items could be made unequivocally true or false:

Most cities with a population over one million have more taxis than private cars. (false)

The majority of cities with populations over one million have a subway system. (false)

Compared to a rural area with dark skies, in most urban areas one can see less than one percent of the stars at night. (true)

8. *Are adjectives and adverbs with absolute meanings avoided?* Statements containing words such as *all, always, every, never,* and *no* are usually found to be false. Students who have not learned the concept being tested answer such items as incorrect because an exception to the *always* or *never* probably exists. Therefore, these words increase the effectiveness of *true* alternate-choice items because students unfamiliar with the concept anticipate the presence of exceptions. Conversely, these words lower the effectiveness of false statements and should not be used when the statement poses a false proposition. However, if absolute words are used too frequently in true statements, students will soon learn to reverse common logic. For this reason, you might occasionally use words with absolute meanings but, in general, should avoid their use in alternate-choice items.

9. *Is the incorrect response plausible?* Test items should be designed so that students who have achieved the relevant skill can easily give the correct answer whereas those who have yet to achieve this skill provide a wrong response. This represents a formidable task for alternate-choice items because students have a reasonable chance of giving the correct answer using only a blind guess. However, because students usually do not guess blindly at test items, the ability of an item to perform properly will be enhanced if the wrong response is plausible. The incorrect response should be at least as believable as the correct response for students who have yet to master the pertinent skill.

As with distractors to multiple-choice items, two techniques are particularly effective at making the incorrect answer more plausible. First, the wrong response can represent a common misconception, as illustrated by the first two items in Figure 9.7. The first item is plausible because people often believe boats float because they are made out of light material. They are surprised that a number of boats have been made out of concrete. (As long as the hull of a boat will displace water that weighs more than the total weight of the boat, the boat will float.) The incorrect response to the second item is also a common misconception in that people often believe diesel engines contain spark plugs. Unlike gasoline engines, diesel engines so highly compress air within the cylinder that it becomes hot enough to ignite the fuel when it is sprayed into the air.

Again, as with multiple-choice distractors, the incorrect responses to alternate-choice items are more plausible if they sound believable. The third and fourth items in Figure 9.7 illustrate this approach. With item 3, superficial reasoning would suggest oxygen, upon which animal life depends, would not be a poison, even under pressure. In reality, oxygen is very poisonous when highly pressurized. This is not a misconception in that it does not involve a commonly learned error. It is simply a statement that, when made, seems reasonable to an unknowledgeable individual. With item 4, superficial reasoning would also suggest a "black hole" contains nothing. Again, it does not represent common misinformation. It is a statement that sounds reasonable even though it is an error. (Black holes are super massive objects in space. Their gravity is so great, more than a billion times that of Earth, that even light cannot escape into space.) A student with limited comprehension of relevant concepts would find these incorrect responses to be attractive.

PRACTICE APPLYING THESE DESIRED QUALITIES TO ALTERNATE-CHOICE ITEMS

Figure 9.8 lists the nine criteria for judging alternate-choice items that we have discussed. This section will help you apply these criteria by examining a series of example items. The objective being assessed and the answer proposed by the item writer are provided to help you evaluate each item. Each example item fails to meet at least one of the criteria. A critique follows each item. Numbers in parentheses preceding each critique indicate the criteria within Figure 9.8 that the example item has failed to achieve. Try to identify these problems before reading the critique.

Examples 9.1 through 9.4 pertain to timing the delay between a lightning strike and the following thunder to determine the distance of the lightning from the observer. Because sound travels a little more than 1,000 feet per second, the distance of a lightning strike can be determined by dividing by five the number of seconds it takes

---

1. Boats float because they are made out of material that weighs less than water. (false)

2. Diesel engines have spark plugs. (false)

3. Oxygen becomes toxic to animals under high pressure. (true)

4. A "black hole" is a location in outer space that contains nothing. (false)

Figure 9.7
Examples of plausible true-false items

1. Does the item measure the specified skill?
2. Is the level of reading skills required by the item below the students' ability?
3. Is one of the two response options unequivocally correct?
4. Does the item present a single proposition?
5. Is the item stated as simply as possible?
6. Are adjectives or adverbs emphasized when they reverse or significantly alter the meaning of an item? Is the word *not* excluded?
7. Are adjectives and adverbs that imply an indefinite degree excluded?
8. Are adjectives and adverbs with absolute meanings avoided?
9. Is the incorrect response plausible?

Figure 9.8
List of criteria for evaluating alternate-choice items

for the sound of thunder to arrive. The performance objective could be stated as follows:

Rule: Given the time delay between a lightning strike and the following thunder, calculate the distance between the lightning strike and the observer.

Example 9.1

If the time between lightning and thunder is 3 seconds, the lightning strike was not as far away as one mile. (true)

Critique of Example 9.1

(5, 6) This item does require the student to apply the rule specified by the performance objective. However, this item should be stated more simply. Also, the word *not* should be excluded from the item because it potentially sets up a confusing double-negative. This item can be stated more simply and *not* can be removed by rewriting the item as a positive statement:

If the time between lightning and thunder is 3 seconds, the lightning strike was <u>less</u> than one mile away. (true)

Example 9.2

The time delay between a lightning strike and the sound of the thunder equals the distance of the lightning strike in miles. (false)

Critique for Example 9.2

(1) This is a well-constructed item, but it does not measure the objective. The item asks whether students can state the relationship between the distance of lightning and time delay of thunder (information), rather than the ability to apply the rule. When measuring student achievement, this distinction between declarative and procedural knowledge is always important.

Example 9.3

If there is little time delay between lightning and the thunder, the distance of the lightning strike is (A. more; B. less) than one mile.

Critique for Example 9.3

(7, 9) The adjective *little* implies an indefinite degree. Such words prevent alternate-choice items from being classified as unequivocally correct or incorrect. Also, the incorrect answer to this item is not plausible. Students who do not know the rule concerning the time relationship between lightning and thunder will probably answer this item correctly. Here is a better alternative to this item

If the time delay between lightning and thunder is 4 seconds, the distance of the lightning strike is (A. more; <u>B</u>. less) than one mile.

Example 9.4

Thunder is louder and follows the lightning more quickly when the lighting strike is closer. (true)

Critique for Example 9.4

(1, 4) This item does not measure the objective. As with Example 9.2, the item measures declarative knowledge (information), not procedural knowledge (rule) as specified in the objective. Also, this true-false item involves more than one proposition: Thunder associated with closer lightning is louder, and thunder associated with closer lightning occurs more quickly. Here is an alternative item that involves a single proposition, although it still does not measure the targeted objective:

The more distant a lightning strike, the (A. sooner; B. later) the thunder is heard.

In many communities within North America, the 9–1–1 phone number is used for summoning emergency assistance. Examples 9.5 through 9.7 pertain to knowledge of when this emergency number is to be used. The performance objective could be stated as follows:

Information: For various emergencies, state whether 9–1–1 is used to summon help.

Example 9.5

You should always use 9–1–1 to call the police. (false)

Critique for Example 9.5

(8) Words with absolute meanings, like *always* and *never,* should be avoided in alternate-choice items, particularly when the proposition posed by the item is false. Because there usually are exceptions, students usually guess the proposition to be false when they do not know the answer. In this case, police usually discourage the use of 9–1–1 for non-emergencies such as requests for information and traffic accidents not involving injuries. Here is how this item could be improved:

One should use 9–1–1 to ask the police about a parking ticket. (false)

Example 9.6

If there is smoke in your house and you do not know what is causing it, you should call 9–1–1. (true)

Critique for Example 9.6

(4, 6) This item involves two propositions: There is smoke in the house, and the cause of the smoke is unknown. More than one proposition should not be included in an alternate-choice item because multiple propositions tend to make the item ambiguous; one proposition may be correct and the other incorrect. Also, the word *not* should be excluded from the item. Here is a way to improve this item:

9–1–1 should be used if you believe your house is on fire. (true)

Example 9.7

Usually, you should not use 9–1–1 to make an emergency call to a plumber. (true)

Critique for Example 9.7

(6, 7) By now you know very well that the word *not* should be excluded, as should words with indefinite meanings such as *usually.* Here is a better wording for this item:

9–1–1 should be used to make an emergency call to a plumber. (false)

Alternate-choice items are useful for measuring declarative knowledge (*information*), and most types of procedural knowledge, including *concepts* and *rules.* For instance, alternate-choice is a good format for determining whether students know the concept of a noun. As we learned, concepts are measured by having students classify previously unused illustrations as examples versus non-examples of the concept. This is what each of the remaining items to be critiqued try to do. The objective they are supposed to measure is as follows:

Concept: Identify whether or not a word is a noun.

Example 9.8

The word *fire* is a noun. (true)

Critique for Example 9.8

(3) This item is not unequivocally correct. Although *fire* is often used as a noun, a sentence such as "He will fire the rocket engine" uses the word as a verb. Providing context can make a proposition indisputably true or false, as is the case with the following item:

In this sentence, is *fire* used as a noun? "Fire was used to cook the food." (yes)

Alternately, embedded alternate-choice items such as illustrated in Figure 9.2 can be used to provide context.

Example 9.9

Often the word *help* is used as a noun. (true)

Critique for Example 9.9

(3, 7) Words such as *often* that imply an indefinite degree should be excluded. Here, *often* could mean "most of the time" or possibly "frequently, but less than half of the time." With indefinite meaning, the item is not unequivocally true or false. The following item avoids this problem:

The word *help* can be used as a noun. (true)

Example 9.10

A noun can be used as the subject within a sentence. (true)

Critique for Example 9.10

(1) Mechanically, this item is well constructed; however, it measures declarative knowledge pertaining to what a noun is. According to performance objective, the item should be concerned

with the *concept* of a noun. Knowledge of a concept is measured by having students classify unused illustrations as examples versus non-examples of the concept.

SUMMARY

The true-false item is the best-known version of an alternate-choice item. Other variations include items where students rewrite false statements to make them true and multiple true-false items that list several true or false statements following a common stem. Embedded items are another variation and involve a series of underlined words or phrases whose accuracy students are asked to judge. Embedded items have the potential advantage of requiring students to make judgments when the stimulus is presented in authentic context. Focused alternate-choice items are similar to the familiar true-false format, except that the specific contrast students are to evaluate is identified.

The alternate-choice format has several advantages. It allows more extensive sampling of content within one test; items using this format are relatively easy to construct, and these items are efficiently and objectively scored. Limitations of alternate-choice items are their susceptibility to guessing, their need for using dichotomous response options, and their use of more indirect measures when assessing intellectual skills. The negative effects of guessing, for the most part, can be offset by the greater number of alternate-choice items that can be included in a test. Problems brought on by the use of dichotomous response options can be addressed by using statements that involve a contrast. Nine qualities that should be incorporated into alternate-choice items were discussed and are listed in Figure 9.8.

ANSWERS: APPLY WHAT YOU ARE LEARNING

9.1. 1. false; 2. false; 3. false; 4. true; 5. true; 6. false; 7. true; 8. true. *Items 1 and 2:* For a given number of items, alternate-choice tests have lower reliability than multiple-choice tests, which in turn have lower reliability than short-answer tests. Reliability is diminished because students often select the correct answer by chance. For this same reason, students tend to get higher scores on alternate-choice than on multiple-choice tests. Increasing the number of items in a test increases reliability. Therefore, one can partially offset the lower reliability of multiple-choice, and particularly alternate-choice, tests by using more items. *Item 3:* Inconsistency in scoring is usually a minor problem for short-answer items but is almost nonexistent for alternate-choice items. This inconsistency does lower the reliability of short-answer tests somewhat. (The overall reliability of multiple-choice and alternate-choice tests is lower than that of short-answer tests because of the impact of selecting correct answers by chance.) Inconsistency in scoring has a major effect on the reliability of essay tests. *Item 4:* Thirty seconds is usually sufficient for completing an alternate-choice item, and 60 seconds for a multiple-choice item. A 30-item multiple-choice test could be completed in 30 minutes, and a 30-item alternate-choice test in 15 minutes. *Item 5:* Almost all the exam time on multiple-choice and alternate-choice tests is spent reading items and solving their problems. A considerable amount of time in an essay test is consumed by writing out the response, as opposed to resolving the mental problem posed by each item. *Item 6:* Alternate-choice and multiple-choice items can indirectly, although accurately, measure procedural knowledge. What is unique to essay items is their ability to determine whether students can express their ideas in writing. *Items 7 and 8:* More time is required to write one essay item than one alternate-choice item, particularly when the time for constructing the essay scoring plan is considered. A test, however, can include many more alternate-choice than essay items, resulting in more

time being required to construct an alternate-choice exam. This shorter time for constructing an essay test is *not* an asset since it results from the essay's weakness with respect to the number of skills that can be measured within one test. With respect to multiple-choice items, alternate-choice items require less time to develop, primarily because of the time required to devise multiple-choice options.

9.2. 1. yes; 2. no; 3. yes. *Item 1:* The two propositions are "Phoenix has higher temperatures than New Orleans" and "New Orleans has more rainy days." This is a poor way to construct an alternate-choice item because conceivably one proposition could be true and the other false. *Item 2:* Although this item involves a contrast (frequency of fog in London versus Paris), only one proposition is stated: "Fog is more common in London than in Paris." *Item 3:* Two propositions are presented in this item. Both happen to be true: One can see mountains from Salt Lake City, and these mountains contain popular ski resorts.

9.3. 1. A; 2. B. Within B of the first pair, the phrase "more so in the United States than some countries" is extraneous to the knowledge being measured. It actually formulates a second proposition in the item. Within item A of the second pair, referring to "one of the rules" does not clarify the proposition and should be eliminated.

SOMETHING TO TRY

- If you have access to some previously written true-false or other alternate-choice items, use the qualities listed in Figure 9.8 to evaluate these items.

- Prepare some alternate choice items that measure this objective:

  Rule: Identify the effect that Earth latitude has on the relative length of a winter day and a summer day for different locales.

(In the northern and southern hemispheres, locales closer to the poles have longer days in their summer and shorter days in their winter than locales closer to the equator. For example, the North Pole has continuous daylight at the beginning of its summer.) Focused alternate-choice items work particularly well with this objective. Use Figure 9.8 to evaluate your items.

• Similarly write and then evaluate several items for an objective within your academic specialization.

ADDITIONAL READING

Carlson, S. B. (1985). *Creative classroom testing*. Princeton, NJ: Educational Testing Service. This book discusses types of objectively scored test items that teachers often overlook when constructing classroom tests. Several of the item types described are variations of the alternate-choice format. A number of examples and worksheets are provided.

Ebel, R. L., & Frisbie, D. A. (1986). *Essentials of educational measurement* (4th ed.). Englewood Cliffs, NJ: Prentice-Hall. Pages 155–157 describe procedures for helping true-false items discriminate between more- and less-knowledgeable students.

Wesman, A. G. (1971). Writing the test item. In R. L. Thorndike (Ed.), *Educational measurement* (2nd ed.). Washington, DC: American Council on Education. This chapter reviews the item-writing literature and discusses ideas for producing various formats of objectively scored test items. Pages 91–94 discuss construction of true-false items.

10

Learning How to Take Written Tests

A variety of factors can influence students' scores on tests. Ideally, the only thing that does affect scores is students' proficiency with the skill the test is supposed to measure. The effects of all other factors decrease the test's validity.

This chapter describes how to reduce the effect of one extraneous factor, specifically, students' ability to take a test. Three aspects of this factor are addressed. The first part of the chapter discusses students' familiarity with the testing medium. The second part of the chapter looks at ways in which students can prepare for a test, including coaching and controlling anxiety. The third section discusses testwiseness; some students score higher on a test simply because they are familiar with procedures that optimize test performance.

Teachers sometimes underestimate the importance of students' learning how to take tests, possibly because teachers are among the most experienced and proficient test takers. Although this chapter is primarily designed to help you help others take tests, you will probably also find some new strategies that will improve your own performance on future tests.

This chapter helps you achieve three skills:

- Identify the effects of familiarity with the testing medium on student performance
- Identify procedures that students should follow when preparing for a test
- Recognize basic components of testwiseness

FAMILIARITY WITH THE TESTING MEDIUM

Two aspects of the testing medium are addressed here. The first is the effect of computer tests versus paper-and-pencil tests. The second pertains to the use of separate answer sheets with elementary school students.

Administering Tests by Computer versus Paper and Pencil

It is becoming increasingly popular to have students take tests using a computer. This procedure has definite advantages, including the ability to administer tests efficiently to individual students. For instance, a computer can individually administer tests to students within a classroom or at remote locations such as within distance-learning settings. In some situations, a computer can adapt the test in realtime, where the specific items administered are adjusted based on how the student is performing.

When the test administered by computer is identical in all ways with the paper-and-pencil version, scores tend to be more comparable. This is what Bugbee (1996) found, and also Zandvliet and Farragher (1997). However, computer-administered tests often are not fully equivalent, such as when computerized tests are adaptive and a student's performance on previous items determines which items are administered subsequently. Inconsistent results have been observed with respect to characteristics of identical items administered within computer adaptive versus conventional paper-and-pencil tests (Hetter, Segall, & Bloxom, 1994; Spray, Ackerman, Reckase, & Carlson, 1989). Computer-adaptive tests are popular with objectively scored college admissions tests. When tests are norm-referenced, separate norms usually have to be established for paper-and-pencil versus computer-administered tests.

Russell and Haney (2000) describe a negative effect that the *lack* of computer-administered tests is having on some high-stakes tests administered in public schools. Increasingly, students are writing papers using a word processor rather than by hand. Simultaneously, high-stakes tests used in many states are relying more on open-ended and performance exercises as opposed to multiple-choice items. However, with these high-stakes tests, students are usually expected to write out their responses by hand. Their research shows that students who are proficient with using word processors perform substantially better on these tests if they are allowed to use a computer to create their response. Russell (1999) observed that some schools are actually requiring students to write more on paper and less on computers simply so that their scores on hand-written tests do not suffer.

Use of Separate Answer Sheets

A second concern is the effect of detached answer sheets on test performance. Some time ago, Gaffney and Maguire (1971) investigated this issue using groups of students enrolled in the second through ninth grades. Students in each grade recorded answers on a separate answer sheet. Each test included seven embedded questions that measured what was common knowledge to these students. Because students would be expected to answer these questions perfectly, wrong answers were assumed to indicate difficulty in using a separate answer sheet. Students were divided into three groups that were given the following types of training in the use of detached answer sheets: (1) minimal instruction with no practice, (2) maximum instruction with no practice, and (3) maximum instruction with practice. The authors conclude that separate answer sheets should not be used before the fourth grade regardless of the amount of instruction and practice. In the fourth and fifth grades, detached answer sheets may be used *if* significant training and practice are provided. After the fifth grade, students do not require training or practice to use detached answer sheets.

Lassiter (1987) questioned whether these findings were realistic because standardized tests (and certainly many classroom tests) do not mea-

sure skills that all students are expected to answer perfectly. She compared the scores of third-grade students when they were administered the Stanford Achievement Test. Consistent with the Gaffney and Maguire (1971) study, she found that students at this grade level performed worse when answers were recorded on a detached answer sheet. On the mathematics and reading subtests, scores dropped between 4% and 6%. This drop in scores was about the same for higher and lower ability students in the third grade.

PREPARING FOR A TEST

The most obvious way to prepare for a test is to study the content the test is expected to measure. For classroom tests, this is probably the single most important aspect of preparation. This section addresses three other topics that affect student preparation for a test: the effect of coaching, conditions that depress test performance, and anxiety.

The Effect of Coaching

Coaching is generally associated with preparing for a specific standardized test. Usually, the coach familiarizes prospective examinees with the type of items expected to be on the test and teaches test-taking strategies (i.e., testwiseness). Sometimes coaching includes instruction about the type of content to be tested and simulates the administration of tests on that content. Coaching has become prevalent for various college admissions tests, such as the SAT, GRE, and LSAT. Many private agencies and even colleges offer courses to help individuals prepare for these exams. Coaching is common at all grade levels, however (e.g., see Smith, 1991).

The issue of coaching is controversial. For instance, developers of college admissions tests characterize their exams as measures of general ability that must be learned over an extended period of time. Historically, these test developers have taken issue with coaching programs, stating that short-term training has a negligible effect on test scores. Agencies that provide coaching have countered by claiming that it substantially increases test scores.

Several careful studies (e.g., Messick & Jungeblut, 1981) have demonstrated that coaching for admissions tests does increase scores to some degree. Powers and Swinton (1984) conducted a highly systematic study involving the Graduate Record Examination (GRE). They mailed self-study preparation materials to approximately 7,000 individuals who had registered to take the GRE. A strongly worded letter encouraging the use of these materials was included for half the participants. The self-study materials were directed at the analytical portion of the exam.

Powers and Swinton found that individuals who used the materials made significant, but not phenomenal, gains in their scores. Also, gains occurred only in the portion of the test to which coaching was directed (scores on the verbal and quantitative sections of the GRE were unaffected). By far, the largest gains in performance were obtained by the participants that had received that letter.

Bangert-Downs, Kulik, and Kulik (1983) reviewed 30 research studies concerned with the effect of coaching on standardized achievement tests. Their review included studies conducted at the elementary through college grade levels. Coaching appears to increase test scores about equally at all grade levels. The typical improvement was enough to change a student's score from the 50th to 60th percentile. (Percentile indicates the percentage of scores below a particular student's performance.)

More recently, coaching, or as it is often called, "teaching to the test," has become more dominant. This is particularly true with public schools preparing for the high-stakes tests used to evaluate the schools and decide whether students will be promoted or graduate. A school might depart from its normal curriculum for several weeks and devote a significant amount of time to prepare students for one standardized test. Teaching to a high-stakes test can be beneficial if the test reflects important standards and the instruction is on the standards rather than the specific content of a test. Teaching to the test,

however, is harmful when it targets specific content from the test such as what appeared on last year's version, when the teaching distorts the curriculum, or when it focuses on memorization.

Conditions That Depress Test Performance

Students have some control over a variety of conditions that affect their performance on both standardized and classroom tests. The first of these is lack of sleep, which impairs the ability to reason, work quickly, and concentrate. A simple but effective study procedure, albeit not the most common strategy, is to prepare over a period of time and get a good night's rest before an important test.

Since eating can make a person drowsy, students should avoid a large meal before a test. Starches, such as bread or french fries, are particularly bad, as are alcoholic beverages. Salads and fruits in moderation are the best bet.

Significant personal and social experiences can also affect concentration and, therefore, performance on a test. Teachers should be aware of this factor and should avoid scheduling tests just before or after a major social event or vacation. Particularly in secondary school, students should be encouraged to avoid scheduling other activities at times when these may affect their concentration on major tests.

The Effects of Anxiety

Research indicates that a low-to-moderate negative correlation exists between anxiety and test performance. That is, as anxiety increases, scores on a test are depressed somewhat. Rocklin and Thompson (1985) conducted a study involving 90 college undergraduates to determine whether the difficulty of a test alters the effect of anxiety on scores. Students were first administered an instrument that measures test anxiety. They were then categorized into high-, medium-, and low-anxiety groups. All students were administered a difficult and an easy verbal aptitude test. Students correctly answered 41% of items on the difficult test and 83% on the easy test.

The least anxious students did best on the difficult test. Their average score on the difficult test was 45%, versus 35% for the other students. The moderately anxious students, however, scored highest on the easier test. They averaged 90% on the easy test, whereas the most and least anxious students averaged approximately 80%.

🌐 10.1   Apply What You Are Learning

Assume that the Rocklin and Thompson study concerning the relationship between anxiety and test performance generalizes to students in elementary and secondary schools. At what anxiety level will students obtain the highest test scores?

Answer can be found at the end of the chapter.

High anxiety is undesirable, particularly in the extreme. Frequent administration of classroom tests should moderate anxiety for two reasons. First, it increases students' familiarity with the examination experience. Second, it reduces the significance of scores on any single exam.

TESTWISENESS

A number of years ago, Millman, Bishop, and Ebel (1965) defined testwiseness as an examinee's ability to use characteristics of either a test or the test-taking situation to obtain a high score. Testwiseness is distinct from skills the test is intended to measure. Therefore, differences in test scores caused by variability in students' testwiseness threaten its validity. Removing testwiseness skills from those who have it is impossible. Teaching it to all students, therefore, reduces variability in testwiseness.

The testwiseness skills discussed here are grouped into the six categories originally proposed by Millman, Bishop, and Ebel. The first four include using time effectively, avoiding errors, eliminating incorrect alternatives, and knowing when to guess. In contrast to these first four, the remaining two categories capitalize on the habits

of the teacher who developed the test, such as being aware of the teacher's intention and the idiosyncrasies the teacher builds into test items.

Sometimes, teachers resist teaching testwiseness because it tends to increase scores without improving comprehension of the knowledge being assessed. For most aspects of testwiseness, the concern is misdirected. Teaching students to use time efficiently and to proof their work carefully is desirable, because these skills are useful in a variety of settings, including testing. A subset of testwiseness skills, however, may appear less noble because they encourage students to profit from inadequacies that teachers build into tests. Examples might include writing long responses to essay questions when the student knows that the teacher favorably grades long answers or avoiding option D on multiple-choice items because the teacher seldom uses that option for the correct answer.

It can be argued that teachers who build inadequacies into a test do a greater disservice than is done by students who use these unintentional cues when trying to perform well on a test. Nevertheless, testwiseness does threaten validity because it represents a skill that a test is not designed to measure. Unless all students are testwise, the teacher cannot determine whether variation in students' scores is due to differences in their level of achievement or their degree of sophistication in test taking. The remainder of this chapter lists advice you can give students to help make them testwise.

Using Time Effectively

Work Quickly and Pace Yourself. Most tests have time limits and, unfortunately, many teachers administer tests that are too long for the time allotted. Many of the standardized tests administered to older students have time limits that do not allow all individuals to complete every item. To maximize scores in these situations, students should customarily work as quickly as possible without making significant errors. They should determine how much time remains at the start of each test and estimate the average amount of time available for each item. Establishing the point in the test when a third or half the time has elapsed may be useful. Of course, increasing the pace beyond reasonable levels when time is running out should be avoided. Students should be taught that in these situations it is important to maintain a quick but sensible pace and that it is crucial to stay on task for the remainder of the test.

Answer Time-Consuming Items Last. When items are weighted equally, items that cannot be answered readily should be marked and answered later. These include difficult items that require more thought to derive an answer and those involving extended computations. If there is any possibility that time will expire before the test is completed, the student should make sure that he or she has answered all easy items.

Answer High-Point Questions First. If time is limited, the student should first answer items that will result in the maximum number of points. If a test includes both essay and objectively scored items, more points per unit of time usually can be obtained by answering the objectively scored items first. This technique is not useful on most standardized tests because items assigned high points and those assigned low points are usually grouped and timed separately.

Answer the Specific Questions Posed by Short-Answer and Essay Items. Especially with essay items, students have a tendency to write everything they know, consuming time that might be used to answer or proof other items. If the teacher is using a carefully developed scoring plan, points are not gained by including information superfluous to the question. Unfortunately, many teachers do not establish a clear scoring plan for essay items and deduct points for erroneous statements even if they are not pertinent to the test item. This increases the importance of answering only the questions addressed by the test item.

Mark Items for Later Review and Changing of Answers. Students should mark and skip over items if they are uncertain of the correct answer. Later terms may give insights on how to solve some of the preceding difficult items. Marking difficult items saves time by making them easier to find when insights occur.

Students often hesitate to change responses when they review previously answered multiple-choice items. Research indicates that students *on an average* gained somewhat more than they lose by changing answers (see Davis, 1975; Fabrey & Case, 1985; Matthews, 1929; Vispoel, 2000). McMorris and Weideman (1986) hypothesized that if students are encouraged to go with their second opinion, they may tend to lose points by changing answers they might not have changed otherwise. Their research, however, found that after being encouraged to go with their second opinion, students still typically gain points by changing answers. The total number of points gained from changing answers is usually small.

Avoiding Errors

Follow Directions Carefully. Directions on standardized tests are generally more involved than are those for classroom tests. Also, the test administrator has less flexibility in clarifying instructions on standardized tests. Particularly at the elementary level, students will be more able to follow directions on standardized tests if similar directions are used and reviewed on several classroom tests.

Students should scan directions quickly on all tests and mark anything that may affect the score, including time limits, how items are to be answered and recorded, what work is to be shown, and whether there is a choice of which items to answer.

Directions for individual items should also be noted. Students have particular problems with directions to essay items. They often lose points simply by not answering the question. They should look for key words and phrases, such as "list," "define," "give two examples," and "compare and contrast." As noted earlier, critical time is frequently lost by writing answers for questions that were not asked.

Estimate Answers. If computations are involved, when possible, the answer should first be approximated and then computed exactly. The correctness of the exact answer can be judged against the approximation. If approximating an answer is impossible or too time-consuming, a likely range should be anticipated. Unfortunately, many students who derive an answer outside the likely range of values simply stay with their answer. At the very least, the item should be marked for review if time remains when the test is completed.

Proof Work. Students often lose points on a test through careless errors. Any time remaining at the end of a test should be used to proof answers. Sitting idly at the conclusion of an exam often amounts to giving away some easily earned points.

If a separate answer sheet is being used, the accuracy of markings should be verified. This can be facilitated if the intended answer can be marked in the test booklet as well as on the answer sheet.

Mark Answers Carefully. Test takers should mark answers carefully when a separate answer sheet is used. Ink should never be used, because it prevents the changing of answers and because some scoring machines cannot read marks made with ink.

The large scoring machines that score standardized tests and those used by centralized testing services in school districts and at colleges are very accurate. Technology is improving the ability to sense even very poorly marked answers.

Relatively inexpensive desktop scanners have become popular for scoring tests. These scanners are very accurate when marks are made clearly. They are also good at distinguishing between poor erasures and new markings, but they sometimes have problems detecting light marks. If the printed answer letter inside the bubble to be marked is visible, the mark may be too light to be scanned. Also, as many desktop scanners read through the center of each bubble space, if the student uses doughnutlike marks, with a hole in the middle, the scanner may not read the mark.

As discussed earlier, elementary students require significant training when first using a separate answer sheet. Games can facilitate this training. The teacher can distribute answer sheets to students and then call out a series of item numbers and answer spaces to be marked. The marks are called out in random order. When the students have finished, the marks form the outline of an object, such as a tree or face. A contest might be held to see who can name the object being drawn first. Special points can be awarded for overall accuracy and adequacy of marks.

Eliminating Incorrect Alternatives

When answering multiple-choice items, test-wise students eliminate distracters that are clearly wrong. If they have to guess, this procedure increases their probability of selecting the correct response. This strategy seems obvious; however, it represents a learned skill. Research as far back as that by Millman and Setijadi (1966) and Lo and Slakter (1973) has indicated that students from diverse cultures obtain lower scores on multiple-choice items, in part because they do not deductively isolate the correct response. Many elementary students also lack this skill until they become experienced with the multiple-choice format. When reviewing a previously completed test, a teacher can help the class reason through multiple-choice options to illustrate how distractors can be eliminated.

Students often read through the options only until they find one that answers the stem. Thus, they may miss a better response that appears later in the list. When answering multiple-choice items, the student should read all options for each item.

Knowing When to Guess

Formula scoring is used with multiple-choice and other objectively scored tests by some teachers and with certain standardized tests. Formula scoring adjusts each student's test score by subtracting points proportional to the number of items answered incorrectly. This procedure encourages students to omit an answer rather than guess when they have no idea what the answer is.

Research such as that by Cross and Frary (1977) and Rowley and Traub (1977) indicates that guessing increases students' scores even when formula scoring is used. Of course, if a student can eliminate one or more of the multiple-choice distractors, guessing among the remaining alternatives is advised. Directions to most standardized tests explicitly give such advice. Research suggests, however, that students underestimate what they know. When students cannot consciously eliminate even one distractor, guessing increases their scores more than can be explained by chance (Cross & Frary, 1977; Rowley & Traub, 1977).

More recent research by Angoff and Schrader (1984) disputes these findings. Using two college admissions tests (the SAT and GMAT), these researchers found that examinees' scores on a formula-scored test did not vary as a function of instructions. When tests were formula scored, students did no better when told to always guess than when told to guess only when one or more distractors could be eliminated. However, students who were told to always guess did no worse than those given more restrictive directions. From the students' perspective, then, probably the best advice is to always guess when necessary. It may help, and it should not hurt.

Budescu and Bar-Hillel (1993) analyzed different formulas for scoring tests in light of guessing and also different guessing styles of examinees. They observed that if an examinee is trying to maximize the score, the best strategy is to answer all items even when answering involves guessing. They concluded that it is best not to correct for guessing but simply to base scores on the number of correct answers. They also concluded that, because of significant variation in how examinees guess when taking a test, test directions should clearly encourage all examinees to answer all items.

Being Responsive to the Teacher's Intentions

Respond to the Teacher's Intended Sophistication. Particularly with essay questions, students must anticipate the degree of sophistication the teacher is seeking in an answer. For example, a thorough response to "Explain the cause of the American Civil War" would require several volumes. Depending on the class, a teacher who asks this question might be looking for a brief response focusing on the slavery controversy, Lincoln's election as President and the resulting secession of Southern states from the Union, or, possibly, events associated with the battle of Fort Sumter. A very brief response such as "Slavery caused the Civil War" may lack the sophistication the teacher is seeking.

The need for students to read into the teacher's intentions can be reduced if the essay item concisely describes the task that students are to complete. When students' responses depart significantly from the intended answer, however, a teacher can improve testwiseness by explaining why, within the context of the class, the intended answer was the expected response.

Respond to the Teacher's Scoring Criteria. Teachers should use a deliberately constructed scoring plan when evaluating answers to essay items. When a careful scoring plan is not developed, however, students can often increase test scores by writing longer responses, using good penmanship, presenting a response that is highly organized, and avoiding spelling errors and faulty grammar.

Accounting for Idiosyncrasies Built into Test Items

Teachers unintentionally build a number of idiosyncrasies into tests. Students can often increase their scores by being aware of these habits. Some examples follow.

Select C as the Correct Multiple-Choice Option. Carter (1986) conducted an interesting experiment to determine whether seventh-grade students were aware of clues that are often embedded in multiple-choice items. One clue is the frequent use of option C as the correct answer. In her experiment, Carter administered the following item to students (p. 21):

Debbie is probably _____ years old.

    A. 5
    B. 8
    C. 12
    D. 16

Although students were provided no information suggesting which option was correct, approximately 70% selected option C. When asked to elaborate on the choice, a student explained:

> My teacher never put the right answer on A. Sometimes it's on B, but most often it lands there (pointing to answer C on test). And the last choice D is usually dumb, especially in Ms. _____'s class.

Selecting the Longest Multiple-Choice Option. Carter also studied the tendency for the correct multiple-choice option to be longer than the distractors. The following item was administered to seventh-grade students:

> The main theme of the story is based on a conflict concerning Debbie's desire
> A. for rain.
> B. to believe that supernatural powers do not influence people and her fear that curses may be impossible.
> C. to watch television.
> D. to be grown.

Half the students selected option B, although a third of the students selected option D. A typical reason given by students for selecting the longest response was, "Look, I figure my teacher doesn't have time to write all that unless it's the right one."

In the previous example, Carter (1986) was interested in why a large percentage of students selected option D, particularly since students generally avoid this choice. Apparently, students had recently read numerous stories about growing up and therefore assumed this would be reflected in the correct answer.

Select the Multiple-Choice Option That is Cued by the Stem. Teachers often give unintentional clues to the correct option through the stem. To illustrate, try to determine the correct answers to the following two items:

1. All but one of the following are parts of a sailboat. The exception is an
    A. halyard.
    B. mainsheet.
    C. outrigger.
    D. shroud.

2. The captain of a ship entering a controlled harbor should contact the
    A. auditor.
    B. harbormaster.
    C. inspector.
    D. monitor.

In the first item, option C is grammatically consistent with the stem. In the second item, option B is similar to a key word contained in the stem. Therefore, both represent the probable (and in these examples, the correct) response.

Quite often, students can pick out the correct answer simply because it sounds right. Teachers frequently give cues to the correct response in the stem content and grammar.

Assume That Options Containing Absolutes Are False. Most concepts taught in schools include exceptions or qualifiers and therefore do not exist as absolutes. Special attention is often and appropriately given to exceptions. Therefore, testwise students correctly anticipate that multiple-choice options and true-false items that contain absolutes such as "always" and "never" represent incorrect statements.

Overview of Testwiseness

Some testwiseness skills simply consist of students' ability to recognize weaknesses that teachers build into tests. Incorporating the characteristics discussed in the last four chapters will help you avoid these deficiencies when developing test items for written tests. The majority of testwiseness skills concern how to work productively when taking a test, such as using time wisely and avoiding errors. Many, but definitely not all, students learn these skills on their own without deliberate training by teachers. Numerous students, particularly those in lower grades or from different cultures, will benefit from deliberate training in testwiseness.

As with other skills, students probably differ in their ability to learn to be testwise. This, and the fact that many students learn such skills on their own, led Scruggs and Lifson (1985) to caution educators not to overemphasize the influence of testwiseness on test validity. Nevertheless, teachers should be alert and responsive to differences in the testwiseness of students.

SUMMARY

Three factors that affect student performance on a test have been addressed: familiarity with the testing medium, preparation for the test, and testwiseness.

Familiarity with the testing medium includes the mode used to present the test and the procedure that students use to record responses. Objectively scored tests are increasingly being administered by computer. When the test administered by the computer is identical to the paper-and-pencil version, little change in student performance is evident. Recent research shows that as students become more dependent on word processors, they perform worse on tests with open-ended items when responses must be written out by hand.

Research regarding detached answer sheets indicates they should not be used before the fourth grade. Students in the fourth and fifth grades benefit from training and experience with detached answer sheets.

Studies show that examinees at all grade levels benefit somewhat from coaching. A variety of other conditions depress test performance, including lack of sleep, eating a heavy meal, and conflicting personal and social events. Test anxiety also affects test performance. Usually, anxiety depresses scores, although moderate anxiety may actually increase scores on classroom tests.

Testwiseness is the ability to improve scores by taking into account the nature of a test and conditions under which it is administered. Skills associated with being testwise were grouped into six categories: using time effectively, avoiding errors, eliminating incorrect alternatives, knowing when to guess, being responsive to the teacher's intentions, and taking into account idiosyncrasies built into a test. The first four categories are essentially good work and study habits. The last two categories pertain to deficiencies that teachers often, although needlessly, build into a test.

ANSWER: APPLY WHAT YOU ARE LEARNING

10.1. The difficulty of most classroom tests is closer to what Rocklin and Thompson referred to as an easy test, on which students, on average, correctly answer 83% of the items. Their study suggests that moderately anxious students will do better on classroom tests than will the most and least anxious students.

SOMETHING TO TRY

• Review the section of this chapter concerned with testwiseness. Then prepare a lesson plan that teaches these skills to your students. Include student activities that provide practice with the test taking you believe to be most important for your students to learn.

- Ask someone who until recently lived in a country where multiple-choice exams are uncommon to describe problems experienced when answering multiple-choice tests administered in this country. Does this experience illustrate how test-taking skills are learned?
- Discuss these questions: What are the differences in skills of a person who is skilled in writing with a word processor versus a student who is proficient with writing by hand. Where these skills are different, which are more important? Upon which of these skills should a test that involves writing skills depend?
- Ask someone who recently participated in a coaching seminar designed to help individuals prepare for a college admissions test to describe activities that occurred in the seminar. What activities seemed to help the most? The least?

ADDITIONAL READING

Educational Research Service. (Undated). Is it OK to teach to the test? *On the Same Page* series, Educational Research Service. Available online: *http://www.ers.org/otsp/otsp1.htm*. This short article suggests how and how not to teach to the test, and identifies commerical test preparation resources.

Smith, M. L. (1991). Meanings of test preparation. *American Educational Research Journal, 28,* 521–542. This article describes techniques used by teachers to help their students perform well on a standardized test. Techniques range from teaching test-taking skills to teaching content known to be on the test.

PART III

How to Develop, Administer, and Score Alternative Assessments

Part II discussed the development, administration, and scoring of written tests. Written tests have a number of advantages, one of which is their efficiency in administration. A written test can be administered simultaneously to a large number of students. Written tests can also be produced and scored more quickly than can many alternative assessments, such as performance assessments and portfolios. Written tests often are as effective as alternative assessments for measuring a student's ability to recall information and to demonstrate knowledge of concepts and rules.

Compared with alternative assessments, however, written tests have some serious limitations. For instance, written tests are very rigid in comparison with informal observation and questions. Informal assessments can be spontaneous, easily incorporated into instruction as it occurs, and quickly modified in response to classroom needs.

Another limitation of written tests is their inability to assess complex skills, specifically problem solving. Written tests can certainly measure a student's ability to solve structured problems, such as many math problems, or problems that can be resolved with well-defined and constrained strategies. However, written tests cannot assess a student's ability to solve problems for which diverse solutions are possible based on the concepts and/or rules the student chooses to use.

These skills require alternative assessments, often referred to as authentic measures because they assess the ultimate performance outcomes generally associated with formal instruction.

Considerable interest has developed in alternative classroom assessments, mainly because written tests cannot be used in many assessment situations. However, as with written tests, alternative assessments will be of low quality if a teacher simply assembles some tasks or other evaluation techniques when it is time to assess students. Instead, assessments must be developed and used within a framework. As noted in Part I, a framework for assessing students includes four interrelated components:

- Purpose, which establishes how results from assessments will be interpreted and used

- Specifications, which establish the knowledge to be assessed and corresponding performance to be observed

- Validity, which is concerned with evidence as to whether appropriate capabilities are being assessed

- Consistency, which is concerned with whether observations of student performance will generalize to other settings

We will be concerned with these framework components as we discuss alternative assessments.

The focus of Part III is on the development, administration, and scoring of alternative assessments. We begin by discussing informal observations and questions. Next, we discuss the more formal performance assessments. Performance assessments are the primary means through which students' ability to solve complex problems is evaluated. Performance assessments are also used with young children and others who are unable to complete written tests, and are used to assess tasks that are heavily dependent on motor skills. The final chapter in Part III discusses portfolios. Portfolio systems in particular address the active and integral role assessments play within learning.

11

Informal Observations and Questions

Observation and oral questions are by far the most common forms of assessment in the classroom. Estimates of the percentage of assessments that are based on observation and questioning are hard to find. Probably more than 90% of all measures of student performance involve casual observation and questioning, as opposed to written tests, performance assessments, and the other more formal types of assessment.

Relative to many other assessments, observation and questioning are efficient and adaptable. For example, numerous observations can occur simultaneously or at least in rapid succession. Subsequent observations can take into account whatever was observed just moments earlier. Similarly, follow-up questions can reflect a student's response to a previous question.

In spite of their tremendous efficiency and adaptability, however, informal observations and questions have significant limitations. Observations tend to be limited to student performances that occur naturally. Failure to see a student demonstrate a particular skill may result because the student lacks the skill or because, although the student has achieved the skill, he or she is not demonstrating it for any number of reasons. Furthermore, the teacher observes only a small proportion of students' behaviors. Because informal observations and questions are spontaneous, these techniques tend to be technically inferior to written tests and performance assessments. Another limita-

tion is that most assessments based on observations and oral questions are undocumented. Unless recorded, the results of these assessments are easily forgotten or distorted.

Despite their limitations, observations and oral questions are absolutely essential to an overall strategy for assessing students. Other techniques do not adequately help the teacher maintain the spontaneity that is crucial to effective instruction. For this reason, it is important to understand the characteristics of informal observations and questions and to review techniques that can help maximize the usefulness of these assessment techniques. This chapter helps you achieve three skills:

- Recognize characteristics of informal observations and questions
- Identify techniques for improving the quality of these observations and questions
- Identify techniques for recording results from informal assessments

CHARACTERISTICS OF INFORMAL OBSERVATIONS AND QUESTIONS

A very important characteristic of both observations and questions is their familiarity. We constantly use observation and questioning as part of virtually everything we do, whether it's spending an afternoon at the shopping mall, being with friends, arriving at an airport, attending a class as a student, or leading a class as a teacher.

Let us review the characteristics of observation and questioning as they occur within two familiar settings: driving a car and talking with friends. As we review these characteristics, ask yourself whether your personal experience confirms their existence. Try to anticipate how these characteristics of observation and questioning apply to informal assessments within the classroom. Later, we will relate these characteristics to the classroom.

First, here are some characteristics of informal observations that occur while driving a car within the busy downtown area of a city.

- *Many events are observed either simultaneously or in very quick succession.* Within seconds, you individually observe a number of cars. You observe traffic signals and road signs. You observe pedestrians, bicycles, parked cars, debris on the road, potholes, and markings on the pavement, such as the centerline. Your observations, however, are not only visual. You listen to the sounds of the car and the wheels on the road. You may be listening to the radio and what passengers in the car are saying. (In the classroom, does a teacher simultaneously observe many events? Can you think of a set of three observations that likely would happen simultaneously or in quick succession?)

- *Events are observed at different levels of detail.* While driving, some observations are detailed, such as when you read street signs. Other observations are more general, such as when you spot a traffic light in the distance.

- *Current observations help select and structure subsequent observations.* Seeing the distant traffic light may cause you to look at how closely cars are following you, just in case you have to stop quickly at a red light. You might also start looking for familiar landmarks to determine whether the approaching intersection is where you plan to turn. (In the classroom, what would be one instance where a current observation structures what you subsequently observe?)

- *Often, observations become focused on one event.* One event may command your complete attention out of necessity (such as when a car suddenly turns in front of you) or out of choice (such as when you hear an interesting announcement on the radio). When attention is focused, fewer or possibly no other events are observed.

- *When observations become focused, observation of other critical events must be maintained.* Many accidents occur when a driver's attention is diverted. For example, cars get rear-ended when the driver in the following car focuses on a single event, such as dialing a number on a cell phone. You establish which critical events must always be observed, even as your observations become more focused.

- *Experience and confidence with a task substantially increase the effectiveness of observations.* When you first learned to drive, you may remember how you focused on things that would affect you immediately, such as the car next to you and the position of your car relative to the edge of the road. When you were a new driver, you probably avoided driving downtown simply because it would require observing too many things in quick succession. With experience, critical observations became more automatic and complex situations were more easily handled. This experience now allows you to go places that new drivers avoid. Confidence, however, must accompany experience. If you lack confidence in your ability to drive, the effectiveness of your observations will not be optimal. For example, after an accident, a driver's confidence is reduced, and for a period of time the person becomes a less-proficient driver until her or his confidence is regained. The effectiveness of observations is highly related to both experience and confidence. (Are experience and confidence relevant to the effectiveness of a teacher's observations in the classroom? The answer is "yes!" Confidence is extremely relevant.)

- *Familiarity with surroundings increases the effectiveness of observations.* Familiarity with surroundings is a special form of experience. Familiarity also influences confidence. An otherwise experienced driver is more proficient when driving in a familiar downtown area than when driving through a new city. When surroundings are familiar, your observations become more automatic, and you can observe more events simultaneously.

- *One depends heavily on the observations of others.* To keep the number of observations manageable, you must often depend on others observing you. You could not safely drive through heavy traffic unless the drivers of other cars were also observing you. Other drivers may have to initiate actions to avoid problems you do not see or alert you to problems that are developing. You usually take actions to help others observe you, such as driving in a predictable manner or using the horn when necessary.

- *Most events are not observed.* Although you observe a phenomenal number of events while driving, you never see most things that occur around you. For example, you probably do not read the license plates of most nearby cars. You do not observe the type of clothes worn by most people in other cars and on the sidewalk. You may not observe that the driver of a car up ahead is trying to get out of a parking space. You cannot possibly observe everything. Many, possibly all, of these events are not relevant to your act of driving the car. Some, however, may be relevant. For instance, if the driver of the car leaving the parking space also has not observed you, your cars may collide.

- *Most observations are not remembered or are distorted when recalled.* Because of the huge number of observations that occur, most details are not remembered. Unlike a tape recorder or CD-ROM, the mind does not retain verbatim what is received. Instead, the mind organizes what is observed in ways that are expected to be useful later. Over time, the mind reorganizes these perceptions. After you arrive home from driving downtown, you retain very few observations. Many of them, such as how long you waited at a traffic light, can be reconstructed, although often inaccurately. Witnesses to an accident similarly construct contradictory descriptions of what recently occurred. Immediately writing down details of what was observed substantially improves the accuracy of recollection. Your idiosyncrasies, such as your values, interests, and habits, influence what you remember and how you remember it. Your idiosyncrasies also influence what you observe in the first place.

Although driving a car is obviously very different from teaching a class, the characteristics of observations that occur in both settings are similar. In both the car and the classroom, *you observe many events simultaneously or in quick succession.* Within a few seconds while walking around in the classroom, you may have looked to see if students are staying on task with seat work, briefly read what a nearby student wrote on her or his paper, noticed the unusual way another student holds a pencil, heard conversation in the hallway, and heard a click over the school intercom suggesting that someone is about to make an announcement.

These events are observed at different levels of detail. Reading what the student wrote on her or his paper, for instance, would be a detailed observation, whereas the overall check of whether students are staying on task would be a general observation. *Current observations help select and structure subsequent observations.* Anticipating an announcement over the intercom may cause you to continue watching students in general rather than to focus attention on the student whose paper you briefly read. The conversation in the hall may cause you to walk closer to the door so that you can observe what is happening.

Classroom observations often become focused on one event. When this happens, the number of other events that can be observed is decreased. For example, if you find it necessary to watch what is happening in the hallway, even if you stay in the classroom, you will be less able to monitor what students are doing in the classroom. Similarly, if you begin working closely with the student whose paper you had scanned, you will be less able to observe what other students are doing. *As you focus your attention, you must maintain your observation of certain critical events.* For instance, if you focus attention on one student's paper, you must continue to observe how much time is passing, what other students are doing, and overall trends in student behavior. When you focus your attention, the tendency will be to stop all other observations. Doing so must be avoided. *Experience and confidence significantly improve the effectiveness of observations in the classroom.* Just as when you first learn to drive a car, your observations are much less effective when you first begin teaching. New teachers tend to focus narrowly on what they will do next. With experience, many actions become automatic, and teachers become able to observe several events simultaneously and handle highly complex situations.

It is ironic that teaching may be the only profession in which responsibilities are as complex if not more complex on the first day as compared to the last day of employment. During the first year of employment, a new teacher typically prepares for and teaches multiple subjects. Often, these preparations are in content areas other than those with which the new teacher is most proficient. Experienced and higher-paid teachers often teach the less-demanding students and classes.

In contrast, when learning to drive a car, a new driver progresses from simpler to more complex situations. After training, the new driver has the option, and usually tries, to avoid complicated situations until he or she gains more experience. Although in some ways an inexperienced driver may be more dangerous than an inexperienced teacher, the classroom environment is much more complex. A teacher who successfully employs informal observations is performing an act more complicated than effectively using observations while driving through downtown traffic.

Confidence, in addition to experience, enhances observation abilities in the classroom. Being comfortable in the classroom setting, being in a school whose administration and other teachers encourage confidence, and being knowledgeable with your subject matter help you effectively observe students.

Teaching students with whom you are familiar helps automate classroom observations. Your observations are less effective if, as is common at the beginning of the year, you confuse students with one another or lack preliminary evaluations of each student's characteristics. Likewise, observations are less effective when new curriculum materials are introduced. After becoming familiar with new materials, your observations tend to be more automatic.

The teacher depends heavily on the observations of students. A teacher has to depend on students' observations to keep events in the classroom manageable, just like a driver in a car has to depend on the observations of others. Students must learn how to observe and be comfortable with initiating observations and taking corrective actions. The teacher can help structure students' observations by asking timely questions, being encouraging, and showing students how and when to get the teacher's attention.

Most events that occur in the classroom go unobserved, and what is observed is often quickly forgotten or distorted when recalled. Writing down what was observed helps retain accuracy, although it is practical to write down only a fraction of what is observed. Careful and continuous observation, as an assessment technique, is unbeatable when it comes to immediate, formative evaluations of student performance. Most classroom assessments are based on informal observations. No other assessment technique provides the information necessary to monitor student progress continually. However, because details are quickly forgotten or distorted, the role of informal observation must diminish when summative evaluations are involved.

🌑 11.1   Apply What You Are Learning

In Chapter 5, we discussed the importance of generalizability (that which we observed generalizing to that which was not observed).

Scan through the 10 characteristics of informal observations we have just discussed, listed in Figure 11.1. Which one of these 10 characteristics makes it so important to determine whether informal observations of student performance will generalize to other settings?

Answer can be found at the end of the chapter.

So far, we have drawn analogies between observations that occur when driving a car and those that occur in the classroom. In the classroom, however, most observations are of an indirect nature. We observe each student's outward performance as an *indication* of the student's internal thoughts and capabilities. We generally

1. Many events are observed either simultaneously or in very quick succession.

2. Events are observed at different levels of detail.

3. Current observations help select and structure subsequent observations.

4. Often, observations become focused on one event.

5. When observations become focused, observation of other critical events must be maintained.

6. Experience and confidence with a task substantially increase the effectiveness of observations.

7. Familiarity with surroundings increases the effectiveness of observations.

8. One depends heavily on the observations of others.

9. Most events are not observed.

10. Most observations are not remembered or are distorted when recalled.

Figure 11.1

Characteristics of informal classroom observations

cannot directly see what students have learned and must depend on outward indications that learning has indeed occurred. Furthermore, in the classroom we often augment these observations with oral questions. Questions can compel, or at least encourage, student actions. Oral questions, so to speak, put you in the driver's seat.

We are going to use as a reference several characteristics of informal observation and questioning that occur when friends interact with each other. We will then relate these characteristics to what goes on in the classroom. It is useful to note that the characteristics discussed previously also apply to our interactions with friends. For instance, when interacting with friends, we observe many events simultaneously or in quick succession. Previous observations affect subsequent observations. Observations often become focused with a

corresponding reduction in other observations. Also, experience and confidence greatly facilitate observations among friends.

Here are some additional characteristics of observations and questioning that occur when interacting with a group of friends:

• *Observations often require inference.* You cannot see what your friends are thinking or what they know. Instead, you have to make inferences from things you can observe, such as what they say, their tone of voice, and their facial expressions. If, for instance, conversation among friends is focusing on a recent video that some members of the group have seen, paying attention to their words and expressions provides only an indication of what they know or are thinking about the video. Inferences drawn from what you observe typically include some distortion of what your friends actually know or are thinking.

• *Subsequent observations substantiate or modify earlier observations.* When interacting with friends, you have opportunities to use additional observations to confirm or modify your judgments. This situation differs from what typically happens with serial activities, such as driving a car. When driving, it is often not practical to go back and make additional observations. When interacting with friends or teaching in a classroom, however, there are many opportunities to follow-up with more observations, and this is important because so many judgments in these cases are based on inference rather than on direct observation. (Can you think of one situation within a classroom where follow-up observations became important to substantiate or modify an earlier observation?)

• *Questioning can set up subsequent observations.* Not only can you make follow-up observations, but you can also ask questions that shape or encourage ensuing observations. For instance, you can ask friends for details about a movie to find out if it is scary or has graphic content.

• *Questions are obtrusive.* When *observations* are *unobtrusive,* they provide an excellent technique for determining typical behaviors, such as attitudes. However, *asking a question* indicates that observations are occurring and identifies what is being observed. Setting up observations, in fact, is often the purpose of asking a question, although posing a question influences what subsequently will be observed. For instance, a question that implies that a movie was boring can cause others to camouflage their real attitudes. A friend might outwardly appear to accept the movie as being somewhat boring if for no other reason than to avoid being offensive.

- *Questions have to be interpreted by others, so clarity is important.* Since you cannot see another's thoughts, you have to infer what thoughts underlie the questions being asked. For instance, you might say, "My parents are visiting. Would renting this video be appropriate?" Possible inferences include "Would I be embarrassed to watch this movie with my parents?" "Would older people enjoy the plot?" or possibly, "Would my parents relate to the issues the movie is raising?" Asking a concise question helps communicate what you are thinking: "My parents enjoy only G-rated movies. What's the rating of this video?" Certainly an advantage of informal questions is the ease with which ambiguous questions can be clarified.

- *Questions can be directed to individuals or to the group.* A question directed at the group encourages others to participate. For instance, you might ask, "Do you all think this video is worth renting?" Most individuals in the group who have seen the movie will at least answer the question to themselves if not verbally. Although questions directed at the group encourage greater participation, this approach reduces control over who will respond to the question. Also, if questions are directed at the group for an extended period, the number of individuals participating tends to decrease because of the lack of personal feedback.

- *Individuals to whom a question is addressed must perceive that their response was listened to and used appropriately.* Because oral questions affect subsequent observations, ignoring or misusing an individual's response is detrimental to later interactions. Friends realize that this is important. They are generally attentive to each other's responses and demonstrate they are empathetic to what is said. (In a classroom, what is one way that a teacher can convey to students that their response was listened to?)

- *Individuals to whom a question is addressed will typically forget their answers, as will the person who asked the question.*
  As we noted earlier, the mind does not memorize knowledge; it organizes knowledge in ways that are expected to be useful later. Writing down what we learn facilitates later recall. Otherwise, the details of even significant events are usually distorted. In casual conversation with friends, forgetting details of what transpired is often of no significance. Questions and observations are used to formulate ideas and impressions rather than to generate a list of details. When details are to be recalled, such as a phone number, a future date, or a joke you wish to tell others, writing it down even in abbreviated form substantially improves the chances that you will recall it.

Each of these characteristics applies to the informal observations and questions that occur in a classroom. For instance, *when observing students, you cannot directly observe what they know or what they are thinking. Instead, you make an inference from what you see—and that inference may be in error.* If you watch a student writing an essay and see that student make a grammatical mistake with subject–verb agreement, you might conclude that the student does not understand how to match the plural form of a verb with a plural subject. It may be, however, that the student mentally switched from a singular to plural subject but forgot to compensate for this switch when writing out the sentence. Similarly, if you happen to see a student holding a pencil incorrectly, you may infer that the student does not know how to hold the pencil, but the student might have just grasped the pencil incorrectly.

Subsequent observations can be used to modify earlier observations. For example, continuing to watch the student write will help clarify whether the student understands rules concerning subject–verb agreement. Likewise, continuing to watch the student hold the pencil will help determine whether he or she typically holds the pencil incorrectly or simply happens to be holding it that way at a particular moment.

Questions directed at students can set up subsequent observations. Asking the first student about subject–verb agreement or talking to the second student about how he or she is holding the pencil can quickly help clarify what these students know. However, questions are obtrusive. The student writing the paper will focus on subject–verb agreement, which in itself might be productive. However, knowing what is being observed, the student is likely to focus on subject–verb agreements and thus might begin to demonstrate maximum rather than typical performance in this area. Similarly, the second student might adjust the pencil grip and later, when you are not observing, revert to the incorrect grasp.

Questions require the students to make inferences from what they observe you saying, since they cannot see what you are thinking. The accuracy of their inferences is influenced by the clarity of your questions.

Questions within a classroom setting are often directed at the group rather than at an individual. For instance, if discussion in the class focuses on how drinking water becomes contaminated, you might ask, "Who can identify a source of water contamination?" Addressing questions to the group tends, at least momentarily, to encourage broader participation. Students who do not respond verbally usually answer the question to themselves. *Individual students, however, must perceive that their response to the teacher was listened to and used appropriately.* Otherwise, students tune out.

With all informal assessments, *the details of what was asked and observed are soon forgotten,* whether they are observations that occur while driving a car, listening to what friends say, or observing students' responses to questions. Students also forget the details of questions they were asked and the responses they gave. Questions are a useful assessment technique only when short-term recall of observations is required (for instance, in assessments used for preliminary, formative, and diagnostic evaluations). Unless students' responses are documented, they are not useful for later summative evaluations.

🌑 11.2   Apply What You Are Learning

In Chapter 4, we discussed types of evidence one uses to establish validity. One of the types is criterion-related evidence, where other observations are used to substantiate what was observed on the test.

Scan through the eight characteristics of informal assessments we have just discussed, which are listed in Figure 11.2. Which one of these eight characteristics is most closely related to gathering evidence that the inference being drawn is valid?

Answer can be found at the end of the chapter.

GUIDELINES FOR USING INFORMAL OBSERVATIONS

We have been looking at characteristics of informal observations and questions. These characteristics have implications as to how one should structure informal assessments. We are going to use these characteristics to establish some guidelines, first for using observations, and later for asking oral questions.

When learning how to drive a car, interacting with friends, or helping students learn, we depend heavily on experience to become proficient at observing. Reading a book cannot provide this experience. However, we can develop some basic principles of observation that can guide what we learn through experience.

1. Observations often require inference.
2. Subsequent observations substantiate or modify earlier observations.
3. Questioning can set up subsequent observations.
4. Questions are obtrusive.
5. Questions have to be interpreted by others, so clarity is important.
6. Questions can be directed to individuals or to the group.
7. Individuals to whom a question is addressed must perceive that their response was listened to and used appropriately.
8. Individuals to whom a question is addressed will typically forget their answers, as will the person who asked the question.

Figure 11.2
Characteristics of interactive observations and questions

Know What to Observe

When we sit around a table with friends, our goal is often simply to enjoy being with each other. We typically are not trying to bring about deliberate changes in our friends. In this respect, a teacher's role is very different. The goals of a teacher are centered on intentionally generating significant improvements in students' capabilities. These goals provide the basis for class activities and should also be the basis for determining what actions are observed.

We have noted the important distinction between students' capabilities and performance. We cannot see what students know and are thinking. Instead, we infer students' capabilities from their performance, which we can see. Our goals for students are typically stated in terms of capabilities. When establishing goals and determining what to observe, we must be careful to select student performances that are reasonable evidence of relevant capabilities. Doing so, in turn,

requires knowledge of the characteristics of capabilities. Matching what we measure to the construct we wish to measure is central to obtaining valid assessments.

Although characteristics of capabilities are not fully understood, classifications such as those we are using in this book provide useful references. For instance, a distinction has been drawn between declarative and procedural knowledge, with procedural knowledge divided into subcategories that include concepts and rules. Most goals involve more than one type of capability. Knowledge of multiplication, for example, includes declarative knowledge ("Tell me how multiplication and addition are similar."), concepts ("Is this an example of multiplication or addition: combining the length of the coastlines of California, Oregon, and Washington to find the length of the Pacific coastline between Mexico and Canada?"), and rules ("Multiply 53 × 3 × 27."). To observe capabilities, we must first identify the characteristics of the capability and then identify which observable student performances will indicate whether a student has achieved that capability.

Declarative knowledge, for instance, can be measured by asking students to recall specific facts, principles, trends, criteria, and ways of organizing events. Continuing the example with multiplication, we can measure declarative knowledge by observing whether a student can recall multiplication tables and by asking students to explain what is meant by multiplication. Concepts can be measured by determining whether students can distinguish between illustrations and non-illustrations of the concept. For multiplication, illustrations of the concept might include finding the area of a rectangle, the total cost of 12 objects costing $3 apiece, or the total number of blocks arranged in 3 rows of 7 blocks. Non-illustrations of multiplication would include the student's indicating that multiplication is used to total the unequal lengths of the California, Oregon, and Washington coastlines. Rules can be measured by observing a student apply appropriate rules. We might observe whether a student can multiply several larger numbers for which multiplication tables are not useful, such as $53 \times 3 \times 27$.

❧ 11.3   Apply What You Are Learning

Here are some observations that might be used to assess a student's knowledge related to placing a fulcrum between two unequal weights so that a bar holding the weights balances. Indicate whether each of the following observations would indicate that the student has learned a skill involving declarative knowledge, a concept, or a rule.

1. Observing whether the student responds correctly when asked, "Where is the *fulcrum* for this lever?"
2. Observing whether the student correctly states the definition of fulcrum
3. Observing whether the student can place the fulcrum so that the bar with the weights is balanced

Answers can be found at the end of the chapter.

Knowing what to observe involves first establishing the goals of instruction and then breaking these goals into meaningful capabilities that students are expected to achieve. In order for our observations and questions to be useful, these capabilities must be classified as representing declarative knowledge, procedural knowledge, or problem solving. As we have noted, different types of behavior must be observed to assess these different types of capability.

The best time for determining what to observe is when the lesson is being planned. At that point, we must establish where problem solving or declarative and procedural knowledge are involved and accordingly select student performances to be observed.

Know When to Limit How Much Is to Be Observed

One of the characteristics of observation is the ability to observe several things simultaneously or in quick succession. Focusing the observations, however, allows you to observe a limited

number of events in greater detail. Focus is often necessary when observing students, especially when the performance being observed is complex or when the observation is critical. A critical observation is one used to determine whether further instruction is necessary.

When planning instructional activities, it is useful to consider whether that day's activities involve complex or critical skills. If they do, you should plan to focus observations on a limited number of skills, possibly on only one. With experience, you learn to observe a number of events simultaneously. At the end of the day, however, if you cannot recall students' performance with a critical skill, the number of skills being observed probably needs to be reduced.

Be Familiar with What Is Being Observed

When driving a car, being experienced and familiar with your surroundings significantly improves the efficiency of your observations. An experienced driver is much more adept at observing what is going on than is a person who is just beginning to drive. Also, a person makes more efficient observations when driving through a familiar but busy area of town than when driving through an unfamiliar but equally busy area of town.

Likewise, familiarity substantially affects a teacher's ability to observe. A teacher who is knowledgeable with the content being taught is much more effective at observing students than a teacher who has superficial content knowledge. An example of superficial knowledge is knowing the content a little bit better than the best students. A teacher who is knowledgeable with content can quickly differentiate between declarative knowledge that students can be asked to explain and procedural knowledge that they must demonstrate through other means. A teacher who is knowledgeable can detect subtle characteristics in student performance that indicate a student is learning a misconception. This level of knowledge is difficult to obtain. Experienced teachers tend to be more knowledgeable than new teachers. To a degree, a teacher's own ability to learn influences the level of knowledge. For the most part, level of knowledge is influenced by persistence, looking for limitations and misconceptions in your own knowledge, talking through ideas with colleagues, and reading ideas described in the several widely available professional magazines. Familiarity is also obtained by gaining experience with a particular set of instructional materials and strategies. However, thorough knowledge of the content being taught is the teacher's single most important means for being familiar with what is to be observed.

Avoid Extended Inferences

Because we cannot see what a student knows or is thinking, inferences are required to make judgments about the student's capabilities. Any inference is based on assumptions. For example, if a student correctly spells the words *achieve* and *receive,* we may infer the student knows how to use *ie* versus *ei* when spelling words. This inference assumes that the student did not simply guess at the order of these letters; it also assumes that the student is applying the rules pertaining to *ie* and *ei* rather than memorizing the spelling of selected words.

Inferences that involve fewer or less-significant assumptions are called *limited inferences.* Those that involve many or highly significant assumptions are called extended inferences. Conclusions drawn from *extended inferences* are more likely to be in error simply because of the increased chance of one or more of the critical assumptions being untrue. Observations that require limited inferences should be favored over those requiring extended inferences. Inferences drawn from multiple observations tend to be more adequately limited than inferences drawn from one observation since more opportunities are provided for detecting false assumptions.

🌏 11.4   Apply What You Are Learning

Listed here are pairs of observations and a resulting inference. Within each pair, identify the observation that involves a more limited inference and is, therefore, the preferred observation.

1. *Observation A:* Gary volunteered to spell hippopotamus. He spelled it correctly.
   Observation B: Gary's portfolio from last year shows that Gary always obtained high scores on spelling tests.
   Inference: Gary is good at spelling.

2. *Observation A:* When asked how to balance a checkbook, Jerome correctly added the deposits and subtracted from that total the amounts for each check.
   Observation B: Jerome explained the importance of balancing a checkbook.
   Inference: Jerome knows how to balance a checkbook.

3. *Observation A:* Ana has a large astronomical telescope at home.
   Observation B: Ana often reads about astronomy and asked if she could do her science report on the reason Saturn has rings.
   Inference: Ana enjoys astronomy.

4. *Observation A:* Gretchen seldom pays attention during history lessons.
   Observation B: Gretchen slept while the class was discussing historical events.
   Inference: Gretchen is not interested in history.

5. *Observation A:* Moesha cannot name the capital of Japan.
   Observation B: After asking three students, you find that no one has named the capital of Japan.
   Inference: Students in the class do not know that Tokyo is the capital of Japan.

Answers can be found at the end of the chapter.

Form and Then Substantiate Hypotheses

When observing students, it is best to form hypotheses concerning what a student or group of students knows. **Hypotheses** are *tentative,* *reasonable explanations* of what we have observed. Hypotheses are not conclusions.

Because what a student knows cannot be seen, it is better to form hypotheses than to draw conclusions from what we observe. By forming hypotheses, we deliberately plan to use additional observations to confirm (or reject) our explanation of student performance. The additional observations may simply be replications of earlier observations. Often they involve different sources of information, such as other things we have seen the student do or possibly information provided by other students, teachers, counselors, and parents.

The use of confirming evidence is an important strategy for establishing the validity of measurements. A significant source of evidence concerning the validity of any measurement is whether interpretations drawn from one observation correlate with, or are confirmed by, other measurements obtained. In Chapter 4, we referred to this technique as *criterion-related evidence of validity*.

Forming and then substantiating hypotheses helps us avoid making extended inferences. The earlier illustrations of extended and limited inferences included the observation that Gretchen fell asleep while the class discussed historical events. The teacher might form several initial hypotheses at this point, such as: Gretchen finds the present discussion boring, Gretchen finds history in general boring, Gretchen is very tired, or Gretchen is protesting some earlier treatment. Each of these hypotheses unfortunately would involve extended inferences. The number of assumptions required to make each inference can be reduced, however, by using additional observations to substantiate or refute each of these hypotheses. As a general rule, an initial hypothesis should be substantiated with at least one additional observation. Interpretations drawn from two or more observations tend to be much more accurate than those drawn from just one observation.

When forming a hypothesis to explain what was observed, the temptation will be to remember the explanation of what we saw and forget the event that helped create the hypothesis. This is an undesirable practice. The appropriateness of a hypothesis assumes a valid interpretation of what was observed. Keeping a clear distinction between what was observed and the interpretation of what was observed makes it much easier to use additional observations to substantiate the hypothesis.

Recognize That Observations Overestimate Achievement

Most observations occur while learning is taking place or shortly thereafter. If observations were made long after instruction, the effects of short-term memory would become apparent. Students soon forget or are unable to recall much of what they have learned. Part of this results from natural forgetfulness. However, retention also drops because many of the cues that supported a student's response are removed, modified, or forgotten within a short period of time. Because most observations occur near the time of instruction, they tend to overestimate student achievement.

Observations also overestimate achievement because knowledgeable students are more likely to be observed than are less-knowledgeable students. When informally observing students, we usually look for evidence of learning rather than evidence of an absence of learning. Students who first learn the skill being taught are more likely to encourage the teacher's observation by answering questions, establishing eye contact, and taking other actions that invite observation.

Help Students Participate in Observations

As when driving a car or interacting with friends, we observe a small fraction of events that occur in the classroom. It is impossible to do otherwise. When driving or when interacting with friends, we depend on the observations of others. For instance, you could not possibly drive safely through a busy downtown district if other drivers were unable or unwilling to observe you. The same situation exists in the classroom.

Students will naturally participate in classroom observations, although a teacher can take steps to encourage and direct this involvement. Students become better observers if they know where the teacher is going, and students are more responsive if the teacher's intentions are concise and predictable. Teachers can provide this information to students in a variety of forms, including statements of goals, advanced organizers, and illustrations of what students will be able to do when skills are learned.

Students can participate in observations only if they have the opportunity to do so. A lecture provides fewer opportunities to participate than does discussion. Asking for recitation provides fewer opportunities to participate than allowing students to originate questions and challenge ideas. Working with a large class as a whole provides fewer opportunities than dividing the class into smaller groups of students.

Students' participation in observation is influenced by their interest in what is going on and by the reinforcement they have received from earlier participation. Knowing the ultimate goal of instruction and its importance increases students' interest. Your present learning about classroom assessment is heavily influenced by you having a clear idea of what you will be learning and the degree to which you believe this knowledge will improve your effectiveness in education.

Students maintain or increase their involvement if rewarded. A student tends to feel rewarded if the teacher values his or her thoughts and if the teacher helps the student determine parts of observations that are insightful and important. Students' active participation in informal observations and other assessments is critical because the teacher, without student help, is able to observe only a small fraction of what occurs in the classroom.

Document Observations That Must Later Be Recalled

We recognize that unless documented, observations are forgotten shortly after they occur, or, at the very least, they become seriously distorted. Documentation usually involves a written or electronic record.

Most observations are not documented because of the amount of time needed to record any more than a small portion of what is observed. Fortunately, most observations in the classroom are for immediate use and need not be retained for extended periods. However, when information needs to be retained, it must be documented or it will be lost.

It is easy to assume that the details of an important event will not be forgotten. Such details are extremely clear at the time the event happens. But within the hour, the details of an important event are gone! Later in this chapter, we will describe some techniques used to document the more-significant observations.

GUIDELINES FOR USING INFORMAL QUESTIONS

By asking questions, a teacher can often quickly gather evidence concerning what students have learned. If only informal observations, but no questions, are used, the teacher might not be able to obtain useful evidence within a reasonable amount of time. Questions greatly expedite informal assessment. However, because questions are obtrusive and can affect what a teacher will be able to observe, they need to be presented carefully and prudently. In this section, we address several guidelines that should facilitate the use of informal questions.

Develop Questions from Instructional Goals

By basing questions on instructional goals, we can anticipate which capabilities need to be assessed. Different capabilities require different kinds of questions. Consider, for example, these two questions about the presidential primary elections in the United States:

What is a primary election?

Which state holds the first presidential primary election?

Now contrast those questions to the following:

> If all states decided to hold their presidential primaries on the same day, how would this influence which candidates are nominated?
>
> If separate primaries in each state were replaced with one national primary, how would this affect where political parties invested their funds?

These two groups of questions assess very different capabilities. The first two questions involve declarative knowledge or recall of information. The second two questions measure procedural knowledge. Both capabilities are important. Unfortunately, we often ask questions that measure one type of capability, and then assume we are measuring both.

By determining what capabilities are implicit in an instructional goal, we can determine which observations need to be made and what questions will facilitate these observations.

As instructional goals often form the basis for planning activities for students, knowing the types of capabilities implicit in each goal can enhance the usefulness of these activities. Informal observations and questions should be established at the same time instructional activities are planned. To be effective, student activities, informal observations, and questions all must reflect the types of capabilities implicit in each instructional goal.

Establish a Clear Problem for Students to Address

Chapters 6 through 9 were concerned with the development of written test items. Considerable emphasis was placed on preparing items that establish a clear problem for the student to address. Doing so is important because one of the major threats to the reliability of students' responses is ambiguity within the items. The quality of informal questions is similarly threatened by this ambiguity.

Informal questions have a major advantage over items in a written test. With written tests, questions must be fully developed before the test is administered. With informal assessments, outlines and a teacher's telegraphic notes are often sufficient for preparing the questions. The specific wording of an informal question is established spontaneously as it is being asked. Questions can be clarified on the spot, and even body language can be used to help communicate the intention of a question.

The spontaneity of informal questions, however, can become a crutch that encourages a lack of planning on the teacher's part. If students often ask for questions to be clarified or if the nature or content of students' responses departs significantly from the intent of the question, it is a warning sign that the questions are failing to present clear problems to be addressed.

As with written tests, questions that measure procedural knowledge, such as concepts and rules, are usually more difficult to create than those that measure recall of information. Therefore, even with informal assessments, it is useful to prepare the details of these more-sophisticated questions prior to class. Think through the list of details the question must communicate to students, the reasoning students should go through in answering the question, and the characteristics of a full and correct answer to the question. A series of related questions must often be asked to assess a skill involving procedural knowledge.

Allow Sufficient Time for Responses

When questions are being asked informally in the classroom, it is common for a teacher to pose several questions within the period of 1 minute. Students also respond quickly to questions; two or three seconds of silence before a student responds is often considered lengthy. To draw an analogy with written tests, many informal questions are similar to completion items, whereas others are more like abbreviated essays. Essay questions cannot be answered at the rate of several a minute, even if we subtract the large amount of time required to write out the answer to the essay question. As with essays, additional time is required to think through the answer to more complex questions. Periods of 5 to 10 seconds of silence prior to a response are reasonable when more complex skills are involved.

Avoid Embarrassing or Intimidating Students

One disadvantage of informal questions is that they are public. When asked within a group, the student needs to respond in front of classmates. This raises the possibility of embarrassing or intimidating the student, often unintentionally. Even when the teacher is working one on one with a student, the student has to perform in front of the teacher. In contrast, with a written test, a student works in almost total privacy. Intimidation or embarrassment can motivate students when used in moderation. However, their effects vary widely across students and can be counterproductive. The teacher's reactions to students' answers tend to be a major source of embarrassment and intimidation.

Recognize the Importance of Reactions to Answers

A teacher's reactions to students' answers are an important part of informal assessments. Many of these reactions do not have counterparts in formal written tests. For example, a teacher can immediately summarize what a student said or ask the student to expand on a point. A teacher can use facial expressions to communicate satisfaction, ask for clarification, or discourage further response.

Kissock and Iyortsuun (1982) believe that listening is the principal tool that teachers have in reacting to students' responses. They propose two parts to effective listening. The first is understanding what a student has said. The second is knowing the feelings of the student who provided the response. Understanding the content of the response and accepting the student's feelings are both important to encouraging further participation by the student.

Kissock and Iyortsuun (1982) also list a number of ways in which a teacher can react to a student's response. Here is a sample from that list:

Acknowledge and reinforce a student's response by rephrasing the answer.

Clarify a student's answer by expanding it or comparing it to another student's answer.

Probe responses by asking for clarification, further evidence, or definitions.

Use nonverbal gestures instead of verbal reactions to encourage other students to respond to what has been said thus far.

Ask another student to evaluate a response.

Use a student's response as the basis for the next question.

Provide an overview of progress that was achieved through discussion.

RECORD KEEPING

The observations from most informal assessments are not documented. To be realistic, far more observations occur than could ever be recorded. There also is no need to record most observations, since information gained from the typical observation is used immediately. Informal observations and questions are used mostly for preliminary, formative, and diagnostic evaluations.

When an observation has unusual significance or when a particular performance is part of a list of important skills the student is expected to demonstrate, however, the details of observations do need to be retained. Thus, they must be documented. Details of observations that are not documented are not usually remembered beyond 1 hour. The basic techniques used to document observations are anecdotal records, checklists, and rating scales.

Anecdotal Records

Anecdotal records are often used to document a student's behavior for later reference by the teacher or by parents, counselors, and other teachers. An anecdotal record consists of a short narrative describing both a behavior and the context in which the behavior occurred. The record may also include an interpretation of that behavior and possibly a recommendation. Figure 11.3 illustrates an anecdotal record. Anecdotal records are often used to describe social adjustments. Unlike checklists and rating scales, anecdotal records are unstructured; therefore, they are particularly useful for describing unanticipated or unusual behaviors. Anecdotal records provide a

```
┌─────────────────────────────────────────────────────────────────┐
│                                                                   │
│   Student   Jimmy Watson                        Date  10/17/03    │
│                                                                   │
│   Observer   H. James                                             │
│                                                                   │
│   This behavior is  (TYPICAL)      ATYPICAL                       │
│   (circle one)                                                    │
│                                                                   │
│   Observation:  The class was asked to orally list causes of the  │
│   Civil War. Students were raising their hands to volunteer a     │
│   possible cause. Jimmy raised his hand. When called on, he       │
│   asked if a movie would be shown in class.                       │
│                                                                   │
│   Interpretation (optional):  Jimmy often becomes detached from   │
│   class activities. This has increased in frequency since the     │
│   beginning of the year and occurs about twice during a class     │
│   period. He does not seem to be trying to disrupt the class or   │
│   draw attention to himself. I presently have no explanation for  │
│   this behavior.                                                  │
│                                                                   │
│   Recommendation (optional):                                      │
│       None                                                        │
│                                                                   │
└─────────────────────────────────────────────────────────────────┘
```

Figure 11.3
Example of an anecdotal record

useful way to record significant observations that are not part of a formal assessment.

Because anecdotal records are unstructured, the following guidelines should be followed so that the record communicates information effectively:

1. The anecdotal record should objectively report specific and observed behaviors.

2. If interpretations of a behavior or recommendations are included in a record, they should be separated from the description of the student's performance.

3. Information contained in a record should be self-sufficient. Whoever reads it later will be unaware of circumstances surrounding the observation; therefore, pertinent information about what was happening just before and during the observation must be provided.

4. There should be a specific reason for writing an anecdotal record. The narrative should make that reason obvious to anyone reading it.

5. An anecdotal record may be read in isolation from other records. Therefore, the narrative should clearly indicate whether the observation represents a typical behavior and should state the nature of any trends relevant to the behavior.

6. Each anecdotal record should record one event pertinent to one student. Separate records should be prepared, if necessary, to describe the actions of more than one student.

Checklists and Rating Scales

A **checklist** is a list of actions or descriptions; a rater checks off items as the particular behavior or outcome is observed. In previous chapters checklists were used to list qualities sought in written test items. Checklists can be used in settings where the presence or absence of a series of conditions is to be established. They also help structure complex observations. For example, pilots use a preflight checklist to verify that an aircraft is ready for takeoff.

Separate copies of a checklist are usually prepared for each student. If the number of items included in the checklist is limited (usually five or fewer), observations of all students in the class can be recorded on a single checklist. For example, students' names might be listed vertically down the left side of the page, and characteristics to be checked listed as column headings. This format is particularly useful when observing the class as a whole rather than individual students.

Cartwright and Cartwright (1984) describe a variation of the checklist in which the frequencies of each student's behaviors are tallied rather than checked as present or absent. They call this variation a "participation chart." All students in the class, or at least a group of students, are listed on one chart. Because several students are being observed simultaneously, the number of behaviors being observed must be limited.

A *rating scale* is another technique for recording the frequency or degree to which a student exhibits a characteristic. Instead of checking for the presence or absence of a characteristic, the teacher uses a scale to describe the student. Such scales often use numbers, such as 1 to 5. Descriptions, for instance, ranging from "never" to "always," are associated with each number. Later chapters describe in some detail the construction and use of checklists and rating scales.

SUMMARY

The vast majority of classroom assessments involve informal observations and questions. These techniques are very efficient and adaptable. Meaningful preliminary, formative, and diagnostic evaluations cannot exist without this type of assessment. However, the technical quality of spontaneous observations and questions tends to be inferior to techniques associated with formal assessments. Informal assessments also tend to overestimate student achievement.

Our experience in using observations and questions in other settings provides a good base for understanding their characteristics when used in the classroom. From this experience, we recognize that many events can be observed quickly. Focusing our observation reduces the number of events that can be observed but increases the amount of detail that is examined. Current observations structure subsequent observations. Experience and confidence are both prerequisites to making efficient observations.

Because of their immense number, most events go unobserved. Many events in the classroom cannot be observed because they are invisible; that is, we cannot directly observe what another person knows or is thinking. Inferences must be made from behaviors that can be observed. Limited inferences are preferred over extended inferences. The use of multiple observations as well as careful selection of what is observed helps limit inferences. A useful strategy for formulating inferences is to form and then substantiate hypotheses that explain what has been observed.

Questions can greatly facilitate observations. Clarity of questions is important since students cannot observe what the teacher is thinking. Each student must perceive that his or her responses are being observed and used appropriately. Questions are obtrusive and tend to encourage maximum rather than typical performance.

Observations and questions should be devised at the same time that student activities are planned. Outlines and telegraphic notes are often sufficient. Instructional goals provide a useful base for this planning; however, capabilities implicit in each goal should be identified. The distinctions between declarative knowledge, procedural knowledge, and problem solving are important, as within all classroom assessments.

Informal assessments are usually not documented, and details of student performance are soon forgotten or distorted. This limitation is often not a concern since information gained through observation is typically used immediately. Information that is to be retained must be documented. Techniques used to record informal observations include anecdotal records, checklists, and rating scales.

ANSWERS: APPLY WHAT YOU ARE LEARNING

11.1. The ninth characteristic is most relevant to generalization: "Most events are not unobserved."

11.2. The second of the eight characteristics is most closely related to gathering criterion-related evidence of validity: "Subsequent observations substantiate or modify earlier observations."

11.3. 1. concept; 2. declarative knowledge; 3. rule.

11.4. 1. B. Gary's portfolio provides multiple observations, which likely involves less inference than simply observing the spelling of hippopotamus. 2. A. Knowing how to balance a checkbook involves knowledge of a rule rather than recall of information. The way to assess knowledge of a rule is to ask the student to demonstrate application of the rule with an example. That is what Jerome was doing when he described how his mother balances her checkbook. Stating the importance of balancing a checkbook involves recall of information. An extended inference is involved when the teacher infers that the student knows the rule simply because the student was able to recall information. 3. B. Ana is directly demonstrating her interest in astronomy by often reading about astronomy and also asking to do a report on Saturn. Having the large astronomical telescope at home may indicate that she or her parents have been interested in astronomy, possibly in the past. 4. A. Gretchen might have slept through the discussion for any of a variety of reasons. Less inference about her interest in history is involved when Gretchen is often observed to be inattentive during history lessons. 5. B. After asking just one student, a more extended inference is being made concerning students' knowledge that Tokyo is the capital of Japan.

SOMETHING TO TRY

• Think of some techniques that you have used to avoid being called on when you did not know the answer. This kind of avoidance procedure is common. What negative consequences do such procedures have on the teacher's ability to assess informally what each student (and the class as a whole) knows and does not know? What techniques can a teacher use to prevent these problems?

• Informal observations often depend on interactions with those being observed. This is necessary to keep the number of observations manageable. List some techniques that a teacher can use to get students to participate actively in the process of informal observations.

ADDITIONAL READING

Cartwright, C. A., & Cartwright, G. P. (1984). *Developing observation skills*. New York: McGraw-Hill. This book discusses principles of observing and recording student behaviors. Many examples are included. Ideas will be most useful to individuals working in special education and with early elementary students.

Cole, K. A. (1999). Walking around: Getting more from informal assessments. *Mathematics Teaching in the Middle School, 4,* 224–227. This article describes techniques some middle school math teachers used to document student progress through informal assessments.

Dillon, J. T. (1989). *The practice of questioning*. London: Routledge. This book provides a research-based discussion of questioning in a variety of settings, including the school classroom, clinical settings in medicine, and the courtroom.

Guerin, G. R., & Maier, A. S. (1983). *Informal assessment in education*. Palo Alto, CA: Mayfield Publishing. This book focuses on the use of day-to-day observations when evaluating students. Skill areas discussed include sensorimotor development, spelling, handwriting, reading, and arithmetic. Various rating forms are illustrated.

Kissock, C., & Iyortsuun, P. (1982). *A guide to questioning: Classroom procedures for teachers*. London: Macmillan Press. This book discusses and illustrates the use of informal questions within each of the six levels of Bloom's cognitive categories and the five levels of Krathwohl's affective categories.

12

Considerations When Using Performance Assessments

Written tests cannot meaningfully measure a number of important skills. Often this is simply because the particular skill does not involve writing, or the students being assessed are unable to write. Certainly written tests cannot measure how well a student can deliver a speech, focus a microscope, play a musical instrument, hold a pencil, or interact socially. Written tests also cannot measure students' ability to solve complex problems when highly diverse solutions to the problems are possible. A well-constructed written test presents students a problem *and* structures how students will resolve the problem. Skills that we have been calling *problem solving* in this book can be assessed only if the structure of the problem's solution is not fixed. For instance, to create a well-written, persuasive letter, two different individuals could and probably would combine different information, concepts, and rules to develop their arguments. The only effective way to measure a complex skill such as this is to give students a task that requires direct, yet flexible application of that skill. One might ask students to do the following:

> Write a letter that could be published in the newspaper about using tax money to support students attending private schools. Your letter should be written to persuade others to agree with your point of view.

This task provides direct observation of student performance and is called a **performance assessment.**

In recent years, considerable attention has been given to what is referred to as **authentic assessment.** All authentic assessments are performance assessments, but the inverse is not true. An authentic assessment involves a real application of a skill beyond its instructional context. In an interview, Shepard (cited in Kirst, 1991) stated that the term *authentic assessment* is intended to convey that the "assessment tasks themselves are real instances of extended criterion performances, rather than proxies or estimators of actual learning goals" (p. 21). Linn, Baker, and Dunbar (1991) describe authentic assessments as involving a "performance of tasks that are valued in their own right. In contrast, paper-and-pencil, multiple-choice tests derive their value primarily as indicators or correlates of other valued performances" (p. 15).

Writing a persuasive letter would be an authentic assessment in a language arts class. In a physics class, an authentic assessment might require students to, from their existing knowledge, create hypotheses that explain why binary stars orbit around each other at a particular rate. In a class concerned with educational measurement, an authentic assessment could involve the development of a classroom test, the creation of a performance assessment, or the interpretation of a score. In each of these cases, one is being asked to perform a real application of a skill outside its instructional context.

Portfolios (discussed in Chapter 14) are sometimes described as authentic assessments. For our purposes, we recognize that portfolios typically include the products of authentic assessments but often include other material, such as annotations written by the student or teacher, paper-and-pencil tests, and other items that help document student progress. We will not equate portfolios with authentic assessments. We will, however, use **performance** and **authentic assessment** interchangeably since our discussion of performance assessments will be limited to situations in which the content of the task that students are asked to perform is authentic.

Performance assessments are typically used in conjunction with written tests. Although performance assessments are needed to measure complex problem-solving skills, written tests tend to be more efficient at assessing the information, concepts, and rules that provide the fundamental knowledge for solving complex problems. For example, before a performance assessment asks students to create hypotheses about the behavior of binary stars, written tests can be used to establish students' knowledge of concepts and rules related to gravitation, mass, and centrifugal force.

Performance assessments have a variety of unique characteristics. For example, they can measure a process as well as products resulting from a process. They can occur in natural or structured settings. Most important, performance assessments can measure skills that written tests cannot. Performance assessments, however, have significant limitations. For instance, they are usually time-consuming to develop, administer, and score. Also, as with essay tests, subjectivity in scoring, unless controlled, results in substantial measurement error.

The next chapter describes how to create performance assessments. In this chapter, we will look at some important characteristics of performance assessments and discuss their implications. We will also describe three procedures for scoring performance assessments: checklists, rating scales, and scoring rubrics. We conclude by discussing some tasks that should precede creation of a performance assessment. This chapter helps you achieve three skills:

- Identify characteristics of performance assessments
- Recognize qualities desired in a performance assessment
- Recognize characteristics that checklists, rating scales, and scoring rubrics should have when used to score performance assessments

CHARACTERISTICS OF PERFORMANCE ASSESSMENTS

Specifying the characteristics of performance assessments depends in part on deciding exactly what a performance assessment is. The qualities associated with written formats such as multiple-choice and essay are more established. The nature of performance assessments is highly diverse and may include observation and evaluation of lab experiments, artwork, speaking, work habits, social interactions, and feelings about issues. For our purposes, a performance assessment will be limited to those situations that meet the following criteria:

1. *Specific* behaviors or outcomes of behaviors are to be observed.

2. It is possible to *judge the appropriateness* of students' actions or at least to identify whether one possible response is more appropriate than some alternative response.

3. The process or outcome cannot be effectively measured using a written test, because of the nature of the task or characteristics of the students.

Defining performance assessments in this manner narrows our focus. For example, determining whether an individual can swim is too global to be evaluated through a performance assessment; determining whether a person can use the breaststroke or can stay afloat without assistance for 5 minutes is specific and thus would represent a performance assessment. To take another example, determining whether a student is more likely to listen to jazz or rap would not be a performance assessment because one response is no more appropriate than another. Narrowing our focus in this way does not imply that observing general behaviors is inappropriate or that providing students with experiences for which there is no correct or preferred solution should be avoided. Our definition of performance assessments is restricted so as to focus on procedures other than written tests to which educational measurement principles can be readily applied.

Categories of Performance Assessments

Performance assessments can be categorized in several ways. This chapter contrasts performance assessments that measure a process versus a product, use simulated versus real settings, and depend on natural versus structured stimuli.

Process versus Product Measures. A *process* is the procedure that a student uses to complete a task. A *product* is a tangible outcome that may be the result of completing a process. For example, the way in which an individual uses woodworking tools to build a piece of furniture would be a process; the piece of furniture resulting from working with the tools would be the product. Generally, the focus of a performance assessment is on either the process or the product. For instance, the completed watercolor might be assessed, but not the student's technique in producing the painting.

Simulated versus Real Settings. Many performance assessments represent simulations because the real situations are unavailable, are too expensive or possibly too dangerous to use, or impractical for other reasons. Some simulations are so realistic that they unquestionably represent adequate substitutes for the real thing. Sophisticated flight simulators train and examine new pilots so thoroughly that the student pilots can safely pilot basic aircraft solo without prior in-flight experience.

Performance assessments in the classroom often depend on simulations. The realism of the simulation may represent an important quality of the performance assessment or may represent nothing more significant than superficial appearance. The need for realism must be judged in light of the reason for giving the assessment. For instance, if the principles that affect stock prices are being taught, a performance assessment need not have any consequences associated with students' investing wisely or poorly. Although the

assessment may seem more realistic and exciting if the exchange of money is simulated, doing so would have little benefit or might even hamper the teacher's ability to determine whether students know what factors influence stock prices. However, including information in the simulation about changes in interest rates and the price of bonds would represent important aspects of the assessment, because these significantly affect the price of stock.

Authentic assessments place considerable emphasis on realism, simulated or otherwise. As with any performance assessment, however, realism must go beyond appearances. Having an assessment look real is not sufficient to make an assessment authentic. The appearance of realism may not even be necessary. Instead, an authentic assessment must incorporate all conditions relevant to the realistic use of the assessed knowledge.

Natural versus Structured Stimuli. A stimulus is natural when it occurs without the intervention of the observer. For instance, a student's social skills are typically evaluated without prompts. In some situations, however, a stimulus may be structured to ensure that the behavior being evaluated occurs, or occurs in a particular setting. Examples of structured stimuli include asking a student to prepare and deliver a speech, perform a lab experiment, or read aloud.

Natural stimuli facilitate observation of typical performance, whereas *structured stimuli* tend to elicit maximum performance. Therefore, natural stimuli are preferred for assessing personality traits, work habits, and willingness to follow prescribed procedures such as safety rules. Structured stimuli are needed to determine how well a student can hold a pencil, write a paper, play a musical instrument, or perform other tasks.

Structuring the stimulus also ensures that the performance to be observed will occur. Observation time can be reduced by asking a student to do something rather than waiting for it to happen naturally. Structuring also helps determine whether the lack of a particular performance results because the student is avoiding a behavior in which he or she is not proficient or because the appropriate condition for eliciting that behavior has yet to occur.

Advantages of Performance Assessments

The most significant advantage of performance assessments is that they allow the evaluation of skills that cannot be assessed by written tests. As we have noted, many skills fall into this category simply because they rely heavily on motor skills; such skills are involved in speech, writing, foreign language, science labs, music, art, and sports. Other skills can be measured only by performance assessments because of constraints posed by written tests; specifically, what we refer to as problem solving. Solving a complex problem draws on previously learned declarative and procedural knowledge, and involves problem situations that can be solved in a variety of ways. A written test can measure students' understanding of grammar rules; however, a performance assessment must be used to determine whether students can incorporate these rules when writing. Parallel examples exist in every academic area. The development of problem-solving skills is often the ultimate justification of many subjects taught in school. Without performance assessments, proficiency with these skills generally cannot be evaluated.

A second basic advantage of performance assessments is their effect on instruction and learning. If, for example, you and I were learning grammar rules, the way in which we expect our grammar skills to be tested will probably influence what we learn. We will be motivated to learn the difference between the active voice and passive voice if we anticipate being asked to make this distinction on a written test. We will learn to write in the active voice if our writing performance is also going to be assessed. Furthermore, our teacher is more likely to teach us how to write in the active voice if the performance assessment is part of the lesson plan. Our teacher may also be more likely to use perfor-

mance assessments if the school district uses standardized tests that incorporate performance assessments to evaluate writing skills. The use of performance assessments can positively influence what is taught and learned.

A third advantage is that performance assessments can be used to evaluate the process as well as the product. Whereas written tests (and portfolio assessments) focus on the product that results from performing the task, the focus of a performance assessment is often on the process a student uses to get to that product. Examples include observing how students formulate a hypothesis or techniques they use in a science lab. Observing the process is particularly important in diagnostic evaluations. If a student is having difficulty solving a math problem, an effective way to diagnosis the problem is for the teacher to watch the student work through the problem. This activity is a performance assessment.

Limitations of Performance Assessments

One major limitation of performance assessments is the considerable amount of time they require to administer. Although written tests are usually administered simultaneously to an entire class, performance assessments often must be administered to one student or to small groups of students. This limitation makes it difficult to use performance assessments for measuring a substantial number of skills. Because administering performance assessments is time intensive, more efficient techniques, such as written tests, should be used when possible.

A second limitation of performance assessments is that the student responses often cannot be scored later. In particular, when a process rather than a product is being assessed, the observer has to score or record events as they happen. If a pertinent behavior goes unobserved, it goes unmeasured.

A third limitation pertains to scoring. Like that of essay tests, the scoring of performance assessments is susceptible to rater error. Bias, expectations, and inconsistent standards can easily cause teachers to interpret the same observation differently. As with essay tests, this problem can be controlled by developing a careful scoring plan.

A fourth limitation involves the inconsistencies in performance on alternative skills within the same domain. Will a student who can deliver a persuasive speech also be able to deliver an entertaining speech? Will a student who is able to create a demonstration of factors affecting electrical voltage also be able to demonstrate factors affecting amperage? Will an individual who can create a good short-answer test also be able to create a good essay test or a good performance assessment? Performance often does not generalize across alternative skills of a domain. The way to resolve this problem is to observe the student performing each task. However, doing so is often not possible because performance assessments are time-consuming to administer.

Performance Assessments in Standardized Tests

A standardized test is a test designed to be administered the same way even when administered by different individuals at different locations. Examples of standardized tests include many of the commercially developed aptitude and achievement tests as well as tests developed and mandated by states or school districts. Historically, standardized achievement tests used multiple-choice items or other written formats exclusively. Most standardized testing programs have now incorporated, or sometimes converted entirely to, performance assessments. As with many fundamental changes in education, using performance assessments with standardized tests brings significant good news and bad news. Let us look at some of the issues.

As with classroom assessments, standardized tests should include performance assessments because important skills in language, science, math, and other basic content areas cannot be assessed using other formats. A traditional written test cannot determine whether students can write

a letter to communicate a point of view, search the Internet for information, or use scientific procedures to compare physical properties of two compounds. Unless performance assessments are used, entire areas of the curriculum go unmeasured. Limiting standardized tests to traditional formats has important implications when these tests are used to certify student achievement or evaluate the effectiveness of instruction. As with classroom assessments, the content of standardized tests not only determines what we know about student achievement, but also influences the content of the curriculum itself.

The limitations of performance assessments also become particularly acute with standardized tests. Performance assessments are expensive to produce and to score. Unless the budget for standardized testing is increased, fewer skills can be assessed when performance assessments are used. In addition, the amount of time allocated to administering standardized tests is restricted. This time constraint, even more than the cost, limits the number of skills that can be assessed when performance assessments are used with standardized tests.

We have learned that limiting the amount of content sampled by a test raises an important question: Does that which we observed generalize to that which we were unable to observe? If the answer is "no," then conclusions we make about each student's achievement would be different had a similar but different sample of content been included in the test. Because the number of observations is so limited when performance assessments are used with standardized tests, this issue of generalization is significant.

Research has shown that generalization is a serious problem. For example, Um (1995) investigated a statewide writing assessment being piloted in Florida. She found that the performance assessment would have to be increased to an impractical length to obtain an acceptable level of generalizability. When Um changed her analysis from individual students to the school as a whole, the results improved, because conclusions about all students in a particular school are based on more observations than are conclusions about each individual student. You may recall that one of the most effective ways to improve reliability or generalizability is to base assessments on more observations. The implication of Um's study is that a standardized test cannot, with confidence, use a performance assessment to certify the writing ability of an individual student, but a standardized test can use a performance assessment format to establish writing performance for the school as a whole.

Similarly, Yen (1997) examined a performance assessment administered annually in Maryland to help evaluate school effectiveness. Performance in this assessment is reported for each of five content areas (math, science, reading, writing, and language usage) along with overall performance. As is common practice, school performance on this assessment was reported in terms of the percentage of students achieving above a cutoff previously established as an acceptable level. An important question is whether the performance observed on this assessment would generalize to a different sample of similar observations. Yen concluded that the enrollment in most elementary schools was too small to obtain the targeted precision for each of the five content areas. Sufficient precision was obtained when observations were combined across the five areas.

As with classroom tests, the performance assessment represents an important item format for standardized tests. Complex problem-solving skills cannot be measured effectively with other formats. Evidence, however, suggests that performance assessments within standardized tests do not generalize adequately unless a large number of observations is involved. Ways to obtain a sufficiently large number of observations include using the performance assessment to evaluate all students in a large school as a group rather than to evaluate individual students. When performance assessments are used to evaluate multiple content areas, it may be necessary to evaluate school performance on the test as a whole rather than for individual content areas. The frequent assessment that occurs within the classroom makes it more likely that teachers can adequately use performance assessments to evaluate the achievement of individual students.

OPTIONS FOR SCORING PERFORMANCE ASSESSMENTS

As with essay tests, performance assessments can be scored analytically or holistically. With analytical scoring, the appropriateness of a student's response is judged on each of a series of attributes. Checklists and rating scales are used with analytical scoring. The scoring of many performance assessments, however, cannot be broken into distinct attributes. Instead, an overall or holistic judgment is made. Scoring rubrics are used to facilitate holistic scoring.

Scoring amounts to making a summary statement concerning a student's performance. This summary may, but does not need to, involve numbers. Although numbers are convenient, the actual descriptions provided by the checklist, rating scale, or scoring rubric are generally more useful than numbers generated through the scoring process. However, numbers are particularly helpful when summative evaluations are involved, such as when grades are to be assigned. With formative evaluations, the completed checklist, rating scale, or scoring rubric provides a framework for providing feedback to students.

Anecdotal records, which are discussed in Chapter 11, can also be used to document a student's behavior and facilitate later feedback. Creating anecdotal records generally does not constitute scoring a performance assessment.

Checklists and Rating Scales

A **checklist** is a list of actions or descriptions; a participant or rater checks off items as the given behavior or outcome is observed. Checklists can be used in a variety of settings to establish the presence or absence of a series of conditions. They also help structure complex observations. We have noted that pilots use a preflight checklist to structure the complex observations that occur before takeoff. A checklist can similarly structure observations of a student within a performance assessment.

The checklist in Figure 12.1 is from part of an assessment of students learning to use a word processor. Students were provided both a disk and a printed copy of a short paper. Changes that the students were to make were handwritten on the paper copy. The checklist was used to observe each student's use of a word processor to make the required changes. Using a checklist is appropriate here because each attribute can be reported as satisfactory or unsatisfactory. Notice that an option is provided for recording an "unobserved."

Rating scales are similar to checklists, except they provide a scale or range of responses for each item. Figure 12.2 illustrates a series of rating scales. In this example, students are assigned a score between 1 and 5 on different qualities associated with delivering a speech.

Rating scales can assume a variety of forms. For instance, the scales in Figure 12.2 use words involving comparisons among students. Ratings such as "exceptional," "good," and "class standards" gain meaning through prior experience with other students. Instead of comparing students with each other, points on a rating scale can reference specific behaviors, as shown in Figure 12.3. The rating scales in Figure 12.2 allow for norm-referenced interpretation. The rating scale in Figure 12.3 provides a criterion-referenced interpretation because it establishes what the student does or does not do.

Rating scales also can differ on how ratings are recorded. For example, the scales in Figure 12.2 are marked by circling the appropriate number. In contrast, a mark can be placed anywhere within the range of the scale in Figure 12.4.

With any rating scale, words used to describe the meaning of various points on the scale should be carefully chosen so that they have the same meaning to different raters. The words must also describe only one dimension or characteristic per scale. Note that in the scale shown in Figure 12.5, two dimensions are addressed. This scale should be divided into two separate scales, one concerned with the adequacy of the sanding and the other with how well the wood was cleaned.

Each rating scale should have four to seven divisions. Words should define the scale at least at its two extremes. Preferably, intermediate points within the scale, the midpoint in particular, should also be defined. If the same descriptions are used for a series of scales, numbers can be associated with descriptions and then used throughout the scales, as in Figure 12.2.

There is a tendency for raters to use only a portion of each scale (for example, to rate more individuals as above average than as below average). This practice negates the usefulness of part of the scale and reduces the reliability of scores. To minimize this problem, verbal descriptions used throughout the full range of a scale should depict plausible behaviors or levels of performance that actually do occur among the students being observed.

Y = Yes
N = No
? = Unobserved

Y N ?   1. Uses ENTER key only at end of paragraphs

Y N ?   2. Uses FORMAT-PARAGRAPH options to control paragraph appearance, not tabs or extra keystrokes

Y N ?   3. Inserts new word within existing text

Y N ?   4. Inserts new paragraph within existing text

Y N ?   5. Uses highlight/drag to move existing word

Y N ?   6. Uses cut/paste to move existing word

Y N ?   7. Uses FIND feature to locate a phrase

Y N ?   8. Uses FIND/REPLACE to change a phrase

Figure 12.1
Partial checklist for scoring performance with a word-processing program

5 = Exceptional, is uncommon to achieve this level at this point
4 = Very good, is superior to what usually is achieved at this point
3 = Good, is typical to what is achieved at this point
2 = Acceptable, meets class standards
1 = Below class standards

1 2 3 4 5   OVERALL RATING

1 2 3 4 5   1. Establishes initial interest

1 2 3 4 5   2. Sustains interest

1 2 3 4 5   3. Organization

1 2 3 4 5   4. Persuasiveness

1 2 3 4 5   5. Dependency on notes

1 2 3 4 5   6. Enunciation

1 2 3 4 5   7. Grammar

1 2 3 4 5   8. Posture

1 2 3 4 5   9. Gestures

Figure 12.2
Illustration of a rating scale

| No further prompting required | Verbal prompting short of repeating assignment was required | Assignment had to be repeated once | Assignment had to be repeated twice | Assignment was not completed after being repeated twice |

Figure 12.3
A scale for rating the amount of additional prompting required before the student completed an assigned task

| Red | Pink | Brown |

Figure 12.4
A scale for rating the color of meat at the center of the steak

| Smoothly sanded and clean | Smoothly sanded but some dust remaining | Smoothly sanded but considerable dust remaining | Minor sanding required | Major sanding required |

Figure 12.5
A scale that is incorrectly constructed because it rates two distinct qualities

The efficiency of a checklist or rating scale has a major impact on how complex the performance assessment can be. The following characteristics improve efficiency:

- The fewest words possible should be used within each item of the checklist or rating scale. Similarly, the fewest words possible should be used to define points on a rating scale. Minimizing the words increases the speed with which the items can be read. Telegraphic phrases that represent incomplete sentences but clearly communicate ideas to the rater are appropriate. Using a redundant phrase in each item, such as "the student will," is inappropriate.

- Key nouns and verbs that indicate the essence of the quality being addressed should appear early within each item. This helps the practiced rater recognize each item within the checklist or rating scale simply by reading the first few words.

- Items should be grouped in the order in which they are likely to be rated. When evaluating a process, the order should correspond to the sequence in which behaviors are likely to be observed. When evaluating a product, items of similar content or various stages of the evaluation should be grouped together.

- All items should have the same polarity. For checklists, all items should describe either a desired quality or an undesired quality. For rating scales, the left end of scales should always describe either the most desired or the least desired performance.[1]

---

[1] In contrast, when developing opinion questionnaires, one should reverse the polarities of some items so that respondents will carefully read each question before answering. Unlike questionnaires, a checklist or rating scale is used repeatedly by the same observer. Once experienced, the observer does not read through items sequentially or in great detail. Reversing the polarity of some items slows down the experienced observer and increases the risk of marking the checklist incorrectly.

- The checklist or rating scale should be easy to mark. The rating scales, along with words used to define points on the scales, typically are listed vertically down the right side of the page. Any narrative used to describe what is being rated is located to the left of each scale.

It is often necessary to write comments on the checklist or rating scale to qualify ratings or to describe significant events. Writing comments on the back of the page slows down the rating process and may draw undesirable attention to the rating procedure. Designating a space for comments or simply using wide margins can solve this problem.

A numerical score for a student's performance can be obtained from a checklist by associating points with each item and then adding up the points associated with items for which the student received credit. With rating scales, a numerical score can be obtained by associating points with each scale, such as 1 through 5, and then summing these points across items. In many situations, such as discussing results with students, ratings on individual items are more informative than is a totaled score.

As illustrated in Figure 12.2, it is often useful to provide an overall or holistic rating in addition to ratings on more narrowly focused items. It is common to place the "overall" rating following the other items, although it is actually better to place such an item at the beginning. When placed at the end, overall ratings are heavily influenced by ratings on the preceding items. In essence it becomes an averaged or totaled rating, which if desired can be obtained by simply summing points across these items. If the overall rating is meant to be holistic, it is better to place it ahead of the other items.

Scoring Rubrics

Performance assessments sometimes must be scored holistically because it is not always possible to analyze performance into a series of separate attributes. Sometimes holistic scoring is used simply because it is faster than analytical scoring;

it is quicker to obtain an overall impression than to make a series of judgments. Scoring rubrics are often used when performance is being holistically scored.

The term **scoring rubric** is sometimes used to reference any scoring plan associated with performance assessments, including checklists and rating scales. In this book, scoring rubric refers specifically to complex and holistic descriptions of performance.

In a way, a scoring rubric is like a rating scale. It consists of a scale with descriptions of performance that range from higher to lower. Unlike a rating scale, though, a scoring rubric addresses several qualities simultaneously within the same scale. Often, only one scoring rubric is used to score a student's performance, whereas a series of rating scales is used to collectively describe the student's performance.

A restaurant uses a scoring rubric, in essence, to describe how meat can be cooked. In the series of descriptions shown in Figure 12.6, notice how the same set of variables—in this case, color and temperature—is present at each level of the rating. Each variable changes from lower to higher as the overall rating changes from one end of the continuum to the other. This use of the same set of variables across the full range of the continuum is a common characteristic of scoring rubrics.

With performance assessments, a scoring rubric provides a series of holistic descriptions of performance. The rater observes the student's performance and then assigns the student to the category that best describes her or his performance.

Figure 12.7 illustrates a rubric for scoring writing samples. Notice, again, that the same set of variables is used across the range of the continuum. When developing a scoring rubric, it is important first to list the variables that are to be judged and then to establish specific descriptions of these characteristics for each point along the continuum.

These characteristics should fit together at each point. That is, it is not sufficient for each variable to change from lower to higher across the continuum. Instead, the description of all variables should match what is typically seen in students performing at a particular level. For instance, in the previous rubric describing how meat is cooked, meat that is light pink in the center will also be expected to have a hot temperature in the center. In Figure 12.7, a student who uses ample supporting ideas or examples (listed in the highest category of the rubric) will typically use words precisely and exhibit few errors in spelling. A student who includes but does not develop supporting ideas (fourth category in the rubric) usually will also demonstrate an adequate but limited word choice and will misspell common words. If descriptions of variables at a particular point on the continuum represent a combination that is unlikely to be seen in students, the scoring rubric will be difficult to use and inconsistencies in scoring will increase.

Scoring rubrics make scoring of student performance more rapid than using a list of items within a checklist or a series of rating scales. A scoring rubric, however, tends to result in greater inconsistencies in scoring than occurs with a series of checklist items or rating scales. Lower consistency reduces the degree to which ratings of student performance will generalize. Therefore, scoring rubrics should be used for less-critical ratings of student performance or in

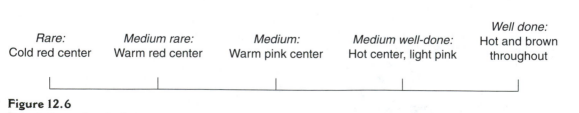

Figure 12.6
Descriptions of cooked meat

Writing is focused on the topic
Logical organization pattern
Ample supporting ideas or examples
Demonstrates sense of wholeness
Word choice is precise
Few errors in spelling
Various kinds of sentence structures used

Writing is focused on the topic
Organization pattern has some lapses
Supporting ideas or examples used
Demonstrates sense of wholeness
Word choice lacks some precision
Errors in spelling uncommon words
Various kinds of sentence structures used

Writing is generally focused on topic
Organizational pattern evident, with lapses
Occasional supporting idea or example
Demonstrates sense of wholeness
Word choice adequate
Errors in spelling mostly uncommon words
Different simple sentence structures used

Writing contains ideas extraneous to topic
Organization pattern attempted, with lapses
Supporting ideas not developed
May lack sense of wholeness
Word choice adequate but limited
Common words misspelled
Different simple sentence structures used

Writing slightly related to topic
Little evidence of organization pattern
Supporting ideas inadequate or illogical
Limited sense of wholeness
Word choice limited or immature
Common words frequently misspelled
Simple sentence structure used

Figure 12.7
Illustration of a rubric for scoring a writing sample

situations where performance must be scored holistically. When scoring rubrics are used in critical situations, consistency in scoring can be improved by averaging the scores assigned by two or more raters.

ACTIONS TO TAKE BEFORE CREATING A PERFORMANCE ASSESSMENT

The next chapter describes how to create performance assessments. Before beginning that discussion, it will be useful to identify other tasks that should be completed before the performance assessment is produced. Performance assessments are a very valuable tool. They can assess skills that other techniques cannot assess, and these skills tend to represent the ultimate goals of instruction. At the same time, performance assessments are our most expensive assessment tool. They should be implemented judiciously. Here are some strategies that can be useful in this regard.

Identify Authentic Tasks

Performance assessments should focus on authentic tasks. Here are the qualities that make a task authentic:

- The task is an actual performance outcome that students are to achieve through your class. The task is not a convenient substitute of that performance or an indirect indication that students have achieved that performance.

- The task requires students to draw on previously learned knowledge.

- The task clearly involves important themes and ideas associated with the content being taught.

- The task involves a real-world application of the content being taught.

This last point is often confusing. Involving real-world applications does not necessarily refer to activities in which students will directly participate later in life. Instead, real-world applications involve direct applications of knowledge that are highly relevant to situations outside the classroom. Authentic tasks in science, for instance, relate to real-world situations in which the science is applied or discussed. Likewise, authentic tasks in math relate to real-world situations in which mathematicians or other consumers of mathematics use math knowledge. This need for authenticity is highly relevant within both elementary and secondary school settings.

Identify Concise Goals That Will Be Assessed

Prior to creating a performance assessment, the goals to be assessed must be identified. Whereas a performance objective identifies the specific behavior, a goal is stated more broadly. Performance assessments normally are used to evaluate broader objectives or goals. An example of a performance objective is

Concept: Circles the sentence within a paragraph that expresses the main idea

An example of a goal is

Writes paragraphs in which the sentences develop each paragraph's main idea

Writes a paper that presents and supports a point of view

A performance objective should establish a behavior that can be directly observed, whereas a goal usually requires inference to judge the adequacy of a student's performance. A goal is often the equivalent of several objectives. Goals rather than performance objectives typically have to be used with performance assessments because the task cannot be meaningfully expressed as a series of specific behaviors. Alternatively, listing the full series of specific performances associated with the task may be impractical.

Nevertheless, to develop a performance assessment, a goal must be expressed in operational terms. The actual task to be performed may represent one of several options for operationally expressing the goal. The task that is selected must be a meaningful representation of the goal.

When constructing performance assessments, there is a temptation to increase realism by involving associated skills irrelevant to the goal being assessed. Including such skills, even when they increase realism, is equivalent to including irrelevant information in a written test item. This extraneous information tends to confuse students and, more important, confounds the assessment. When a student performs unsatisfactorily, the teacher cannot determine whether the student has yet to achieve the goal being assessed or simply is unable to work through the irrelevant material. When determining content to be included in a performance assessment, keep it free of irrelevant skills.

Determine Whether the Assessment Will Focus on Process or Product

As we have noted, a performance assessment is uniquely able to evaluate the process that a student uses as well as the product that results from completing the task. The process is particularly important for diagnostic evaluations when a teacher is trying to find out why a student is having difficulty. For some tasks, the way in which a student tackles the problem is more relevant to the instructional goal than is the specific solution the student derives.

Generally, the performance assessment focuses on either process or product, but not both. The particular focus affects the directions given to students and the plan you must devise to score students' responses.

Tell Students What Will Be Expected of Them

One advantage of performance assessments is that you usually can tell students exactly what is on the test. This cannot be done with a written test. With performance assessments, telling students what they will be asked to do, right down to the actual scoring criteria, is a very effective way of communicating instructional goals. (This also is an effective way to help assure that your instruction is consistent with your goals!) Telling students what they are to do also increases the likelihood that they will successfully perform the task. Given that performance assessments are time-consuming to administer, you can save yourself and your students considerable time by explaining what you expect them to accomplish. Performance assessments on which students have performed well are much more quickly scored than performance assessments with which students have had significant problems.

Determine That Students Have Mastered Prerequisite Skills

When used appropriately, performance assessments require students to integrate knowledge. Obviously, without knowledge of prerequisite information, concepts, and rules, students will not succeed with the performance assessment. Considerable time will be saved if prerequisite skills are identified and students' achievement of these skills is evaluated before the performance assessment is administered. Again, performance assessments on which students perform well are much more quickly scored.

SUMMARY

A performance assessment is the only way to measure many skills. A performance assessment is authentic when the performance to be observed consists of actual versus indirect indications that a student has achieved an instructional goal and involves a direct application of knowledge that is highly relevant to situations outside the classroom. Performance assessments can be used to evaluate a process or a product. They can assess behaviors resulting from natural or structured stimuli. Performance assessments are considerably more expensive than written tests to develop, administer, and score. They effectively communicate instructional goals to students, and can assess capabilities, including complex intellectual skills, that cannot be evaluated through written tests.

The generalizability of performance assessments tends to be lower than that of written tests. Students are more likely to perform differently had a different task been used to assess the same goal. Increasing the number of tasks that are observed is an effective way to improve generalizability. Therefore, observations from well-constructed performance assessments used by teachers are more likely to generalize than those obtained through standardized tests. For the same reason, performance assessments used within standardized tests lack sufficient generalizability when used to evaluate the achievement of individual students.

Checklists, rating scales, and scoring rubrics facilitate judging and recording observations from performance assessments. Checklists are appropriate when the process or product can be broken into components that are judged to be present or absent, or adequate or inadequate. A scoring rubric is used when performance is to be scored holistically. Performance assessments usually are scored more quickly with scoring rubrics, although the resulting scores tend to have lower reliability than when checklists or rating scales are used. Scoring procedures should be constructed to facilitate the efficient use of these scoring instruments. Checklists, rating scales, and performance assessments should be formatted so that brief comments can be quickly inserted during observations. Usually, qualitative scoring of performance assessments is preferable, although numerical scores can be derived when needed, such as for assigning letter grades.

SOMETHING TO TRY

• List three instructional goals for a class you might teach that would be assessed with a performance assessment. Using criteria provided in this chapter, do you believe the student performance used to assess each of these goals would be considered authentic? Why or why not?

• Figure 12.2 contains rating scales for assessing a speech. The ratings involve comparing a student's performance to that which is typical. In essence, the ratings are norm-referenced. Try to revise this rating scale so that it becomes criterion-referenced. Be sure to write each rating so that it addresses a single quality. (You may have to use more narrowly focused statements to accomplish this.)

ADDITIONAL READING

Flexer, R. J., & Gerstner, E. A. (1993). *Dilemmas and issues for teachers developing performance assessments in mathematics.* (CSE Technical Report 364). Los Angeles: University of California, National Center for Research on Evaluation, Standards, and Student Testing. This case study examines issues related to implementing alternative assessments in the classroom, including logistics, changes in teachers' instructional and assessment practices, and effects on student learning. Articles such as this report are available from the CRESST web site.

Messick, S. (1994). The interplay of evidence and consequences in the validation of performance assessments. *Educational Researcher, 23*(2), 13–23. This article provides a detailed discussion of validity issues related to performance assessments. Topics addressed include the need for targeting the underlying capability when designing an assessment rather than focusing on students' outward performance. The article also discusses the role of structured assessments such as objectively scored tests.

Shavelson, R. J., Baxter, G. P., & Pine, J. (1992). Performance assessments: Political rhetoric and measurement reality. *Educational Researcher, 21*(4), 22–27. This article summarizes research studies by the authors related to performance assessments. Issues addressed include factors affecting student performance on the assessments, reliability of scores, and correlation of scores on performance assessments with traditional written tests. Their research involved fifth- and sixth-grade students participating in a special hands-on science curriculum.

Solano-Flores, G., Shavelson, R. J., Ruiz-Primo, M. A., Schultz, S. E., & Wiley, E. W. (1997). *On the development and scoring of classification and observation science performance assessments*. (CSE Report 458.) Los Angeles: University of California, National Center for Research on Evaluation, Standards, and Student Testing/Center for the Study of Evaluation (Available online at *http://www.cse.ucla.edu/ CRESST/Reports/TECH458.pdf*). This report describes how to conceptualize hands-on performance assessments in science. The report also illustrates the problem performance assessments often have with generalizability across tasks; altering what students are asked to do changes which students perform well.

13

Creating Performance Assessments

The previous chapter discussed considerations when using performance assessments, including options for scoring results. This chapter uses this information to describe how to create performance assessments. This creation involves three basic steps. First, the capability to be assessed is established. Then, the performance students will use to demonstrate proficiency with the capability is determined. Finally, a plan for scoring students' performance is created.

We are going to use a *performance assessment specification* to guide the development of performance assessments. The elements of this specification are listed in Figure 13.1, and follow the three basic steps noted above. Our strategy in this chapter is to first talk through these three basic steps, applying our discussion to the development of an initial performance assessment. Later in the chapter we create the specification for some additional performance assessments.

Performance assessments can be used to measure any type of capability, although their cost requires us to use them judiciously. When a performance assessment is used to measure information, a concept, or a rule, we will call it a *single-task* performance assessment. Single-task performance assessments are easy to set up, although they usually require more time to administer than do their written-test counterparts. When problem solving is involved, we will call the assessment a *complex-task* performance assessment because the student is being asked to

apply a complex combination of information, concepts, and rules to solve the problem. Our first illustration involves the creation of a single-task performance assessment.

As we discuss the creation of performance assessments, it is useful to keep in mind considerations that should precede their development. As is true with instruction, our assessments of student performance must be goal driven. We also should limit performance assessments to tasks that are authentic, that is, these assessments should involve real-world applications of the content being taught. For each goal, we need to determine whether the focus of instruction and, likewise, the assessment is on the process or the resulting product. We need to establish for each goal what is expected of students, again to both guide instruction and provide the basis for designing and scoring the assessment. Because of the relatively high cost of performance assessments, we should identify prerequisite skills so that the teacher and students do not devote time to the present assessment without first establishing proficiency with other skills critical to the present task.

CAPABILITY TO BE ASSESSED

- *Goal to be assessed*
- *Type of capability involved*

PERFORMANCE TO BE OBSERVED

- *Domain of tasks associated with goal being assessed*
- *Description of task to be performed*
- *Focus on process or product?*
- *Prerequisite skills to be verified*
- *Required materials*
- *Guidelines for administration*
- *Instructions to students*

SCORING PLAN

Figure 13.1

Elements of a performance assessment specification

This chapter helps you achieve two skills:

- Recognize the three basic steps to producing a performance assessment
- Apply these steps to the creation of single-task and complex-task performance assessments

ESTABLISHING THE CAPABILITY TO BE ASSESSED

Specifying the capability to be assessed is the first and most fundamental step in creating a performance assessment. Throughout this book, a very deliberate distinction has been made between the student's *capability* and the student's *performance*. The capability is the student's knowledge that we would like to assess but cannot observe directly, because we cannot see what another person knows or is thinking. Instead, we must identify a performance that provides an *indication* of the student's knowledge.

A performance assessment is used to observe this performance systematically. The selection of the performance to be observed must be based on a clear awareness of the capability being assessed. Identifying that capability helps us determine the type of behavior we should observe and how broadly our observation must generalize. For instance, if we are trying to learn whether a student can find the meaning of an unknown word without the help of others, we might ask the student to look up a few words in a dictionary. However, we may want our observations to generalize to both paper and electronic dictionaries and possibly to other resources. We must clearly establish the capabilities we are trying to assess and use the performance assessment specification to control the content of our assessments.

With performance assessments, the capability is often expressed as a goal. Goals involve statements such as these:

1. Using commercial references, find the meaning of unknown words
2. Using Internet search engines, locate web sites containing information on a specified topic
3. Summarize the plot of a short story
4. Calculate the volume of an irregularly shaped object
5. Use ratios of area to solve common problems

As noted earlier, goals may incorporate several performance objectives. Goals generally do not identify the specific behavior that will be observed but often represent a summary statement or a title for the capability we are trying to assess.

When establishing the capability to be assessed, we must also identify the type of knowledge involved. We know that the basic types are declarative knowledge, procedural knowledge, and problem solving. In this book, the term *information* is used to reference declarative knowledge and the terms *discrimination, concept,* and *rule* are used to represent subtypes of procedural knowledge. Identifying the type of knowledge involved is important, because different types of student performance are used to indicate whether a particular type of capability has been learned.

Table 13.1 lists examples of each type of capability along with the type of performance that can be used to indicate achievement of these capabilities. In casual conversation, the term *problem solving* is often used broadly. For instance, when providing students some simple division problems, a teacher might use the phrase "I would like you to solve these problems." When discussing types of cognitive knowledge as we are doing here, "problem solving" involves *creating a solution to a problem that involves a goal for which a means for reaching that goal has yet to be identified.* In order to determine whether students can identify a means of reaching the goal, they must have the flexibility to use their choice of appropriate and previously learned information, concepts, and rules to solve the problem presented in the assessment. Only performance assessments are able to measure this type of problem solving. Written tests do not provide the required flexibility and therefore are not useful for this purpose. Written tests can, however, measure

Table 13.1

Techniques for assessing various capabilities

Capability	Examples of Goals	Performance Used to Assess Capability
Declarative Knowledge		
Information	Name the vowels within the alphabet	Ask students to state what they know
	Recall the plot of important short stories	
Procedural Knowledge		
Discrimination	When shown a series of letters, all the same except for one that is different, identifies the letter that is different	Ask students to identify the object that is different in some relevant but unspecified way
	When presented with a series of audio tones, all the same pitch except for one that is different, identifies the tone that is different	
Concept	Identify triangles among previously unseenobjects	Ask students to classify diverse and previously unused illustrations as examples versus non-examples of the concept
	Identify the statement of the plot within descriptions of previously untold short stories	
Rule	Using Internet search engines, locate web sites containing information on a specified topic	Provide students a relevant but previously unused example and ask them to apply the rule
	Correctly use *ei* and *ie* when spelling unknown words	
Problem Solving	Read and then summarize the plot of a previously unseen short story	Ask students to generate solutions to a relevant previously unused problem
	Calculate the volume of a previously unseenirregularly shaped object	

information, concepts, and rules and should be used instead of performance assessments whenever possible because of their efficiency.

As noted in Figure 13.2, our first performance assessment will be designed to assess this goal: "Using Internet search engines, locate web sites containing information on a specified topic." This goal is *not* an example of problem solving. Instead, it involves applying a *rule.* Once one learns how to use a search engine, that procedure can be reused again and again in new searches. (When a goal involves *problem solving,* the student has to create a means for reaching

that goal. Whenever the goal involves a *rule,* the application of the rule *is* the means for reaching the goal.)

Although written tests can measure procedural knowledge, performance assessments often have to be used instead because of the characteristics of students, or because of the characteristics of the skills being assessed. For example, written tests cannot be used to test young children or to test older students who have conditions that make written tests inappropriate. Likewise, many goals involving procedural knowledge require the use of performance assessments simply because the goal involves extensive motor skills. Examples include many skills learned in music, art, sports, science labs, speech, language acquisition and using an Internet search engine.

⬢ 13.1 Apply What You Are Learning

Which of the following skills must be evaluated using a performance assessment?

1. Identifying characteristics of different elements within a periodic table
2. Running the 40-yard dash
3. Writing a play
4. Communicating orally in Spanish
5. Determining how individual words are used in a sentence (identifying a noun, verb, or adjective)
6. Knowing what is meant by *tardy*

Answers can be found at the end of the chapter.

ESTABLISHING THE PERFORMANCE TO BE OBSERVED

The second major step in creating a performance assessment involves establishing the performance to be observed. As indicated in Figure 13.1, establishing this performance involves seven parts. We are going to illustrate how to apply each of these seven parts through the creation of our first performance assessment.

Domain of Tasks Associated with Goal Being Assessed

Typically, a number of different tasks can be used to assess a particular goal. For instance, with respect to knowing how to use Internet search engines, a student might be observed using any of a variety of different options such as Google and Yahoo! Or a student could be asked to search for web sites relevant to any of a number of topics, such as locating an online store for purchasing a particular product versus determining the local time in various cities around the word.

A very important question is whether performance on one task generalizes to another. If

the student is able to use Google, can one assume the student is equally proficient with using Yahoo!? If a student is able to use the search engine to locate web sites for online stores that sell a particular product, can one assume the student is equally proficient at finding a web site that provides the local time for various cities? If performance *does* generalize, there is no need to observe students performing every task. However, if how a student performs on one task *does not* generalize to performance on another, then a student must be observed performing each of the tasks, or one must limit the inference of what it is we know a student can or cannot do. Figure 13.2 briefly describes types of tasks associated with using an Internet search engine to locate web sites.

Research referenced in Chapter 5 suggests we should be very concerned with how well performance assessments generalize. For example, research suggests the students who can write good papers on one topic are different from the students who will write good papers were the topic to be changed. That is, writing ability often does not generalize when the writing prompt changes. Similarly, students who can correctly apply techniques of scientific inquiry to answer one research question are different from the students who will correctly apply scientific inquiry were the research question changed. Again, this is a critical issue because the results from a performance assessment often change if the specific behavior observed through the assessment is changed, even when both behaviors are legitimate indicators of students' achievement of the same instructional goal.

The ideal way to determine whether performance generalizes is to ask students to perform all tasks that are legitimate indicators of the goal, and establish whether the behavior on each task does or does not generalize to the other tasks. In a classroom, however, this empirical approach is impractical. Although not as good, a reasonable option for teachers is to list the tasks that are legitimate indicators of the goal, and from experience and professional judgment decide whether behaviors on these tasks will generalize. That is, judge whether

CAPABILITY TO BE ASSESSED

- *Goal to be assessed:* Using Internet search engines, locate web sites containing information on a specified topic
- *Type of capability involved:* Rule

PERFORMANCE TO BE OBSERVED

- *Domain of tasks associated with goal being assessed*

  Locate web sites using the various search engines, such as Google and Yahoo!

  Locate web sites relevant to different content areas, such as an online store that sells a specified product, or a site that provides the local time at various cities around the world

  Using information provided by the search engine, identify the subset of listed web sites that are likely to contain the sought-after information

  Recognize duplicate links (i.e., URLs that are associated with the same web site)

  Using links provided by the search engine, go to the subset of the listed web sites thought to contain sought-after information

- *Description of task to be performed:* Students will be asked to use the Google search engine to locate two web sites: (a) a site that provides the current time in Johannesburg, Madrid, New Delhi, Quebec, Tokyo, and Vancouver; (b) an online store that sells commonly available light bulbs at a discount

- *Focus on process or product?* Process

- *Prerequisite skills to be verified*

  Ability to right-click (or Control-click) on a link in order to open it as a new window

  Ability to read a URL, identifying when two somewhat different URLs are to the same site

- *Required materials*

  Computer, connected to Internet, Web browser open

  A paper listing the above cities, with space to write their current local times

- *Guidelines for administration*

  Once the Web browser is open, students are not to be provided information related to
  Using the computer or its software
  Using Google
  Interpreting information provided by Google

  While within a web site accessed through Google, help can be provided to the student with navigating within the web site, or with answers to any questions that pertain to content contained in the website

  The instructions to students can be repeated or paraphrased

- *Instructions to students*

  Ask the student to use Google to locate the best site that tells what time it presently is in each of the cities listed on the paper

  Then ask the student to use Google to locate an online site that has discounted prices on light bulbs

Figure 13.2   *(continued)*

Performance assessment specification related to using Internet search engines

---

SCORING PLAN

This checklist is used with both Google searches:

__ Opens Google successfully

__ Enters phrase or multiple words for search phrase

__ Use all words relevant to the search, (e.g., *local time in cities,* and *discount light bulbs*)

__ Uses right-click (or Control-click) to open linked site in a new window.

__ Clicks only on links to sites with descriptions relevant to search

__ Avoids opening alternate listings for same web site

__ Selects web site that contains searched-for information (i.e., local times for cities; discount price for light bulbs)

Figure 13.2
Continued

the students who perform well on one task will likely be the same students who perform well on the alternate tasks that could serve as indicators.

This is why our performance assessment specification includes the *Domain of tasks associated with the goal being assessed.* If it is judged that performance will generalize to all tasks in this domain, then the performance assessment created through the present specification will be assumed to be adequate. However, if it is judged that performance on the task included in the present performance assessment will not generalize to the other tasks that could have been used, then additional performance assessments should be created that utilize those tasks. Or alternately, one should more narrowly define the instructional goal that is being assessed.

Description of Task to Be Performed

In the last section (*Domain of tasks associated with goal being assessed*), we listed in abbreviated form the various tasks that could be used to assess the current instructional goal. Now we describe in greater detail the task that will actually be included within the present performance assessment.

In the specification we are developing in Figure 13.2, students will be asked to use the Google search engine to locate web sites contain-

ing information on two topics: (a) the current time in Johannesburg, Madrid, New Delhi, Quebec, Tokyo, and Vancouver; and (b) online stores that sell light bulbs at a discount. They will be asked to locate three good sites for each of these two topics.

With the task to be performed now described in greater detail, the teacher has to make an important judgment as to how well performance on this specific task would generalize to performance assessments that involve other tasks listed earlier in the specification. The teacher might conclude, for instance, that students' performance with the Google search engine *might not* generalize to other search engines, but then judge this as acceptable as long as students know how to use at least one of the major search engines. The teacher might also conclude that if students can use Google to find online stores that sell light bulbs at a discount, *and* also to find the local time for the six cities listed, the students should be successful at using Google to perform most any other typical search; these two searches are very different from each other, and involve searches on specific topics students probably have not conducted previously. Because the teacher is focusing on the *process* students' use, judgments can be made as to whether students selected the best sites provided by the Google search engine, and whether students avoid going to links that have near-identical URL addresses. If this teacher's reasoning makes sense, the teacher may conclude that performance on this performance assessment *will* generalize to other relevant tasks, at least as they relate to using the Google search engine.

When establishing the task to be performed, two issues have to be considered.

1. *Does this performance assessment present a task relevant to the instructional goal?* As with all tests, to be valid, a performance assessment must involve an appropriate behavior. This means that the student performance to be observed must correspond to the goal being assessed, including the type of capability represented by the goal. The performance assessment we are developing involves the use of an Internet search engine to locate relevant web sites. This goal involves procedural knowledge, specifically a rule. Table 13.1 indicates that to assess a rule, the student should be asked to apply the procedural rule to a relevant but previously unused example. In this case, students should be asked to find relevant web sites by using a search engine. In order for this task to represent a *new* example, the students should be asked to search for web sites containing information they had not previously been asked to seek.

2. *Are the number and nature of qualities to be observed at one time sufficiently limited to allow accurate assessment?* It is possible to assess too many qualities. This is more of a concern when the focus of the performance assessment is on the student's process rather than on the product. If an assessment is too comprehensive and the process being observed occurs rapidly, it may not be possible to judge all behaviors simultaneously.

One technique for observing a complex process is to score it at its conclusion. This procedure is used in some competitive sports, such as gymnastics and diving. When ratings are assigned at the conclusion of the performance, the duration of the observation must be short so that the rater can remember exactly what occurred. The number of qualities being observed is less critical when a product rather than a process is being scored.

Often, the complexity of assessments can increase as you become more proficient with the rating procedures. You should initially use performance assessments that measure few qualities. If a complicated assessment must be used, you often can improve your assessment skills by first rehearsing its administration.

Focus on Process or Product?

Typically a performance assessment is concerned with either the *process* used to complete the task, or the *product* that results from completing that task, but not both. If both process and product are observed, emphasis should be given to one or the other. When there is a preferred way to complete a task, the focus will be on the process. When the specific process used is of minimal concern, focus is on the product of the performance.

With the performance assessment we are presently creating, the focus is going to be on the process. Certainly we are interested in the product; that is, whether or not students can use the search engine to locate good web sites, but if we were to only look at the web sites the students ultimately selected, we would not know whether a student had made appropriate choices during the search process. For instance, did the student provide the search engine the best words with which to search? Did the student look beyond the first page of web sites the search engine listed? Among the sites listed by the search engine, did the student miss any that would have likely been more relevant than those that were chosen? Had these considerations not been relevant, the focus of our present performance assessment would be on the product rather than the process.

Prerequisite Skills to Be Verified

Performance assessments are relatively expensive to administer in terms of time and resources. Therefore, it is prudent to verify that students have achieved any skills that are prerequisite to the task being observed. Determining which prerequisite skills should be checked relies on a teacher's professional judgment. With the performance assessment we are presently developing, the teacher may be able to assume students can use the computer keyboard and can navigate the Web using a browser. But it may be inappropriate to assume students know how to right-click (or Control-click) to open links in a new window, or to determine whether two somewhat different URL addresses pertain to the same web address. These skills make using a Web search engine more efficient and are identified in Figure 13.2 as prerequisite skills to be verified.

Required Materials

The purpose of listing required materials is to think through what must be at hand before the performance assessment begins. As shown in Figure 13.2, these materials can be quickly identified through a list.

Guidelines for Administration

With a performance assessment, it is important to establish beforehand any conditions associated with its administration. Again, a teacher's professional judgment is critical as to what is to be included here. Types of questions to be addressed include prompts or other help that can be given students as they complete the assessment, conditions that must exist in the room, amount of time allowed for completing the task, and actions or other circumstances that nullify or stop the assessment. Only the important and non-obvious conditions need to be addressed.

Figure 13.2 lists the guidelines for our present performance assessment, and primarily identifies what assistance the student may and may not receive. However, none of the other questions raised in the prior paragraph was judged relevant, or at least it seemed obvious how the issues should be addressed. For instance, no time limit is to be applied, although it seems obvious that if a student clearly cannot proceed, the assessment will be stopped.

Instructions to Students

These instructions indicate what students will be told during the assessment. It sometimes may be useful to write out verbatim instructions, but that usually is not necessary as long as your guidelines are concise.

These instructions should cause a proficient student to meet all the qualities listed in the scoring criteria. Professional judgment is used to determine the adequacy of instructions. In Figure 13.2, the instructions indicate that students will use Google to first locate a web site that provides local times for various cities, and then use Google to locate an online store that sells light bulbs at a discount.

ESTABLISHING A PLAN FOR SCORING STUDENTS' PERFORMANCE

As illustrated in Figure 13.2, the third major step in creating a performance assessment is development of the scoring plan. The scoring plan may result in a numerical score, but often, particularly in classroom assessments, it produces a qualitative description of a student's performance. The scoring plan establishes what the teacher will observe within each student's performance.

The content of a scoring plan is heavily dependent on whether the process or product of a student's response is to be scored. As we noted earlier, the process should be scored if generally accepted procedures for completing the task have been taught and a student's departure from these procedures can be detected. In contrast, the product should be scored if a variety of procedures are appropriate, particular procedures have not been explicitly taught, or the use of appropriate procedures cannot be ascertained by watching the student's performance. With respect to the illustration in Figure 13.2, the *process* the student follows with the Internet search engine is observed.

This particular scoring plan uses a checklist, which is simpler and more widely used with classroom performance assessments than are rating scales.

Three issues should be considered when establishing a scoring plan.

1. *Is each quality to be measured directly observable?* A process or product can be measured only if it can be observed. When possible, qualities to be scored should be described so that no inference is required to determine that the quality being scored does in fact exist. Note that most of the descriptions given in the scoring criteria within Figure 13.2 are directly observable. One can determine, without inference, whether the student right-clicks on links to open them in a new window. Some inference is required, however, to determine whether the web sites that were selected contain the searched-for information.

🌑 13.2 Apply What You Are Learning

The following are descriptions used to judge the adequacy of student performance with various skills. The first five descriptions pertain to process assessments and the second five to product assessments. Within each group of five, three of the descriptions require inferences because the specified qualities are not directly observable. Therefore, those descriptions are less desirable as scoring criteria in a performance assessment. Which descriptions require an inference?

Process Assessments

1. The student demonstrates good sportsmanship.
2. The student uses fingertips to depress valves on the trumpet.
3. The student knows how to sand a piece of wood.
4. The student places a lighted match next to the burner before turning on the gas.
5. The student correctly views the needle on the voltage meter.

Product Assessments

1. The painted piece of wood is free of brush marks.
2. The chair is solidly constructed.
3. The steak is properly cooked.
4. The fingernails are free of dirt.
5. The student understands the directions.

Answers can be found at the end of the chapter.

2. *Does the scoring plan delineate essential qualities of a satisfactory performance?* The importance of this characteristic to a scoring plan is obvious. Particularly with complex performance assessments, it is easy to accidentally exclude some essential qualities in the scoring plan. A way to reduce this problem is to ask a colleague to look at your performance assessment and independently list important qualities to be scored or at least provide feedback to your scoring criteria.

3. *Will the scoring plan result in different observers assigning similar scores to a student's performance?* Once the desired characteristics of a performance are established, the scoring plan should result in independent observers giving consistent ratings to a particular performance. When the scoring plan involves directly observable qualities, different observers are more likely to assign similar scores.

ADDITIONAL EXAMPLES OF CREATING PERFORMANCE ASSESSMENTS

The preceding sections divided the creation of a performance assessment specification into three basic steps:

1. Establishing the capability to be assessed
2. Establishing the performance to be observed
3. Establishing procedures for scoring the performance

These three steps were illustrated with a performance assessment that involved using an Internet search engine. In this section, these three steps are used to create three single-task and one complex-task performance assessment. Recall that a *single-task* assessment is used to measure knowledge of information, concepts, and rules. A *complex-task* performance assessment involves the application of problem solving, where students create solutions to a problem that involves a goal for which a means of reaching that goal has yet to be identified.

Both single-task and complex-task performance assessments are formal assessments in that they are created before they are used. In contrast, the teacher's large number of informal assessments involves casual observations and oral questions. Although informal assessments are (or should be) systematically planned, they are improvised as instruction progresses. Many informal assessments are like informal versions of a performance assessment, in that they involve students performing tasks, and often are heavily dependent on motor skills.

When formal performance assessments are involved, the teacher generally has no choice but to carefully think through or even write out the full performance assessment specification. As illustrated in Figure 13.2, this includes listing a description of the performance, required materials, and guidelines for administration, along with the scoring plan. Particularly with complex-task performance assessments, there is too much involved to develop the performance assessment without written specifications.

With single-task assessments, these same specifications can often be devised mentally and not written out. Nonetheless, the teacher should probably formally state the goal to be assessed and prepare a formal, albeit brief, scoring plan. In the following examples of performance assessments, we will write out the entire specification to facilitate discussion.

Example 1: Knowing Tense of a Verb within a Sentence

Capability to Be Measured. As Figure 13.3 indicates, the goal to be measured by this performance assessment is identifying the tense of a verb within a sentence. The type of capability is a *concept* which, according to Table 13.1, can be assessed by asking students to classify various illustrations. (Notice that if students were instead asked to recall their own illustrations of verb tense, the performance assessment could be testing information rather than a concept. The choice of task that the performance assessment asks students to perform is always a critical decision.)

Performance to Be Observed. Knowledge of verb tense is an important communication skill within reading, writing, and speaking. It is also very broad in terms of its potential application. The instructional goal to be assessed, as stated in Figure 13.2, narrows the context down to identifying verb tense within a sentence that is written or spoken by another individual. Were the instructional goal stated in a less-narrow sense, the *domain of tasks associated with goal being assessed* would become a much more extensive list. For instance, were the goal stated more broadly, possible tasks would include rewriting paragraphs in a different tense, or listening to a story and determining whether past, present, or future events are being described. Of course, by making the goal narrower, we are explicitly recognizing that students' performance on this assessment does not generalize broadly.

Notice that the teacher will be reading the sentences from a set of cue cards. Given the number of factors to be considered, writing out sentences prior to the performance assessment will make its administration easier and more consistent with the specification.

In this performance assessment, the product rather than the process will be scored. The assessment is examining whether students recognize the appropriate tense, not the logic they apply to make their determination.

Scoring Plan. The scoring plan is very simple, consisting of a one-item checklist. For each sentence, the teacher simply determines whether the student identified the appropriate verb tense. This scoring plan appropriately involves a *directly observable* event; the student states the tense of the verb. As a result, different observers who are knowledgeable about verb tense will similarly score each student's performance.

This skill could also be assessed by a written test. After reading each sentence, the student would specify the verb tense. Short-answer,

CAPABILITY TO BE ASSESSED

- *Goal to be assessed:* Identifies tense of a verb within a sentence
- *Type of capability involved:* Concept

PERFORMANCE TO BE OBSERVED

- *Domain of tasks associated with goal being assessed*

    Classifies verbs as past, past perfect, present, future, or future perfect tense

    Identifies tense of verbs within printed and spoken sentences

    Identifies tense without the verb being explicitly identified

- *Description of task to be performed:* Student indicates whether the verb in the sentence is past, past perfect, present, future, or future perfect tense. Sentence does not include an infinitive or gerund. Sentence can involve past or future perfect tense. Sentence presented orally without visual cues. Verb within sentence identified to student

- *Focus on process or product?* Product

- *Prerequisite skills to be verified*

    Ability to differentiate between a verb and other parts of speech

- *Required materials*

    Cue cards for teacher from which sentences are read

- *Guidelines for administration*

    Administer 10 sentences in random order, two each representing past, past perfect, present, future, and future perfect tense

    Name but do not provide the meaning of the five verb tenses

    Sentences can be reread when necessary

- *Instructions to students*

    At the beginning of assessment, tell the student that you will read some sentences and ask the student to name the tense of the verb

    After reading each sentence, restate the verb and ask the student what tense it is

SCORING PLAN

    Student correctly identified the verb tense (Yes or No)

Figure 13.3
Performance assessment specification related to identifying tense of a verb

multiple-choice, or alternate-choice formats could be used. By orally stating the sentences, this performance assessment involves listening rather than reading skills. As with many single-task performance assessments, this one could be administered simultaneously to a number of students, with students writing their responses on paper rather than responding orally.

Example 2: Telling Time with a Clock

Capability to Be Assessed. Figure 13.4 provides the specification for this performance assessment. The goal being assessed is telling time using a clock. The capability is a rule, because the student can apply the same procedural knowledge to tell the time in each situation. Because the goal involves a rule, this

CAPABILITY TO BE ASSESSED

- *Goal to be assessed:* Establishes the time using a clock
- *Type of capability involved:* Rule

PERFORMANCE TO BE OBSERVED

- *Domain of tasks associated with goal being assessed*

    Tells time using a digital or analog clock

    With an analog clock, tells time with numbers or other markings on the face

    With digital or analog clocks, tells time with or without seconds indicated

    With digital or analog clocks, tells time with different shapes, sizes, and colors used for the clock face

- *Description of task to be performed:* Student views the face of an analog clock and states the displayed time
- *Focus on process or product?* Product
- *Prerequisite skills to be verified*

    The student can read numbers

- *Required materials*

    Clock face with movable hour and minute hands. The face should contain numbers to designate hours. The clock should not have a second hand.

- *Guidelines for administration*

    Use eight different time settings, two times with the minute hand within each of the quarter hours

    Vary the hour hand through its full range

    The minute and hour hands should be distinctly visible in all settings

- *Instructions to students*

    Say to the student, "What time does this clock show?"

SCORING PLAN

    Time stated by student is correct within 1 minute

Figure 13.4
Performance assessment specification related to telling time with a clock

capability should be assessed by providing students previously unused examples of time on a clock face and asking them to establish the time.

Performance to Be Observed. This performance assessment requires students to state the time displayed on a clock face. As the domain description in Figure 13.4 suggests, one has to learn how to tell time with very diverse clocks. As you rec-

ognize, there are digital and analog clocks; clocks including watches that involve widely different shapes, colors, and sizes; analog clocks that do and do not have numbers on their face, and so on. An important question is whether performance observed with one clock generalizes. For instance, if a student can read a digital clock, does that mean the student can also read an analog clock, and vice versa? Would the absence of numbers on the face of an analog clock change a student's performance?

In Figure 13.4, the description of the task and the list of required materials indicate the specific type of clock to be used in this performance assessment. If, for example, students are also expected to use digital clocks, a separate parallel performance assessment must be established for that task since performance with analog clocks probably will not generalize to performance with digital clocks. A teacher could use professional experience to decide whether a student's performance with analog clocks generalizes to clocks that also have a second hand, or that do not include numbers on the clock face. Or the teacher can more narrowly interpret performance related to the goal being assessed (for instance, limiting interpretation to performance with analog clocks with a particular type of face).

The specification calls for a physical clock with movable hands. Alternatively, clock faces drawn on cards should work. This particular performance assessment can be administered simultaneously to a group of students. If appropriate for the students, the assessment could be replaced with a written test in which students view the pictures of clock faces and indicate the displayed times.

In this performance assessment, the product rather than the process will be scored, because somewhat different but acceptable procedures can be used to derive time from the clock display. Correctness of each student's procedure is determined from the outcome or product of that procedure.

Scoring Plan. Figure 13.4 indicates that a one-item checklist is used to score a student's response. The scoring plan specifies that an answer within 1 minute of the displayed time be scored as correct.

Example 3: Getting Help by Phone in an Emergency

Capability to Be Assessed. This example (Figure 13.5) involves using the phone to get help in an emergency. This involves procedural knowledge, specifically a *rule* in which the learned procedure can be applied to a variety of related situations.

Performance to Be Observed. As indicated in the domain of tasks, there are a number of elements associated with placing an emergency call. These range from knowing when to use 9–1–1 or other emergency numbers, to accurately communicating critical information to the dispatcher. In this performance assessment, a student is only expected to quickly go to the phone and dial the appropriate number. Will performance on this task generalize to the actions that must occur within an emergency call? Will a student be able to recognize whether or not an emergency situation truly exists? To the extent that performance on this assessment does not generalize, other assessments may have to be created to evaluate the other skills associated with placing emergency calls.

Parts of the assessment might also be handled with written tests. For instance, a series of alternate-choice items often can be used to determine, for instance, that the student knows the emergency number is called if unexplained smoke is detected but is not called if there is a broken water pipe. As often is the case, the present performance assessment clearly has to be simulated; an actual emergency cannot be created nor can an actual dispatcher who handles emergencies be contacted. Experience does show that learning how to dial the emergency number fortunately does generalize to other aspects of getting help by phone in an emergency. Many young children have demonstrated this in numerous occasions, often better than adults.

With this performance assessment, the process rather than the product is scored. The emergency dispatcher is not actually contacted; therefore, the teacher is not focusing on the product. Students are being tested to determine whether they follow a specifically taught procedure.

Scoring Plan. Figure 13.5 shows the rating scales used to score students' performance. A checklist could have been used to indicate whether or not students adequately met the criteria. The rating scales allow the observer to specify the degree to which the criteria are met.

The rating scales in Figure 13.5 include numbers. The use of numbers is not necessary,

CAPABILITY TO BE ASSESSED

- *Goal to be assessed:* Uses the phone to get help in an emergency
- *Type of capability involved:* Rule

PERFORMANCE TO BE OBSERVED

- *Domain of tasks associated with goal being assessed*

    Distinguishes between situations for which the use of the emergency number is appropriate versus inappropriate

    Dials 9–1–1 (or other emergency number) in response to an emergency situation

    Is responsive to questions asked by the emergency dispatcher

    Accurately communicates information pertaining to the emergency

- *Description of task to be performed:* Student dials 9–1–1 on a phone in response to an emergency situation
- *Focus on process or product?* Process
- *Prerequisite skills to be verified*

    The student can distinguish between an emergency and non-emergency situation

    The student can state the appropriate emergency number (e.g., 9–1–1)

- *Required materials*

    A disconnected phone, similar to what the student has access to at home

- *Guidelines for administration*

    The assessment begins with the telephone clearly visible but approximately 10 feet away from the student

    Student is to be aware of the phone's presence

    Instructions are to be clearly stated to the student but not repeated

    No cues are to be provided

- *Instructions to students*

    Say to the student, "Using the phone in this room, show how you would call the police in an emergency. Do this right now."

SCORING PLAN

	Less than 5 second delay [2]	5 to 15 second delay [1]	More than 15 second delay [0]
How quickly does student go to the phone?			

	Before dialing [2]	During or after dialing [1]	Not at all [0]
When does student pick up handset?			

	Dials correct number quickly [2]	Dials correct number, but slowly [1]	Does not complete dialing correct number [0]
How efficiently does student dial emergency number?			

Figure 13.5

Performance assessment specification related to getting help by phone in an emergency although numbers can expedite recording the observed performance. As is often the case with performance assessments, performance on this particular assessment provides a criterion-referenced interpretation. (Recall that criterion-referenced interpretations indicate what a student can or cannot do.) Using numbers to score this assessment does not facilitate or detract from its being criterion-referenced. However, were the numbers recorded and the descriptions associated with the numbers removed, the numbers by themselves would not be interpretable, at least not in a criterion-referenced sense.

Example 4: Using Ratios of Area to Solve Common Problems

Capability to Be Assessed. The last example involves using ratios of area to solve common problems. To assess this skill, students might be asked to compute the area of a field to be planted with seed and, using directions provided with the seed, to determine how many packages of seed are needed to plant the entire field. Alternatively, students might be asked to use information provided on a paint can to determine how many cans are required to paint the interior walls of several rooms. In each case, students would not be told what quantity they need to calculate nor that a ratio must be determined in order to solve the problem.

In this example (Figure 13.6), students are asked to create a gauge for measuring rain to the nearest 0.1 inch. A problem with measuring rain is that high accuracy is usually required; in this case, within 0.1 inch. The solution to this problem is to collect rain using an object with a cross-section of relatively large area—in this case a funnel's large opening—and to let the rain flow into an object with a cross-section of relatively small area—a tall glass cylinder such as may be found in most chemistry labs. The ratio of the areas of the funnel and glass cylinder is used to calibrate the cylinder. For instance, if the top of the funnel has 10 times the area of a cross-section of the cylinder, then 1 inch of water in the cylin-

der corresponds to 0.1 inch of rain falling into the funnel.

Performance to Be Observed. The capability being measured here is an example of problem solving. That is, students are being provided a goal but not a means for reaching that goal. Problem solving is the one type of capability that only performance assessments can adequately measure. To demonstrate proficiency with solving the problem, the student must have flexibility with respect to applying previously learned information, concepts, and rules to solve the problem. With this and any problem-solving skill, two students relying on somewhat, or possibly quite, different knowledge may both derive perfect solutions to the problem. For instance, options for measuring area at the open end of a funnel include starting with a measure of the funnel's diameter or with a measure of its volume. Traditional written tests, including multiple choice and essay, do not provide students this flexibility. The structure that is inherent in well-constructed written tests should actually structure the solution to whatever task they present.

In this book, considerable importance has been given to matching the test item to the category of capability being measured. Had we asked students, for instance, to explain how they would construct a rain gauge, we would have been requiring students to recall declarative knowledge and state what they know. Such a test item would likely be measuring information rather than problem solving. Similarly, had we asked students to contrast the advantages of alternative ways of constructing a rain gauge, we again would have been asking students to declare what they know. Knowledge of information as well as concepts and rules is always essential, and likewise the assessment of these categories of knowledge is very important. However, the assessment of these categories with the exclusion of problem solving is a mistake. The assessment of capabilities involving problem solving requires the use of performance assessments in which students use previous knowledge to solve an authentic problem,

CAPABILITY TO BE ASSESSED

- *Goal to be assessed:* Uses ratios to solve common problems
- *Type of capability involved:* Problem solving

PERFORMANCE TO BE OBSERVED

- *Domain of tasks associated with goal being assessed*

  The focus of the domain is solving problems where the use of a ratio is critical to the problem's solution

  The need for using a ratio to solve the problem is to be deducted by the student

  Ratios can involve any physical measurements such as those associated with lengths, areas, volumes, weights, forces, and intensities

  Knowledge directly related to a measurement such as how one computes volume or the concept of pressure, although often prerequisite, is not part of the domain being assessed

- *Description of task to be performed:* The student creates a rain gauge using a funnel and a tall glass cylinder. The task is to calibrate the rain gauge. This involves establishing the cross-sectional area of both the cylinder and the top of the funnel, and using the ratio of their areas to place calibration marks on the cylinder so that rainfall can be measured.

- *Focus on process or product?* Process

- *Prerequisite skills to be verified*

  The student can derive area of a circle

  The student knows the concept of measured rainfall

- *Required materials*

  Twelve-inch ruler, funnel, tall and narrow non-graduated glass cylinder, hand calculator, paper, pencil, and transparent tape

- *Guidelines for administration*

  The required materials are to be placed on a table in front of the student such that it is obvious that all of the materials are part of the assessment.

  The teacher may answer questions not relevant to the goal being assessed. Other than the above information and the instructions that follow, no additional information is provided to the student.

  The teacher is not to indicate that solving the problem will involve the use of ratios.

- *Instructions to students*

  Use the funnel and glass cylinder to create a rain gauge

  The rain is to fall through the funnel and collect in the cylinder

  Calibrate your gauge so that it measures rainfall to the nearest 0.1 inch

  Mark your calibrations on the paper

Figure 13.6   *(continued)*

Performance assessment specification related to using ratios to solve common problems

SCORING PLAN

Area of cross-section of cylinder	Computed with major error (more than 50%, or not computed)	Computed with moderate error (20% to 50%)	Computed with minor error (10% to 20%)	Computed with no significant error (less than 10%)
Area of cross-section of top of funnel	Computed with major error (more than 50%, or not computed)	Computed with moderate error (20% to 50%)	Computed with minor error (10% to 20%)	Computed with no significant error (less than 10%)
Ratio of areas of funnel to cylinder, using whatever areas were computed[1]	Ratio is not computed	Ratio is computed with error that affects results by more than 10%	Ratio is computed with error that affects results by less than 10%	Ratio is computed with no error
Calibration of cylinder throughout the scale, using whatever ratio was computed[2]	Cylinder not calibrated	Measures differences in rainfall with less than 0.1 inch precision	Measures differences in rainfall with 0.1 inch precision	Measures absolute rainfall with 0.1 inch precision

[1]When computing ratios, use student's erroneous areas if errors were made in their computation.
[2]When calibrating cylinder, use student's erroneous ratio if error was made in its computation.

Figure 13.6
Continued

one for which the means for its solution has not yet been taught or identified.

As with any assessment, an important question is whether the observed performance will generalize to relevant performances that were not observed. The present performance assessment is trying to determine whether students can use ratios to solve common problems. Will our observations generalize? If students can satisfactorily use ratios of areas to calibrate a rain gauge, will they also be able to determine how much paint they should purchase to paint the interior walls of a house, or how much the throughput of cable modems would decrease if the number of users sharing the coax cable increased by some magnitude? Likewise, if we find that a student is unable to use ratios to calibrate the rain gauge, will this student also be unable to determine the required amount of paint

or reduction in modem throughput? We conceivably might answer this important question of generalizability by administering multiple assessments to assess students' ability to solve problems involving ratios, but would this be practical? Would we have sufficient time, given that other skills must also be assessed? The issue of generalizability is important, but it is also especially problematic with the assessment of problem solving.

Scoring Plan. Satisfactorily completing this particular performance assessment results in a product; specifically, a calibrated rain gauge. The focus of the scoring plan for this assessment, however, is on the process. Can the student use ratios of area to calibrate the rain gauge?

The scoring plan shown in Figure 13.6 indicates that four steps within the process are examined, beginning with computing the cross-section areas for the funnel and cylinder and concluding with the calibration of the glass cylinder. Arguably, the rating scales focus on the product at various points within a student's solution of the problem, as opposed to the process the student is using. The scoring plan does, however, attend to the process of using ratios of areas to create the rain gauge rather than focusing on characteristics of the completed rain gauge.

The scoring plan appropriately uses qualities that are directly observable. The plan also attempts to delineate qualities essential to a satisfactory performance. The rating does not dictate how cross-section areas of the funnel and glass cylinder will be computed, but does stipulate that the process of producing the rain gauge will involve a ratio of areas that is appropriately determined. Each rating scale addresses a single dimension. Each scale is constructed so that different observers would likely assign similar ratings to a student's performance.

SUMMARY

The creation and scoring of a performance assessment is divided into three basic steps. First, one establishes the capability to be assessed. Although the assessment requires observation of each student's performance, that performance only *indicates* the degree to which a student has achieved the targeted capability; we cannot directly observe knowledge. We use our understanding of the capability being measured to identify performances that will provide good indications of a student's knowledge.

The category of capability is also very important. We have used five categories. If the capability is declarative knowledge, we call the capability *information*. Procedural knowledge has been divided into three subcategories: *discriminations, concepts,* and *rules*. The remaining category is problem solving. Table 13.1 provides examples of instructional goals involving these five categories, along with types of performance that can be used to assess knowledge within each category.

The second step in developing a performance assessment is establishing the performance to be observed. This performance must be relevant to the capability being evaluated and must be practical in terms of the number and nature of qualities that must be scored. Conditions under which the performance will occur must be clear, and instructions to the student need to be concise and complete. A performance assessment *specification* helps guide the establishment of a performance that achieves these qualities. Specifications are illustrated in Figures 13.2 through 13.6.

The third step in developing a performance assessment is the creation of a scoring plan. This plan should involve qualities that are directly observable and that collectively represent the essential qualities of a satisfactory performance. The scoring plan should result in different observers' assigning similar scores to a student's performance. A scoring plan typically involves a checklist, rating scales, or a scoring rubric.

ANSWERS: APPLY WHAT YOU ARE LEARNING

13.1. Skills 2, 3, and 4 must be evaluated using a performance assessment. They cannot be assessed with written tests. Skill 2 requires a performance assessment because it is a motor skill. Communicating orally in Spanish (skill 4) is also dependent on motor skills that cannot be assessed in writing, but in addition involves problem-solving skills that rely on the use of numerous, previously learned concepts and rules; very diverse strategies or dialogues provide a correct response. Skill 3, writing a play, similarly represents problem solving and cannot be assessed with a written test. In contrast, skills 1, 5, and 6 can be evaluated using a written test. Skill 1 involves recall of information, skill 5 requires application of rules, and skill 6 pertains to a concept. With these skills, a written test should be used unless inappropriate for the abilities of the student.

13.2. Among the process descriptions, items 1, 3, and 5 require an inference about what is being observed. The following revisions represent improvements because they directly describe what is to be observed: *Item 1:* The student helps teammates score points. *Item 3:* The student sands the wood parallel to the grain. *Item 5:* The student views the voltage meter in a way that will eliminate parallax error. Among the product descriptions, items 2, 3, and 5 require inferences. Improvements to these items include the following: *Item 2:* The chair supports 500 pounds. *Item 3:* The steak is pink in the center. *Item 5:* The broom was placed (as directed) in the closet.

SOMETHING TO TRY

- Devise a performance assessment for assessing this instructional goal: Be able to determine the density of a solid object. (Density is defined here as an object's mass relative to water. An object with twice the mass of water would have a density of 2.0. Similarly, an object with half the mass of water would have a density of 0.5.) Using criteria given in this chapter, select an authentic task to assess achievement of this instructional goal.
- Prepare a performance assessment for a class you might teach. Use the specification format illustrated in Figures 13.2 through 13.6.

ADDITIONAL READING

Berk, R. A. (Ed.). (1986). *Performance assessment: Methods and applications.* Baltimore, MD: Johns Hopkins University Press. This book includes several chapters on the development and use of performance assessments. Specific chapters discuss listening, speaking, and writing assessments.

Cartwright, C. A., & Cartwright, G. P. (1984). *Developing observation skills* (2nd ed.). New York: McGraw-Hill. Chapters 2 through 4 include examples of checklists, rating scales, and other techniques for recording observations during performance assessments, particularly at elementary grade levels.

Fitzpatrick, R., & Morrison, E. J. (1971). Performance and product evaluation. In R. L. Thorndike (Ed.), *Educational measurement* (2nd ed., pp. 237–270). Washington, DC: American Council on Education. This chapter discusses the development and production of performance assessments. Examples are provided in a variety of content areas. Issues such as the reality of simulations, reliability, validity, and cost factors are addressed.

Zigmond, N., Vallecorsa, A., & Silverman, R. (1983). *Assessment for instructional planning in special education.* Upper Saddle River, NJ: Prentice Hall. This book presents a 12-step process for developing, administering, and interpreting an assessment of individual students. The process is then illustrated in the areas of reading skills, written expression, and mathematics.

14

Portfolios

In recent years, portfolios have become widely used in many elementary and secondary schools. In some classrooms, they have become the only procedure for formally assessing students.

The practice of developing a portfolio comes from professions such as architecture, advertising, art, photography, and journalism. In these professions, a person assembles a portfolio containing examples of work to be shown to prospective clients and employers, which generally includes the person's best work. The content of the portfolio, however, must also be responsive to the interests and needs of the client or employer.

A student's portfolio also contains samples of work. Within guidelines established by the teacher, the student typically selects the material to be included. As with professional portfolios, this material tends to represent the student's best work. Often, the material is placed in an expandable file folder that is maintained for each student. Electronic portfolios are another option. The portfolio becomes the basis on which the teacher and student collaboratively assess the student's achievement.

Many characteristics of portfolios match qualities often sought in education. For example, the preparation and evaluation of a portfolio emphasizes the performance of the *individual* student. A portfolio also focuses on the *accomplishments* of the student, with particular emphasis on the student's best work. The evaluation of a student's work is collaborative in that it involves both the student and teacher.

Some characteristics of student portfolios are fundamentally different from those of portfolios prepared for prospective clients or employers. For instance, professional portfolios are ultimately evaluated by clients and employers, not by the person who developed the portfolio; in the classroom, the teacher and student develop and evaluate the portfolio. The teacher and student must assume a fuller responsibility for determining the appropriateness of the portfolio's content and also for scoring the content. Validity and generalizability are crucial issues within this responsibility.

Professional and student portfolios also differ with respect to their roles. Professional portfolios emphasize summative evaluations, whereas student portfolios often emphasize formative evaluations. That is, with student portfolios, emphasis is given to determining what instruction should occur next. To play this formative role, student portfolios must be evaluated frequently and they must contain more detailed examples of work than are required for summative evaluations.

This chapter helps you achieve two skills related to student portfolios:

- Recognize characteristics of portfolios when used for student assessment
- Become familiar with procedures for designing portfolios

CHARACTERISTICS OF PORTFOLIOS

As with any assessment technique, the characteristics of student portfolios include both advantages and limitations. Some of these advantages and limitations are unique to portfolios. Because portfolios represent a relatively new approach to assessing students and because their popularity has grown rapidly in recent years, their use in the classroom is sometimes accepted without critical evaluation. Ignoring significant limitations then causes critics to reject portfolios as a useful tool for assessing students. As we review some of the main characteristics of portfolios, it is important to keep a balanced perspective. We will observe that portfolios represent a very useful assessment technique when their unique advantages are relevant to the teacher's instructional goals. However, their limitations must also be addressed. Because of these limitations, portfolios often must be supplemented with other formal, and certainly with many informal, assessments of student achievement. We will discuss the advantages and limitations of portfolios in the context of seven qualities.

Adaptable to Individualized Instructional Goals

Portfolios can be easily adapted to the instructional goals of individual students because each student prepares a separate portfolio, and the teacher reviews the portfolio with the individual student. Written tests and performance assessments, in contrast, are more difficult to individualize.

Written tests often involve a common set of items administered simultaneously to a group of students. Even when instruction is individually paced, a common or similar form of the written test is administered to each student. Sometimes written tests are adapted to individuals, such as tests administered by computer. Such adaptive tests, however, usually involve different subsets of test items common to all students.

Portfolios can be totally individualized. Each portfolio can be responsive to unique instructional goals established for the particular student. Individualizing portfolios usually pertains more to *how* rather than to *what* instructional goals are being assessed. For example, students who are learning writing skills typically share common instructional goals, although the specific level of performance each student is expected to achieve and the writings each student creates may vary widely. Portfolios can easily accommodate these differences, whereas other assessments, particularly objectively scored tests, often cannot.

Focus on Assessment of Products

A portfolio consists primarily of *products* representing samples of the student's work. The *process* used to create the product usually must be inferred. Obviously, products are relevant to instructional goals. In writing, for example, instructional goals include being able to produce essays, poems, letters, and other forms of communication. Products similarly are important outcomes in science, math, social studies, speech, and art—virtually all academic disciplines.

The process by which a product is achieved, however, is also important. Sometimes the process is more important than the product. The teacher and student, when they review the products contained in a portfolio, usually cannot directly view the procedures that were used to produce the products. Even when a portfolio includes earlier drafts or versions of a product, someone reviewing the materials must infer the processes that joined each stage in the development of the final product. Changes in the process that led to changes in the product are usually not directly observed from the samples of work included in the portfolio. Even when portfolios incorporate the products resulting from performance assessments, it is the products associated with the assessment and not observations of the student's process during the performance that is placed within the portfolio. Portfolios provide a more direct assessment of student products than of the processes leading up to the product.

A student's process can be assessed by a variety of alternative techniques. Informal observations and questions are particularly useful, although, as noted in Chapter 11, informal assessments also have significant limitations. For example, they usually lack documentation and overestimate student achievement. Performance assessments represent a useful formal assessment technique for observing a student's process. Written tests can also measure aspects of the process a student is using. If portfolios are the only formal technique used to assess students' work, the teacher must remember that most judgments concerning the process a student is using are based on inferences rather than on direct observations.

Identify Students' Strengths Rather Than Weaknesses

Many formal assessments focus on students' mistakes rather than on their accomplishments. For example, marks made by a teacher on a written test usually identify errors. When a teacher hands back a multiple-choice test, most of the discussion concerns the incorrect answers. Perhaps one reason students do not look forward to taking tests is that the focus of results is on bad news—it is natural to avoid punishment.

Standardized tests also emphasize negatives. When criterion-referenced interpretations are used, standardized tests tend to focus on identifying skills in which students are deficient. With norm-referenced interpretations, scoring below average is perceived as more significant than is scoring above average, even though half the students taking the test would be expected to perform below the middle or average score.

Portfolios, however, emphasize student strengths rather than weaknesses. Students are encouraged to submit examples of their best work. Within this context, discussion easily focuses on what has been accomplished. A student's deficiencies are addressed in terms of new goals rather than in terms of inadequacies in current performance. Students usually enjoy producing portfolios more than taking tests, and this form of assessment tends to be a positive and constructive aspect of learning.

Two additional points are relevant here. First, portfolios do not necessarily have a monopoly on positive experiences within assessments. Although it is natural to emphasize the positive when using portfolios, a teacher has, and can take advantage of, the numerous opportunities within all formal and informal assessments to emphasize what students have achieved. As with portfolios, this encouragement must be specific and sincere. The student must perceive that the encouragement is relevant to her or his performance. Important errors need to be addressed; however, their relevance can be demonstrated by using them to plan instruction rather than presenting them merely as deficiencies in students' performance.

The second point pertains to the need for portfolios to be sensitive to errors. When students present their best work, they will avoid products that demonstrate problems. For example, a student will avoid using sentence structures or discussing an aspect of history that he or she does not understand. Carefully constructed written tests and performance assessments require a student to demonstrate proficiency with important skills. The content of a portfolio has to be similarly structured so that problems that a student is experiencing become apparent.

Actively Involve Students in the Evaluation Process

In professions that use portfolios, it is common for a teacher or mentor to help the student develop the portfolio. For example, the mentor of an aspiring artist, collaboratively with the student, will identify what the portfolio must contain and provide advice in selecting specific samples of work. Ultimately, however, the portfolio belongs to the student. It is evidence for prospective clients and employers of what the student—and not the mentor—can do. The aspiring artist must therefore be actively involved in the evaluation of products included in the portfolio.

A parallel situation exists when portfolios are used within the classroom. Student ownership is important to the process. The teacher provides guidelines and, in collaboration with the student, identifies goals to be met and the types of samples the portfolio will contain. The student is responsible for actually selecting the materials for inclusion. The teacher then helps the student evaluate the materials that are included.

Since the student owns the portfolio, the student as well as the teacher has continuous access to it, although physical portfolios (versus Web-based electronic portfolios) typically remain in the classroom. The student can show the portfolio to other students or to whomever he or she chooses. This approach to documenting student achievement contrasts noticeably with that of a teacher maintaining a private grade book. The assessment process is more student centered and less teacher centered.

Communicate Student Achievement to Others

The purpose of professional portfolios is to communicate to others what a person can do. It is natural for prospective clients or employers to ask an individual for her or his portfolio, that is, for examples of previous work.

In a similar manner, student portfolios provide teachers with a useful framework for discussing students' progress with parents, counselors, and administrators. A student's portfolio contains examples of what the student is able to do. A portfolio is generally a more effective reference for discussing the student's progress than are examples of written quizzes and exams or scores on standardized tests.

As discussed later in this chapter, a student portfolio also contains a list of goals toward which the student is working; captions, such as notes provided by the student explaining the reason for including particular work in the portfolio; and evaluative comments by the student and teacher. All these elements can facilitate communication of the student's achievement to others.

The student can also use a portfolio to show others what he or she has achieved. Hebert (1992), principal of the Crow Island Elementary School in Winnetka, Illinois, describes how this is done each spring through a Portfolio Evening, when students discuss their portfolios with their parents. Prior to the evening, students review their portfolios, guided by questions such as

How has your writing changed since last September?

What do you know about numbers that you did not know in September?

What do you want to tell your parents about your portfolio?

How should you organize your portfolio to show your parents these things?

On the given evening, for about an hour, students sit individually with their parents and use the portfolio to describe what they have learned. The teacher circulates and highlights particularly important information for the parents.

Time Intensive

The *preparation* of a portfolio generally does not involve much additional time, since most of the material included in a portfolio would be prepared anyway. The *periodic joint reviews* of the portfolio are what can make the use of portfolios time intensive. At scheduled intervals, the teacher and student review the portfolio. Typically, the teacher first examines a portfolio alone, then meets with the student to discuss the portfolio. Although time estimates vary, a common practice is to take about 30 minutes for the initial review and an additional 30 minutes to meet with the student. Therefore, approximately an hour per student is required each time portfolios are reviewed.

There are different views concerning the significant amount of time involved in this type of assessment. For example, in their book about the use of portfolio assessment in the teaching of reading and writing, Tierney, Carter, and Desal (1991) suggest that after a transitional period, the use of portfolios requires no additional time. They propose the use of portfolios ". . . involves a refocusing. Instead of doing a lot of group things or working out of a particular textbook or workbook, time can be allotted differently so that teachers are using that time to work with individuals, conferencing with individuals; maybe working with some small groups. It's a question of setting priorities differently and using the classroom time differently, more than it is taking more time" (pp. 7–8).

Moss and colleagues (1992) suggest that the use of portfolios "will clearly add to teachers' workloads. . . . Schools and districts interested in fostering the professionalization of teaching in this and other ways must seriously rethink the way teachers' workloads are structured. Disciplined inquiry and collaboration, both of which are essential to professional practice, require time" (pp. 19–20).

The amount of time associated with the use of portfolios depends largely on how often the teacher formally reviews portfolios with each student. At the elementary school level, it is reasonable to expect a total of 20 to 30 hours for each of these reviews. The amount of time would typically be greater at the secondary school level because of the nature of the content and the larger number of students. Teachers generally review portfolios individually with students every 4 to 6 weeks.

Frequent reviews of portfolios are preferable. A primary role of student portfolios—which is not a role of professional portfolios—is to determine what, in terms of instruction, should occur next. If this formative role is to be emphasized, 4 to 6 weeks between reviews represents an excessive time interval. If portfolios constitute the only formal assessment a teacher is using, reviews need to occur much more frequently, although that may be impractical. If, however, portfolios are used for general planning, and other assessments are used for more detailed planning, a 4- to 6-week interval between portfolio reviews may be appropriate.

Generalizability

As with any educational measure, generalizability is important to portfolio assessments. Judgments of student achievement should be reasonably consistent if different teachers assess a student's work, or if different examples of work are included in the portfolio.

When portfolios are used to assess a student's writing skills, the student is usually responsible for selecting the samples of writing to be included in the portfolio. Typically, work is selected from among a number of papers. The teacher's judgment of that student's writing skills *should* not be affected by the particular sample of papers the student happened to select; otherwise, the teacher's judgment is being influenced by characteristics of the specific writing sample rather than by the student's proficiency with writing skills. Similarly, if two teachers agree on the criteria for scoring writing skills, they should assign the same scores to an individual student's portfolio; if they do not, it would suggest that characteristics of the teachers, separate from the student's writing skills, are influencing the judgment of each student's achievement. Similar illustrations can be drawn from any content area.

Little is known about how well judgments derived from portfolios generalize, particularly within the context of the classroom. Other formal assessments, including written tests and even performance assessments, also have a longer history within both classroom assessments and standardized testing programs.

The Rand Corporation (Koretz, McCaffrey, Klein, Bell, & Stecher, 1992) studied the generalizability of portfolios used in a large assessment program. Their study involved a statewide program in Vermont that used portfolios to assess writing and math skills at the fourth- and eighth-grade levels. Results of the study raised some important concerns. Average reliability coefficients ranged from 0.33 to 0.43. (Reliability coefficients range from zero to one, with 1.00 indicating perfect reliability.) In contrast, standardized performance assessments involving writing samples tend to have reliabilities greater than 0.70. Conventional standardized achievement tests usually have reliabilities near 0.90. These low portfolio reliabilities are of concern because, if the reliability coefficient is below 0.50, the performance of an individual student cannot be differentiated from the overall average performance of students (Kane, 1986).

The reliability of scores on a classroom assessment tends to be lower than that of scores on standardized assessments, largely because of the high amount of effort associated with developing and scoring standardized assessments.

For example, in the Vermont assessment program, scoring criteria were established through extended discussions, and teachers involved with scoring the portfolios were given special training. This level of preparation generally does not occur with classroom-level assessments.

Moss and other researchers (1992) examined the writing portfolios of 10 high school students, which were being used for classroom assessments. As with the Vermont study, inter-rater reliabilities were very low. In their discussion of these low reliabilities, however, Moss and others pointed out that the use of independent raters to establish the reliability of portfolio scores might be inappropriate. With classroom assessments, the teacher, who generally has extensive knowledge about each student, scores portfolios. Unlike independent scorers, the teacher can use this knowledge to augment the scoring process. This, in turn, may improve the consistency of ratings across different samples of work, or conceivably across ratings by different teachers assuming these other teachers were similarly familiar with each student.

Knowledge about the consistency of portfolio ratings is very limited. Current evidence indicates that the generalizability of ratings may be low. Therefore, we need to be cautious when using portfolios to assess the achievement of individual students, particularly if the portfolios serve as the teacher's only formal assessment of student achievement.

DESIGNING STUDENT PORTFOLIOS

To some extent, the content of portfolios can be thought of as a series of performance assessments. In this sense, the procedures for producing a performance assessment apply to designing portfolios; thus, the design of student portfolios can build on procedures already discussed. Portfolios, however, allow students to choose the products upon which they will be evaluated. Portfolios also go beyond assessing students. They represent an instructional system and integrate student assessment into student learning. Because of this broader role, the design of portfolios depends heavily on how they are to be used.

Establish How the Portfolio Will Be Used

Because of the popularity of portfolios, it is fairly common to start placing student work into folders with the intent of implementing a portfolio system, but without really knowing what is to be done with all the material. This practice plays into one of the major weaknesses of portfolios: the substantial amount of time required for teachers to review portfolio contents. By first establishing how the portfolio will be used, one can restrict its contents to what is relevant and design its structure to facilitate its intended use.

A student's portfolio is potentially used for any of a variety of purposes. The more common purposes include the following:

- Growth monitoring, in which portfolio content is used to document student *progress* toward goals or improvements in proficiency

- Skill certification, in which the portfolio is used to establish which instructional goals the student has adequately accomplished

- Evidence of best work, in which the portfolio contains a student's exemplary work and presents the highest level of proficiency the student has achieved with each goal

- External assessment, in which the portfolio is used to establish student proficiency by agencies outside the classroom, such as the school, school district, or a state agency

- Communication with parents, in which a portfolio is taken home or maintained at home to convey how the child is performing at school

The purpose of a portfolio should significantly affect its contents. For example, a portfolio used to monitor growth requires examples of work over time that substantiate growth toward various goals. A portfolio used for skill certification, in contrast, requires only work samples that establish the status with each goal. Prior work can be located elsewhere. A portfolio used to illustrate a student's best work also will contain only samples of work related to each goal.

When the purpose is clear, the content of a portfolio largely establishes itself. Designing a portfolio is much like planning for a meeting. When scheduling a meeting with another person, the purpose of that meeting dictates your preparation, including the supporting materials you bring along. You will be less effective in meetings when the purpose is unclear and you come unprepared. The contents of a portfolio are supporting materials that will be used in your meeting or interaction with the student. Those materials will not be useful unless their content is driven (and limited) by how they will be used in that meeting.

The purpose and content of portfolios used for external assessments is largely driven by the agency dictating their use. Particularly when the agency is the school or even the school district, the characteristics of the portfolio can be designed with local teacher input or negotiation. The content of portfolios used with external assessments has to be limited; however, a clear understanding of how the portfolios will be used is central to establishing the usefulness of their contents.

The content of portfolios used to communicate with parents also must be limited. Parents are not involved in the day-to-day happenings in the classroom and will be overwhelmed unless portfolio content is restricted. Again, the purpose must drive the content. Generally the purpose is to show the student's progress with particularly important skills. The portfolio may also guide parents into actions that help the child achieve particular goals. Parents' ability to understand the relevance of the student's work to a particular instructional goal strongly influences how parents will use information provided through the portfolio.

The portfolio is not simply a place to put students' work. It is an integral part of instruction that is used to facilitate assessment. The portfolio is most commonly used to prepare for meetings between the student and teacher. A clear understanding of how the portfolio is to be used should drive its design and contents. A separate binder, or working portfolio, might be used for collecting all work, with appropriate samples of that work placed in the portfolio reviewed by the teacher, parent, or others. Some samples of work may be moved from one portfolio to another, as needs dictate. However, the clear understanding of each portfolio's use must control its content.

Center the Content of Portfolios on Instructional Goals

The instructional goals to be assessed constitute the second major factor driving portfolio design. The list of goals provides the framework for selecting and evaluating work samples. This list of goals specifies what the student is striving to achieve and indicates which skills the student should try to document through the portfolio. Similarly, the list of goals guides the teacher's and student's evaluation of the portfolio.

As discussed in previous chapters, goals are broader than performance objectives. A performance objective specifies the specific *behavior* that indicates that the student has obtained the capability being assessed. For instance, here is a performance objective:

> *Rule:* Given the relative location of adjacent centers of low and high pressure in Earth's atmosphere, indicate the direction of the wind between these two centers.

Goals are stated more generally than objectives. An example of a goal would be

> Understand the relation between atmospheric pressure and airflow

Valencia (1990) names the following as examples of goals in reading:

> Understanding the author's message
> Learning new information from expository texts
> Summarizing the plot of a story
> Using word identification skills flexibly to construct meaning

Reading fluently

Exhibiting an interest and desire to read

A goal is often the equivalent of several objectives. Inferences are required to assess whether a student has achieved a goal. As with performance assessments, instructional goals rather than performance objectives are normally used with portfolios, in part because of the complexity of skills being assessed. Goals also are used with portfolios and performance assessments because they often provide a simpler and more manageable framework.

Within a portfolio, the list of goals should be placed in a prominent place, usually at the front, so that the student and teacher see them each time the portfolio is opened. *The goals must provide the basis for including each entry and all assessments*. To help focus attention, the list of goals can also be used as a log. Students can be asked to document in a space next to the relevant goal each sample of work they insert into the portfolio.

Translate Instructional Goals into Student Performance

As with written tests and performance assessments, portfolios *do not* directly measure student knowledge, but use student behaviors as an *indication* of what students know. Throughout this book, *capability* is used to represent the knowledge we are trying to assess. We cannot see this capability because we cannot see what another person knows or is thinking. Therefore, we depend on a student's *performance* to provide an indication of the student's capability.

We also realize that there are different types of capabilities. Depending on the type of capability involved, different types of performance are particularly effective for assessing student knowledge. Psychologists organize knowledge and skills into three basic types: declarative knowledge, procedural knowledge, and problem solving. In this book we have referred to declarative knowledge as *information,* and subdivide procedural knowledge into *discriminations, concepts,* and *rules*. Table 14.1 summarizes the types of performance we typically use to provide an indication of each type of knowledge. (Table 13.1 provides parallel illustrations in the previous chapter.)

Although effectively used portfolios are an integral part of instruction and go beyond strictly assessing knowledge, the assessment components of portfolios can typically be thought of as a series of performance assessments. Our discussion concerning the design of performance assessments thus has direct relevance to the design of portfolios. In that discussion, the creation of a performance assessment was divided into three basic steps:

1. Establishing the capability to be assessed

2. Establishing the performance to be observed

3. Establishing procedures for scoring the performance

With portfolios and performance assessments, instructional goals must be examined in terms of the capabilities they represent. The nature of the capability must drive the type of performance used to assess students' knowledge. The products included in a portfolio are the outcomes of that performance. A scoring procedure must be established for each product. A checklist, rating scales, or a scoring rubric is commonly used to guide the scoring process.

Figure 14.1 illustrates a checklist used in a portfolio to score expository writing. This checklist is part of a cover sheet that accompanies each student's paper. Because expository writing is a complex activity we refer to as *problem solving,* it is measured by asking students to generate solutions to the problem that requires use of previously learned information, concepts, and rules. In this case, students are asked to generate an expository essay. As with the assessment of all problem solving skills, students must be given flexibility in how they create this essay. As illustrated in Figure 14.1, the scoring plan references the characteristics that should be present within the essay, or whatever product students are expected to produce. As with

Table 14.1

Techniques for assessing various capabilities

Capability	Examples of Goals	Performance Used to Assess Capability
Declarative Knowledge		
Information	Describe the purpose of a science experiment	Ask students to state what they know
Procedural Knowledge		
Discrimination	When shown four pictures of a small animal, three of the pictures identical and the fourth different in a certain way, select the picture of an animal that is different	Ask students to identify the object that is different in some relevant but unspecified way
Concept	Circle words within a paragraph that function as verbs	Ask students to classify diverse and previously unused illustrations as examples versus non-examples of the concept
Rule	Use the Web to find the address and phone number of a business	Provide students a relevant but previously unused example and ask them to apply the rule
Problem Solving	Write an expository essay	Ask students to generate solutions to a relevant previously unused problem

performance assessments, portfolios can assess students' knowledge of information, concepts, and rules as well as complex skills.

Plan the Student into the Assessment Process

A major advantage of portfolios is that they actively involve students in the assessment process. Portfolios should be designed with this in mind.

The checklist within Figure 14.1 includes a place for students to assess their own performance. As with performance assessments, students are typically given the scoring plan prior to the assessment. With portfolios, the scoring plan helps guide the learning process and also allows students to assess their own knowledge. A problem with self-assessment is that some students do not have a basis for evaluating qualities included in the scoring plan. At the very least, though, the scoring plan

structures learning. A more advanced student can assist another student, often to the benefit of both.

With portfolios, students can be planned into the assessment process in a variety of other ways. For instance, the cover sheet illustrated in Figure 14.1 includes a place for students to indicate strengths and problems experienced with writing the paper. The teacher's comments can be written after the teacher and student *jointly* establish the strengths of the paper and the appropriate focus for subsequent work.

Students also are actively involved with portfolios when *they* select products to be included. Although the criteria for including a product are established by the teacher or by the teacher and student together, it is the student who applies the criteria. In addition, the student owns the portfolio, which is typically kept in the classroom, and has ready access to its contents. The student can, and is encouraged to, share the contents of the portfolio with others.

Name:_____ Date: _____

Title of this paper: _____

_____

Expository Writing

	Self-Assessment	Teacher Assessment
Focus stays on the topic	Y ? N	Y ? N
Organization proceeds logically	Y ? N	Y ? N
Supporting ideas or examples are used	Y ? N	Y ? N
Sentences are complete except for deliberate fragments	Y ? N	Y ? N
Sentences have subject/verb agreement	Y ? N	Y ? N
Words with appropriate meaning are used	Y ? N	Y ? N
Words are correctly spelled	Y ? N	Y ? N

What I like best about this paper: _____

_____

_____

My greatest problem when writing this paper: _____

_____

_____

My teacher's comments on the strengths of this paper: _____

_____

_____

My teacher's comments on where to place focus: _____

_____

_____

Figure 14.1
Cover page for expository writing

Students are actively involved when they provide annotations to support these products. They can use annotations to describe the process used to produce a product. For example, students can describe the process used to devise the main idea of a reading or they can explain how hypotheses were formed and conclusions drawn when performing a science experiment. The use of annotations can broaden the scope of portfolios, which are generally limited to product rather than process assessments—a significant limitation when importance is placed on the procedure or process students use to arrive at the product. Annotations can be written in the margins of papers, integrated within the body of text, or attached, like endnotes. As with any self-report, students, and older students in particular, may be influenced by what they think the teacher wants to hear. The quality of annotations also varies widely across students.

Figure 14.2 illustrates another way to involve students. These rating scales allow students to score the adequacy with which they implement good learning and work strategies. Specific behaviors included in the rating scales can change from day to day. The teacher and student together can establish the action that becomes the focus for the next day. The teacher can also convey agreement or disagreement with the student's ratings.

Take Steps to Make Review of Portfolios More Efficient

A major disadvantage of portfolios is that considerable time is required to review them and update students' records. This is particularly true in high school and often in middle schools, where subject matter and assessments are more complex and teachers work with a greater number of students. Often, changing classroom routines (for example, having students spend more time working individually or in small groups) can provide time to discuss evaluations with students. Such changes do not work equally well with all subject areas, nor with all students or all teachers. The bottom line is that portfolio assessments are generally time inten-

sive. Whenever possible, steps should be taken to make the review of portfolios more efficient.

One strategy is to design portfolios and their review with efficiency in mind. Here are some techniques that can help. Place goal statements that guide the review at the front of each portfolio. If all portfolio content is not being included in a particular review, direct students to move products that are to be reviewed to the front. Alternatively, have students temporarily move material to be scored into an "active review" folder. A preprinted checklist, such as the one shown in Figure 14.1, or other scoring aid should be stapled by students to the front of each product so that it is immediately accessible. Similar products should be reviewed together, much as all students' responses to the same item are scored together when grading essay tests. (This strategy increases scoring reliability while reducing reading time.)

A second strategy to increase efficiency is to plan for success. When a student fails to meet standards, an additional review will be required unless the student's failure is to be ignored. Also, portfolios with high-quality products require less time to review. Anything that will enhance the quality of products contained in portfolios will significantly increase the efficiency of their review. Techniques that will help include clearly communicating expectations to students by prominently displaying examples of good work that can serve as models, sharing with students the carefully constructed checklists or rating scales that will be used to score their work, and verbally stressing the importance and efficiency of good work. Another way to enhance the quality of work is to have advanced students monitor less-advanced students and help them preview their portfolios.

Another strategy for reducing scoring time is to limit the number of goals that are assessed using portfolios. Portfolios can be used to assess almost any capability involving cognitive skills. Skills involving information, concepts, and rules, however, can often be assessed with conventional written tests. These tests are not authentic in the sense of being direct measures of targeted performance outcomes, but keep in mind that no test directly

Name _____ Date _____

What is most important for me to improve today?

Here Is How I Did Today

	Always	Usually	Sometimes	Never	Teacher Agrees
Follow directions without being reminded	★	☺	☺	☹	Y ? N

Today's best example:

Ask for help when needed	★	☺	☺	☹	Y ? N

Today's best example:

Keep working until finished with task	★	☺	☺	☹	Y ? N

Today's best example:

Do something nice for others	★	☺	☺	☹	Y ? N

Today's best example:

Here is what I am most proud of today:

What is most important for me to improve tomorrow?

Figure 14.2
Behavior rating scales

measures knowledge. All assessments are limited to being indicators of what students know. If portfolios were direct assessments of knowledge taught in schools, we would not be concerned with whether observed performance generalized to unobserved performance. Yet we need to be very concerned about the generalizability of portfolio assessments and performance assessments, as well as any educational measure. By depending in part on traditional written assessments and using portfolios or performance assessments with *problem solving* and other skills that can be assessed no other way, we can improve the overall efficiency of assessment.

Commercial computer software is available to help manage portfolios. The features and cost of such software have to be evaluated in the context of local needs and resources. For more information you may look under "Education" using Yahoo!, enter the search phrase "electronic portfolio" within Google, or look through the CRESST or ERIC Assessment and Evaluation web sites.

In a college-level course concerned with classroom assessment that I teach, we depend heavily on portfolio assessments. Partly to increase efficiency, the portfolios are maintained on a computer and accessed through the Internet. Portfolios are established for projects rather than for students. That is, all students place in one portfolio their work related to one project. Approximately 25 portfolios are maintained for the same number of projects. All portfolios, including my reviews, are open to all members of the class. Personal information is sent directly to individual students using e-mail or face-to-face contacts. Software such as WebBoard, the forum feature within Blackboard, and the file-sharing features of Oracle's Internet File System can be used to transfer and organize student work that can be represented within computer files.

Use Multiple Observations to Increase Generalizability

With portfolios, as with many classroom assessments, a teacher generally does not formally establish how well performance will generalize to other measures. Doing so is usually impractical. However, a teacher can follow procedures that facilitate consistent observations. Two procedures are particularly appropriate with portfolios. The first, addressed earlier, involves carefully specifying the characteristics within students' work samples that are to be judged. This can be accomplished by developing a scoring plan for each goal, usually by devising a checklist, rating scales, or a scoring rubric. The second procedure involves applying this scoring procedure to multiple observations of student work.

The number of observations can be increased in a variety of ways. Students can be asked to include more samples of work, or to submit *diverse* samples that demonstrate proficiency with an instructional goal. For instance, in reading, students can be asked to show that they can determine the message the author is trying to convey, not only in short stories, but also in a newspaper article or a poem. In science, students can be asked to demonstrate that pollution harms organisms by finding multiple news articles that describe the effects of pollution on diverse animals and plants. The number of observations can also be increased by having more than one person judge each student's work sample. The additional reviewer can be another teacher or even another student.

Each of these techniques increases the number of observations and, therefore, tends to improve the consistency with which portfolios are scored. Using all the techniques improves consistency more than using just one of the techniques. However, the single best technique is to base judgments of performance on diverse samples of work. Using diverse samples substantially improves the degree to which observations will generalize to other settings.

Because consistency improves when the number of observations is increased, judgments regarding a group of students are much more reliable than are judgments about individual students. Even though the reliability of judgments made about individual students can be quite low, portfolios can provide highly reliable judgments concerning the achievement of the class as a whole.

GUIDING STUDENTS' USE OF PORTFOLIOS

The validity of assessments, in part, depends on what a student includes in the portfolio. Students may vary in terms of the quality of work samples they include. Quality can vary both on whether it truly represents the student's best work and whether it allows assessment of the specific skills the teacher is trying to evaluate.

Moss, with others (1992), closely examined the work of 10 students enrolled in a high school writing class, for which the teacher used portfolios to assess student achievement. The researchers examined the contents of both the students' portfolios and their comprehensive writing folders. The comprehensive folders contained all the writing that the students completed during the year. The researchers found that the work samples included in portfolios sometimes provided in-depth information concerning some qualities of the writing being assessed, but inadequate information about other qualities. In other cases, work samples provided a broader demonstration of the characteristics being assessed, but insufficient detail to detect changes in student performance with respect to individual characteristics. In some cases, students failed to include samples of writing that the researchers judged to be their best work.

Professionals and students alike must be taught how to prepare a portfolio. Professionals such as architects, artists, and models are usually guided early on in the selection of materials to be included, learning to recognize the types of capabilities sought by prospective clients and employers and how to select the best work to illustrate each of these capabilities. Students must be similarly guided. Otherwise, judgments of the student's achievement are influenced by the ability to develop the portfolio rather than by the degree to which the instructional goals have been achieved. For portfolios to be effective, the student must clearly understand the goals of instruction. The student must also understand the criteria that are to be used to score the portfolio. When the teacher reviews the portfolio with the student, the teacher should score the quality with which the portfolio is constructed as well as the quality of the work samples. Separate scores should be provided for the quality of the portfolio and for the quality of the work samples.

SUMMARY

Portfolios have become a widely used alternative for assessing student achievement. The concept of portfolios comes from professions in which portfolios are used to show examples of work to prospective clients and employers.

Student portfolios share some characteristics with their professional counterparts. For example, they are individualized, emphasize one's best work, and focus on products rather than on the process leading up to the products. Student and professional portfolios also have fundamental differences. Professional portfolios play a summative role, whereas student portfolios generally are used in formative evaluations. Others ultimately judge the content of professional portfolios, whereas the student and teacher judge student portfolios.

The use of portfolios to assess student achievement is time-consuming. No additional time is associated with producing products to be included in the portfolio if producing these products is already part of the students' activities. The increased time involves regularly discussing portfolios with each student. Unless smaller samples of work are involved, portfolios are very time-consuming in the higher grades. Because of the amount of time involved, teachers generally review a portfolio with a student once every 4 to 6 weeks. This represents a particularly long interval when portfolios provide the basis for formative evaluations. It is best to supplement portfolio assessments with other formal and informal assessments.

The first step in designing portfolios is clearly establishing how they will be used. The content of portfolios is then based on the instructional goals they will be used to assess. As with performance assessments, these goals must be translated into student performance, that is, establishing the performance to be observed. Establishing the scoring procedures is also part of the portfolio's design. In order for portfolios to be effective, students must be designed into the assessment process as active partners. Generalizability of observations is a major concern with portfolio assessments. To minimize this problem, multiple and diverse products should be used to assess each instructional goal.

SOMETHING TO TRY

• Many teachers, especially in early elementary grades, are using portfolios extensively, and often effectively. If the class includes practicing teachers, identify teachers who are currently using portfolios. Ask them to describe and, preferably, to show examples of their portfolios. Discuss with these teachers some of the issues presented in this chapter regarding advantages and limitations of portfolios. (Particularly because of the recent popularity of portfolios, there is a tendency to describe portfolios in positive but very general terms. Keep the discussion responsive to specific characteristics of portfolios. Find specific strengths and limitations.)

• Individually (or with a small group) prepare a plan for scoring a portfolio in your academic area. The scoring plan should list the instructional goals that the portfolio is designed to assess. For each goal, a list of characteristics that would be used to judge each student's samples of work should be established. These characteristics could be developed as a checklist, rating scales, or a scoring rubric. This scoring plan should facilitate consistent scoring. That is, the checklist, rating scales, or scoring rubric should specify student characteristics that can be observed directly or involve only minimal inference. The scoring plan should involve judgments of multiple work samples. To facilitate generalizability, diverse samples of each student's work should be judged.

• When portfolios are used, a teacher discusses each portfolio with the student approximately every 4 to 6 weeks. This represents a long interval if portfolios are being used in a formative as opposed to a summative role. For a class you might teach, list some specific ways to supplement these discussions with feedback from other formal and informal assessments.

ADDITIONAL READING

National Center for Research on Evaluation, Standards, and Student Testing. (1992). Portfolio assessment and high technology videotape. Los Angeles: Author. This 10-minute video illustrates the setup and use of classroom portfolios. The video and companion *Guidebook for the Video Program* are available from the CRESST web site, or can be purchased from CRESST on CD-ROM. The Guidebook includes an annotated list of references concerned with alternative assessment.

Paris, S. G., & Ayres, L. R. (1994). *Becoming reflective students and teachers with portfolios and authentic assessment.* Washington, DC: American Psychological Association. This book describes advantages typically sought when portfolios are used in the classroom. It includes a number of illustrations of the types of forms students and teachers can use when assessing portfolio work.

Tierney, R. J., Carter, M. A., & Desal, L. E. (1991). *Portfolio assessment in the reading-writing classroom.* Norwood, MA: Christopher-Gordon. This book deals exclusively with the philosophy, development, and use of portfolios. Focus is on assessment of reading and writing, although ideas discussed in the book generalize fairly well to other content areas. The authors' illustrations throughout the book are particularly useful. An annotated bibliography concerning portfolios is included.

Underwood, T. (1998). The consequences of portfolio assessment: A case study. *Educational Assessment, 5,* 147–194. This article describes a 1-year study of three teachers' use of a portfolio system in their language-arts classes.

PART IV

How to Use Assessments

. . . including a careful discussion of the integral role assessment plays within learning. . . .

In Parts II and III, we discussed the development, administration, and scoring of classroom assessments. The assessment techniques considered have been quite varied and include the teacher's informal observations and questioning of students, various formats of written tests, performance assessments, and portfolios. In Part IV, our focus is on the *use* of these assessments.

Chapter 15 is concerned with integrating assessment into instruction. Particular attention is given to the roles of assessment within a cognitivist approach to instruction, where the focus is on helping learners become experts; and within a constructivist approach, where the focus is on helping learners construct new knowledge. Chapter 15 addresses two other topics: the relevance of validity and generalizability to integrating assessment into instruction, and the implications to standardized testing if these external assessments are to play an integral role in instruction.

Chapter 16 is concerned with reporting student performance to parents and other individuals outside the classroom. This reporting is accomplished through a variety of techniques, often including letter grades, conferences, written communications, and increasingly through the use of checklists. We discuss the characteristics of these techniques and briefly describe procedures for establishing standards.

Chapter 17 addresses the interpretation of standardized tests. This discussion is limited to issues directly relevant to the classroom teacher. Distinctions between standardized achievement and aptitude tests are drawn to help you use results of these tests in classroom decisions as well as interpret test results to parents. Specific procedures are provided for interpreting the scores most commonly used with standardized tests, including percentile ranks and grade equivalents. Finally, information is provided to help you critically evaluate and respond to the uses of standardized tests that are typical in most schools.

15

Integrating Assessment into Instruction

For some time, it has been common to separate discussions of assessment from those of instruction. This has not happened because instruction and assessment have been seen as independent events; quite the contrary, educational reform efforts tend to emphasize the importance of integrating assessment into instruction. Take, for example, mastery learning, an approach to instruction proposed by Bloom some time ago, where formative assessments play a dominant and inseparable role within the instructional process.

Shepard (2000) proposes that, beginning in the 1980s, the approach taken in instruction and curriculum separated from that of educational testing as a result of the constructivist movement. Prior to that time, behaviorism was the dominant theory of learning, which in turn was closely matched to what Shepard refers to as a curriculum of social efficiency. Much like the detailed task analyses that were used to improve the efficiency of factories and business, curriculums were organized into specific skills expressed as a series of behavioral objectives. In turn, precise measurement specifications were required to ensure that each skill was appropriately assessed.

A parallel existed at that time in the design of instruction. Instructional design models, which were successfully applied first to training in the military but later to many other areas including continuing education efforts within business,

began with a task analysis to determine what skills would have to be learned in order for trainees to become successful at what they were being trained to do. Once these skills were identified, behaviors that would indicate the skill had been learned were identified and expressed as behavioral objectives. Test items were developed that measured proficiency with each behavior. Then, finally, instruction was designed that efficiently brought about the behaviors that would be measured by the tests.

The development of constructivist and cognitive learning theories altered views as to how learning most effectively took place. Both placed the focus on how the mind works and how one learns rather than on the behaviors that would be the anticipated outcomes of learning. The research strategy widely used by cognitive psychologists has been to identify differences used by experts versus novices to solve problems within a particular domain. For instance, playing the game of chess involves problem solving. To better understand the functioning of the mind, cognitive psychologists would investigate the differences in mental processes used by expert and novice chess players. Consistent with this research strategy, the goal of learning becomes one of helping the learner acquire the mental capabilities used by experts to solve problems.

The constructivist model proposes that learned knowledge is constructed out of existing knowledge. The effectiveness and the efficiency of instruction are viewed as being heavily dependent on the student's existing knowledge and values. Particularly in contrast to behaviorists, constructivists emphasized the active involvement of the learner in the learning process as opposed to focusing on the development of a carefully detailed set of instructional activities to which learners would be exposed. Likewise, constructivists tended to build instructional activities around broad themes rather than detailed lists of specific skills.

As Shepard (2000) notes, dominant testing practices associated with the behaviorist learning theory have continued to remain prevalent while focus within instruction has largely switched to cognitive and constructivist approaches. The result has been a disconnect between testing and instructional practices, particularly with external assessments. This disconnect unfortunately often shows up in the training teachers and prospective teachers receive in assessment. For instance, a common approach taken in measurement textbooks is to encourage teachers to start with a set of behavioral objectives, create test items or performance assessments that correspond to those objectives, and treat the match between objectives and the content of assessments as the most fundamental evidence of test validity. Within that approach, little or no attempt is made to match the performance to be observed to the type of capability being learned, such as recognizing the differences in tasks that should be used to assess declarative versus procedural knowledge. Likewise, minimal attention is usually given to informal assessments and other techniques that facilitate formative evaluations, which is unfortunate because this is where assessment is most commonly used within instruction to closely monitor learning while it occurs.

In the present chapter, we review some key elements of cognitive and constructivist theories and look at the implications to assessment. Although providing a full introduction to these models is outside the scope of this book, additional readings listed at the end of the chapter provide options for further study. This chapter helps you achieve four skills:

- Integrate assessment into instruction within a cognitive approach, where the focus is on helping learners become an expert

- Integrate assessment into instruction within a constructivist approach, where the focus is on helping learners construct new knowledge

- Recognize the relevance of validity and generalizability to integrating assessment into instruction

- Recognize the implications to external assessments of integrating assessment into instruction

INTEGRATING ASSESSMENT WHEN HELPING LEARNERS BECOME EXPERTS

As we have noted, the research strategy widely used by cognitive psychologists has been to identify differences in how experts versus novices solve problems within a particular domain. The expectation is that if one has an understanding of the cognitive processes employed by an expert, these same processes can be learned by others. In essence, the intended outcome of instruction is for learners to become experts.

Findings from this research suggest that experts use two basic types of knowledge when solving problems: *declarative knowledge* and *procedural knowledge.* As you recognize from earlier discussion, declarative knowledge refers to information one can state verbally; it involves knowing that something is the case. Declarative knowledge goes way beyond content that one can memorize. It includes the recall of specific facts, but also principles, trends, criteria, and ways of organizing events. We have indicated that declarative knowledge is assessed by having students state what they know.

Procedural knowledge is knowledge of how to do things. In earlier chapters, we have divided procedural knowledge into *discriminations, concepts,* and *rules,* and have identified techniques for assessing each. For instance, knowledge of a concept can be assessed by providing students with new illustrations and asking them to classify each as an example or non-example of the concept. For example, knowledge of the concept of "odd versus even" numbers can be assessed by asking students to categorize several numbers as odd or even. In contrast, asking students to explain the difference between odd and even numbers, while involving an important skill, is assessing declarative rather than procedural knowledge.

Any of a variety of test formats can be used to assess both declarative and procedural forms of knowledge. For instance, to assess knowledge of the concept of a robin (a common type of bird in

Canada and the United States), one can casually observe the name students use when they see a robin versus other kinds of birds; the students are in essence classifying birds as examples and non-examples of a robin. Alternately, one could ask students to point to robins within a picture. If students can handle written tests, knowledge of the same concept can be assessed even with multiple-choice items, where the multiple-choice options list names of various birds. In each of these examples, the concept of a robin is legitimately being assessed because students are being provided examples that they are asked to classify.

Cognitive psychologists view declarative and procedural knowledge as a means to something else, specifically, solving problems. Gagné, Yekovich, and Yekovich (1993) state, "A problem is said to exist whenever one has a goal and has not yet identified a means for reaching that goal" (p. 211). Even when mechanically well constructed, items within written tests cannot assess a student's ability to solve this kind of problem. Nor can listening to students' responses to oral questions. Performance assessments, or portfolios that incorporate performance assessments, are needed for assessing problem-solving skills.

Let us look more closely at how declarative and procedural knowledge is learned, and how that knowledge is then used to solve problems. We will look also at the implications this has to classroom assessment if assessments are to be integrated into instruction.

Declarative and Procedural Knowledge

Declarative Knowledge. Declarative knowledge can be thought of as a series of propositions or ideas that reside in long-term memory. In order to be retained for more than a short period of time, any new proposition must become linked to other ideas. For instance, if told somebody's name or phone number, you will not remember that information for long unless you deliberately or sub-consciously associate it with other information that you already know. For example, when introduced to a new person, you might associate that person with another individual who shares the same name and also shares some other unique characteristic, such as being particularly tall or short or having a special mannerism, to help you remember the name. You are establishing an important linkage between new and existing knowledge. The acquisition and retrieval of propositions requires these linkages. Two processes that facilitate these linkages within declarative knowledge are *organization* and *elaboration*.

Organization involves dividing information into subsets and establishing a relationship among the subsets. To illustrate, stop a moment to look at the figure below and describe to yourself what you see.

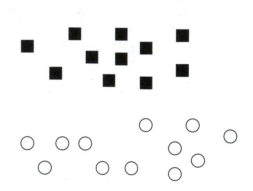

In the figure, did you see two groups of objects or did you instead see the 23 separate objects? Did you notice that one group consisted of filled-in squares and the other of circles with no shading? By imposing some kind of organization, tomorrow you are more likely to recall some of the content of this figure. We naturally categorize characteristics of cities, weather patterns, people we meet or hear about, events we go to, and so forth. Typically, multiple classifications are involved, all helping us link new information to what we already know *and* helping us retrieve that information when we need it.

In learning, there are numerous ways to help students organize information. Teachers can provide advanced organizers, provide a topic outline, or encourage students to outline what is being discussed. Presentations can be presented so that the organizational structure is obvious. Chapter titles and headings within a reading can provide structure, as can the placement at the beginning of each chapter of a list of topics to be addressed.

A second process that facilitates the creation of linkages within declarative knowledge is *elaboration*. Consider the following information:

You are driving quickly to a friend's house because you are late.

There is a police car parked just over the hill.

You probably have already added to this story. That is, you have elaborated upon the information provided in order to establish meaning to two otherwise isolated statements. Your elaboration has in various ways involved linkages to other information or declarative knowledge that you already possess.

As with organization, there are numerous ways to use elaboration to help students establish linkages. One is for the teacher to use analogies. You probably have on a number of occasions used analogies to help a friend understand a point you are making, such as relating a situation to one that occurred earlier. Alternately, a teacher can ask students to create their own examples or analogies. Or, as with the above story relating the parked police car to driving quickly to the friend's house, students can be asked to anticipate missing information.

Procedural Knowledge. Beginning in Chapter 3, we have subdivided procedural knowledge into discriminations, concepts, and rules. Discriminations are a very basic type of procedural knowledge and involve sensitivity to some attribute that is critical to later understanding of a particular concept. For instance, the concept of "small" involves sensitivity to differences in size, such as being presented with four objects that are identical in every way except that one is a different size than the other three. *Discrimination,* however, involves only the ability to point to or identify in some way the object that is different. Discrimination would not involve describing the difference or even recognizing it by name as would be required in response to the question, "Which one is smaller?"

A *concept* requires using a set of discriminations and meaningfully associating a name with these characteristics. The concept of "small," for example, involves sensitivity to size and being able to associate the word *small* within the context of different sizes. Concepts typically involve linkages to a series of discriminations, as well as to other concepts. The concept of "small" involves discriminations associated with the concept of "typical" because, for instance, a particular car and a particular ant must both be understood as "small" relative to other cars and other ants, even though a small car is very large compared to a small ant.

Rules are relationships that govern or predict actions, such as the formula governing the conversion of temperatures from the Celsius to Fahrenheit scale; or the rule that governs the use of the indefinite article *a* or *an* in a sentence; or a particular procedure in algebra used to isolate a single unknown on one side of the equation.

Two important qualities of procedural knowledge from the perspective of both instruction and assessment are that (1) procedural knowledge always involves *doing* something; and (2) procedural knowledge, as learners gain experience, changes with respect to its automaticity. With respect to procedural knowledge involving the act of doing something, assessment of discriminations must involve learners reacting to a difference, even if that difference cannot be described or given a name. Assessing knowledge of concepts also requires learners to do something more than stating what they know; students must classify things. With concepts, students must be able to establish an object or abstraction as belonging or not belonging to the particular category represented by the concept.

Procedural knowledge often becomes, and in many cases actually *must* become, automatic to be useful. To illustrate, a strategy used in algebra to separate an unknown within equations involving fractions is to multiply both sides of the equation by the respective denominators. For instance, in this equation

$$\frac{4}{X} = \frac{7}{20}$$

multiplying both sides of the equation by X changes the equation to

$$4 = \frac{7X}{20}$$

Then multiplying both sides by 20 changes the equation to

$$20 \times 4 = 7X \text{ or } 80 = 7X$$

By isolating X in this way, its value can easily be determined to be $80 \div 7$, or approximately 11.4. One can automate this procedure, doing what is often called "cross-multiplication," which involves simply multiplying each numerator by the denominator that is diagonally across the equal sign. Applying this to the original equation above changes that equation to the one which we eventually obtained, $80 = 7X$. This automation has a major advantage in that, once learned, one does not have to think through what is happening; the process is completed much more quickly. The automation, of course, has a major disadvantage, this being that the process is no longer being thought through with respect to why it works. However, when a process becomes automated, one does not have to think it through to employ it. This is what happens to countless procedures we learn, such as those associated with driving a car, conversing with friends, brushing our teeth, preparing food, and instructing and assessing students.

Like rules, concepts are procedural knowledge that also can become automated. When automated, concepts can be represented by their name and the verbal descriptions we use to elaborate upon that name. For instance, you and I have automated knowledge of the concept "small." We can convince each other of our understanding by expressing in words what it

means for something to be small. Because of both of our levels of sophistication, you can listen to my verbal description of what small means and quickly determine whether or not I know the concept "small." Because a sophisticated level of knowledge of a concept often can be assessed using verbal statements (the very same strategy we use to test knowledge of information), many cognitive psychologists believe that automated concepts are declarative knowledge. In fact, much of declarative knowledge is referred to as *conceptual understandings*. When knowledge of a concept has reached this automated state, it can be assessed as if it were declarative knowledge. However, when a concept is being learned, such as when a child is learning the meaning of "small," it should be assessed as procedural knowledge, by providing the child diverse objects not previously used in this context and having the child indicate which objects are small.

Rules, when automated, become procedures that cognitive psychologists call *automated basic skills*. Gagné, Yekovich, and Yekovich (1993) identify three things teachers can do to help students automate rules. The first is to identify prerequisite procedures or subskills and help students automate those skills. The second is to help students to combine small procedures into larger composite procedures. The third is to help students "proceduralize" their skills so that they can exploit the goal–subgoal structure of the procedure without thinking about it.

However, not all cognitive skills do or should become automated. Certain subsets must remain at the level where they are consciously employed as strategies for solving problems within specific content domains. Physicians use strategies to establish a diagnosis. Mechanical engineers use a different set of strategies to solve structural problems. Likewise, other sets of strategies are used by biologists, electricians, carpenters, pilots, or teachers. Because a particular set of strategies is unique to a given content domain, they are referred to as *domain-specific strategies* and are an essential part to becoming an expert within that domain. Again, an expert consciously uses domain-specific strategies, determining when it is appropriate to use a particular strategy, and continuously evaluating whether the strategy is providing its expected results with respect to solving the problem.

Problem Solving and Transfer

As noted previously, problem solving as conceptualized here is different from applying known procedures to solve a problem, such as using a formula to convert Fahrenheit temperatures to Celsius. That activity involves applying a rule, in this case the rule being represented by the formula used for this temperature conversion. Knowledge of rules is an important element for obtaining solutions to problems, but it is not what we are referring to here as problem solving.

A problem exists when one has a goal but has not yet identified a means for reaching that goal. Problem solving involves establishing that means. An example of problem solving is determining what an unknown liquid is, or determining which paint is best for use on the exterior of one's house, or determining the next move in a game of chess, or determining how to return home when a connecting flight has been missed.

The process of solving a problem always takes the same form. First, one creates a representation of the problem that establishes the "givens" to the problem. For instance, if you missed a connecting flight, you will have to secure a seat on another flight. Most likely, only certain airlines serve your home airport (declarative knowledge that will influence how you solve your problem). You may be carrying with you only certain items that will influence your options should it be necessary to stay overnight. These givens activate knowledge, including strategies that may help establish a solution, such as recognizing the need to recall what you know about later flights into your home airport, and recalling strategies for contacting an airline agent to check on available flights. A possible solution for your problem is then established and evaluated. For any problem, this sequence may be repeated several times until the problem is solved, or until one gives up seeking a solution.

Our present focus is on the integration of assessment into instruction when the purpose of instruction is to help learners become experts. In this context, a relevant question pertains to what an expert does to solve problems. In a broad sense, the answer is that an expert uses a high level of three types of knowledge: *conceptual understanding* specific to the domain in which the problem exists; *automated basic skills* within that domain; and *knowledge of strategies* used to solve problems within that domain. Conceptual understanding refers to the declarative knowledge we have discussed previously. It includes knowledge of facts, trends, and principles. It probably includes concepts that can be quickly represented as words and ideas. This conceptual understanding helps one establish a clear representation of the problem and narrows the search for procedures that can be used in its solution. Automated basic skills involve procedural knowledge such as rules. Through experience, these learned routines can be applied without thinking much about them, which in turn frees up mental capacity to concentrate on other aspects of determining a solution to the problem. Finally, domain-specific strategies help make the search for and application of a solution more efficient and effective.

However, from an instructional and assessment perspective, learning is effective only if students are able to *transfer* application of knowledge from the context in which it was learned to situations within which they later are expected to solve problems. Let us look at how one facilitates transfer within the three types of knowledge we have identified.

Conceptual Understanding. With conceptual understanding, one significant issue is determining what declarative knowledge is critical to solving problems. There is general agreement that teachers must themselves be experts within the content domain they are teaching. A science teacher, for instance, must be knowledgeable with relevant science. However, this content expertise is often insufficient. Cognitive psychologists have found that an effective way to identify which conceptual understandings are required for transfer is to establish the kinds of declarative knowledge experts invoke when they actually solve real-world problems. That is, simply asking scientists what they believe is important knowledge is not enough. Instead, one would observe what knowledge scientists use when they go about solving scientific problems. To know which conceptual understandings are crucial, science teachers must be content experts not just with important scientific principles, but also with *real-world applications* of the science they are teaching. The same is true, of course, with teachers of math, of history, of foreign language and writing, and certainly also teachers of educational pedagogy, including assessment.

Even if a student learns appropriate declarative knowledge for a given problem-solving domain, it is quite possible the student will be unable to activate that knowledge when it is needed. It is believed that a learner is more likely to activate the necessary knowledge if that knowledge is learned within a problem-solving context. Probably the reason is that if declarative knowledge is learned in that context, it is more probable that useful linkages will be made within propositions that make up this conceptual understanding. One strategy proposed for doing this is to provide instruction within a problem context. That is, establish a problem that is to be addressed and help students achieve declarative knowledge that helps address that problem. Another strategy is for instruction to take on the form of an apprenticeship. The teacher initially presents problems and models solutions, and gradually shifts problem-solving responsibility to the students.

Automated Basic Skills. The advantage of automated basic skills is that they are procedural techniques that can be applied efficiently, therefore allowing mental capabilities to focus on other aspects of solving the problem. Driving a car on a busy road would be impossible were a number of procedural skills not automated. A procedural skill generalizes to many problem settings and does not have to be relearned for each. As with

conceptual understanding, however, one must activate an appropriate basic skill when needed. Part of knowing which basic skills to use involves knowledge of strategies, which we address next. However, it also involves establishing linkages between the skills and their various applications. Again, a teacher must be familiar with diverse real-world settings to which a particular procedure applies, and help students learn procedures within those varied contexts.

Strategies. When solving a problem, an expert develops and uses strategies to make more efficient and effective the search for relevant knowledge and the evaluation of possible solutions. A detective employs strategies to solve a mystery. A scientist uses strategies when conducting research. Historians, writers, composers, architects, and physicians all use strategies in their work. An important characteristic of experts within these and other fields is that they know useful strategies for getting the work done (that is, solving problems), *and* they know when to apply a particular strategy.

When learning strategies, in order to assist with transfer, students must learn when and how to use strategies. In part, learning a strategy involves knowing the steps to follow. However, unlike automated basic skills, with strategies it is important to remain mentally involved when they are used. One must evaluate whether steps are being applied appropriately, whether they are having the intended effect, and whether in fact they appear appropriate within the context of the problem being solved. Gagné, Yekovich, and Yekovich (1993) state that a possible reason many people fail to transfer strategies is that they do not know when the strategy should be used. They point out the need to show students why a strategy works and provide understanding associated with implementing the strategy effectively.

Some Implications to Classroom Assessment

When the focus is on helping learners become experts, there are a number of implications to how one assesses students if the assessment is to be integrated into instruction. First, experts rely heavily on declarative and procedural knowledge. Although problem-solving skills are the ultimate goal, such skills cannot be realized without the essential declarative and procedural knowledge. Declarative and procedural knowledge must be assessed along with problem-solving skills. Declarative knowledge is assessed by having students state or explain what they know. Procedural knowledge, in contrast, is assessed by having students perform the procedure.

Procedural knowledge involves discriminations, concepts, and rules. With discriminations, students are not expected to describe the difference or even recognize the difference by name. Recently learned concepts are assessed by providing students with diverse illustrations not previously used within the present context and having them classify the illustrations as examples and nonexamples of the concept. Rules are assessed by observing students perform previously unused tasks that involve application of the rule. Declarative and procedural knowledge can generally be measured using any of the formats discussed in this book, including informal observations and questions, written tests, performance assessments, and portfolios that employ these formats. Our first implication, therefore, is recognizing the importance of assessing declarative and procedural knowledge, including the types of performance used as indicators of declarative and procedural knowledge.

A second implication is the need to rely heavily on informal assessments to verify students are forming linkages necessary to retain information in long-term memory. To be useful, students must be able to recall declarative knowledge when it is needed for solving problems. To allow this to happen, students must establish, for each idea they learn, links to existing knowledge. Two techniques we have identified that help establish links are organization of knowledge and elaboration. Because links to existing knowledge must be established simul-

taneous to learning new information, a teacher needs to rely on informal assessments. (Formal assessments do not have the spontaneity to monitor learning while it is occurring.) Informal assessments can involve oral questions that cause students to state elaborations they are generating and describe how they are organizing what they understand. Recall, however, that informal assessments tend to overestimate what students have learned. To ensure useful linkages are being established, one should err on the side of over-assessment. Links tend to be more useful if instruction occurs in the context of real-world problem situations.

A third implication pertains to procedural knowledge that *should not* become automated. Many procedural skills do become automated. However, procedural rules that become domain-specific strategies should not. Through informal assessments, a teacher needs to establish that students are learning when to apply a given strategy, and that students are deliberately evaluating whether the strategy is achieving its anticipated outcome.

A fourth implication is that assessments, particularly those that are informal, must be non-threatening to students. One of the characteristics of informal assessments addressed in Chapter 11 is that they are interactive between the teacher and students, and among students. This characteristic is necessary, for instance, for assessing students' elaborations when they establish linkages between new declarative knowledge and existing knowledge. It is also necessary when students are learning how and when to apply strategies when solving problems. In order to sustain students' participation, they must be comfortable making and learning from mistakes. The focus of assessment must, from the perspective of students, obviously be one of facilitating learning rather than one of making judgments.

A fifth implication is that the outcomes of assessments should involve qualitative descriptions of what students do and do not do. It is common to think of a numerical score as the end result of an assessment. Certainly that is not the case with informal assessments, but even with formal performance assessments, the scoring plan can be a checklist, or a scoring rubric. These might be transformed into a summary numerical score to facilitate record keeping or grading, but qualitative descriptions provide a much more useful basis for interacting with students. A numerical score does not add information that is not already contained in a careful qualitative statement of what is observed, and can be dispensed with unless a summary record must be retained in that form. Focusing on the qualitative interpretations of student performance makes it easier to blur the distinction between instruction and assessment, which is good. It also makes it easier for a teacher to establish that the assessments are being used to facilitate learning rather than focus on inadequacies.

A final implication addressed here is that performance assessments should be a significant assessment tool at all grade levels and within all content areas. What ultimately distinguishes a person as having expertise is that individual's ability to solve authentic problems within a particular content domain. Performance assessments, whether administered informally or formally, are the only assessment option for evaluating problem-solving skills.

Performance assessments can be incorporated into a portfolio system. They also can involve homework, various projects, and group activities. As with any test, a performance assessment is an indirect indication of what a student knows and what the student is thinking. In the same sense, one cannot see a person solve a problem. Of course, we can observe behaviors and outcomes that again serve as indicators of the mental processes that constitute problem solving. The implication is that a performance assessment needs to be structured so that the behaviors observed provide a valid indication of those processes, and one that generalizes reasonably well to other performances the student might have been asked to perform. Using the performance assessment specifications illustrated in Chapter 13

can help structure the assessments so that they have these attributes.

INTEGRATING ASSESSMENT WHEN HELPING LEARNERS CONSTRUCT NEW KNOWLEDGE

A major difference between the learning theories of behaviorists, cognitivists, and constructivists is the frame of reference from which each theory evolves. Each frame of reference is defensible, although this does not mean one would be equally comfortable with the application of each theory within a classroom environment. As with all learning theories, behaviorists recognize that one cannot see another person's knowledge or what the person is thinking. Instead one uses behaviors as an indication of what an individual knows and is thinking. Behaviorists try to identify the behaviors that serve as good indicators of knowledge that is to be learned, and then focus on techniques that bring about those behaviors. Although some behaviorists take an extreme view that behaviors should be the only focus of instruction, no behaviorist seriously takes a view so extreme as to suggest the nature and functioning of the mind are insignificant factors. The behaviorist's view that the purpose of instruction is to help students perform in ways that are consistent with the performance of knowledgeable individuals is a goal that, from an instructional point of view, is difficult to argue against.

As with other learning theories, cognitivists recognize that the way one's mind functions is highly relevant to the learning process. To help determine how the mind functions, a common research approach taken by cognitivists is to contrast how experts versus novices solve problems. That research has been highly useful in establishing the nature of knowledge from the perspective of what the mind does. From an instructional point of view, helping students become more like experts than novices is also a goal that is difficult to argue against.

Again, as with other learning theories, constructivists recognize that the purpose of learning, and likewise the major role of formal education, is to help students develop new knowledge. Behaviorists, cognitivists, and constructivists all recognize the active participation of the learner as critical to acquiring new knowledge. No learning theorist believes deep learning will be realized through passive involvement of students.

It is wishful thinking to anticipate that listening to taped lectures in our sleep will provide a deep understanding, or hoping that a special pill, if swallowed, will provide encyclopedic knowledge! Possibly in the future, there will be a way to manipulate the structure of the brain such that one can achieve knowledge without having to work long and hard as we do today. The possibility of manipulating a person's knowledge while that individual remains passive is a scary thought, and is also inconsistent with present understandings of how the brain and nervous system function. However, through technology we almost certainly will continue to develop and learn how to apply new tools, such as the computer, through which we can extend and substantially augment our mental capabilities.

As their name indicates, constructivists focus on how a learner constructs new knowledge. This focus is obviously very useful to the practice of instruction and that of integrating assessment into instruction. The contributions of constructivists are significant yet not totally unique. We will look at two issues they raise: the role of prior knowledge to constructing new knowledge, and the role of feedback in facilitating learning.

The Role of Prior Knowledge

A constructivist view of learning is that one creates new knowledge out of existing knowledge. How one learns new knowledge is heavily dependent on the knowledge one presently has. There is evidence that supports this. For instance, a student's learning of the chemical makeup of water as H_2O is going to be heavily influenced and potentially restricted by that student's awareness of the existence of water, of the elements hydrogen and oxygen, and of the process by which elements combine into compounds. Learning the meaning of jazz is similarly going to be influenced by awareness of various instruments such as piano and clarinet, of rhythms such as syncopation, and also by learned attitudes toward these instruments and various kinds of music. The conflicts in the Middle East and elsewhere in the World are vivid examples of how previous learning, including attitudes, heavily influence what individuals and groups of people learn and what they are willing to learn.

From a constructivist perspective, one builds on prior knowledge and cultural perspectives. *Scaffolding* is an important concept among constructivists. Scaffolding is much like an effective tutor, working one on one with a student. The tutor conceivably could tell the student what needs to be known; in essence, he or she could provide an individualized lecture. Usually the more effective strategy is for the tutor to identify the limits of the student's knowledge, and provide prompts that provide sufficient structure for the student to discover the new knowledge on her or his own. Scaffolding is that structure, provided by the teacher. When the student discovers the knowledge, or is able to solve the new problem unaided, the temporary scaffolding is no longer needed and is removed. New scaffolding is then created by the teacher to aid the student in constructing still additional knowledge, building on earlier and recently learned knowledge.

The process of scaffolding actively involves the student and relies heavily on each student using prior knowledge. The process requires the teacher, through assessment, to establish a clear understanding of the student's current knowledge. It also requires the teacher to have a high level of competence with the content being learned, including a detailed and working understanding of the structures of that content.

The Role of Feedback

Shepard (2000), in her discussion of the role of assessment in teaching and learning, contrasts two approaches to providing feedback. She illustrates one approach with a study by Elawar and Corno (1985) in which teachers were trained to provide written feedback on math homework that identified specific errors, poor strategies, and gave suggestions for improvement. Emphasis of the feedback was on understanding rather than superficial knowledge. This approach was found to improve students' math achievement. In contrast, a separate study by Lepper, Drake, and O'Donnell-Johnson (1997) examined techniques used by successful tutors. It was observed that the more effective tutors did not provide students the correct answer when errors occurred. Often errors were ignored when they were not critical. Instead, the effective tutors used questions designed to cause the student to self-correct.

Shepard states that these two studies illustrate a tension among constructivists with respect to the role of informal assessment and feedback. Should the feedback be explicit or should it be indirect, allowing students to reexamine their own ideas? Shepard identifies this as an important question that needs to be examined through research. Regardless of how this issue is resolved, continuous feedback is an essential element within a constructivist approach to instruction. If feedback is to be continuous, it will have to be based largely on informal assessments.

Some Additional Implications to Classroom Assessment

Constructivists place heavy emphasis on the learner as an active participant. Few if any educators would argue for students playing a passive role within formal education, but constructivists give more attention to the need for the learner's active involvement. Constructivists also place heavy emphasis on the role of the teacher as a scaffolder, providing the temporary structure needed for a student to establish new ideas and construct new knowledge from within the context of present knowledge. Providing this scaffolding requires understanding at all times what it is the student knows and does not know. This goes way beyond simply using pretests. Assess-

ments and interactions with students must also occur more frequently than that afforded by portfolios. Pretests and portfolios can both be useful assessment tools, but informal assessments must play the major role. The implication is that the more active one wants students to be within the learning process, the more extensive the use of systematic informal assessments must become.

As in most settings, the majority of assessments within a constructivist approach are used formatively rather than summatively. As opposed to a summative role, formative assessments are used to immediately redirect instructional activities. For this to happen, students must receive substantial feedback from the assessments. Shepard (2000) raises the question as to whether feedback to students should be explicit, or more indirect, placing more demands on students' self-evaluation. Possibly the answer depends in part on characteristics of students, with those who have developed higher levels of confidence and self-motivation able to play a more independent role within the feedback process.

RELEVANCE OF VALIDITY AND GENERALIZABILITY TO INTEGRATING ASSESSMENT

Chapters 4 and 5 introduced two extremely important concepts: validity and generalizability. Validity is concerned with the degree to which an assessment is measuring what it should measure. If it does not, then the assessment is useless.

Generalizability is concerned with whether that which is observed within an assessment generalizes to that which was not observed. Any assessment involves only a sample of possible observations. In writing assessments, the topic upon which a student writes is a small sample of the variety of topics that could have been chosen. Likewise, the teacher who happens to be scoring a student's writing is a small sample of the teachers that conceivably could have been the ones reading the paper. If changing the topic *or* the reader changes the conclusion about a student's writing proficiency, then the judgment of that student's proficiency is really a function of the topic that happens to be chosen or the teacher who happens to be involved; the student's writing proficiency does not generalize. Observations that do not generalize are of limited use because conclusions drawn from the observation are limited to a very specific situation. Furthermore, lack of generalizability also limits the validity of an assessment. This is because something other than what is supposed to be assessed is influencing observed performance. For example, if two teachers assign different scores when they read a student's paper, the change in scores is not due to changes in the student's writing performance, but rather something other than what the assessment is supposed to be measuring, such as idiosyncrasies in the teachers' scoring procedures.

Because of the importance of validity and generalizability, it is appropriate that we review these concepts within the present context of integrating assessment into instruction.

Establishing Evidence of Validity

Validity evidence has to be established for an assessment because indirect measures are involved; one is not able to directly see what another person knows or is thinking. A teacher depends on students' performances to provide an *indication* of their knowledge and thinking. Because inferences are involved, it is not just prudent but also essential that we have evidence that conclusions drawn from what is observed are legitimate statements about students' knowledge and thought processes.

There is a tendency to equate students' performance with knowledge. This seems to be particularly true when using more authentic measures such as performance assessments where the performance used in the assessment can be very close to what people do in real-world settings. It is as if the "behavior" rather than the knowledge underlying the behavior is what we are trying to instill in students. But that position represents the most extreme behaviorist point of view by suggesting

what is in the mind is irrelevant; that only outward behaviors matter. Most behaviorists recognize that behaviors are only indicators of knowledge, with the latter being what human learning is about. Unless one's point of view is that of extreme behaviorists, then we must recognize the importance of using evidence to establish that appropriate interpretations and uses are being made of the behaviors observed throughout assessments.

When integrated into instruction, most assessments are informal. Because these assessments happen so quickly and are often spontaneous in nature, it is very easy to forget the fact that the performance being observed is only an indicator of knowledge. Therefore, it is appropriate that we review briefly the topic of validity evidence within our present discussion. Our discussion of validity has been organized into three types of evidence: *construct-related, content-related,* and *criterion-related evidence.*[1]

Construct-Related Evidence. Construct-related evidence establishes a link between the underlying but invisible construct we wish to measure and the visible performance we choose to observe. To establish this link, one has to identify the nature of the construct being assessed and select behaviors that serve as good indicators of status with that construct. Within the classroom, the construct we generally are most concerned with is learned knowledge and its uses. From cognitive research, we believe knowledge involves declarative and procedural components, with this knowledge used to solve problems.

Establishing the nature of the knowledge being assessed requires a teacher to have in-depth

---

[1]The categories of validity evidence used here, construct-, content-, and criterion-related, are those suggested in the 1985 *Standards for Educational and Psychological Testing* (AERA, APA, & NCME, 1985). Chapter 4 explains why this, rather than the more recent 1999 version of the *Standards,* is referenced in this book.

knowledge of the content being assessed. The type of behavior that should be used in an assessment depends on the type of capability. Declarative knowledge, or information, is assessed by having the student state what he or she knows; that is, "declare" what is known. Procedural knowledge should involve having the student perform a procedure. For instance, concepts, before the knowledge becomes automated, should be assessed by having students classify diverse and previously unused illustrations as examples and non-examples of the concept. Knowledge of a rule should similarly be assessed by having students apply the rule with previously unused examples.

To illustrate, let us use the *concept* of a prime number. (An integer is called a prime number if the only positive whole numbers that equally divide that integer are 1 and the integer itself.) Being a concept, one would provide students diverse and previously unused numbers and have students classify them as examples and non-examples of a prime number. To help ensure the examples are diverse, one could include smaller and larger numbers such as 2 and 97, and also numbers that included some of the same digits but would be classified differently, such as 5 and 15. In order to limit the examples to illustrations previously unused, 3 rather than 2 could be used if 2 had been used earlier as an example of a prime number but 3 had not. Although it would be important for students to be able to explain what prime numbers are and to be able to illustrate this understanding with their own examples, this could be assessing declarative knowledge rather than procedural knowledge.

Within an informal assessment, a teacher might have students quiz each other, taking turns providing numbers and having the other person indicate whether or not the number was prime. To assure the assessment had construct-related evidence of validity, the teacher would monitor not only the correctness of the answers, but also make sure that the numbers used were diverse and were not repeats of earlier examples.

Content-Related Evidence. Content-related evidence of validity is concerned with how well the content of the assessment incorporates the tasks that have been identified as appropriate for measuring the present construct. When developing a written test, for instance, a teacher might be fully aware of the types of performance that would provide good indicators of the knowledge being assessed, but then fail to include in the test those items that actually require students to perform that behavior. In fact, this happens all the time. Teachers often select items that appear to intellectually challenge students, or are novel or even clever, but really do not closely match the task that goes with the construct the test is supposed to assess. For written tests, Chapter 4 encourages the use of a table of specifications or possibly a list of performance objectives to help ensure a match between test content and the skills associated with the construct.

When assessments are integrated into instruction, their informal nature can easily result in failing to plan the content of assessments. If one is serious about integrating assessments into instruction, then the planning of assessments must also be integrated into the planning of the instructional activities. In addition to having a clear idea of what the goals are for the day and the nature of the constructs to be learned, the content of assessments to be included that day should also be carefully outlined.

With formal written tests and performance assessments, it is common to involve all students in an assessment. For instance, when a written quiz is administered, the teacher is careful that all students who are to be involved complete the quiz. With informal assessment, it is not as easy to involve all students, partly because some students will try to participate and others will avoid it. If the purpose of an assessment is to determine the overall status of the class, partial participation is adequate as long as participating students are representative of the class as a whole. But often, the intent is to assess individual students. Content-related evidence of validity must then be evaluated at the individual student level.

Criterion-Related Evidence. Criterion-related evidence pertains to how well performance on a given assessment correlates with performance on relevant external or criterion measures. It is common for measurement specialists to measure this correlation statistically, but within the classroom, teachers are more likely to use qualitative judgments of relationships. With either approach, the question being addressed is the same, "If an assessment truly is valid, with what other things should performance on this assessment correlate?"

Shepard (2000) addresses the appropriateness of triangulation within informal assessments, a technique often used in qualitative research where the researcher looks for multiple indicators that are basically independent of each other but support the same conclusion. This is a legitimate approach to establishing criterion-related validity evidence. If a student in chemistry demonstrates knowledge of the difference between elements and compounds using examples available in the lab, does the student correctly recognize which are referenced in the periodic table and also which are involved in spectroscopic studies? Criterion-related evidence is gathered over time, with the teacher looking for consistencies or inconsistencies in what the assessments suggest a particular student knows. Criterion-related evidence is something good teachers continuously do intuitively.

Generalizing Observed Performance to Unobserved Performance

Whenever a student is assessed, only a small sample of potential performances can be included within the assessment. This is not unlike sampling that goes on in statistical studies, such as opinion polling. An opinion poll involves a proportionally small sample of people from the population being studied. That which is observed in the poll is useful only if the results would have been about the same had a different sample of people been used.

In Chapter 5 we noted that in classroom assessments, although all students in the class might be sampled, only a small proportion of potential tasks are included within any given assessment. If a different sample of tasks had been used, would the same conclusions be drawn with respect to what the student knows? Unless the answer is "yes," the assessment will be of very limited use; observed samples of performance need to generalize to relevant unobserved samples of performance.

Our discussion of generalizability addressed several facets of the problem. For instance, will a student's performance generalize to other instances of the same task? Skills as basic as multiplication with single digits often do not generalize; for instance, multiplying 5×4 is usually easier than multiplying 8×7. Will student's performance generalize to *different* tasks within the same domain? With reading comprehension, students who are best at outlining a short story they read are often different from the students who are best at establishing the main idea of the story. Will different teachers reading students' essays consistently score the students' papers? Different readers are often assigned different scores to the same set of papers.

Studies such as by Shavelson et al. (1997) suggest that when scoring plans are carefully devised and used, performance scores assigned by one rater are about as good for one rater as for an average of several raters. Studies, however, suggest that ratings do not generalize very well across tasks. Including a greater number of tasks within an assessment is needed for performance to generalize very well.

When informal assessments are integrated into instruction, one can expect different teachers simultaneously observing student performance to come to the same conclusion regarding the performance of the students, as long as they clearly establish what they are looking for. However, if these teachers were to observe students performing another related task, it is likely their conclusions would be inconsistent from those drawn from observing the other task. The only solution here is to increase the number of tasks. As with all assessments, multiple observations of student performance usually are necessary for the assessments to generalize.

Because informal assessments such as oral questions often involve only a sample of students, one needs to be concerned about how well these observations will generalize. Typically, informal assessments overestimate what students can do, because the more proficient students are more likely to actively participate.

IMPLICATIONS TO EXTERNAL ASSESSMENTS

External assessments, often referred to as standardized tests, play a very visible role within education. An appropriate question is what the implications to external assessments are if assessments are to be integrated into instruction.

In Chapter 17, we look at some issues related to standardized tests, including how to interpret scores commonly used to report results on external assessments. As you probably recognize, standardized tests presently play a number of roles, although as we will later note, some of the roles are incompatible with each other, and some are simply beyond the role that current standardized tests can play. Common among present roles of external assessments are certifying student achievement, placing students into instructional groups, and evaluating the effectiveness of teachers and schools.

As presently designed, standardized tests cannot be used to facilitate the integration of assessments into instruction. To a large degree, the reason for this is that several characteristics of standardized tests are exactly opposite those that tests must have if they are to play an integral role within instruction. Here are some examples:

- Assessments that are integrated into instruction must be highly responsive to the immediate needs of students; the tests would have to be available for use *when* they are needed. Instead, the administration of standardized tests is scheduled months in advance.

- Results from the test would need to be available immediately if they are going to be used to help redirect current instruction. Instead, results from standardized tests are distributed weeks after their administration.

- In order to redirect learning in terms of specific skills students have yet to learn, content measured by a test must be highly focused and detailed in its coverage of the curriculum. Instead, standardized tests tend to measure broad samples of content.

- Related to the previous point, assessments need to provide predominantly criterion-referenced interpretations, establishing what students can and cannot do if an assessment is to play an integral role within instruction. In contrast, standardized tests predominantly provide norm-referenced interpretations.

This list could go on, but you get the idea. Integrating assessments into instruction relies heavily on informal assessments. External assessments cannot play the same role, at least not directly.

There is, however, a very valuable instructional role external assessments can play. If configured and used appropriately, external assessments can identify content areas within which instruction is strong and where it is weak. They also can identify trends over time, to help determine whether the quality of learning is increasing or possibly decreasing, and to facilitate evaluation of instructional innovations. Current external assessments do not allow this to happen. By repeatedly using the same test for several years, and using the results to evaluate teachers and individual schools, external assessments have the predictable effect of teaching to the test and biasing the curriculum toward the sample of skills measured by the test. Understandably, if your teaching is judged to a large degree by how your students do on a test that is re-administered each year for a period of time, consciously or unconsciously you are going to give particular attention to whatever skills are measured by the test.

If the purpose of external assessments is to improve learning rather than simply improve test scores, there are changes that can be made to external assessments that will help accomplish this. One change is to stop administering a given test every year to all students in selected grades. The achievement of students within a school district (not the achievement of individual students but the overall achievement of students within the district) can be determined by administering a test to a *sample* of students in the district. Furthermore, significant changes in achievement usually do not occur within a period of 1 year; administering a test every other year or even every third year is adequate for detecting changes in achievement. By using samples of classrooms, with the sample used changing from year to year, and by administering a test less frequently than every year, one no longer is able to establish how students within every class "scored on the test." From the point of view of many, the inability to compare teachers in terms of how their students performed on the test *causes its own problem,* but one that is addressed shortly. However, by disallowing the use of external assessments to evaluate teachers, the temptation of teaching to the test is diminished substantially. Also, if a given test is administered less frequently and to only samples of students, it is possible to create multiple tests and administer different tests to different samples of students, allowing an increase in detail with which the curriculum is assessed, and in turn facilitating a criterion-referenced interpretation of test results.

This alternate approach to external assessments would not allow the external assessments to establish what individual students had learned. However, the broad sampling of content these assessments measure does not let them do this presently, at least not nearly as well as individual teachers can through their more frequent and extensive formal and informal assessments. This alternate approach also does not allow the external assessments to be used to evaluate individual teachers. However, the repeated use of the same test and then using scores from those tests to evaluate individual teachers provides a false accountability, because the natural and strong tendency for teachers to emphasize the subset of skills measured by the test *will* result in test scores improving, but not as a result of overall improvements in student learning.

Through more detailed testing of content, including the option of relying more heavily on performance assessments, this alternate approach does allow an individual school district, or group of school districts such as those within a particular state, to identify more specifically where their greatest instructional needs are, and cooperatively with teachers, establish strategies for addressing those needs. This alternate approach also allows the external assessments to help determine the effectiveness of interventions used for addressing instructional needs.

If we know what constitutes effective teaching, and in a number of critical areas research has established instructional strategies that are effective, teachers can be evaluated in terms of how adequately they adhere to proven strategies. There are many aspects of teaching for which we do not know what works best because research findings are less conclusive. Quite appropriately, for areas where research is not conclusive, we must recognize that different approaches to teaching may work well, with the selection of the best option often depending on characteristics of the students and teachers who are involved.

This alternate approach allows external assessments to play a highly useful role within instruction. This role is different from that played by a teacher's own formal and informal assessments, but nevertheless it provides a better opportunity for identifying needs and facilitating instruction than does the approach that is more typically now taken with standardized tests. There is a strong tendency, however, to continue testing every student at a given grade level with the same standardized test administered every year. Because the expected outcome of formal education is for students to achieve, administering a test to all students and holding teachers accountable for results seems like such a direct approach to ensuring success in education. This success is more likely to be realized if educators are working cooperatively to find and implement solutions to instructional needs rather than allowing results on external assessments to become the goal of formal education. The quality of learning continues to rely heavily on the ability of teachers to effectively integrate assessment into instruction.

SUMMARY

Although it is common to separate discussions of assessment from those of instruction, this chapter gives particular emphasis to their integration. Part of this disconnect between assessment and instruction is associated with educational measurement maintaining its roots within behavioral psychology while curriculum and instruction have moved on to paradigms associated with cognitive psychology and constructivism.

Researchers in cognitive psychology often contrast how experts versus novices within a content domain solve problems. Problem solving appears to involve declarative and procedural knowledge. To learn and later retrieve declarative knowledge, one must establish linkages among propositions which make up that knowledge. Organization and elaboration are two procedures that facilitate establishment of these linkages. To assess procedural knowledge, a student must be asked to do something as opposed to describing how to do it. To solve problems, some procedural knowledge must become automated basic skills whereas other procedural knowledge becomes domain-specific strategies. Declarative and procedural knowledge must be learned in a manner that allows transfer to the solution of various problems.

Several implications to classroom assessment were addressed. One is recognizing the need for declarative and procedural knowledge and knowing how to assess them. Also, knowledge should be learned and assessed within the context of problem-solving situations. Assessments should be non-threatening to students to encourage, for example, students' use of elaborations. Assessments should generate qualitative descriptions of what students can and cannot do. Performance assessments must play a dominant role at all grade levels.

A constructivist view of learning states one creates new knowledge out of existing knowledge. Scaffolding is an important principle within this paradigm, and involves a teacher providing the learner a temporary structure through which insights into new knowledge are achieved. When the new knowledge is learned, the teacher removes the temporary structure and replaces it with different scaffolding that is used for the construction of subsequent knowledge. Providing this scaffolding requires continuous awareness of a student's knowledge, which in turn relies heavily on extensive informal assessments. Feedback to the learner plays an important role, but within the constructivist's approach, it is unclear whether the feedback should be explicit or indirect.

Validity and generalizability are issues important to integrating assessments into instruction. Establishing evidence of validity is necessary because assessments, including those that are informal or more authentic, always involve indirect measures of knowledge and its use. Evidence of validity can be organized into construct-, content-, and criterion-related categories. Generalizability is a relevant issue because only samples of observations are involved in either formal or informal assessments. Generalizability across tasks is more difficult to achieve than is generalizability across raters.

External assessments, as presently used, do not facilitate integration of assessment into instruction. In part, this is because some characteristics of standardized tests are opposite from those that tests must have if they are to play an integral role. Also, as currently used, external assessments tend to narrow instruction to the set of skills measured by the tests. An alternative approach is to increase the detail of the curriculum that is assessed by administering different external assessments to different samples of students. This does not allow using external assessments to evaluate individual teachers. However, teachers should be evaluated in terms of whether they employ instructional strategies that have been proven to be effective rather than whether they can manipulate instruction to improve scores on tests. To more effectively use external assessments as an integral part of instruction, external assessments should be used to identify instructional needs and to help evaluate how effectively innovations are responding to those needs.

SOMETHING TO TRY

- Rent the DVD or videotape of the movie *Music of the Heart, Dead Poets Society,* or another movie that is centered around a teacher and students interacting. While enjoying the movie, identify some examples of informal assessment that occur, which commonly do or realistically could occur within many classrooms. What role does each of these assessments play, and why was it important for that assessment to occur?

- Identify a specific instructional goal. Examples could include, within algebra, being able to solve for one unknown; within astronomy, being able to locate an object in the night sky; and within letter writing, being able to write an e-mail to an online retailer who shipped a purchased product that was found to be inadequate. Within the context of the instructional goal, identify a couple of examples of both declarative and procedural knowledge that are critical to solving the problem being addressed. In light of the type of capability involved, describe how one would assess each of those skills. How could it be done informally within the context of classroom activities?

- Read the article entitled *Constructivist Learning Theory* written by George E. Hein; available online at *http://www.exploratorium.edu/*

IFI/resources/constructivistlearning.html. (If the web address changes, conduct an Internet search on the name of the article's title and author.) This article provides a nice overview of constructivism, and discusses implications to the audience intended for the article: museum educators. Because this probably represents a different audience than yourself (although you probably have benefited from the work of a number of educators working at museums), you can easily read the article as a reasonably informed outsider. From that perspective, do you agree with the point of view of the author? Look carefully, and determine whether informal assessment is a significant part of the approach proposed by the author. Identify the key issues that generalize to assessment in the classroom.

ADDITIONAL READING

Gagné, E. D., Yekovich, C. W., & Yekovich, F. R. (1993). *The cognitive psychology of school learning.* New York: Harper Collins. This book provides a very readable discussion of cognitive psychology, and carefully discusses implications to learning in classroom settings. Separate sections are devoted to learning mathematics, science, reading, and writing.

Gagné, R. M. (1985). *The conditions of learning* (4th ed.). New York: Holt, Rinehart, and Winston. Discusses the nature of learned capabilities and conditions required for students to learn each capability.

Shepard, L. A. (2000). *The role of classroom assessment in teaching and learning.* CSE Technical Report 517, CRESST. Available online at *http://www.cse. ucla.edu/CRESST/Reports/TECH517.pdf.* This report proposes reforms in classroom assessment that are consistent with constructivist paradigms.

Snow, R. E., & Lohman, D. F. (1989). Implications of cognitive psychology for educational measurement. In R. L. Linn (Ed.), *Educational measurement* (3rd ed., pp. 263–331). New York: Macmillan Publishing. This chapter provides a detailed introduction to research in cognitive psychology and discusses implications this research could have to research in educational measurement.

16

Assigning Grades and Reporting Student Performance

Schools use a variety of systems to report student progress. The most common are conferences; narrative systems, such as letters to parents; checklists; and letter grades. These systems are often used in combination to supplement one another; for instance, parent conferences may be used in combination with letter grades.

Particularly with older students, letter grades are the most widely used system for reporting performance. Letter grades are vaguely defined; therefore, important considerations include determining on what to base grades and the levels of proficiency to be associated with each grade.

Achievement of course objectives is usually listed as the major consideration when assigning grades. Other factors often include student motivation, attitude, and effort. Grades sometimes also reflect discipline, such as when they are adjusted because a student handed an assignment in late or cheated on a test. Incorporating achievement, motivation, attitude, effort, and discipline into a single grade may broaden the meaning of grades, but it also complicates their interpretation.

In addition to determining what should be included in grades, a teacher must establish criteria for each grade and weights to associate with individual assessments.

This chapter helps you achieve three skills:

- Recognize advantages and limitations of alternative systems for reporting student performance outside the classroom

- Establish criteria when assigning letter grades
- Determine the role of grades in motivating and disciplining students

ALTERNATIVE REPORTING SYSTEMS

Schools use a variety of systems to report student performance. The individual teacher typically does not have control over which system is used. However, by briefly describing each system and identifying its major advantages and limitations, this chapter will help you recognize the capabilities of whatever system you are expected to use. The systems discussed here are percentage grades, letter and number grades, pass–fail marks, checklists, written descriptions, and conferences with parents.

Percentage Grades

Percentage grades assign each student a number between 0 and 100. Within the United States in the early 1900s, this system was the most popular grading system. Most schools no longer assign percentage grades; however, many teachers use percentage grades to report students' performance on individual tests and assignments. Also, school districts often use percentage grades to communicate standards that teachers are to use when assigning letter grades. The term *percentage* is used because these grades are assumed to represent the percentage of content a student has mastered.

Advantages. The major advantage of percentage grades is that they provide a convenient summary of student performance. They can be recorded and processed quickly. If the distribution of grades for a given class is known, percentage grades provide a quick overview for a counselor or other audiences of student performance relative to others in the class.

Limitations. One limitation of this reporting system is that the name itself is misleading. A student who receives a 100 probably has not mastered 100% of course content in the sense that further improvement is impossible. Nor is it correct to state that a person who receives a 75 has learned three-fourths of the content. Simply changing the difficulty of the tests or class assignments will significantly alter students' percentage scores.

A second limitation of percentage grades is that they imply a degree of precision that cannot be justified given the reliability of grades. Although percentage scores outside the range of 50% to 100% are rarely assigned, teachers cannot distinguish among levels of student achievement as accurately as the scores suggest.

A third limitation is that percentage grades do not indicate the combination of skills that a student has achieved. Instead, the percentage grade provides an overall indication of student achievement.

Letter Grades

Letter grades consist of a series of letters; typically, five letters are used. Sometimes letters are selected that correspond to certain adjectives (e.g., **E**xcellent, **G**ood, **A**verage, **P**oor, **U**nacceptable). The most common series is A, B, C, D, and F. The vast majority of schools and post-secondary institutions use letter grades.

Some teachers and many school systems relate letter grades to percentage grades. For instance, the range of 90% to 100% might be equated to an A. As indicated previously, percentage grades really do not represent percentage of mastery. Therefore, associating a range of scores with each grade poorly defines letter grades. Unfortunately, this point is often ignored. A teacher or school district may be thought to have higher grading standards than another if higher percentages are associated with respective grades. Because the difficulty of tests and assignments significantly affects the percentage of maximum points that students receive, letter grades cannot be meaningfully associated with percentage scores.

Advantages. As with percentage grades, the major advantage of letter grades is that they provide a convenient summary of student performance. A second advantage is that they approach the optimal number of categories for reporting student progress. If a grading system has too many categories, such as with percentage grades, the system implies precision that does not exist. A grading system with too few categories has reduced reliability and fails to report meaningful distinctions among students.

Mitchelmore (1981) proposed a strategy for establishing the appropriate number of grade categories. He proposed that the optimal number of categories should result in assigning grades within one value of their true grade to at least 90% of students. (A *true grade* is the grade each student would receive if grades were perfectly reliable.) For individual tests and assignments the maximum acceptable number of grades would vary from three to nine. The number of grades in letter-grading systems fits within this range.

A third advantage of using the letter grades A to F is their prevalence and hence familiarity in the United States and some other countries. However, this familiarity can lead to making claims for grades that are unfounded. Letter grades derive much of their meaning from their *relative* positions on a scale or from what we have come to expect of students who have received a particular grade. This is how values on other scales, such as temperature and weight, derive much of their meaning. The principal meaning of the grade B is derived from it being below an A and above a C. With experience, teachers and students learn to anticipate the specific level of performance associated with a given grade, much as we learn to anticipate how comfortable the outside air will be when we are simply told the temperature. Unlike grades, however, a temperature is tied to absolute events (e.g., the freezing and boiling points of water). As we note later, letter grades more adequately communicate student performance when teachers strive to use common grading standards.

Limitations. As with percentage grades, one limitation of letter grades is that they do not indicate the combination of skills that a student has achieved. They provide only a general indication of performance.

A second limitation is that a letter grade by itself does not provide sufficient information to determine whether a student should be promoted to the next grade level in school. Nevertheless, schools typically identify a specific letter grade, which, if assigned, prevents the student from advancing. F is often used for that purpose. If a minimally acceptable level of performance that was educationally meaningful were established, teachers could reserve the F grade for students who achieved below that standard.

A variety of procedures have been proposed for setting minimum standards. (See, for example, reviews by Berk, 1986; Shepard, 1984; and an instructional module on standard setting by Cizek, 1996.) For our purposes, a *minimum standard* is defined as the point below which students have been shown to be unable to learn subsequent material effectively. If a grade such as F is used to indicate that a student is performing below the minimum standard, that grade should be reserved for identifying such students. Because of its meaning, an F grade in particular should not be assigned to some predetermined percentage of students.

A related problem arises when grades are averaged. In college, for example, an F usually indicates that a student has not gained sufficient proficiency to be given credit for a course. However, a C average is usually required to graduate or advance past a particular year in school. A similar procedure is used in high schools, but with different cutoff requirements. This approach assumes that low achievement in one area can be counterbalanced by high achievement elsewhere. Little attention is given to the issue of in which areas, specifically, the low and high achievement appears and whether this combination indicates that the student would benefit more from

retention or promotion. This issue is especially relevant given that the benefits of retaining students have not been established (see, for example, Holmes & Matthews, 1984; and McCoy & Reynolds, 1999).

Pass–Fail Marks

A pass–fail marking system collapses all letter grades into two categories. For example, the F grade could represent failing status, with all other letter grades considered a pass. Sometimes a D, or a C in graduate school, is assumed to represent failing status. Beginning in the 1960s, pass–fail marks gained considerable popularity. Their intent was to encourage students to explore academic subjects they would otherwise avoid because of anticipated low grades (Weller, 1983). One is more likely to find pass–fail grades in use within post-secondary institutions. Usually, pass–fail is offered as an optional grade, although some institutions use this marking system exclusively. A variation of pass–fail is a pass/no-pass policy in which a student's record lists only the courses that a student has passed.

Advantages. As already noted, pass–fail marks have been proposed as a means of encouraging students to take courses in content areas they might otherwise avoid. However, studies indicate that students do not vary the courses they select when given the pass–fail option (Stallings & Smock, 1971).

Limitations. Pass–fail grades have a number of significant disadvantages not shared by other marking systems. One general limitation of pass–fail marks is that they reduce the utility of grades. Advisors are less able to determine how students are achieving in courses when the pass–fail option is used. Colleges are less able to estimate how well an admissions applicant will succeed when a transcript contains a substantial number of pass–fail grades. Students tend to use the pass–fail option to avoid low grades in courses they would take regardless of the grading options. Research suggests that students achieve less when a pass–fail system is used (Karlins, Kaplan, & Stuart, 1969; and Suddick & Kelly, 1981).

A second limitation is that pass–fail grades tend to have low reliability. Ebel (1965) estimated that if the reliability of grades using a five-category system were 0.85, reducing the number of categories to two would reduce the reliability to 0.63. This lower reliability of pass–fail grades was also observed in research by Millman, Slovacek, Kulick, and Mitchell (1983).

Checklists

A checklist allows a teacher to indicate which of a variety of statements describes a given student. Statements on the checklist may pertain to specific academic skills, behavioral and attitudinal traits, or some combination of these. A distinct checklist can be established for each course to reflect the content of the subject area. Checklists are often used to report student attitude and work habits in addition to academic skills. The use of checklists is normally limited to elementary and some secondary schools.

Advantages. The major advantage of checklists is that they more adequately communicate student performance. Lack of specific information is a significant limitation of the preceding systems. A second advantage is that checklists allow the teacher to report separately a variety of traits relevant to instruction. With letter grades, teachers are tempted to combine multiple, unrelated qualities into a single grade, with a resulting decrease in reliability. Checklists circumvent this problem.

Limitations. Checklists are more time-consuming to prepare and process. Computers can alleviate this problem, particularly as handheld computers become more widely used for recording observations and other assessments of student performance. Incorporating a summary grade into checklists enables school personnel and staff at other institutions to process them more efficiently.

Another concern is that great care must be taken to construct a checklist with statements that clearly describe pertinent behaviors. As with checklists used for scoring performance assessments and portfolios, statements should express behaviors and traits that are directly observable. Inference should not be required. For example, "The student uses appropriate punctuation when writing sentences" is more useful than "The student writes well." (Chapter 12 provides guidelines for constructing checklists.) Because checklists are used to provide information to parents, parents should assist in the development and revision of checklists used for grading.

Particularly in elementary and middle schools, checklists are increasingly being used as a substitute for letter grades. This change often is initiated by teachers who, with at least some justification, are concerned about the negative effects that letter grades have, particularly on less proficient students. When parents are not heavily involved in the development and ongoing evaluation of the checklists, little or nothing is gained by giving parents the detailed information that a checklist can provide. Often, parents cannot effectively use the detailed information unless it is accompanied by a narrative from the teacher. Checklists can also be misleading, as they sometimes appear to present inconsistent information. For example, early in the year, a checklist might indicate that a student is using correct punctuation when writing sentences. Later in the year, when more complex punctuation skills are taught, the same checklist might indicate that the same student is not using punctuation correctly. The parents will likely conclude that the child is losing rather than gaining proficiency.

Typically, parents are unable to use highly detailed information about a child's achievement. They do not observe the day-to-day details of classroom work and often are unaware of the pedagogy critical to effective learning. Usually, parents want to know whether everything is all right in general and what they can do to facilitate the child's achievement in school. This information may best be conveyed through a general rating of performance within each academic area, accompanied by brief written descriptions that help the parents interpret and use these ratings.

Written Descriptions

An alternative or supplement to assigning grades is to write a narrative description of each student's work. The narrative can describe traits that facilitate or restrict learning, in addition to the student's accomplishments. As with a checklist, the primary audience for written descriptions is parents.

Advantages. The major advantage of written descriptions is their flexibility. They can include whatever is relevant, and can focus the reader's attention on the most significant issues.

Limitations. The flexibility of written descriptions is also their greatest limitation. Considerable care must be taken to write clearly and to provide a comprehensive description of each student. Both what is and what is not included in the description can be misconstrued. For example, when an ongoing trait has not been mentioned in previous narratives or by prior teachers, this trait may be assumed by the reader to be a new or developing quality when it is first reported. Similarly, a previous description that is absent from a present report can be assumed to represent a change in the student's performance. This limitation can be reduced by reading previous written descriptions, a time-consuming process.

The consistency of written descriptions can be improved by following an outline agreed to by all teachers. As with checklists, it is best if the outline is developed jointly with parents. By following the outline, the reader knows what is being rated. This approach avoids misinterpretations from the omission of information.

Another limitation of written descriptions is that they are time-consuming to prepare and read. For this reason, they are generally impractical for teachers at secondary schools and for others who evaluate a large number of students. Written descriptions also pose problems for counselors and others who review a large number of student progress reports; the volume of reading can be substantial, and reports from different teachers are usually written without a common framework.

Parent Conferences

Many schools supplement written grade reports with conferences between teachers and parents. These conferences are most successful when ideas expressed are supported by concrete illustrations, such as portfolios or other examples of work. Particularly when examples of work are involved, students can be effectively involved as participants in these conferences with parents.

Advantages. The major advantage of parent conferences is direct communication with the teacher. As opposed to writing a letter, a conference allows the teacher to use feedback from the parent to assure that ideas are being communicated accurately and with appropriate emphasis. A conference can also increase parents' involvement in the child's schooling, both directly and psychologically, resulting in benefits to the instructional process.

Limitations. Parent conferences share two important limitations with written descriptions. First, because they often are unstructured, care must be taken to provide a representative description of the student. This problem is minimal, however, because conferences usually play a supplementary role in reporting student progress. Also, the direct communication with parents allows the teacher to sense inadequate communication.

A second limitation common to written descriptions is that parent conferences are time-consuming. Conferences require considerable planning time on the part of teachers, in addition to the time needed for the conference itself. It is often difficult for parents to come to regular conferences at times that are convenient for teachers.

A limitation unique to conferences is that they usually provide no permanent documentation of what was communicated. The supplemental role of parent conferences minimizes this concern.

❧ 16.1 Apply What You Are Learning

Indicate (A or B) which reporting system is superior with respect to the characteristics being questioned.

Which reporting system provides a record that is easier to average across subject areas?

1. A. Letter grades
   B. Written descriptions
2. A. Percentage grades
   B. Parent conferences

Which reporting system provides precision more consistent with classroom measures of student achievement?

3. A. Letter grades
   B. Percentage grades
4. A. Letter grades
   B. Pass–fail marks

Which reporting system best indicates the specific skills a student has learned?

5. A. Checklists
   B. Percentage grades
6. A. Letter grades
   B. Parent conferences

When each student has several teachers, which reporting system is more likely to identify the subject in which a particular student is having the greatest difficulty?

7. A. Letter grades
   B. Pass–fail marks

Which reporting system is most likely to help a counselor recommend the colleges to which a student should apply for admission?

8. A. Checklists
   B. Letter grades

Answers can be found at the end of the chapter.

ESTABLISHING GRADING CRITERIA

Most schools use letter grades to report student performance. The meaning of letter grades is often vague, since a single letter is used to communicate very complex information. Teachers can offset this vagueness by carefully establishing grading criteria. Doing so involves (1) determining the nature and number of assessments on which to base grades, (2) selecting the weight to be given each assessment, and (3) setting the performance standard for each grade.

Nature and Number of Assessments

In most elementary and secondary schools, the content of the curriculum is set by others, either the school district or a state agency. Teachers are usually responsible for determining how to teach and assess this content and for assigning grades.

If the primary function of these grades is to communicate students' academic proficiency, assessments on which grades are based must be measures of what students have learned. These assessments may involve diverse measures obtained throughout the school term. However, only a content expert, typically the teacher, can determine the nature and number of assessments that should be used to establish student proficiency. Here are some factors to consider.

1. As a whole, items included in grades should provide a representative sampling of all the instructional objectives covered during the term. Thus, a variety of measures, such as written tests, performance assessments, and assignments, can be included.

2. A grade should be based on multiple observations of achievement. The reliability of scores on one project or one written test is usually no better than moderate. Increasing the number of observations is one of the most effective techniques for increasing the reliability of grades or of any assessment.

3. A grade need not include all items for which student scores have been retained. Most seat work, homework, and quizzes are used for formative rather than summative roles. When their role is formative, these assessments generally should not be considered when assigning grades.

4. Items that are unrelated to instructional objectives should be excluded from grades. For instance, unless promptness and participation are specifically identified as instructional objectives, they should be excluded from grades, or at least their influence should be minimized when weights are determined for each assessment.

Determining the Weight to Be Given Each Assessment

The weight given each assessment is also based on the professional judgment of the teacher. Quite obviously, more significant assessments are weighted more heavily. Weights should correspond to the relative importance of the instructional objectives being assessed. Weights should not be based on amount of student effort, class time, or time required to assess student work unless these variables are important to the instructional objectives being assessed. Taken as a whole, the weights assigned to various assessments should make logical sense in terms of overall instructional objectives.

In addition to influencing the grade each student receives, giving additional weight to a test, project, or other measure affects the reliability and validity of the grade. If additional weight is given to a measure that has low reliability or validity, the reliability and validity of the overall grade is reduced. Therefore, if you heavily weigh an assessment when assigning grades, take particular care to ensure that this assessment is reliable and valid.

When less than 10% of the overall grade is based on a particular assessment, that assessment has a minimal and usually negligible effect on the overall grade. For this reason, variables not directly related to instructional objectives, such as

participation and promptness, can be included within the grading scheme without actually affecting the grades that are assigned. I am not encouraging inclusion of such variables, but simply acknowledging that, to an extent, one can get away with it. (Authors also walk fine lines!) Watch out for cumulative effects. If, for example, participation and promptness are *each* given 10%, their cumulative effect becomes more substantial. If they are included, minimal weight should be assigned to variables indirectly related to instructional objectives.

Establishing Performance Standards

Establishing performance standards for grades requires selection of a reference to which student performance will be compared. Four references are often considered:

1. A student's ability to learn
2. A student's prior performance
3. The performance of other students
4. Predefined levels of performance

Teachers often try to combine references (Nava & Loyd, 1991). For example, a teacher might use predefined levels of performance, such as 90% for an A, 80% for a B, and so on, but then adjust each student's grade based on an estimate of how much the student has improved. This procedure results in a grade that lacks meaning. By combining the two references, the grade can no longer be interpreted in light of either reference: It no longer describes student performance in terms of the predefined levels, and it no longer describes how much the student has improved. The simultaneous use of two or more references usually makes it impossible to interpret the grade. When assigning grades, select and use one reference exclusively.

Ability to Learn. Using student ability as a reference for setting performance standards is intuitively appealing, but it has some serious problems. It is appealing because all students have an equal chance of receiving a high grade. However, here are the problems:

1. A teacher does not typically have reliable and valid measures of students' capacity to learn skills within each content area.

2. When reasonable measures of ability do exist, they predict which students are likely to achieve the most. They do not indicate the *maximum* achievement a student can obtain. A teacher cannot use these measures to determine the fraction of potential a student has achieved.

3. Individuals interpreting grades generally are not provided measures of student potential. Without such information, it is not possible to interpret grades referenced to student potential.

Prior Performance. How much a student has improved over prior performance also provides an appealing reference for setting performance standards. Using this reference, a student who begins with less achievement does not have to learn more in order to receive the same grade as a student who began with a higher level of achievement. However, basing grades on how much students have improved results in grades being largely controlled by the error that is inherent in every teacher's assessments. Here is why.

Because of their less-than-perfect reliability, the scores on even the best assessments have some error. This error is then transferred to student grades that are based on these assessments. Although we hope that the differences in the grades students receive reflect real differences that exist among students, some of the differences in grades will always be caused by errors within the assessments. If a teacher adjusts grades based on students' prior performance, this in effect removes differences in grades associated with real differences that exist among students. This adjustment does not remove errors inherent in each assessment. Consequently, by removing real differences among students, a much larger portion of differences in grades becomes associated with errors in the assessments. This problem becomes even worse when a teacher's measurement of students' prior performance is based on

a recollection of earlier performance rather than on a formal assessment of student achievement prior to instruction. Grades should not be based on the improvement of each student's performance because of the substantial effect errors in assessment have on these grades.

Performance of Other Students. Using the performance of others as the standard of performance involves presetting the distribution of letter grades. For example, a teacher might assign an A to the top 15% of the students, B to the next 25%, and so on. This is sometimes called *grading on the curve.* Three concerns are often associated with basing standards on the performance of other students:

1. Standards may vary depending on which students are enrolled in the class. This is particularly true for small classes and is always somewhat of a problem unless several sections of a class can be combined for grading purposes.

2. The performance of other students provides a vague and often hard to defend performance standard. Simply telling a student or parent that a lower grade was assigned because others performed better lacks clarity.

3. Using the performance of others as a reference encourages competitive rather than cooperative learning. Competitive learning is sometimes supported on the basis that it is more like the real world, although teachers generally favor cooperative learning.

Predefined Levels of Performance. Assigning grades based on predefined levels of performance associates each grade with a fixed performance regardless of the distribution of grades ultimately assigned in the class.

School districts, as well as colleges, use different techniques to establish performance levels for each grade. Often percentages are associated with each grade. For instance, 90% to 100% might correspond to an A; 80% to 90%, a B; and so on. Recall that grades historically were reported as percentages rather than as letters. As we noted, these percentages *do not* refer to percentage of mastery. Simply using easier or more difficult assignments or tests significantly changes students' percentage scores. Therefore, teachers who associate the same percentages with each grade are likely not using the same grading standards. Teachers who are teaching similar classes and whose students end up with *approximately* the same distribution of grades are more likely to be using similar grading standards.

Although the distribution of grades is not the reference when grades are based on predefined levels of performance, the distribution of grades can help teachers determine whether they are using equivalent levels of performance for assigning grades. If grade distributions vary dramatically among teachers, this information can be used to help evaluate grading standards for the next term.

A second approach to defining performance standards is to associate adjectives with each letter grade. Common associations are A = outstanding, B = very good, C = satisfactory, D = weak, and F = unsatisfactory. Schools often use these or similar descriptions on grade reports. Certainly, these words are limited by their vagueness, but so are percentage scores, although less obviously so. (For instance, the interpretation of 90% depends as much on the difficulty of the task that students are asked to complete as the interpretation of "outstanding" depends on the meaning a teacher attaches to this adjective.)

A third and superior approach to defining preset performance standards is to describe the characteristics of students associated with each letter grade. This is similar to establishing the descriptions associated with a scoring rubric (see Chapter 12).

One technique for establishing these descriptions is first to identify which students were assigned each letter grade during the previous comparable term or year. Then, the subset of students who scored within the middle of each grade range is selected. Approximately the middle 50% of students *within* each grade range is appropriate. Finally, the performance of each of these sub-

sets of students is described in terms of the broad instructional goals of the content being taught. As with a scoring rubric, it is best to use the same variables when describing performance within each of these subsets of students. These descriptions become the preset performance standards for assigning grades to subsequent students.

Letter grades assigned using preset standards will communicate student performance to parents and others only if these preset standards are meaningfully communicated along with the dissemination of the letter grades. This is most effectively done by establishing and distributing descriptions of standards such as we have just discussed. Although such descriptions can be readily distributed to parents and made available to school personnel, they cannot generally be distributed to other audiences who have to interpret grades. For those audiences, grades must be interpreted through reference to more vague standards, such as how students with a particular average of grades tend to perform.

ROLE OF GRADES IN MOTIVATING AND DISCIPLINING STUDENTS

Grades can strongly motivate students. (To illustrate, how alert are you when the instructor explains how grades will be assigned?) The motivational role of grades comes quite naturally. High grades are continually associated with desirable qualities, such as good work. Low grades are related to less-desirable outcomes, such as low performance. Sometimes low grades are used to punish students; for instance, to show disapproval of students' turning in assignments late or cheating on tests. The motivating potential of grades, however, is not universal. Particularly among students who have had limited success in school, the possibility of a high grade or the threat of a low grade has a negligible effect.

Use of Grades to Motivate Students

Deutsch (1979) referred to grades as "the basic currency of our educational system." Not unlike monetary outcomes, the positive associations with high grades can result in grades being perceived as an end unto themselves. Educators generally resist excessive emphasis on grades. Some recommend that they be abolished. Nonetheless, grades in some form are likely to continue. Accountability has always been regarded as a necessary part of education at all levels. Assessment of student learning will always be a significant aspect of accountability. Students will learn to associate values with any index of achievement, no matter what form it takes or how abstract it becomes. Grades, or their substitute, will always elicit some motivational qualities.

We can debate whether teachers should use grades to motivate students. Obtaining a high grade should be synonymous with achieving a high degree of course objectives. We can argue that motivating students to obtain high grades is equivalent to encouraging high achievement. However, grades have no intrinsic value. The extrinsic value they obtain is conveyed, in part, by teachers who themselves typically completed a baccalaureate degree or beyond. Teachers have had an above-average success with grades and are likely to reinforce motivational attributes they themselves have associated with grades.

Use of Grades to Discipline Students

Grades serve as a convenient and often effective disciplinary tool. Cullen, Cullen, Hayhow, and Plouffe (1975) found that students were more likely to avoid a low grade than work for a high grade. This facilitates teachers' use of grades as punishment. Particularly at the secondary and post-secondary levels, grades have been used to discipline students for a variety of actions, including delinquent homework, truancy, and cheating on tests.

In spite of their convenience, grades *should not* be used to discipline students. Previous discussion has indicated the need for grades or any scores to measure a single trait. The internal consistency or reliability of grades is reduced when used to communicate multiple characteristics that are unrelated. Individuals who later interpret grades without direct knowledge of the student typically assume that the grades indicate

degree of academic competence. Disciplining students through grades, therefore, invalidates their interpretation.

Two disciplinary actions involving grades have a particularly significant negative impact on the usefulness of grades: assigning zero credit for incomplete work, and lowering grades in response to cheating.

Zero Credit for Incomplete Work. Teachers often reduce the credit that students receive on an assignment when the work is turned in late. As indicated previously, the practice of incorporating unrelated qualities into a grade reduces the usefulness of grades when interpreted by others. This effect is particularly profound when the teacher assigns a score of zero to missing or incomplete work. A teacher may perceive the assignment of a zero to be an appropriate punishment for not completing a task. The teacher might also assign a zero score as a nonpunitive response to the student's failure to earn any points on the test or assignment. However, the fact that a student is missing a score is not synonymous with the student's having zero achievement with the competency represented by the score. (An analogy that comes to mind is the weather service's recording today's maximum temperature as zero whenever the maximum reading is missing.) A zero score has a very potent effect on a student's grade because its numerical value usually deviates considerably from other scores assigned the student. The effect is so strong that using a zero to indicate a missing score in essence may override all other assessments you have obtained for that student. If the zero is being given for disciplinary purposes, the assigned grade may have little relation to the student's achievement of instructional goals.

Obviously, the best resolution of a missing score is to have the student complete the missing assignment. If this is not possible, an alternative is to obtain some indirect estimate of that student's proficiency. A substitute score may be established by reviewing the student's performance with similar skills and substituting this performance for the missing score. If the missing score represents a heavily weighted component of course grades, a grade of "incomplete" might be assigned until the student has completed the missing activity, if the school provides this option. To reiterate, a major reason for not assigning a score of zero when a score is missing is that the zero probably does not represent a best estimate of the student's achievement with the skills represented by that score.

Lowering Grades in Response to Cheating. Cheating on tests or other class activities is usually viewed as a serious offense, and rightfully so. Disciplinary action is appropriate. However, lowering grades is an inappropriate response to cheating, again because of the negative impact of such action on the interpretation of grades.

Assigning an F grade is a common response to cheating on a test. Honor codes established at some schools even support this reaction. Hills (1981) reviewed the legal implications of failing students caught cheating. Courts interpret cheating as a disciplinary, not an academic, matter and do not support a disciplinary role for grades.

From a measurement perspective, grades should reflect the teacher's best assessment of each student's achievement. If a test score is assumed to be invalid because a student cheated, the student should be reexamined, using a test of similar difficulty. Unless instruction is individually paced, the student may be asked to complete the same or a parallel test without further preparation.

SUMMARY

Schools use a variety of systems to communicate students' performance to parents and others. These systems include conferences, narrative reports, checklists, percentage grades, letter grades, and pass–fail marks. The most commonly used system is letter grades. A number of school systems use checklists to augment or replace letter grades, particularly at the early elementary levels. Most schools use conferences, usually between a teacher and parent. The use of checklists and conferences was addressed in earlier chapters.

When interpreted by others, letter grades generally are assumed to report a student's achievement of instructional goals. Including other factors in grades, such as disciplinary actions, makes grades more difficult or impossible to interpret. Grades should rely on a number of assessments, which collectively represent a broad cross-section of instructional objectives covered during the term. Particular attention should be given to the reliability and validity of assessments assigned the heavier weights.

A single reference should be used when assigning grades. One reference might be students' ability to learn; however, appropriate measures of ability to learn do not exist. Improvement over prior performance represents another reference, but grades based on improvement often are influenced entirely by errors in the assessments. The performance of other students can be used as a reference for grading, although many teachers prefer not to use this approach. Also, unless large numbers of students are involved, the performance of the class may vary widely from one year to another. Assigning grades based on predefined levels of performance is generally the most preferred option. These levels of performance might be established using percentages, although it is better to establish descriptions of performance associated with each letter grade, much like a scoring rubric.

Grades motivate many students. The consequences of depending heavily on grades to motivate students are unknown, but strong dependence on grades to motivate students is generally regarded as undesirable. Grades should not be used to discipline students.

ANSWERS: APPLY WHAT YOU ARE LEARNING

16.1. 1. A; 2. A; 3. A; 4. A; 5. A; 6. B; 7. A; 8. B.

SOMETHING TO TRY

- How would you determine what you should discuss during a conference with parents? Name specific ways in which planning for a parent conference is similar to planning portfolios.
- Design a checklist that could be used to report student performance in a class you might teach. Use guidelines for constructing a checklist discussed in Chapter 12.
- List some specific techniques sometimes used by teachers to assign grades that makes it difficult for parents and others to interpret the grades. Relate these techniques to points addressed in this chapter.
- Should letter grades be eliminated? If yes, what should replace them? If no, what specific changes should be made to how letter grades are assigned and used?
- A common procedure for establishing minimum scores for each grade is to look for breaks in the distributions of students' scores. Do you see any significant problems with using this procedure to assign grades?
- Design a plan for assigning end-of-term grades for a class you might teach. Your plan should identify specific assessments on which grades would be based.

ADDITIONAL READING

Brookhart, S. M. (1994). Teachers' grading: Practice and theory. *Applied Measurement in Education, 7,* 279–301. Reviews grading practices used by teachers, and discusses the implications of grading practices to motivation and evaluation theory.

Geisinger, K. F. (1982). Marking systems. In H. E. Mitzel (Ed.), *Encyclopedia of educational research* (5th ed., pp. 1139–1145). New York: Free Press. This selection reviews research pertaining to grading and focuses on the purpose of grades, discussion of alternative marking systems, and psychometric qualities of grades.

Hills, J. R. (1981). *Measurement and evaluation in the classroom* (2nd ed.). Columbus, OH: Merrill. Pages 345–357 discuss legal aspects of grading.

Stiggins, R. J. (1991). *A practical guide for developing sound grading practices*. Portland, OR: Northwest Regional Educational Laboratory. This is a handbook of approximately 50 pages used in a workshop in the NWREL Classroom Training Program. The handbook discusses (1) the importance of grades to students, (2) the role of student achievement, effort, and other characteristics in the assignment of grades, (3) alternative means of gathering data on student achievement, and (4) determining grading standards.

17

Interpreting and Using Standardized Tests

tations and even wrong decisions that are harmful to the student.

This chapter helps you achieve three skills:

- Identify basic distinctions between aptitude and achievement tests
- Interpret scores commonly used with standardized tests
- Evaluate selected uses of standardized tests that are particularly relevant to the classroom environment

Standardized tests originate outside the school, but significantly affect what goes on in the classroom. In most schools and classrooms, standardized tests are a very visible and often controversial part of the assessment process. School principals often minimize the role standardized achievement tests have on classroom activities, but, at the same time, strongly praise teachers whose students perform well on these tests. Newspapers and real-estate agents attach considerable importance to standardized test scores, as do many parents, school superintendents, community leaders, and politicans.

A teacher needs to be knowledgeable about standardized tests, not only to defend against their misuse, but also to take advantage of the information they can provide. An appropriately selected standardized test can furnish a snapshot of students' abilities, identifying areas of probable strength or weakness. Standardized tests often are used to help establish instructional groups within a classroom or to help identify students likely to benefit from special instruction.

To use standardized tests and to guard against their misinterpretation, a teacher must recognize the basic distinctions between aptitude and achievement tests. A teacher must also know characteristics of scores used to report test results. The interpretation of some of these scores is intuitive, although the commonsense interpretation of some scores leads to incorrect interpre-

DISTINCTION BETWEEN APTITUDE AND ACHIEVEMENT TESTS

For our discussion, the most useful distinctions between aptitude and achievement tests are found in their purpose and the types of skills they measure.

Purpose of Aptitude and Achievement Tests

The overall purpose of aptitude tests is to estimate how well students will learn. Such estimates facilitate a variety of decisions, such as how to group students or how to identify students who will benefit from special types of instruction. Aptitude tests also help select students for admission to academically competitive schools, and may help students formulate realistic educational and vocational goals.

Achievement tests measure students' present status with a set of skills. When scores are compared to norms, achievement tests indicate strengths and weaknesses of a student or group of students compared with those of the norm group. In conjunction with aptitude measures, achievement tests are used to evaluate the effectiveness of instructional programs and to identify students with learning disabilities. Standardized tests help ensure that students are taught critical skills. They are used to exempt students from instruction in skills they have already learned or to group students based on what they have yet to learn.

Skills Measured by Aptitude and Achievement Tests

Although the uses of aptitude and achievement tests are generally different, both types of tests measure previously learned skills. In fact, tests have no choice but to measure learned skills. Even though we often try to make inferences to underlying or even innate capabilities, we are always limited to measuring student behaviors that we can see. *All behaviors that are measurable are learned.*

Aptitude and achievement tests tend to measure different behaviors, however. Aptitude tests tend to measure more general abilities that are learned over an extended period of time, whereas achievement tests typically measure more specific and recently acquired skills. Aptitude tests tend to measure skills learned informally, such as knowledge of vocabulary and the ability to solve problems involving spatial relationships between objects. Achievement tests measure skills taught in school, such as mathematics and reading.

Sometimes people are surprised that aptitude tests do not measure innate abilities but rather measure what a student has learned. It is important to recognize that all psychological and educational tests must measure observable behaviors. How well a student has learned skills in the past often provides a good estimate of skills the student will learn in the future. Given that the purpose of aptitude tests is to estimate a student's ability to learn new material, using measures of prior learning is a reasonable strategy for predicting subsequent learning.

Any achievement test can conceivably be used as an aptitude test in the sense that it will predict future achievement. However, as the skills tested by the achievement test become a smaller subset of skills essential to learning later skills, the ability of the achievement test to predict later achievement will decrease. For example, an achievement test measuring multiplication skills will more accurately predict a student's ability to learn exponents than to solve quadratic equations, even though multiplication is an integral part of both skills. An appropriate achievement test provides the better short-range prediction of

students' ability to learn a specific skill; an aptitude test provides the better long-range prediction of students' ability to learn material in a variety of school subjects.

By measuring broad skills, aptitude tests are less affected by experiences specific to a particular classroom or year in school. However, aptitude measures do reflect learning that occurs informally, particularly in the home and community. Consequently, scores on aptitude tests are influenced by a variety of cultural factors. Physical impairments, particularly those of sight and hearing, also affect scores on aptitude tests. Some tests such as "culture-fair" tests attempt to better measure latent aptitude, typically by using pictures or diagrams to minimize language-dependent skills. However, nonverbal aptitude tests are less able to predict how well students will learn in a school setting simply because academic tasks are highly verbal. As with all tests, nonverbal aptitude tests measure learned skills, and therefore performance on these tests is still influenced by cultural factors.

A school district typically decides which standardized tests will be used in its schools. A committee that includes teacher representatives usually makes this decision. Test reports are given to teachers both to facilitate instruction in the classroom and to interpret test scores to parents. School districts administer more standardized achievement tests than aptitude tests. Most of the achievement tests are *achievement batteries,* a series of tests covering several broad content areas, such as reading, writing, mathematics, science, and social studies.

INTERPRETING SCORES COMMONLY USED WITH STANDARDIZED TESTS

Several different types of scores are used to report results on standardized tests. In a broad sense, these scores are very similar; the same students obtain the highest scores on a particular test, regardless of which type of score is used. These types of scores differ, however, with respect to some important characteristics of which you should be aware. It is convenient to group these types of scores into four categories: standard scores, percentile ranks, grade equivalents, and scaled scores.

Standard Scores

Standard scores are so named because their interpretation is based on a statistical measure called *standard deviation*.[1] You do not need to know how to compute standard deviation to use standard scores; however, being able to interpret standard deviation is important for using standard scores. The web site designed for use with this book shows how to interpret standard deviation.

Standard deviation (referred to as SD in Figure 17.1) basically indicates how far a particular score is above or below the *arithmetic mean* of a group of scores. (When you think of the word *average,* you are probably thinking about the arithmetic mean. The arithmetic mean is computed simply by adding up all the scores and dividing this total by the number of scores.) Figure 17.1 shows the approximate proportion of scores within 1, 2, and 3 standard deviations of the mean. Usually all scores are within 3 standard deviations of the mean.

Imagine cars driving on a highway where the arithmetic mean was 70 mph (miles per hour), and the standard deviation was 5 mph. Were this the case, one would expect that somewhere in the neighborhood of 68% of the cars would be traveling within 1 standard deviation (5 mph) of 70; that is, between 65 and 75 mph. Likewise, about 95% of the cars would be traveling within 2 standard deviations of the mean (60 to 80 mph), and almost all cars to be traveling within 3 standard deviations (55 to 85 mph). The mean and standard deviation do not establish whether these cars are driving at a reasonable speed. They do establish the speed of cars with respect to what is typical for this particular section of the highway. With a mean and standard deviation of 70 and 5, you probably would agree with the verbal descriptions given in Figure 17.1. The average speed of 70 could be called "at the middle," while speeds of 65 and 75 could be described as "somewhat below" and "somewhat above" the middle. Likewise, 80 would be judged as "significantly above the middle," and 55 as "far below the middle." Relative to other cars on this highway, those traveling at 65 or 75 would not be considered far from what is typical, but cars traveling at 55 or 85 would be.

The performance of a student relative to how others scored on the test can also be expressed in terms of standard deviation. For example, a score that is 1 standard deviation below the arithmetic mean is somewhat below middle. A score that is 3 standard deviations above the mean is far above the middle. Scores can be expressed in fractions of a standard deviation unit. For instance, a particular score could be 2.4 standard deviations above the mean.

❧ 17.1   Apply What You Are Learning

Here are some brainteasers. A large number of students completed a test. In terms of standard deviation units, here are the scores for four of these students:

> Laura's score is 1 SD below the mean.
> Manuel's score is at the mean.
> Monique's score is 1 SD above the mean.
> Vincent's score is 2 SDs above the mean.

1. What fraction of all students scored higher than Laura but lower than Monique?
2. What fraction scored outside this range; that is, scored either lower than Laura or higher than Monique?
3. What fraction scored lower than Laura?
4. What fraction scored higher than Monique?
5. What fraction of all students scored lower than Manuel?

---

[1]Here is a point that is often confusing: The meaning of the word *standardized* as in standardized test has little to do with the meaning of *standard* in standard score. Calling a test "standardized" indicates its administration is carefully prescribed so that the test is administered the same way at different locations or at different times. A score is said to be a "standard score" if it refers to standard deviation units. Although standard scores are often used to report results on standardized tests, standard scores are used in a variety of settings unrelated to educational testing.

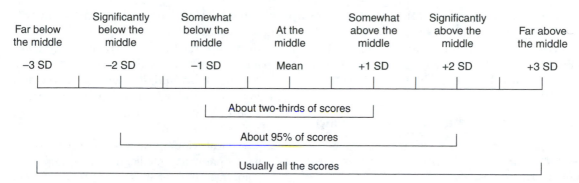

Figure 17.1
Approximate fraction of test scores within 1, 2, and 3 standard deviations of the mean and narrative descriptions of these prints.

	Far below the middle	Significantly below the middle	Somewhat below the middle	At the middle	Somewhat above the middle	Significantly above the middle	Far above the middle
	−3 SD	−2 SD	−1 SD	Mean	+1 SD	+2 SD	+3 SD
T-scores	20	30	40	50	60	70	80
Deviation IQs	52	68	84	100	116	132	148
Stanines		1 2	3	4 5 6	7	8 9	

About two-thirds of scores

About 95% of scores

Usually all the scores

Figure 17.2
Selected standard scores on a scale that is 3 standard deviations below to 3 standard deviations above the mean

6. What fraction scored higher than Manuel but lower than Monique?
7. What fraction of all students scored higher than Vincent?

Answers can be found at the end of the chapter.

A standard score has a preset mean and standard deviation. Those used with educational tests usually involve a scale that has a convenient mean and standard deviation. We will look at the four standard-score scales you are likely to see used in schools. Each of these scales is illustrated in Figure 17.2.

T-Scores. The *T*-score is a standard score with a mean equal to 50 and standard deviation equal to 10. A student whose score on the test is equal to the test mean will obtain a *T*-score of 50. Likewise, a student whose score is 1 standard deviation below the mean will obtain a *T*-score of 40.

A student who scored 2 standard deviations above the mean will have a *T*-score of 70. *T*-scores are used to report results on the Preliminary SAT/National Merit Scholarship Qualifying Test, also known as the PSAT/NMSQT.

🌐 17.2 Apply What You Are Learning

Here is how each of several students performed on the PSAT/NMSQT. What *T*-score did each of these students obtain?

1. Michael scored 1 standard deviation *above* the mean.
2. Stephen scored 2 standard deviations *below* the mean.
3. Seth scored 0.5 standard deviations *above* the mean.
4. Lisa scored 1.5 standard deviations *above* the mean.
5. Randall scored 2.5 standard deviations *below* the mean.

Answers can be found at the end of the chapter.

Deviation IQ Scores. Earlier intelligence tests derived a mental age score for a child and compared that score to the individual's chronological age. The ratio of mental age to chronological age, when multiplied by 100, became the child's intelligence quotient, or IQ. The concept of an intelligence quotient was not useful for older adolescents or adults because a person's intellectual capabilities were believed to cease development before the age of 20.

Analysis of scores of the then-dominant intelligence test indicated that the mean and standard deviation of IQs were approximately 100 and 16, respectively. Therefore, to get around the problem of comparing mental age to chronological age, performance on intelligence tests was expressed using a standard score with mean and standard deviation preset at 100 and 16. This standard score was referred to as a *deviation IQ* score. A person whose performance on the intelligence test was at the mean was assigned a deviation IQ score of 100. Similarly, an individual whose performance was 1 standard deviation above the mean was assigned a score of 116.

Virtually all tests that report results as IQ scores are using *deviation IQ* scores. Any values can be used for the mean and standard deviation of a standard-score scale. Publishers of intelligence tests quite consistently use a mean of 100; however, standard deviation values other than 16 are sometimes used. Knowing the standard deviation being used with a particular intelligence test is important to the interpretation of its scores. Also, different intelligence tests measure different abilities. Therefore, knowing what an intelligence test measures is also highly relevant to its interpretation.

Stanine Scores. The term *stanine* is an abbreviation of the words "*sta*ndard *nine*," and its value is limited to the range of 1 to 9. Stanine is a standard score with a mean equal to 5 and standard deviation equal to 2. A student whose raw score equals the average for the test will obtain a stanine score of 5. A score that is 1 standard deviation below the mean equals a stanine of 3. Students who score 2 (or more) standard deviations below and above the mean are assigned stanines of 1 and 9, respectively.

Because only nine numbers are associated with stanine scores, more than one raw score often ends up being assigned the same stanine. As illustrated in Figure 17.2, each stanine score refers to a small range of ability.

A score that is 3 standard deviations above the mean is assigned a stanine of 9, not 11, because stanines are limited to a range of 1 to 9. A stanine of 9 thus refers to a wider range of scores because it includes all scores from the highest score to a score approximately 2 standard deviations above the mean. A stanine of 1 represents a similarly wide range of scores.

🌐 17.3 Apply What You Are Learning

Here is how several individuals performed on a standardized test. What stanine did each of these students obtain?

1. Miles scored 1 standard deviation *above* the mean.
2. Natasha scored 2 standard deviations *below* the mean.

3. Chris scored 0.5 standard deviations *above* the mean.
4. Greg scored 1.5 standard deviations *above* the mean.
5. Mindy scored 2.5 standard deviations *below* the mean.

Answers can be found at the end of the chapter.

NCE Scores. One additional standard score that is commonly used is called the normal curve equivalent score, usually referred to as the NCE score. NCE scores have a preset mean of 50 and a rather unusual standard deviation of 21.06. This standard deviation value was selected so that students obtain the same score at three points on both the percentile rank and NCE scales, these points being 1, 50, and 99. Scores on both the NCE scale and percentile ranks range from 1 to 99, but the interpretation of scores on each scale is different. This difference will become apparent when we later discuss percentile ranks.

Considerations When Interpreting Standard Scores. A standard score indicates how many standard deviations a student's score is below or above the mean. Visualizing a standard score as a point on one of the scales in Figure 17.2 can facilitate its interpretation. Knowing the mean and standard deviation of a standard score locates the score on its scale. For example, because T-scores have a mean and standard deviation of 50 and 10, a T-score of 35 is 1.5 standard deviations below the mean.

Converting students' raw scores on a test (for instance, the number of items each student answered correctly) to standard scores does not change the meaning of the students' performance on that test. The conversion simply changes the reporting of the performance from one scale to another. The conversion is very similar to converting temperatures from Fahrenheit to Celsius. Temperature measurements on one scale have the same meaning as on the other, even though the numerical values change.

As noted earlier, the interpretation of standard scores depends in part on the nature of the norm group. For instance, even if a high school achievement test and a college admissions test both use T-scores to report results, the scores are not interchangeable. Although a T-score of 50 would represent the mean on both tests, average high school and average college applicants are not equivalent. However, standard scores can be used to compare a student's performance on different tests if the tests use the same norm group. An achievement battery, for example, consists of several subtests, each measuring a different academic content area. Because all subtests were administered to the same norm group, a student's relative performance in each content area can be directly compared. Standard scores (and percentiles) allow such comparisons as long as a common norm group is involved with all tests.

When comparing standard scores from different tests, one must also recognize that the abilities measured by the respective instruments are different. Therefore, it is not surprising if a student obtains different scores in math and reading even if the tests use the same standard scores. It is similarly not surprising if a student obtains different deviation IQs on two aptitude tests, even if both tests include "Intelligence" in their names. Tests must be interpreted in light of the specific skills measured by the instrument.

When interpreting standard scores, one must take into account the precision of the test. Horst, Tallmadge, and Wood (1975) suggest using one-third of a standard deviation as the minimum difference of educational significance. Differences of less than that are usually not measurable; thus, differences of less than 3 points on the T-score scale and less than 5 points in deviation IQs are not meaningful. Stanines do not share this problem, since each point corresponds to half a standard deviation unit.

It is also useful to always associate descriptive words, such as those included in Figure 17.2, when using scores that rely on standard deviation. For instance, since a T-score of 40 is one standard deviation below the mean, referring to it as "somewhat below the middle" helps establish what the score represents. Likewise, a

T-score of 70 would be described as "significantly above the middle."

Percentile Ranks

Student performance on standardized tests is often expressed as a percentile rank. The percentile rank of a score is the percentage of scores falling below that score. If a student who correctly answered 40 items is at the 78 percentile rank, then 78% of individuals in the norm group correctly answered fewer than 40 items. Percentile rank is often used to help interpret scores because its meaning is easy to conceptualize. Percentile ranks are expressed as whole numbers ranging from 1 to 99.

An important consideration when interpreting percentile ranks is recognizing that they do not represent equal intervals. This is illustrated in Figure 17.3. For example, locate the 5th and 10th percentile ranks and also the 45th and 50th percentile ranks. Notice how the distance between the 5th and 10th is much more significant than the distance between the 45th and 50th. Percentile ranks represent inconsistent intervals because more students achieve middle versus low or high scores on most tests. Because relatively few students obtain the lowest and highest scores, a student with low (or high) scores has to improve substantially on the test to surpass another 5% of other students. In contrast, most students obtain near average scores on a typical test. A student with an average score, therefore, has to improve only slightly on the test to surpass another 5% of other students. When interpreting scores on standardized tests, remember to treat changes in near-average percentile scores as less significant than changes near the bottom and top of the percentile scale.

Look closely in Figure 17.3 at the relationship between percentile ranks and the standard deviation units we were discussing earlier. As you would expect, the 50th percentile represents the middle score, a score that is at or close to the arithmetic mean. Because percentile ranks change so rapidly for scores near the middle, 1 standard deviation below the mean is near the 15th percentile. Likewise, 1 standard deviation above the mean is near the 85th percentile. That is, the 15th percentile, although it sounds like a low score, is only "somewhat below the middle," and the 85th percentile is only "somewhat above the middle." However, percentile ranks change much more slowly for relatively high and low scores. A score 2 standard deviations below the mean would be near the 2nd or 3rd percentile, and a score 3 standard deviations below the mean would be at the lowest or 1st percentile. Similarly, scores 2 standard deviations above the mean would be near the 97th or 98th percentile, and a score 3 standard

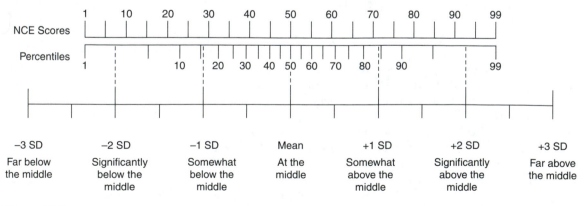

Figure 17.3
Percentile rank and NCE score intervals, compared with standard deviation units

deviations above the mean would be at the 99th percentile. A lot of people are not aware of this. For example, intuitively they believe the 15th percentile is a low score when in fact it represents a level of performance much closer to the middle than to a score that is at the 1st percentile.

In Figure 17.3, compare percentile ranks to NCE scores. Both scales range from 1 to 99. Over that range, NCE scores change at a constant rate but percentile ranks do not.

Because percentile ranks and percentage scores are both based on percentages, they are sometimes confused with each other. The distinction between these two types of scores is important. A student's percentile and percentage scores on a test are usually quite different. Also, percentile scores are used in a norm-referenced context, whereas percentage scores are applicable to criterion-referenced interpretations. As indicated previously, percentile rank indicates the percentage of scores falling below a given score. A student scores at the 20th percentile by outperforming 20% of other individuals in the comparison group. However, the students scoring at the 20th percentile probably answered other than 20% of the test items correctly. If the test consisted of easy items, the lowest scoring 20% of examinees conceivably could have correctly answered more than 90% of the items. Or if the test items were difficult, students scoring at the 95th percentile could have incorrectly answered many or even most of the items.

🌀 17.4   Apply What You Are Learning

Indicate whether each of the following statements is true or not necessarily true:

1. A student scoring at the 80th percentile correctly answered the majority of items on the test.
2. A student scoring at the 80th percentile correctly answered more items than a student scoring at the 60th percentile.
3. A student who correctly answered 80% of the items scored somewhere above the 20th percentile.

4. If students scoring at the 70th percentile correctly answered 70% of the items, then students scoring at the 80th percentile correctly answered 80% of the items.
5. A student scoring at the 15th percentile scored far below the middle of the scores.

Answers can be found at the end of the chapter.

Grade Equivalents

Unlike standard scores and percentile ranks, grade-equivalent scores convey growth. For example, at every grade level, the average student within the norm group scores at the 50th percentile. In contrast, this average student's grade-equivalent score increases by 1.0 every year. This reflection of academic growth in a test score is appealing. However, there are some natural interpretations given to grade-equivalent scores that represent serious errors. You need to be aware of this problem.

Grade Equivalents Identify Median Scores. A grade equivalent represents the median test score for that particular grade. Fifty percent of the students in a typical fourth grade are expected to score below the fourth-grade equivalent, 50% of seventh graders are expected to score below the seventh-grade equivalent, and so on. Therefore, large portions of students in a typical school invariably will be above and below these median values.

Negative connotations are often associated with scores below grade level. A fourth-grade student whose grade equivalent is 3.0 might be considered to be falling below reasonable expectations. However, *grade-equivalent scores do not represent standards that students should be expected to achieve.* They simply identify the midpoint of scores at a particular grade level.

Grade Equivalents Do Not Convey Months of the Year. A common practice with grade equivalent scores is to think of the number to the right of the decimal as representing months of the school year. For example, a grade equivalent of 7.1 is thought to represent the average seventh-grade performance in October. A grade equivalent of

7.9 would refer to June in the seventh grade, and 8.0 would then identify average performance at the beginning of the eighth grade. Students, however, do not learn at the constant rate that these numbers suggest. Also, achievement probably decreases rather than increases over the summer. Because student growth in the course of a year is not linear, equating grade equivalents to specific months of the year should be avoided.

Grade Equivalents Exceed Grade Levels at Which Skills Are Taught. Grade equivalents on most standardized tests are established for a wide range of grade levels, even though the tests focus on skills taught predominantly in one particular grade. For instance, a mathematics test designed for the sixth grade may report grade-equivalent scores ranging from 2.0 to 10.0, even though material covered on the test is not taught at these grade levels. Grade equivalents *do* indicate a student's *relative* performance. The score of 6.5 on a given test is higher than that of 5.5 and lower than that of 7.5. This characteristic is shared by all other types of scores, including percentile ranks and standard scores. *Grade equivalents are not designed to indicate whether a student is achieving skills taught at a particular grade level.* Always remember that grade equivalents provide a norm-referenced interpretation.

Grade Equivalents Do Not Allow Comparisons across Content Areas. One of the advantages of achievement batteries is that they can help determine a student's relative strengths or weaknesses. Standard scores and percentile ranks allow a teacher to make these comparisons. For example, if a second-grade student scored at the 84th percentile in spelling and at the 98th percentile in computations, it would indicate that, relative to other students, this individual is stronger in computations.

Comparison across content areas should not be performed with grade-equivalent scores. Table 17.1 lists grade equivalents that correspond to selected percentile ranks for the spelling and computation subtest within an achievement bat-

Table 17.1

Grade-equivalent scores in spelling and computation at selected percentile ranks

Percentile Ranks	Grade Equivalent	
	Spelling	Computation
99	5.5	3.8
98	4.7	3.4
84	3.8	2.9
50	2.4	2.4
16	1.6	1.8
2	1.1	1.5
1	K.8	1.2

tery widely used in elementary schools. Notice the grade equivalents that our second grader obtained. The 84th percentile in spelling corresponds to a grade equivalent of 3.8. The 98th percentile in computation corresponds to a grade equivalent of 3.4. The grade equivalents suggest that this student's greater strength is in spelling, opposite to the indication provided by percentile ranks.

Remember that grade equivalents do not indicate the grade level at which students are mastering skills. As with standard scores and percentiles, grade equivalents only indicate *relative* performance. Grade equivalents are derived from median scores. There is a reason for the different conclusions suggested by grade equivalents and percentiles regarding the relative strengths of our second-grade student. Percentiles and standard scores use the same range of scores across subject areas. For instance, percentiles range from 1 to 99 in spelling, computations, and all content areas. Grade equivalents do not. In Table 17.1, grade equivalents for spelling range from K.8 to 5.5. For computation, the grade equivalents have quite a different range. Because different scales are used in each content area, grade equivalents cannot indicate the relative strengths of students across different content areas.

Scaled Scores

Scaled scores are a set of numbers used across multiple levels of an achievement test. Like grade equivalents, scaled scores increase over time as a student progresses through school; unlike standard scores and percentiles, scaled scores portray growth in achievement across grades.

Scaled scores usually involve three digits and an arbitrary range. For example, the scaled scores for an achievement battery might use 100 to represent low achievement in early elementary grades and 900 to represent high achievement in high school.

Scaled scores avoid some problems of grade-equivalent scores by using arbitrary numbers. With grade equivalents, it is easy (but erroneous) to interpret a score of 8.3 as representing the third month of eighth-grade work. A scaled score of 630 suggests no inherent meaning. The interpretation of scaled scores is gained only through experience in working the test and learning what students typically are achieving when they obtain a scaled score close to 630. (Incidentally, "experience" is probably how you learned to give meaning to many scales, including those used to indicate air temperature, heights of people, or size of cities.)

Scaled scores do share a disadvantage with grade equivalents. Unlike standard scores and percentile ranks, scaled scores cannot be used to compare performance across content areas. For instance, if a student obtains a scaled score of 630 in reading and 650 in math, one cannot determine which of these two areas represents the student's relative strength.

USING STANDARDIZED TESTS IN THE CLASSROOM

Standardized tests play a variety of roles in education. They help determine when early elementary students are ready to be taught reading. They help identify students to be placed in special ability groupings. They are used to monitor student achievement and facilitate evaluation of instructional programs.

Standardized tests can and often do represent a positive resource in education. Unfortunately, their use can lead to erroneous conclusions and actions. In part, this happens because users are unfamiliar with the characteristics of the scale being used to report results, such as percentiles or grade equivalents. Sometimes a particular application is simply not compatible with the test's capabilities.

Our attention will focus on three roles that standardized tests often play in the classroom: placing students into instructional groups, determining the needs of individual students, and identifying students who may benefit from special-education classes.

Grouping Students According to Ability

Teachers and administrators use aptitude and achievement tests to group students at all elementary and secondary grade levels. Aptitude tests are typically used for comprehensive groupings in which the same ability groups are maintained for instruction in several content areas. Standardized achievement tests are more likely used when groupings are formed for a specific subject, such as reading or mathematics.

The issue of grouping students has been debated for some time. Proposed advantages include better matching of the content and pace of instruction to students' needs, better motivating more capable students with higher goals, and reducing frustrations of less-able students. Proposed disadvantages often parallel the advantages. For instance, lower aspirations are often set for lower ability groups and students segregated in lower ability groups when separated may miss stimulation provided by higher-achieving students.

The issue of grouping has been researched for some time and the results, in general, have not been promising. In extensive reviews of the research, both the National Education Association (1968) and Esposito (1973) failed to identify overall gains in achievement resulting from placing students in ability groups. Slavin (1987) proposed that the reason prior research reviews did not find benefits is that these studies failed to distinguish between various approaches to grouping students. In his review of research within elementary schools, Slavin found that research consistently demonstrated no improvement from placing students in comprehensive groupings, that is, placing students into ability groups for instruction across several content areas did not improve student performance. However, maintaining heterogeneous classes and regrouping students when teaching specific mathematics and reading skills improved achievement in those areas. Although not addressed by Slavin's research, one would expect a teacher's own tests, if well constructed, to provide a better basis for grouping students relative to specific skills. Classroom tests tend to measure more narrowly focused skills than do standardized achievement tests and, in particular, standardized aptitude tests. Slavin (1990) found no evidence in the research that indicates grouping students in secondary school benefits achievement.

Lou and others (1996) focused on research that had been conducted when students were grouped *within* classes. This research is more common in elementary school settings, although their review of the research encompassed all grade levels. They found benefits in achievement when homogeneous groups were formed within a classroom, although these results were not consistent. Low-ability students learned significantly more in heterogeneous groups, whereas medium-ability students learned more in homogeneous groups. High-ability students learned equally well either way. The size of the groups was important. Achievement improved when groups involved three or four students, but not when groups involved 6 to 10 members. Greater benefits from grouping were realized in math and science than in reading and other subjects.

The widespread practice of placing students into comprehensive ability groups apparently does not improve student achievement. However, grouping students for instruction in selected content areas, often temporarily, along with making adjustments to how instruction is delivered may result in significant achievement gains.

Determining the Needs of Individual Students

Practicing teachers know very well the limitations of standardized tests with respect to identifying instructional needs of individual students. LeMahieu and Wallace (1986) some time ago identified three conditions prerequisite to diagnosing instructional needs that are problematic with standardized achievement tests. First, assessments must measure carefully articulated learning outcomes. This need requires a more detailed coverage of content than is usually provided by standardized tests. Second, test results must be provided to teachers within days following the test administration, rather than the several weeks normally taken to process most standardized tests. Third, tests designed for diagnostic purposes should be administered at several points during the school year to monitor growth and identify students whose achievement patterns are changing. Classroom assessments clearly have the potential to address all three conditions identified by LeMahieu and Wallace.

Test publishers generate detailed student reports for teachers and parents. From the nature of these reports it is easy to determine whether a publisher is conveying realistic expectations. The more appropriate reports keep the analysis of student achievement general. They describe student performance on clusters of skills, each measured by a number of test items. Reports are not realistic when they judge whether each student has mastered specific skills, with mastery decisions often based on one to three test items.

Standardized achievement batteries can provide the teacher with an important planning tool when they suggest content areas in which the class or individual students are relatively strong or weak. However, the teacher needs access to the content of the test to determine exactly what the test is measuring in a particular area. Access is problematic if the same test is being used to evaluate schools or teachers. In essence, if standardized achievement batteries are expected to help teachers address the needs of individual students, these tests should be distinct from instruments that are used outside the classroom to evaluate the effectiveness of instruction.

Identifying Students Who Will Receive Special Education

When a student's abilities are sufficiently exceptional, augmented or alternative instructional procedures are required. The classification of exceptionalities is complex and includes physical and emotional as well as mental qualities.

The process of classifying students as well as the act of labeling students as a result of this classification is controversial. Ysseldyke and Algozzine (1982) state that the major advantage of labeling students is their subsequent admission to a special service. Gallagher (1976) identifies other advantages of labeling: (1) as a means of initiating plans to counteract negative conditions, (2) as a means of calling attention to a specific problem to obtain additional resources, and (3) as a basis for conducting research into procedures that prevent or treat negative conditions.

Labeling students clearly has disadvantages. Algozzine and Mercer (1980) address two problems. First, labeling often does not result in differential treatment for individuals and therefore fails its most basic function. Second, when labels are perceived as negative, they affect the perceptions of the student and others in a way that may limit social, emotional, and academic growth. Certainly, not all labels are negative. For instance, the designation *gifted* is generally perceived as an asset. Certain labels for the same condition are often preferred over others. Salvia and Ysseldyke (1998) indicate, for instance, that parents may prefer *autistic* or *learning disabled* to *mentally retarded*.

Bias in Placement Procedures. Disproportionate numbers of minority students are in special education. On the one hand, this represents an advantage for minorities because of increased expenditures per student. On the other hand, as academic expectations are often lower in special-education curricula, long-term placement in special education may promote greater discrepancies in achievement rather than remediating deficiencies. This possibility is an area of significant concern. The disproportionate number of minorities placed in special education and the role of intelligence testing rightfully remains an important topic (see for example, de la Cruz, 1996).

Standardized tests, aptitude tests in particular, are a natural target of this concern. In an important legal case in California (*Larry P. v. Riles,* 1972), the court ruled that intelligence tests could not serve as the basis for placing African American students in classes for the mentally handicapped.[2] As we have noted, all tests measure learned behaviors, which in turn are influenced by culture and other experiences. Concerns about placement of minorities in special education and potential bias in aptitude tests were instrumental in passing Public Law 94-142. Among other things, this law stipulates that

1. Tests and other diagnostic procedures used to evaluate students must be free of cultural bias.

2. Each student must be regularly reevaluated.

3. Students with handicaps must be taught in regular classes, or mainstreamed, whenever possible.

Considerable attention has been given to techniques for detecting and preventing bias within standardized tests. These techniques are helpful, but can never fully remove bias from instruments. However, an apparent bias in test scores can be due to conditions distinct from the test. In such circumstances, adjusting or removing the test will only remove symptoms of the problem.

---

[2]In a contradictory case in Illinois (*Parents in Action on Special Education [PACE] v. Hannon,* 1980), after reviewing items on commonly used intelligence tests, the judge ruled that these tests could be used with African Americans for placement purposes because the items that behaved most suspiciously involved the subset of items that appeared nondiscriminatory in content.

It must also be understood that tests are not the only potential source of bias when placing students. For example, Ross and Salvia (1975) provided teachers with reports describing the aptitude and achievement of anonymous third-grade children. Although the test data indicated that each child was borderline mentally handicapped, simply attaching a photograph of a physically more or less attractive child to the report significantly affected the teachers' diagnosis of each child's mental capability.

Failing to understand characteristics of test scores leads to errors when classifying students. Characteristics of standard scores, percentiles, and grade equivalents were discussed earlier in this chapter. We noted that percentiles represent unequal units because their values change very rapidly near the average of scores and very slowly near the top and bottom of the range of scores. We also noted that grade equivalents do not represent standards or expectations, but instead represent median values; half the students within a typical school fall below grade level.

Shepard (1984) surveyed 2,000 psychologists and learning-disability teachers and found many of them unaware of these characteristics of percentile and grade-equivalent scores. For instance, half these specialists judged an IQ of 90 to be within the normal range, which it certainly is, but considered the 25th percentile rank on an achievement test to be within a fairly low range. (Recall our discussion of percentiles; the 15th percentile rank is about 1 standard deviation below the mean, or "somewhat below the middle." Both an IQ of 90 and the 25th percentile are approximately two-thirds of 1 standard deviation below the mean.) Consequently, a student with this combination of scores might be diagnosed with a learning disability because of the apparent discrepancy between aptitude and achievement.

Until fairly recently, a widely used indication of a learning disability was a performance 1.5 to 2 years below "expected" performance. We have learned, however, that grade equivalents do not address the issue of reasonable expectations and that many normal students obtain grade-equivalent scores more than 2 years below their current grade in school. This proportion actually increases in higher grades (Oosterhof, 2001).

When grouping and categorizing students, teachers and all educators should be familiar with the characteristics of scores used with standardized tests. One should be able to identify equivalent scores across commonly used scores and to recognize the advantages and limitations of these scales.

SUMMARY

A standardized test is a test designed to be administered consistently across a variety of settings. In schools, most standarized tests are aptitude and achievement measures. An aptitude test is designed to predict future achievement, whereas an achievement test is used to measure current performance. Both aptitude and achievement tests measure skills that students have learned. Aptitude tests tend to measure more general skills that are learned informally, whereas achievement tests measure more specific skills, such as those taught in a particular grade in school.

The four categories of scores commonly used with standardized tests are standard scores, percentile ranks, grade equivalents, and scaled scores. Standard scores describe a student's performance in terms of standard deviation units. Standard scores most commonly used in schools are T-scores, stanines, deviation IQs, and NCE scores. Percentile ranks indicate the percentage of examinees in the norm group who scored below each score. Percentile ranks represent unequal intervals, with differences in the midrange of the scale much less significant than differences near the bottom and top of the scale.

Grade-equivalent scores indicate the median performance of students from different grades on a single test. Unlike standard scores and percentile ranks, grade-equivalent scores are designed to reflect student growth. However, by associating test scores with one's grade in school, grade-equivalent scores invite erroneous interpretations. They do not represent standards that students should achieve, and they do not identify the grade at which content is or should be taught. Grade equivalents often exceed the range of grades at which skills measured by the test are taught. Skills on a test designed for the fourth grade, for instance, are usually not taught in kindergarten or eighth grade, even though grade equivalents for one test usually have a range beyond this magnitude.

Scaled scores are similar to grade equivalents in that they reflect student growth. The numerical values of scaled scores are not associated with grade placement in school and therefore avoid some of the natural misinterpretations associated with grade equivalents. Unlike standard scores and percentile ranks, grade equivalents and scaled scores cannot be used to compare student performance across content areas, such as within an achievement battery.

ANSWERS: APPLY WHAT YOU ARE LEARNING

17.1. 1. Approximately 68% or about two-thirds are between 1 SD below the mean and 1 SD above the mean. 2. The remaining one-third of scores are outside the range between Laura and Monique. 3. If approximately one-third of the scores are outside the range between Laura and Monique, approximately one-sixth of the scores—half that fraction—are lower than Laura's score. 4. Similarly, approximately one-sixth of the scores are above Monique's score. 5. Approximately half the scores are lower than the mean score. 6. If approximately two-thirds of the scores are between 1 SD below the mean and 1 SD above, then approximately half that number of scores, or one-third of the scores, are between Manuel's and Monique's scores. 7. Approximately 95% of the scores are between 2 SDs below the mean to 2 SDs above the mean. This leaves 5% of the scores outside that range. Half the percentage, or approximately 2% or 3%, are therefore higher than Vincent's score. If you correctly answered most of the seven questions, that is not bad. If you correctly answered all seven questions without help, then you may be more than 3 standard deviations from the mean on this one.

17.2. 1. 60; 2. 30; 3. 55; 4. 65; 5. 25.

17.3. 1. 7; 2. 1; 3. 6; 4. 8; 5. 1.

17.4. *Item 1:* Not necessarily true. If a test is difficult, an individual scoring higher than 80% of other examinees may have correctly answered fewer than half the items. Conceivably, even a person scoring at the 99th percentile could have answered fewer than half the items. *Item 2:* True. The 80th percentile corresponds to a higher score than the 60th percentile. *Item 3:* Not necessarily true. For instance, if the test is easy and the individual with the lowest score correctly answered 80% of the items, then this student scored below the 20th percentile. *Item 4:* Not necessarily true. Percentile rank does not indicate percentage of items that were answered correctly. Even if by coincidence students scoring at the 70th percentile correctly answered 70% of the items, this coincidence would probably not continue with other scores. For example, if the highest scoring student correctly answered 75% of the items, the 80th percentile could not correspond to a score of 80%. *Item 5:* Definitely false. A student scoring at the 15th percentile is "somewhat below the middle. Look closely at Figure 17.3.

SOMETHING TO TRY

- Obtain actual or simulated score reports on a standardized achievement battery for several students. Try to select reports that include at least one standard score, percentile ranks, and grade equivalents. State for each student what the scores do and do not tell you about the student. Your interpretation should be consistent with characteristics of each type of score. If you personally know the students, evaluate their scores, taking into account what you know about them through other sources of information.

- Obtain norm tables for a standardized achievement battery that includes these three scores within the same table: a standard score (such as *T*-scores or stanines), percentile rank, and grade equivalents. Using the standard scores, find the scores that are 1, 2, and 3 standard deviations above and below the mean. Look at the percentile equivalents to these scores and see if this helps demonstrate that percentile ranks change rapidly near the center and slowly for higher and lower scores. Check the grade-equivalent scores. What is their range? What grade equivalents are 1 standard deviation above and below the mean? (Remember, 1 standard deviation from the mean is "somewhat" above or below the middle.)

- Select two feature articles from newspapers or magazines, or select two professional articles or technical reports published on the Web or in journals. The two articles should be complementary. Prepare a one or two page summary and personal reaction to the two articles.

ADDITIONAL READING

Haladyna, T. M. (2002). *Essentials of standardized achievement testing.* Boston: Allyn and Bacon. This book devotes chapters to several current issues related to standardized achievement testing, including their use for high-stakes testing, testing of students at risk, and pollution of test score interpretations and uses.

Hills, J. R. (1986). *All of Hills' handy hints.* Washington, DC: National Council on Measurement in Education. This booklet is a compilation of articles previously written by Hills regarding the interpretation of selected standard scores, percentile ranks, and grade equivalents. Each article presents a series of true-false items followed by an explanation of these answers.

Mehrens, W. A., & Lehmann, I. J. (1986). *Using standardized tests in education* (4th ed.). New York: Longman. This book provides an extended discussion of the selection and use of standardized tests in schools.

Wagner, R. K., & Sternberg, R. J. (1984). Alternative conceptions of intelligence and their implications for education. *Review of Educational Research, 54,* 179–223. This article provides a good overview of how intelligence has been conceptualized and discusses implications these views have for teaching declarative and procedural knowledge.

APPENDIX
Professional Opportunities in Assessment

An expanding number of career opportunities are available in assessment. Specialists work in a variety of areas to identify better techniques for measuring student performance, help educators become familiar with capabilities and constraints of educational measurement, improve the accuracy of tests, research statistical properties of tests, and investigate ways to use computers in assessment.

Individuals with master's and doctoral degrees in measurement are employed by schools, universities, research and development institutes, private industry, and state and federal governments.

Information concerning career opportunities, application procedures, and financial aid can be obtained directly from university departments offering graduate programs in educational measurement. For addresses and other material, consult the catalogs of universities. On the Internet, also check the *Opportunities* section of the National Council for Measurement in Education (*http://ncme.org*). Graduate students in educational measurement typically have undergraduate majors or substantive work in mathematics, statistics, psychology, sociology, or education, although undergraduate majors in other areas are common.

REFERENCES

Airasian, P. W. (1997). *Classroom assessment* (3rd ed.). New York: McGraw-Hill.

Algozzine, B., & Mercer, C. D. (1980). Labels and expectancies for handicapped children and youth. In L. Mann & D. A. Sabatino (Eds.), *Fourth review of special education*. New York: Grune & Stratton.

American Educational Research Association, American Psychological Association, & National Council on Measurement in Education. (1985). *Standards for educational and psychological testing*. Washington, DC: APA.

American Educational Research Association, American Psychological Association, & National Council on Measurement in Education. (1999). *Standards for educational and psychological testing*. Washington, DC: AERA.

Angoff, W. H., & Schrader, W. B. (1984). A study of hypotheses basic to the use of rights and formula scores. *Journal of Educational Measurement, 21,* 1–17.

Bangert-Downs, R. L., Kulik, J. A., & Kulik, C. C. (1983). Effects of coaching programs on achievement test performance. *Review of Educational Research, 53,* 571–585.

Berk, R. A. (1986). A consumer's guide to setting performance standards on criterion-referenced tests. *Review of Educational Research, 56,* 137–172.

Bloom, B. S. (Ed.). (1956). *Taxonomy of educational objectives: Handbook 1. Cognitive domain*. New York: McKay.

Bloom, B. S., Hastings, J. T., & Madaus, G. F. (1981). *Evaluation to improve learning*. New York: McGraw-Hill.

Brown, F. G. (1983). *Principles of educational and psychological testing* (3rd ed.). New York: Holt, Rinehart & Winston.

Budescu, D., & Bar-Hillel, M. (1993). To guess or not to guess: A decision-theoretic view of formula scoring. *Journal of Educational Measurement, 30*(4), 277–291.

Budescu, D., & Nevo, B. (1985). Optimal number of options: An investigation of the assumption of proportionality. *Journal of Educational Measurement, 22,* 183–196.

Bugbee, A. C. (1996). The equivalence of paper-and-pencil and computer-based testing. *Journal of Research on Computing in Education, 28,* 282–299.

Carter, K. (1986, Winter). Test-wiseness for teachers and students. *Educational Measurement: Issues and Practice, 5,* 20–23.

Cartwright, C. A., & Cartwright, G. P. (1984). *Developing observation skills*. New York: McGraw-Hill.

Chase, C. I. (1979). Impact of achievement expectations and handwriting quality on scoring essay tests. *Journal of Educational Measurement, 16,* 39–42.

Chase, C. I. (1986). Essay test scoring: Interaction of relevant variables. *Journal of Educational Measurement, 23,* 33–41.

Cizik, G. J. (1996). Setting passing scores. *Educational Measurement: Issues and Practice, 15*(2), 20–31.

Coffman, W. E. (1971). Essay examinations. In R. L. Thorndike (Ed.), *Educational measurement* (2nd ed.). Washington, DC: American Council on Education.

Confrey, J. (1990). A review of the research on student conceptions in mathematics, science, and programming. In C. B. Cazden (Ed.), *Review of research in education: Vol. 16* (pp. 3–56). Washington, DC: American Educational Research Association.

Cross, L. H., & Frary, R. B. (1977). An empirical test of Lord's theoretical results regarding formula scoring of multiple-choice tests. *Journal of Educational Measurement, 14,* 313–321.

Cullen, F. T., Cullen, J. B., Hayhow, V. L., & Plouffe, J. T. (1975). The effects of the use of grades as an incentive. *Journal of Educational Research, 68,* 277–279.

Daly, J. A., & Dickson-Markman, F. (1982). Contrast effects in evaluating essays. *Journal of Educational Measurement, 19,* 309–316.

Davis, R. E. (1975). Changing examination answers: An educational myth? *Journal of Medical Education, 50,* 685–687.

de la Cruz, R. E. (1996). *Assessment-bias issues in special education: A review of literature.* (ERIC Document Reproduction Service No. ED 390246).

Deutsch, M. (1979). Education and distributive justice. *American Psychologist, 34,* 391–401.

Diederich, P. A. (1973). *Short-cut statistics for teacher-made tests.* Princeton, NJ: Educational Testing Service.

Duchastel, P. C., & Merrill, P. F. (1973). The effects of behavioral objectives on learning: A review of empirical studies. *Review of Educational Research, 43,* 53–70.

Ebel, R. L. (1965). *Measuring educational achievement.* Upper Saddle River, NJ: Prentice Hall.

Ebel, R. L. (1982). Proposed solutions to two problems of test construction. *Journal of Educational Measurement, 19,* 267–278.

Ebel, R. L., & Frisbie, D. A. (1986). *Essentials of educational measurement* (4th ed.). Upper Saddle River, NJ: Prentice Hall.

Elawar, M. C., & Corno, L. (1985). A factorial experiment in teachers' written feedback on student homework: Changing teacher behavior a little rather than a lot. *Journal of Educational Psychology, 77,* 162–173.

Esposito, D. (1973). Homogeneous and heterogeneous ability grouping: Principal findings and implications for evaluating and designing more effective educational environments. *Review of Educational Research, 43,* 163–179.

Fabrey, L. J., & Case, S. M. (1985). Further support for changing multiple-choice answers. *Journal of Medical Education, 60,* 488–490.

Fremer, J. (2000a). A message from your president. *NCME Newsletter, 8*(3), 1.

Fremer, J. (2000b). A message from your president. *NCME Newsletter, 8*(4), 1–2.

Frisbie, D. A. (1973). Multiple-choice vs. true-false: A comparison of reliabilities and concurrent validities. *Journal of Educational Measurement, 10,* 297–304.

Gaffney, R. F., & Maguire, T. O. (1971). Use of optically scored test answer sheets with young children. *Journal of Educational Measurement, 8,* 103–106.

Gagné, E. D., Yekovich, C. W., & Yekovich, F. R. (1993). *The cognitive psychology of school learning.* New York: Harper Collins.

Gagné, R. M. (1985). *The conditions of learning and theory of instruction.* New York: Holt, Rinehart & Winston.

Gallagher, J. J. (1976). The sacred and profane uses of labeling. *Mental Retardation, 14,* 3–7.

Gierl, M. J. (1997). Comparing cognitive representations of test developers and students on a mathematics test with Bloom's taxonomy. *Journal of Educational Research, 91,* 26–32.

Glaser, R. (1963). Instructional technology and the measurement of learning outcomes. *American Psychologist, 18,* 519–521.

Hebert, E. A. (1992). Portfolios invite reflection—from students and staff. *Educational Leadership, 49,* 58–61.

Heppner, F. H., Anderson, J. G. T., Farstrup, A. E., & Weiderman, N. H. (1985). Reading performance on a standardized test is better from print than from computer display. *Journal of Reading, 28,* 321–325.

Hetter, R. D., Segall, D. O., & Bloxom, B. (1994). A comparison of item calibration media in computerized adaptive testing. *Applied Psychological Measurement, 18,* 197–204.

Hills, J. R. (1981). *Measurement and evaluation in the classroom* (2nd ed.). Columbus, OH: Merrill.

Holmes, C. T., & Matthews, K. M. (1984). The effects of nonpromotion on elementary and junior high school pupils: A meta-analysis. *Review of Educational Research, 54,* 225–236.

Horst, D. P., Tallmadge, G. K., & Wood, C. T. (1975). *A practical guide to measuring project impact on student achievement.* Washington, DC: United States Department of Health, Education, and Welfare, Office of Education.

Hughes, D. C., & Keeling, B. (1984). The use of model essays to reduce context effects in essay scoring. *Journal of Educational Measurement, 21*(3), 277–281.

Hughes, D. C., Keeling, B., & Tuck, B. F. (1980). The influence of context position and scoring method on essay scoring. *Journal of Educational Measurement, 17,* 131–135.

Kane, M. T. (1986). The role of reliability in criterion-referenced tests. *Journal of Educational Measurement, 23,* 221–224.

Karlins, J. K., Kaplan, M., & Stuart, W. (1969). Academic attitudes and performance as a function of a differential grading system: An evaluation of Princeton's pass-fail system. *Journal of Experimental Education, 37,* 38–50.

Kirst, M. (1991). Interview on assessment issues with Lorrie Shepard. *Educational Researcher, 20*(2), 21–23.

Kissock, C., & Iyortsuun, P. (1982). *A guide to questioning: Classroom procedures for teachers*. London: Macmillan Press.

Koretz, D., McCaffrey, D., Klein, S., Bell, R., & Stecher, B. (1992). *The reliability of scores from the 1992 Vermont portfolio assessment program: Interim report*. RAND Institute on Education and Training, National Center for Research on Evaluation, Standards, and Student Testing. (ERIC Document Reproduction Service No. ED 355 284.)

Kuder, G. F., & Richardson, M. W. (1937). The theory of the estimation of test reliability. *Psychometrika, 2,* 151–160.

Larry P. v. Riles, 343 F. Supp. 1396 (N. D. Calif. 1972).

Lassiter, K. (1987, April). *An examination of performance differences of third graders using two types of answer media*. Paper presented at the annual meeting of the National Council on Measurement in Education, Washington, DC.

Lee, J. A., Moreno, K. E., & Sympson, J. B. (1986). The effects of mode of test administration on test performance. *Educational and Psychological Measurement, 46,* 467–474.

LeMahieu, P. G., & Wallace, R. C., Jr. (1986). Up against the wall: Psychometrics meets praxis. *Educational Measurement: Issues and Practice, 5*(1), 12–16.

Lepper, M. R., Drake, M. F., & O'Donnell-Johnson, T. (1997). Scaffolding techniques of expert human tutors. In K. Hogan & M. Pressley (Eds.), *Scaffolding student learning: Instructional approaches and issues* (pp. 108–144). Cambridge, MA: Brookline Books.

Linn, R. L., Baker, E. L., & Dunbar, B. D. (1991). Complex, performance-based assessment: Expectations and validation criteria. *Educational Researcher, 20*(8), 15–21.

Linn, R. L., & Gronlund, N. E. (2000). *Measurement and assessment in teaching* (8th ed.). Upper Saddle River, NJ: Merrill/Prentice Hall.

Lo, M. Y., & Slakter, M. J. (1973). Risk taking and test-wiseness of Chinese students. *Journal of Experimental Education, 42,* 56–59.

Lord, F. M. (1977). Optimal number of choices per item: A comparison of four approaches. *Journal of Educational Measurement, 14,* 33–38.

Lou, Y., Abrami, P. C., Spence, J. C., Poulsen, C., Chambers, B., & d'Apollonia, S. (1996). Within-class grouping: A meta-analysis. *Review of Educational Research, 66,* 423–458.

Mager, R. (1984). *Preparing instructional objectives* (2nd ed.). Belmont, CA: David S. Lake.

Marso, R. N. (1970). Test item arrangement, testing time, and performance. *Journal of Educational Measurement, 7,* 113–118.

Matthews, C. O. (1929). Erroneous first impressions on objective tests. *Journal of Educational Psychology, 20,* 280–286.

McCoy, A. R., & Reynolds, A. J. (1999). Grade retention and school performance: An extended investigation. *Journal of School Psychology, 37,* 273–298.

McMorris, R. F., & Weideman, A. H. (1986). Answer changing after instruction on answer changing. *Measurement and Evaluation in Counseling and Development, 19,* 93–101.

Melton, R. F. (1978). Resolution of conflicting claims concerning the effect of behavioral objectives on student learning. *Review of Educational Research, 48,* 291–302.

Messick, S. (1989a). Meaning and values in test validation: The science and ethics of assessment. *Educational Researcher, 18*(2), 5–11.

Messick, S. (1989b). Validity. In R. L. Linn (Ed.), *Educational measurement* (3rd ed., pp. 13–103). New York: American Council on Education.

Messick, S., & Jungeblut, A. (1981). Time and method in coaching for the SAT. *Psychological Bulletin, 89,* 191–216.

Millman, J., Bishop, C. H., & Ebel, R. L. (1965). An analysis of test-wiseness. *Educational and Psychological Measurement, 25,* 707–726.

Millman, J., & Setijadi. (1966). A comparison of the performance of American and Indonesian students on three types of test items. *Journal of Educational Research, 59,* 315–319.

Millman, J., Slovacek, S. P., Kulick, E., & Mitchell, K. J. (1983). Does grade inflation affect the reliability of grades? *Research in Higher Education, 19,* 423–429.

Mitchelmore, M. C. (1981). Reporting student achievement: How many grades? *British Journal of Educational Psychology, 51,* 218–227.

Moss, P. A., Beck, J. S., Ebbs, C., Matson, B., Muchmore, J., Steele, D., Taylor, C., & Herter, R. (1992). Portfolios, accountability, and an interpretive approach to validity. *Educational Measurement: Issues and Practice, 11*(3), 12–21.

National Education Association. (1968). *Ability grouping research summary*. Washington, DC: Author.

Nava, F. J. G., & Loyd, B. H. (1991). *The effect of student characteristics on the grading process*. Paper presented at the annual meeting of the National Council on Measurement in Education, San Francisco.

Nitko, A. J. (1984). Defining "criterion-referenced test." In R. A. Berk (Ed.), *A guide to criterion-referenced test construction* (pp. 8–23). Baltimore, MD: Johns Hopkins University Press.

Oosterhof, A. C. (2001). *Classroom applications of educational measurement* (3rd ed.). Upper Saddle River, NJ: Merrill/Prentice Hall.

Oosterhof, A. C., & Coats, P. K. (1984). Comparison of difficulties and reliabilities of quantitative word problems in completion and multiple-choice item formats. *Applied Psychological Measurement, 8,* 287–294.

Oosterhof, A. C., & Glasnapp, D. R. (1974). Comparative reliabilities and difficulties of the multiple-choice and true-false formats. *Journal of Experimental Education, 42,* 62–64.

Posey, C. (1932). Luck and examination grades. *Journal of Engineering Education, 23,* 292–296.

Powers, D. E., & Swinton, S. S. (1984). Effects of self-study for coachable test item types. *Journal of Educational Psychology, 76,* 266–278.

Rafoth, B. A., & Rubin, D. L. (1984). The impact of content and mechanics on judgments of writing quality. *Written Communications, 1,* 446–458.

Rocklin, T., & Thompson, J. M. (1985). Interactive effects of test anxiety, test difficulty, and feedback. *Journal of Educational Psychology, 77,* 368–372.

Ross, M. B., & Salvia, J. (1975). Attractiveness as a biasing factor in teacher judgments. *American Journal of Mental Deficiency, 80,* 96–98.

Rowley, G. L., & Traub, R. E. (1977). Formula scoring, number-right scoring, and test-taking strategy. *Journal of Educational Measurement, 14,* 15–22.

Russell, M. (1999). Testing writing on computers: A follow-up study comparing performance on computer and on paper. *Educational Policy Analysis Archives, 7*(20). Available online: *http://epaa.asu.edu/epaa/v7n20/.*

Russell, M., & Haney, W. (2000). Bridging the gap between testing and technology in schools. *Education Policy Analysis Archives, 8*(19). Available online: *http://epaa.asu.edu/epaa/v8n19/.*

Salvia, J., & Ysseldyke, J. E. (1998). *Assessment* (7th ed.). Boston: Houghton Mifflin.

Scruggs, T. E., & Lifson, S. A. (1985). Current conceptions of test-wiseness: Myths and realities. *School Psychology Review, 14,* 339–350.

Shavelson, R. J., Ruiz-Primo, M. A., Schultz, S. E., & Wiley, E. W. (1997). *On the development and scoring of classification and observation science performance assessments* (CSE Technical Report 458). Los Angeles: University of California, National Center for Research on Evaluation, Standards, and Student Testing.

Shepard, L. A. (1984). Setting performance standards. In R. A. Berk (Ed.), *A guide to criterion-referenced test construction* (pp. 169–198). Baltimore, MD: Johns Hopkins University Press.

Shepard, L. A. (2000). *The role of classroom assessment in teaching and learning* (CSE Technical Report 517). Los Angeles: University of California, Center for Research on Evaluation, Standards, and Student Testing.

Slavin, R. E. (1987). Ability grouping and student achievement in elementary schools: A best-evidence synthesis. *Review of Educational Research, 57,* 293–336.

Slavin, R. E. (1990). Achievement effects of ability grouping in secondary schools: A best-evidence synthesis. *Review of Educational Research, 60,* 471–499.

Smith, M. L. (1991). Meanings of test preparation. *American Educational Research Journal, 28,* 521–542.

Snow, R. E. (1989). Toward assessment of cognitive and conative structure in learning. *Educational Research, 18*(9), 8–14.

Spray, J. A., Ackerman, T. A., Reckase, M. D., & Carlson, J. E. (1989). Effect of the medium of item presentation on examinee performance and item characteristics. *Journal of Educational Measurement, 26,* 261–271.

Stallings, W. M., & Smock, H. R. (1971). The pass-fail grading option at a state university: A five-semester evaluation. *Journal of Educational Measurement, 8,* 153–160.

Suddick, D. E., & Kelly, R. E. (1981). Effects of transition from pass/no credit to traditional letter grade system. *Journal of Experimental Education, 50,* 88–90.

Taylor, W. L. (1953). Cloze procedure: A new tool for measuring readability. *Journalism Quarterly, 30,* 415–433.

Tierney, R. J., Carter, M. A., & Desal, L. E. (1991). *Portfolio assessment in the reading-writing classroom.* Norwood, MA: Christopher-Gordon.

Tittle, C. K., Hecht, D., & Moore, P. (1993). Assessment theory and research for classrooms: From *taxonomies* to constructing meaning in context. *Educational Measurement: Issues and Practice, 12*(4), 13–19.

Um, K. R. (1995). Sampling effects of writing topics and discourse modes on generalizability of individual student and school writing performance on a standardized fourth grade writing assessment. Unpublished doctoral dissertation, Florida State University, Tallahassee.

Valencia, S. (1990). A portfolio approach to classroom reading assessment: The whys, whats, and hows, *The Reading Teacher, 43,* 338–340.

Vispoel, W. P. (2000). Reviewing and changing answers on computerized fixed-item vocabulary tests. *Educational and Psychological Measurement, 60,* 371–384.

Weller, L. D. (1983). The grading nemesis: An historical overview and a current look at pass-fail grading. *Journal of Research and Development in Education, 17,* 39–45.

Wesman, A. G. (1971). Writing the test item. In R. L. Thorndike (Ed.), *Educational measurement* (2nd ed.). Washington, DC: American Council on Education.

Yen, W. M. (1997). The technical quality of performance assessments: Standard errors of percents of pupils reaching standards. *Educational Measurement: Issues and Practice, 16*(3), 5–15.

Ysseldyke, J. E., & Algozzine, B. (1982). *Critical issues in special and remedial education.* Boston: Houghton Mifflin.

Zandvliet, D., & Farragher, P. (1997). A comparison of computer-administered and written tests. *Journal of Research on Computing in Education, 29,* 423–438.

NAME INDEX

SUBJECT INDEX